SPATIAL STATISTICS AND MODELS

THEORY AND DECISION LIBRARY

AN INTERNATIONAL SERIES
IN THE PHILOSOPHY AND METHODOLOGY OF THE
SOCIAL AND BEHAVIORAL SCIENCES

Editors

GERALD EBERLEIN, *University of Technology, Munich*
WERNER LEINFELLNER, *University of Nebraska*

VOLUME 40

SPATIAL STATISTICS
AND MODELS

Edited by

GARY L. GAILE

Department of Geography, University of Connecticut, Storrs, Connecticut, U.S.A.

and

CORT J. WILLMOTT

Department of Geography, University of Delaware, Newark, Delaware, U.S.A.

D. REIDEL PUBLISHING COMPANY

A MEMBER OF THE KLUWER ACADEMIC PUBLISHERS GROUP

DORDRECHT / BOSTON / LANCASTER

Library of Congress Cataloging in Publication Data

Main entry under title:

Spatial statistics and models.

    (Theory and decision library ; v. 40)
    Includes bibliographies and index.
     1.   Geography—Statistical methods—Addresses, essays, lectures.
2.   Spatial analysis (Statistics)—Addresses, essays, lectures.   I.   Gaile,
Gary L.   II.   Willmott, Cort J., 1946—   III.   Series.
G70.3.S6 1984   910'.01'51   83—22984
ISBN 90—277—1618—8

Published by D. Reidel Publishing Company,
P.O. Box 17, 3300 AA Dordrecht, Holland

Sold and distributed in the U.S.A. and Canada
by Kluwer Boston Academic Publishers,
190 Old Derby Street, Hingham, MA 02043, U.S.A.

In all other countries, sold and distributed
by Kluwer Academic Publishers Group,
P.O. Box 322, 3300 AH Dordrecht, Holland

Printed in The Netherlands

To William A. V. Clark

TABLE OF CONTENTS

GARY L. GAILE AND CORT J. WILLMOTT

INTRODUCTION

The quantitative revolution in geography has passed. The spirited debates of the past decades have, in one sense, been resolved by the inclusion of quantitative techniques into the typical geographer's set of methodological tools. A new decade is upon us.

Throughout the quantitative revolution, geographers ransacked related disciplines and mathematics in order to find tools which might be applicable to problems of a spatial nature. The early success of Berry and Marble's *Spatial Analysis* and Garrison and Marble's volumes on *Quantitative Geography* is testimony to their accomplished search. New developments often depend heavily on borrowed ideas. It is only after these developments have been established that the necessary groundwork for true innovation obtains.

In the last decade, geographers significantly augmented their methodological base by developing quantitative techniques which are specifically directed towards analysis of explicitly spatial problems. It should be pointed out, however, that the explicit incorporation of space into quantitative techniques has not been the sole domain of geographers. Mathematicians, geologists, meteorologists, economists, and regional scientists have shared the geographer's interest in the spatial component of their analytical tools.

This volume is a sampling of state-of-the-art papers on topics biased towards those dealing directly or indirectly with spatial phenomena or processes. The substantive interests of the contributors are highly diverse, e.g., geology (Agterberg, Krumbein and Schuenemeyer), geomorphology (Jarvis and Mark), climatology (Balling, Rayner and Willmott), cartography (Moellering and Shepard), human geography (Gould), population and migration (Austin, Davies, Huff, Miron and Pickles), urban geography (White), economic geography (Gaile, Green, Griffith, Sheppard and Semple) and, of course, methodology (Bennett and Goodchild). Nonetheless, the authors are united in their interest in the description and explanation of spatial structure and processes through the use, development and evaluation of statistical, numerical and analytic methods. For purposes of presentation, these approaches have been segregated into predominantly process-based quantitative descriptions, i.e., "models", and predominantly general or mathematically-based

ix

Gary L. Gaile and Cort J. Willmott (eds.), Spatial Statistics and Models, ix—x.
© 1984 *by D. Reidel Publishing Company.*

descriptions, i.e., "statistics". The latter category most often is derived from probability theory. Models and statistics are, by no means, mutually exclusive areas of inquiry, however.

Several main themes can be found in this volume. The vast majority of papers, for example, discuss fitting equations to data. Even though regression analyses and trend surface techniques have been around for some time, important methodological problems still have not been fully solved, e.g., estimating parameters in gravity models (Sheppard) and in linear regression (Mark) to name but a few. Simulation modeling (Rayner and White) is developing into an important spatial tool, although the methods are not as well-known or refined as traditional statistical methods. Spatial autocorrelation is a "hot topic" and it is thought to confound many spatial statistics. Miron's paper and others address this topic which until now has only been surveyed in widely scattered readings. The computer-assisted presentation of spatial data in two-space is a recurring theme — cartography in the computer age. Several of the authors herein are particularly concerned with better ways to conceptualize and operationalize this process. Classification or regionalization is a traditional and important spatial theme which, by no means, is nearly fully developed. Only recently have the methods, data and facilities (computers) become sophisticated enough to undertake these problems. Most work in this area remains to be done.

Any field of inquiry is in constant need of reanalysis and criticism. It was with this in mind that Peter Gould was invited to contribute a general commentary on the theoretical underpinnings of quantitative geography. Gould's early call for a paradigm shift in human geography provides some thoughts on the directions and challenges of the next decade.

ACKNOWLEDGEMENTS

The editors gratefully acknowledge Susan Clarke, Benito Cribari, Jeff Gaile, Dean Hanink, Clint Rowe, Junior Wells and Pat and Abby Willmott for being great people.

PART I

SPATIAL STATISTICS

DANIEL A. GRIFFITH

THEORY OF SPATIAL STATISTICS

1. INTRODUCTION

Classical statistics is based upon sampling theory. This theory involves artic-
ulations of the concepts of statistical population, sample, sample space and
probability. Meanwhile, spatial statistics is concerned with the application
of sampling theory to geographic situations. It involves a translation of these
four notions into a geographic context. The primary objective of this paper is
to discuss these translations.

Classical statistics also deals with measurements that provide useful
information about a statistical population and the convolution of these
measures with sampling theory. The result is a sampling distribution from
which probabilities can be derived. A second objective of this essay is to
review measures that furnish useful information about statistical geographic
populations.

2. DEFINING A GEOGRAPHIC POPULATION

A population is the total set of items for which a measurement is to be
obtained. This set must be defined in such a way that one can clearly specify
whether or not any item is a member of it. For example, all people who reside
in the United States is a population that the United States Census Bureau
seeks to study. A statistical population is the set of measures corresponding
to a population. If a population has N items, and some attribute is measured,
then the statistical population will include N measures, one for each item in
the parent population. For instance, the income of each person who resides in
the United States is a statistical population corresponding to the foregoing
parent population. Once a locational context is attached to measures, the
total set constitutes a statistical geographic population. Popular examples
here include average income for each county in the United States or population density for each census tract in a metropolitan area.

A number of less familiar geographic populations are infrequently or often
unknowingly used, too. First, consider a planar surface that is partitioned into
four mutually exclusive and collectively exhaustive areal units, such as that

Gary L. Gaile and Cort J. Willmott (eds.), Spatial Statistics and Models, 3–15.

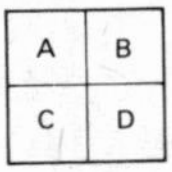

Fig. 1. One partitioning of a planar surface into four mutually exclusive and collectively exhaustive areal units.

appearing in Figure 1. The spatial distribution of values for some phenomenon over this surface constitutes a statistical geographic population. Another type of population emerges from the manner in which this planar surface was partitioned into areal units. A third type alludes to the idea of random noise versus systematic pattern in a geographic landscape.

This last category of geographic population requires additional explanation, whereas the nature of the other three populations should be self-evident. Suppose one is driving away from an urban area into a desolate region with his radio tuned into some radio station. This radio receives distinct signals in the urban area, while these signals become increasingly weaker as distance from the urban area increases. These signals represent a discernable, understandable pattern. Meanwhile, since the radio remains capable of receiving signals, it continues to pick up sound waves. But, these sound waves are from many sources, none of which is dominant, and when they mix together they are received as static, or noise. Analogously, social, economic, physical or other forces induce a given spatial distribution over a planar surface. Other factors, however, operate independent of one another, and mix with these aforementioned forces, introducing noise that yields a modified resultant distribution. Hence, the geographic population is, in reference to either this random noise component or this systematic pattern component, based upon a spatial distribution.

3. SPATIAL SAMPLING PERSPECTIVES

The first spatial sampling perspective is a classical sampling approach where replacement occurs and order is important. As such there are N^n possible samples, where n denotes the sample size. For example, if one wanted to consider all samples of size 2 for the geographic configuration appearing in Figure 1, then the areal unit combinations would be:

A,A	B,A	C,A	D,A
A,B	B,B	C,B	D,B
A,C	B,C	C,C	D,C
A,D	B,D	C,D	D,D

These sixteen pairs of areal units constitute the sample space in this case. Probabilities and the sampling distribution of measures here are described by the Central Limit Theorem and the Law of Large Numbers. This perspective is rarely used because most regions are partitioned into relatively few areal units. Urban geographers who want to say something about spatial distributions within, say, the United States urban system have employed it with census tracts as areal units, though. Their parent population is all census tracts in United States SMSAs.

The second spatial sampling perspective is similar to the classical sampling approach having no replacement and order being important. Accordingly, there are $n!/\Pi_{i=1}^{i=k}(n_i!)$ possible spatial distributions, where k denotes the number of distinct values. For instance, consider the set of values $\{0, 2, 3, 3\}$. The possible number of spatial distributions that could be constructed by convoluting this set with the geographic configuration given in Figure 1 is $4!/[(1!)\,(1!)\,(2!)] = 12$. These twelve possible arrangements, consitituting the sample space for this case, are presented in Figure 2. The sampling distribution here for any traditional statistic is a spike, as can be seen from the reporting of arithmetic means in Figure 2. In other words, since most

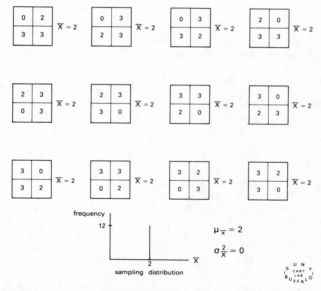

Fig. 2. All possible spatial distributions, based upon the configuration in Figure 1 and the set of values $\{0, 2, 3, 3\}$.

traditional statistics involve summation, and addition is commutative, then these statistics fail to provide any information about the spatial distribution in question. This shortcoming has led to the development of geostatistics and statistical theory based upon spatial autocorrelation. This perspective is used primarily in the latter of these two situations.

The third spatial sampling perspective refers to the manner in which a planar surface is partitioned into areal units. It is affiliated with the classical sampling approach having no replacement and order being unimportant. Consider the aforementioned set of values to refer to total population counts in areal units. Then, the total population for the region is $0 + 2 + 3 + 3 = 8$. Here, the pertinent question asks how many ways these eight people could be grouped into four areal units. The answer for this specific example is given in Table I. In general the number of possible groupings is given by

$$\sum_{i=1}^{i=k} \prod_{j=1}^{j=m} C(a_{ij}, b_{ij})$$

subject to $\sum_{j=1}^{j=m} b_{ij} = n$ and $a_{i1} = n$ where k is the number of possible compositions, and m is the number of combination terms for each composition.

TABLE I

The number of ways eight items can be allocated to four areal units

Composition	Combination			Spatial distributions
8, 0, 0, 0	$C(8, 8)$	=	1	4
7, 1, 0, 0	$C(8, 7) C(1, 1)$	=	8	12
6, 2, 0, 0	$C(8, 6) C(2, 2)$	=	28	12
6, 1, 1, 0	$C(8, 6) C(2, 1) C(1, 1)$	=	56	24
5, 3, 0, 0	$C(8, 5) C(3, 3)$	=	56	12
5, 2, 1, 0	$C(8, 5) C(3, 2) C(1, 1)$	=	168	24
5, 1, 1, 1	$C(8, 5) C(3, 1) C(2, 1) C(1, 1)$	=	336	24
4, 4, 0, 0	$C(8, 4) C(4, 4)$	=	70	12
4, 3, 1, 0	$C(8, 4) C(4, 3) C(1, 1)$	=	280	24
4, 2, 2, 0	$C(8, 4) C(4, 2) C(2, 2)$	=	420	24
4, 2, 1, 1	$C(8, 4) C(4, 2) C(2, 1) C(1, 1)$	=	840	24
3, 3, 2, 0	$C(8, 3) C(5, 3) C(2, 2)$	=	560	24
3, 3, 1, 1	$C(8, 3) C(5, 3) C(2, 1) C(1, 1)$	= 1120		24
3, 2, 2, 1	$C(8, 3) C(5, 2) C(3, 2) C(1, 1)$	= 1680		24
2, 2, 2, 2	$C(8, 2) C(6, 2) C(4, 2) C(2, 2)$	= 2520		24
Total			8143	***

Constructing the corresponding sampling distribution is a very tedious task, especially without the aid of a computer.

The fourth spatial sampling perspective to be outlined here stems from the classical stratified sampling approach. A sample space is constructed for each of p areal units where replacement occurs and order is important. For any areal unit i, then, there are $N_i^{n_i}$ possible samples of size n_i. The total number of spatial distributions in this case is $\Pi_{i=1}^{i=p} N_i^{n_i}$. One simple example for this perspective is presented in Figure 3. Because $N_i = 2$ and $n_i = 2$ $\forall i$, there are 256 possible values. Since some values repeat, though, only 81 distinct spatial distributions exist. The probability of observing these distributions is not the same; in other words, they are not equally likely distributions. The resulting sampling distribution is not a spike, and is associated with the Central Limit Theorem for multivariate analysis. It is employed extensively in research based upon information collected on the "long form" the United States Bureau of the Census distributes for selected attributes, and then compiles and publishes at the census tract or block level.

The last major spatial sampling perspective shares a close affinity with stochastic processes theory. It views any value x_i in a geographic distribution as being the weighted average of neighboring areal unit values, plus a random or noise component. Moreover,

$$x_i = \rho \sum_{j=1}^{j=p} w_{ij}x_j + u_i \tag{1}$$

where ρ = the degree of similarity for juxtaposed areal unit values; $\sum_{j=1}^{j=p} w_{ij} = 1$, $w_{ij} \geq 0$ $\forall_{i,j}$; x_j = the value for areal unit j; p = the number of areal units; and, u_i = a noise component associated with areal unit i. The parameter ρ in equation (1) is related to the notion of spatial autocorrelation, and determines the prominance of pattern in a spatial distribution. Using matrix notation equation (1) becomes $X = \rho WX + U$. Hence, U is given by

$$X = (I - \rho W)^{-1} U \tag{2}$$

where I is the identity matrix. Because ρ is unknown in most cases, spatial autocorrelation indices may be used to obtain $\hat{\rho}$, and then $\hat{U}$. Measures calculated for all possible vectors $\hat{U}$ compose the sampling distribution. This perspective is exemplified in Figure 3, which is the sample space of noise term spatial distributions corresponding to the sample space presented in Figure 2. The sampling distribution for $\bar{u}$ is not a spike, as can be seen from the reporting of these arithmetic means in Figure 4. In other words, although

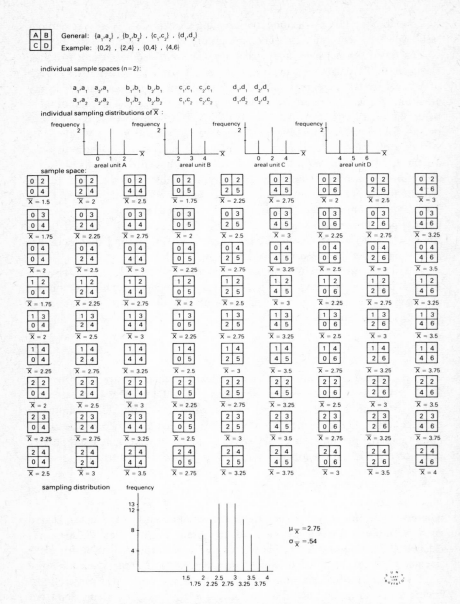

Fig. 3. All possible spatial distributions for a stratified random sample example.

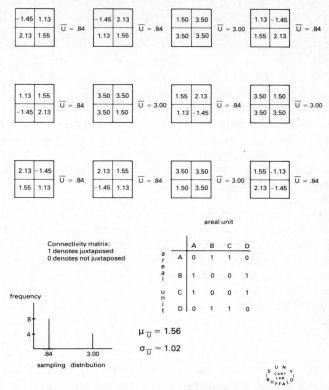

Fig. 4. The noise component for those spatial distributions appearing in Figure 2.

$\mu_{\bar{x}} \equiv \bar{x}$, the accompanying $\mu_{\bar{u}} \not\equiv \bar{u}$. This perspective has been utilized to compare statistics such as $\bar{x}$ and $\bar{u}$ in order to determine how important the spatial pattern component is.

4. SPATIAL AUTOCORRELATION

As the last sampling perspective indicates, classical statistics fail to provide any information about geographic distributions. Figure 2 exemplifies this problem. Regardless of which of the twelve possible spatial distributions is considered $\bar{x} = 2$, $s^2 = 2$, and so forth. Attempts to take the underlying configuration into account have led to the development of geostatistics, planar statistics, and directional statistics. Each of these three types will be subsequently discussed.

Another problem that became recognized is associated with the nature of information rendered by an application of classical statistics to geographic situations. One of the fundamental assumptions of classical statistics is that the elements of some population take on numerical values in an independent fashion. This assumption frequently is violated in spatial statistical situations. Moreover, the value of some phenomenon in a given areal unit tends to be related to those values of this phenomenon taken on by juxtaposed areal units. The last sampling perspective is the one basically employed here. That area of spatial statistics that has emerged is known as spatial autocorrelation. Literally speaking, the spatial term of this phrase refers to a geographical dependence structure for observations. The term correlation refers to a relationship between entities, and the prefix auto- refers to the fact that a single variable is being related to itself. The body of spatial statistics that is evolving through this conception characterizes a statistical distribution not only by its mean μ and its variance σ^2, but also by its geographic configuration $\mathbf{W}$ and its spatial autocorrelation ρ. This topic of spatial statistics is treated first because it has profound implications for geostatistics, planar statistics, and directional statistics. A more detailed discussion of it appears elsewhere in this volume (Miron, 1984).

The spatial autocorrelation viewpoint does not ignore randomness. Rather, it maintains that a geographic distribution is composed of both pattern and random error. Consequently, x_i may be decomposed in accordance with equation (1), where ρ is the spatial autocorrelation parameter. Equation (2) uses the spatial linear operator $(\mathbf{I} - \rho\mathbf{W})^{-1}$, which is like an input/output multiplier in that it accounts for all direct and indirect effects flowing over a surface, transforming a random distribution into a partially patterned one. This transformation affects the type of information yielded by a statistical analysis.

Using the calculus of expectations, let $E(x_i) = \mu_x$ and $E(u_i) = \mu_u$. Now from equation (1)

$$E(x_i) = E(\rho \sum_{j=1}^{j=p} w_{ij}x_j + u_i)$$

$$\mu_x = \rho \sum_{j=1}^{j=p} w_{ij} E(x_j) + E(u_i) = \rho\mu_x + \mu_u$$

$$\mu_x - \rho\mu_x = \mu_u$$

$$\therefore \mu_x = (1 - \rho)^{-1} \mu_u. \tag{3}$$

If $-1 < \rho < 0$, then $\mu_u > \mu_x$; if $0 < \rho < 1$, then $\mu_u < \mu_x$. The simple result presented in equation (3) will be used to illustrate spatial statistical aspects of geostatistics, planar statistics, and directional statistics.

5. GEOSTATISTICS

The development of geostatistics was an attempt to take geographic configuration into account during statistical analysis. The three popular statistics are the spatial mean, standard distance and areal frequency distribution. These concepts have provided few insights because little is understood about their sampling distributions. Rather, moments have been derived for special spatial distributions from which they are assumed to be calculated (Neft, 1966).

Let z_i be a value for some attribute measured on areal unit i. This areal unit can be assigned a Cartesian co-ordinate (x_i, y_i). If the areal unit is something other than a point, then usually its centroid is the (x_i, y_i) point assumed. Hence, the spatial mean is defined as the Cartesian co-ordinate point $(\bar{x}, \bar{y})$, where

$$\bar{x} = (\sum_{i=1}^{i=n} z_i x_i)/(\sum_{i=1}^{i=n} z_i) \tag{4}$$

and

$$\bar{y} = (\sum_{i=1}^{i=n} z_i y_i)/(\sum_{i=1}^{i=n} z_i). \tag{5}$$

The standard distance is defined as

$$SD = \{[\sum_{i=1}^{i=n} z_i(x_i - \bar{x})^2]/(\sum_{i=1}^{i=n} z_i) + [\sum_{i=1}^{i=n} z_i(y_i - \bar{y})^2]/(\sum_{i=1}^{i=n} z_i)\}^{\frac{1}{2}}.$$

An areal frequency distribution can be constructed by obliquely rotating an outline map upon which the areal unit centroids have been plotted, and constructing a line proportional to z_i at the centroid location (x_i, y_i) of areal unit i.

The appropriate population sampled from here is either the partitioning of a planar surface, or the spatial distribution approximated in a stratified random sample. If the entire population of entities is used, then this first perspective applies. Otherwise, the second perspective may be applicable.

Few interesting questions can be addressed with geostatistics. The United States Census Bureau plots the spatial mean of the geographic population distribution after each census. One could hypothesize

$$H_0 : \mu_{(\bar{x}_t, \, \bar{y}_t)} = \mu_{(\bar{x}_{t-1}, \, \bar{y}_{t-1})}. \tag{6}$$

In other words, given the partitioning of the planar surface, do the two spatial means come from the same spatial distribution? Because the same set of areal units is used in both time periods t and $t - 1$, then this problem reduces to one of the difference between two means for correlated samples.

Returning to equation (3), if non-zero spatial autocorrelation is present in variate Z, then the information provided by equations (4) and (5) is not readily interpretable. Now the sampling perspective changes, and null hypothesis (6) takes on a new meaning. Here, the question asked is whether or not the two spatial means come from the same spatial distribution of noise. Further, SD becomes inflated or deflated in the presence of non-zero spatial autocorrelation, and systematic geographic patterns are observable in the areal frequency distribution that distort the underlying random areal frequency distribution.

6. PLANAR STATISTICS

A parallel attempt to extend classical statistics into the arena of constellations of observations resulted in the nearest neighbor statistic, quadrat analysis, and sundry ordered statistics such as the runs statistic. Null hypothesis sampling perspectives for these first two concepts assume that random noise generates a geographic distribution of points over a planar surface, and hence the points observed are but a sample of the infinite number of points located on this planar surface. The generator is assumed to be Poisson in nature. A reasonable survey of these statistics may be found in Getis and Boots (1978). The runs statistic is associated with a permutation sampling perspective.

The nearest neighbor statistic provides information that helps to answer the question of how punctations are spaced on a punctiform planar surface. Spacing is defined in terms of distance between dyads of nearest points, sometimes in k directions. Its equation is

$$R = 2 \times (n/A)^{1/2} \times \left(\sum_{j=1}^{j=k} \sum_{i=1}^{i=n} d_{ij}/n\sqrt{k} \right), \tag{7}$$

whère n = the number of points located on the planar surface; A = the area of the planar surface; and d_{ij} = the distance to the i-th nearest neighbor in the j-th direction. Clearly as all points cluster together, $d_{ij} \rightarrow 0$ and thus $R \rightarrow 0$. Given the null hypothesis of a Poisson point generator, $\bar{d} = \frac{1}{2}(A/n)^{\frac{1}{2}}$, and hence $R = 1$. Further, as points become uniformly distributed, $\bar{d} \rightarrow (2\sqrt{3})^{\frac{1}{2}} \times (A/n)^{\frac{1}{2}}$, and thus $R \rightarrow 2 \times (2/\sqrt{3})^{\frac{1}{2}}$. Many of the shortcomings of this statistic are spelled out by Vincent (1976), Sibley (1976), Ebdon (1976), and Haworth and Vincent (1976). Its principal drawback stems from the geographical boundary value problem.

Quadrat analysis provides information that helps to answer the question of how densely punctations are located on a planar surface. This technique together with all of its pecularities is treated at length in Rogers (1974). Density is defined in terms of quadrat counts, and then evaluated by constructing a frequency distribution for these counts, followed by a statistical comparing of it with that for a Poisson distribution. Two sampling perspectives may be employed here. First, randomly located quadrats can be used to estimate density profiles. Second, the surface may be partitioned into mutually exclusive and collectively exhaustive quadrats, with the superimposition of this grid being placed at random.

The runs statistic uncovers information about lateral relations. A run is a sequence of data that possesses a common binary trait. One run ends and another starts when the sequence of data no longer displays one of these binary traits, and begins to display the other. The random variable, say V then, is the number of runs that are observed. The sampling perspective is that of randomization, with a sampling distribution whose attributes are summarized as

$$\mu_V = (2 \times n_0 \times n_1) / (n_0 + n_1) + 1,$$

$$\sigma_V^2 = [(2 \times n_0 \times n_1) \times (2 \times n_0 \times n_1 - n_0 - n_1)] / [(n_0 + n_1)^2 \times (n_0 + n_1 + 1)]],$$

and

$$Z = (V - \mu_V)/\sigma_V,$$

where n_0 = the number of observations having property "0," and n_1 = the number of observations having property "1."

For each of these three situations the presence of non-zero spatial autocorrelation is complicating. For instance, in equation (7) is one measuring the clustering of points due to some external factor, or the gravitation of points towards one another? Consider the simplest case of equation (7), namely $k = 1$ and

$$R = 2 \times (\sum_{i=1}^{i=n} d_{ij}/n) \times (n/A)^{1/2} .$$

Next, let $d_i = \rho \sum_{j=1}^{j=n} w_{ij} d_j + \delta_i$. Then,

$$R = 2 \times (\rho \sum_{i=1}^{i=n} \sum_{j=1}^{j=n} w_{ij} d_j/n) \times (n/A)^{1/2} + 2 \times (\sum_{i=1}^{i=n} \delta_i/n) \times (n/A)^{1/2}.$$

Only the second expression on the right hand side of this equation is interpretable within the context of nearest neighbor theory.

Similarly, with quadrat analysis, one does not know whether or not a statistical decision is attributable to the presence or absence of an external factor, or the gravitational attraction of points. Spatial autocorrelation can be tested for directly here by treating quadrats as areal units and calculating any of the myriad spatial autocorrelation indices.

The runs statistic would reduce to a linear geographic two-color map problem. Again, one would have difficulty extracting meaningful conclusions.

7. DIRECTIONAL STATISTICS

Directional statistics pertain to observations that are angles measured with respect to a reference axis. This topic also will be treated at greater length in this volume (Schuenemeyer, 1984), and is thoroughly discussed in Gaile and Burt (1980). To exemplify the relationship between spatial statistical theory and directional statistics, consider the directional mean

$$\bar{x}_0 = \tan^{-1} [(\sum_{i=1}^{i=n} \sin \theta_i) / (\sum_{i=1}^{i=n} \cos \theta_i)] ,$$

where θ_i denotes the i-th observed angle. If points have a propensity to gravitate towards one another, then

$$\theta_i = \rho \sum_{j=1}^{j=n} w_{ij} \theta_j + \psi_i.$$

The convolution of autocorrelation effects are crystal clear here, since for example

$$\sin (\theta_i) = \sin (\rho \sum_{j=1}^{j=n} w_{ij} \theta_j) \times \cos (\psi_i) + \cos (\rho \sum_{j=1}^{j=n} w_{ij} \theta_j) \times \sin (\psi_i).$$

Once again, then the interpretation of results is not straightforward.

8. CONCLUSIONS

This paper supplies an introduction to the theory of spatial statistics from an intuitive point of view by first surveying appropriate sampling perspectives, and then emphasizing the viewpoint of random noise in a geographic landscape. Next the fundamental areas of spatial analysis are related to this random noise perspective with a judicious selection of representative statistics. Although spatial statistics is in its infancy, discussions presented here provide a taste of its content. Hopefully this taste will whet one's appetite, and provide an impetus for pursuing a more indepth study of the topic (see Griffith, 1980; Ord, 1981; and Griffith, 1981).

Dept. of Geography
State University of New York at Buffalo

BIBLIOGRAPHY

Ebdon, D: 1976, 'On the underestimation inherent in the commonly used formulae', *Area* 8(3), 165–169.

Gaile, G. and J. Burt: 1980, *Directional Statistics*, Geo Abstracts, Norwich.

Getis, A. and B. Boots: 1978, *Models of Spatial Processes*, Cambridge University Press, Cambridge.

Griffith, D.: 1980, 'Towards a theory of spatial statistics', *Geographical Analysis* 12(4), 325–339.

Griffith, D.: 1981, 'Towards a theory of spatial statistics: a rejoinder', *Geographical Analysis* 13(1), 91–93.

Haworth, J. and P. Vincent: 1976, 'Maximizing the nearest-neighbor statistic', *Area* 8(4), 299–302.

Miron, J.: 1984, 'Spatial autocorrelation in regression analysis: a beginner's guide', in G. L. Gaile and C. J. Willmott (eds.), *Spatial Statistics and Models*, this volume.

Neft, D.: 1966, *Statistical Analysis for Areal Distributions*, Regional Science Research Institute, Philadelphia.

Ord, J.: 1981, 'Towards a theory of spatial statistics: a comment', *Geographical Analysis* 13(1), 86–91.

Rogers, A.: 1974, *Statistical Analysis of Spatial Dispersion*, Pion, London.

Schuenemeyer, J.: 1984, 'Directional data analysis', in G. L. Gaile and C. J. Willmott (eds.) *Spatial Statistics and Models*, this volume.

Sibley, D.: 1976, 'On pattern and dispersion', *Area* 8(3), 163–165.

Vincent, P.: 1976, 'The general case: how not to measure spatial point patterns', *Area* 8(3), 161–163.

PETER GOULD

STATISTICS AND HUMAN GEOGRAPHY
Historical, Philosophical, and Algebraic Reflections

> But philosophical knowledge can become
> genuinely relevant and fertile for ... [a]
> positive science *only when* ... [the geog-
> rapher] comes across the basic traditional
> concepts and, furthermore, questions their
> suitability for that which is made the theme
> of his science.
>
> Martin Heidegger, *The Piety of Thinking*, p. 21.

1. LOOKING BACK

Starting dates are often difficult to pinpoint exactly, but the "mid-Fifties"
were certainly the time when statistical methodology began to burgeon in
human geography. Although there was a lot of cross-fertilization and independent experimentation, the main strands can be picked out quite easily:
the universities of Washington (Garrison, 1955; Berry and Garrison, 1958)
and Lund (Hägerstand, 1952; Godlund, 1956a, b), and through the latter the
remarkable and lonely efforts of one man in Finland (Ajo, 1953); some
parallel efforts at Iowa (McCarty, 1956) and Northwestern (Taaffe, 1958;
Thomas, 1960); and then one or two individuals who saw in genuine stochastic modeling a different and fruitful way of looking at the world (Curry,
1960). Years later a pioneering paper in Japan was recovered Matui (1932),
but by then the particular statistical question had been asked again, and the
answers greatly extended (Clark and Evans, 1954; Dacey, 1960). Most of
the early statistical experiments were based upon regression analysis, representing attempts to estimate empirical relationships (usually linear), while
maps of residuals were used to highlight the exceptions to such generalizations. No one had heard of such things as spatial autocorrelation in those
days — including the statisticians, who were still helping the econometricians
worry about the independence of their observations in time series. Spatial
statistics were very much an open question, and more extended multivariate
approaches, such as factor analytic and numerical taxonomic methods, were
only just becoming practical possibilities with the growth of large computing
facilities (Berry, 1960, 1961).

17

Gary L. Gaile and Cort J. Willmott (eds.), Spatial Statistics and Models, 17–32.
© 1984 *by D. Reidel Publishing Company.*

For all the naivety and mistakes of those days, it was a time of great intellectual excitement (Gould, 1979), generated by people who had been completely conventionally trained, and who felt a sense of disappointment and frustration upon entering *graduate* work. Having been conducted through the factual compilations of conventional undergraduate curricula, they had looked forward to genuine challenge as they entered graduate programs that were meant to represent intellectually demanding, respected, and professional research perspectives. Instead, they found more of the same undemanding memorization characteristic of a field that still had not gained even a foothold in many universities with high intellectual standards, and research programs in which the methodological frontiers were the plane table, a visually incoherent fractional code, and maps constructed by transfering census data to paper with the aid of colored pencils. Many felt it was not good enough, and here and there a few people finally decided to do something about it.

Given the deep dissatisfaction of a small, but growing group of young geographers with the state of geographic methodology in those days, it was almost inevitable that many turned to statistics, although pioneering efforts were also made in optimization (Morrill and Garrison, 1960), computer simulation (Hägerstrand, 1953; Morrill, 1965), and stochastic models of both natural and human phenomena (Curry, 1962, 1964). Economists on the human side of the discipline, as well as a number of geologists on the physical side, seemed well-versed in methods with half a century of proven worth behind them in research areas as diverse as agriculture, pharmacology, biology and industrial quality control. Moreover, such methods appeared to demand measurement, a hallmark of the physical sciences, which were becoming a rich source of analogy in human affairs (Stewart, 1947; Stewart and Warntz, 1958; Carrothers, 1956). Statistical methods also raised the question of experimental design, and indicated how hypotheses might be formulated and tested, not upon the touchstone of certainty — after all, Science is always open, nothing is ever certain, the sun may not rise tomorrow — but at assigned levels of probability. Footnotes reported that if you regressed the square root of X_2 and the arcsin of X_3 against the log of X_1, that all the beta coefficients were significant at the one percent level. It was difficult to know exactly what this meant, but at least you might be able to *predict* X_1 from X_2 and X_3. Since prediction was declared to be the *sine qua non* of the Scientific Method, it all seemed so much better than what had gone before. The fact that new terms were required, along with the latest computing facilities, did nothing but reinforce the feeling that real methodological advances were being made.

And there is no question that learning such approaches *did* make quite genuine intellectual demands for a change. One had to start at the beginning, and actually build up expertise through least-squares (calculus), eigenvalues and eigenvectors (linear algebra), and the double-Poisson distribution (probability theory). A person had to work hard, and invest time and considerable intellectual effort to learn these things, an experience very different from wrestling with the demanding details of coconut production in Palu-Guava, or following, with a sense of growing anticipation and almost unbearable intellectual excitement, the delimitation of yet another CBD in yet another American city. We also found many colleagues in adjacent fields of the social sciences who were employing statistical methodology, and we began to share ideas and exchange techniques, thus breaking down the distressing sense of isolation and disconnection that geography had created for itself over the previous half-century. There is no question about it: this was an important facet of the development of statistical methodology in the field.

In fundamental conceptual terms, the new methods did not move that far from the usual approaches. If there was an important synthetic component in the traditional geographic perspective, then employing factor analytic methods, with their huge numbers of variables, seemed totally appropriate. That dozens of urban factorial ecologies finally uncovered the structure of the US Census should not necessarily be disparaged (Marchand, 1979): we now know why American cities, considered as points, have locations in a three-dimensional, orthogonal, and Euclidean space created from the enormous redundancy contained in the original choice of the census variables themselves. And if another strong tradition in geography was regionalization, then the computerized algorithms of numerical taxonomy were strong enough to tear apart and partition any geographic space, often in dozens of different ways depending upon which psychologist wrote the algorithm, what constraints of contiguity and compactness you invoked, and what you wanted to show in the first place. But it all seemed so much more "objective" and scientific than the old exercises of human judgment that ended with imprecise and overlapping boundary zones, so that an area might end up belonging to two or more regions at once. This, by definition, was not good classification, and *therefore* (?), not good regionalization either.

As for statistical, that is to say probabilistic, *models,* these too were seized upon and employed with enthusiasm. People and neighborhoods in a city went from one state to another, and we tied down the rich historical experience with our Markov chains, and talked of fixed-point vectors and convergence to steady states, implying (did we actually *grasp* what we were implying?) that people and their creations would follow the clockwork mechanism of liquid-vapor exchanges, with a bit of probabilistic smudging at the edges. Whoever saw a city actually converge to an equilibrium state? Or think that it could?

And then we discovered Fourier analysis, and pretended that we observed functions describing some aspects of the human condition that were continuously differentiable — not such a bad assumption, because even when we thought we were observing a continuous function, we always broke it up into finite pieces for the Fast Fourier algorithms required by our digital machines. The fact that we could seldom make much sense out of the power spectra, that we could seldom interpret and give *meaning* to the pure cosine components into which we partitioned our variance in a linear additive fashion, seemed to matter less than the fact that we were employing the same methods as our examplars — the physical sciences. Unfortunately, I know of no example where we could make the claim of even modestly extending our understanding of the human spatial condition through these methods.

The same authority of the physical analogy underlies our use of entropy modeling. Unable to determine what we might mean by the total energy available to the "system", the total amount of money rich people and poor people might allocate to their daily journeys-to-work, we iterate our doubly-constrained models back and forth until we find the best fit, an empirical gauging that is finally expressed as a single value describing the effect of distance or cost on all the people of a region. The fits are invariably good: with a Lagrangian available as a balancing parameter for each origin and destination, it would be surprising if they were not.

With so many $(n+m+1)$ parameters, most of the distributions describing mass human movements in an urban region are satisfactory by any reasonable standards: but the assumptions are heroic; the analogy of trip-distributions to a classical conservative field is false; the *structure*, the sheer connectivity, of the region is ignored; independent allocations cannot possibly be justified; and maximizing the entropy is "pointless, since the 'general case' is pointless" (Atkin, 1977a, p. 100). In other words, we have a more complex version of extrapolation from a linear regression equation without any understanding of the actual problem. Once again, we have an elaborate statistical "fit", which might be used for short-term extrapolation (a task for which it is, in essence, *not* required), but far from enhancing our genuine understanding of the "system", the false statistical mechanical analogy actually smothers the real problem so that it slips back into concealment where our thinking cannot reach it. Given some change in the "system", we will undoubtedly be able to recalibrate our distance parameter and the $(n+m)$ Lagrangians, but we have absolutely no understanding of the process of genuine spatial and human readjustment represented by the mapping $W: S_t \rightarrow S_{t+1}$ since we have ignored fundamental structural properties in our initial description.

2. TURNING POINT

Why would someone who had the privilege of being in "at the beginning" at Northwestern in 1956, and who shared the deep intellectual excitement of those early days and their subsequent development, do such an apparent about face, and become so critical of statistical methods and models? Why would the same person, who had taught every variety of multivariate statistical methods and numerical taxonomy with conviction and enthusiasm, find himself unable to stand in front of students and lecture about these things with the same sense of intellectual honesty as he had before? The reasons are difficult to explicate succinctly, but they are rooted in mathematics and philosophy, two traditional areas of concern that we may legitimately call "higher". I am acutely aware that in using such an adjective I may raise feelings of disquiet, even hostility, so let me abjure immediately any notion that these ancient and highly developed fields are somehow "better" than others. That is not the point: they are simply different, and in the strict sense that I want to employ them here they are genuinely higher in the same way that some things form cover sets in an algebraic hierarchy for other sets at lower levels. All the sciences (an archaic and often dysfunctional designation today), all areas of human inquiry, may be related to these cover sets, and when we are prepared to "move to higher ground", we often gain a perspective on our own work that was concealed from us before. Reflecting upon what we are doing, bringing out of concealment that which was previously hidden from us, can be an unnerving experience — when anchors give way we drift in an open sea of new possibilities, but our secure and snug haven sinks quickly below the horizon. Nevertheless, the questions often possess an insistence that cannot be ignored. Philosophers and mathematicians are dangerous, because in rather different ways they are relentless and ruthless in their concern for the foundations of knowing. And if we begin to share their astringent viewpoints, we shall sometimes see our own foundations crumble.

The problem initially was a mathematician, an algebraic topologist who began to turn his attention from the deep structures of the physical realm (Atkin, 1965) to the apparently ubiquitous sense of structure in the human world (Atkin, 1972). No matter where one looked — chess, psychiatry, literature, urban planning, the university ... the list is endless — people were constantly using the term *structure*. Often without any real sense of what they were talking about in any well-defined, operational way, but one could hardly deny the sheer and constant presence of the *word* itself in so many areas of human discourse and inquiry. The fact that we are prepared to name, to give a word to that which we see only ghost-like through the mist, points to an intuitive sensing whose further and more formal clarification can deepen our understanding. And so a search for a well-defined structural language began (Atkin, 1974), and its fount was eventually cast in the metal of algebraic topology.

It was no accident: as an area of mathematics deeply concerned with structure, as an area providing a more general and enriching perspective on many conventional parts of mathematics itself, it was founded on the definitions of the set and the relation — two of the most unconstrained and fundamental concepts in mathematics itself. Two further fount-a-metal ideas were added: first, the realization that the words we use take on meanings of different degrees of generality, and that some of them form cover sets at the N level (the designation is arbitrary), for those at lower $N-k$ levels in the hierarchy. And if we confuse sets with the elements of sets we are in trouble (Russell, 1956), which is precisely where many of the human sciences are today. We must not only make our sets and relations well-defined, but sort out with extreme care the hierarchy of algebraic relations contained in the words we employ for our descriptions. Secondly, we must make the careful conceptual distinction between the geometrical structures that form the multidimensional spaces of our inquiries, and the things that are supported, whose existence is *allowed,* by such geometries. This is the critical distinction between backcloth and traffic.

It is not possible to explore these fundamental ideas here at any length; a number of elementary expositions are available (Atkin, 1974, 1977b, 1981; Gould, 1980), but a few brief examples may be helpful. The critical shift, the critical enlargement of perspective, occurs when the conventional function is seen as a highly constrained form of the more general relation. Relations describe connections between elements of sets, and provide us with a particularly rich geometric picture in the form of a simplicial complex. For example, in a poor rural region, we may have a well-defined set of farmers **F**, and a set of agricultural things **A** (irrigation pumps, rented land, cooperative markets ...) at some well-defined hierarchical level (Gaspar and Gould, 1981). A relation $\lambda \subset F \otimes A$ defines each farmer as a simplex, a polyhedron whose vertices are in the agricultural set. Farmers sharing vertices are connected by faces of varying dimensionality to form a complex — a simplicial complex — that defines the backcloth, and makes operational the intuitive notion that there is some *structure,* some coherence and connectivity, to agriculture in the region. Of what could such a sturcture be composed except the connections between the set of people who farm and the set of agricultural things that define them *as farmers*? And it is not obvious that the geometry, the agricultural backcloth, can forbid and allow traffic on the structure — namely, the crops and animals that must have certain minimal geometries to exist at all?

Out of these apparently simple concepts, we can create a perspective that is very different from conventional approaches — methodologies which would take the rich multidimensional complexity of our agricultural world, and squeeze it through that constrained mathematical concept called the function. Out of our concern for rigorous definition of set and relation, we can make operational our intuitive ideas of structure, and begin to understand how these multidimensional geometries influence the things that exist upon them. Seeing the function now for the constrained descriptive tool it actually is, even the traditional geographic analogy between particle physics and innovation diffusion has to be discarded (Hägerstrand, 1967). When Portuguese farmers live in small villages, and exchange information over a glass of wine in the evening, we can see how the restricted and unreflective tradition of functional thinking that leads to a least-squares estimation of a mean information field actually crushes down, and totally misrepresents, their multidimensional complexity (Gasper and Gould, 1981, p. 111). We also see that innovations, considered as transmitted traffic, must have some *structure,* some backcloth of face-to-face communication upon which they can move, and that this geometry of connections will severely shape the actual course of diffusion. If the simplicial complex forming the connections between the farmers is highly fragmented, there will be high values at many dimensional levels in the obstruction vector $\hat{Q}$, a measure of the global properties of the complex. Local structure may also be of crucial importance, and a careful examination of individual components will disclose whether farmers form long q-chains or a compact algebraic star. Or perhaps they are connected in such a way that q-holes appear in the geometry — topological objects that information about innovations must work its way around. And what will happen if a high-dimensional farmer (the adjective itself discloses a very different way of *thinking* about the people who make the geometry) dies, retires, or moves away from the region? It will depend upon his own degree of connection and eccentricity, two concepts made precise and well-defined in the algebraic language. The concept of eccentricity reflects the common meaning of the word, for an eccentric farmer is different from the rest, does not share connections, and "sticks out like a sore thumb" from the complex. If he is totally eccentric and disconnected, the structure is not affected very much if he disappears, in contrast to another who may form a highly connected part of the fabric, and whose absence will be felt in greater fragmentation and higher obstruction. What q-holes will such a farmer leave behind? What forces will be felt as a result of such changes in the structure?

And so we are led to a very different view of dynamics and change, and, in fact, of time itself. Change implies forces at work — graded t-forces working at different dimensional levels on the structure — and we can describe such forces by observing change, just as any classical physicist tautologically measures force by recording change (a ball rolling down an inclined plane, a weight extending a spring, a dial moving on a volt meter), and then immediately turns around to *ascribe* change to a force! But while the geometry of the physical world appears to be totally stable (and since we are embedded in it, could we even *be* on-the-outside-looking-in and tell if it were otherwise?), the geometries of the human world are frequently *not* stable, and may actually be changed by purposeful human action based upon reflection that is informed by ethical and moral considerations. Traffic on a stable backcloth can change, giving us what we might call a classical Newtonian view, but backcloths describing the human world may themselves change, with severe consequences for the traffic that lives upon them. When a high-dimensional faculty member retires, ask the graduate students who "live" on that part of the departmental structure whether they feel t-forces of stress — forces that are dimensionally graded to the simplices they affect. And what stresses do they feel when a whole graduate department disappears? Then the cover sets higher in the hierarchy, the larger backcloth of academic geography, has to be considered as the students are q-transmitted to other departments, departments chosen presumably because they contain in their local structures faculty-simplices who *connect* with the intellectual interests and capabilities of the now-departed department. Such views of radical backcloth change give us an Einsteinian view, and from this perspective comes a radically different way of thinking about time as a multidimensional structure that must exist for a certain p-event (an event of a particular dimensionality and significance) to appear. If we want a p-event of a certain dimensionality to happen, we may have to start building the structure for it now in order for it to appear later.

These brief and fleeting glimpses of a totally different methodological world provide us with a perspective that departs radically from the conventional statistical view, whether our concern is for multivariate description based on forcing rich human data through constrained functional filters (leaving most of the insight behind?); or for taxonomic approaches that tear apart highly connected structures with deterministic partitional machines in order to stuff the broken pieces into 18th Century boxes; or for statistical models that seductively obliterate our questioning by giving us good fits — but little true understanding. The problem is now quite clear, if only we are willing to stand open to it and reflect upon it. Unlike the physical sciences, which generated descriptive mathematical structures out of a contemplation of the things themselves, we in human geography (and all the others who share our concern to describe different facets of the human condition), have borrowed our mathematical apparatus in a totally blind and unreflective way. And without excusing it, how could it be otherwise when there was virtually no significant tradition of careful philosophic reflection in the field of human geography — or in any other human science for that matter? Like fledglings in the nest with gaping beaks, we take as given the highly constrained, essentially functional, structures of the calculus (with the continuum as a *mathematical* definition), linear algebra, and probability, with all the supporting mechanical theories of error, entropy, linear decomposition, and so on, and we use these as our *a priori* frameworks upon which we force the rich multidimensional complexity of *human* geography.

Upon hindsight, we can now see the methodological developments of the past quarter of a century as a sad story of intellectual distortion, a history made even more grotesque in light of the continuous and meticulous example of the physical sciences to generate the mathematical structures appropriate for their own descriptive tasks *out of the things themselves*. Newton, Leibnitz, Gauss, Hamilton, Maxwell, the tensors of Ricci and Levi-Civita employed by Einstein ... all part of a long tradition, still continuing today with the creation of appropriate algebraic structures by Penrose (1974) to describe the quantum level when conventional structures break down, and the use of Regge lattices by Misner, Thorne and Wheeler (1974) for the cosmological scale. The physical scientists reflect upon things physical, and they attempt to find or generate the mathematical languages and structures to describe them appropriately, yet always contingently. Taking the history of the physical sciences as a whole, their example of making the mathematics fit the descriptive needs has been a glorious one of open intellectual endeavor. In contrast, the human sciences plod along a century (or two) behind, forcing their human materials on mathematical forms that contain within their origins the simpler analogies and structures of the classical physical world from which they were originally derived.

3. LOOKING FORWARD

Out of the quite understandable misappropriation and misapplication of statistical methods in human geography, a transitory phase we can now see as almost inevitable, and perhaps even necessary given the tradition of unreflecting acceptance of the historical matrix (Scott, 1982), a deep division has developed, usually characterized as the humanist-scientist split (Christensen, 1982). Of course, such a bare dichotomy distorts the subtle gradations of reality almost to the point of caricature, but we need some general term for the problem. In the same way that the geographers of one generation reacted to the unstructured, factual tradition of their intellectual inheritance, so a later one reacted instinctively against the mechanistic analogies that were often implicit in the statistical methodologies arising out of the physical and biological worlds of the late 19th and early 20th centuries. But such a comparison is too glib, and it obscures as much as it reveals: without exception, those who reacted against the older compilative tradition had been deeply schooled within it, and they knew only too well what they were reacting against. In contrast, few of those who reacted against the later mathematical methodologies knew what they were really dealing with, if for no other reason than they had little or no mathematics as a linguistic key to gain entry to a different framework, and no thoughtful experience in the actual employment of such techniques to judge in an informed and reasoned way. Furthermore, by associating mathematics with the devil incarnate, they evinced little desire to comprehend. As a result, they constantly appeared to be *against* something, but could seldom articulate their reasons except in distressingly emotional terms — hardly the best conveyance for clear and reasoned criticism. Of course, those of an earlier generation had been just as polemic and just as negative in their reactions against the established order, but whatever one's views about them may be, it must be granted that they were also genuinely and positively *for* a more demanding and challenging approach to geographic inquiry — no matter how misguided some of the results now appear upon hindsight. In contrast, some of those who reacted against them appeared to be *for* very little, except perhaps the expression of individual feelings and emotions as part of a research endeavor that presumably must lead to intersubjectively shared and testable knowledge.

And I hope that no reader of this essay misunderstands such criticism: individual feelings and emotions obviously underpin our human world. I personally delight in travel and the wonder of new landscapes; I adore poetry and literature and music and dance, and engage myself as participant or audience at every possible opportunity (and find opera and architecture excruciatingly dull — we are all flawed vessels); I rejoice to see the bulbs that my wife and I have planted in the Fall appear in all their sweetness in the Spring; we create in our own garden a mass of flowers from April to October ... and all the highly particular emotions and feelings I have are *totally irrelevant* to an act of inquiry that I undertake as a professional scholar. I would not dream of making my deeply personal, private, and emotional life and feelings an integral part of my professional research, nor would I have the impertinence to believe that these could be of the slightest interest (except prurient) to anyone else as part of our shared, intersubjectively verifiable knowledge. For my fundamental and deep concern as a scholar is to "gain the assent of the reader", no matter how contingently, with a descriptive story well and convincingly told so that it illuminates for others a part of our human world not seen in such a way before. What else *is* Science?

Unfortunately, the humanist-scientist split obscures even more; by implying an either-or, one or the other choice, it fails to illuminate the possibility that both perspectives, when reflected upon and modified, may be crucially necessary for a deep and explicating act of understanding. In fact, we might reflect upon three possible perspectives (Gould, 1982), and consider their appropriateness for any act of genuine inquiry. Such an act seems to be essentially ingestive, for the Greek-founded curiosity of our Western world makes inquiry a devouring act, no matter how gentle and patient the questioning (Steiner, 1978). In contrast, our personal *ex*-pressions of emotion, right down to their etymological roots, represent a pushing out from ourselves those aesthetic and ethical sensibilities we *choose* to declare to others — an act of declaration that can never represent a sharing of the deep, and quite personal, meaning that is quite particular to ourselves.

The first tradition or perspective has been labeled by the philosopher Jürgen Habermas as the *technical* (Habermas, 1968), an inescapable starting point to any genuine act of inquiry, since, at the very least, we must choose what it is that we will actually observe. More formally, it demands of us that we make the sets of things we observe as well-defined as possible, and display an equal concern for the definition of the relations that will connect the elements of our sets. Without a concern for *relating* some things to others there can be no real description; we would just be left with lists standing by themselves with no relation to *structure* them. The same perspective should also make us think about the words we choose to describe our sets, and ask whether we have sorted these fundamental building blocks into a proper hierarchy of covers. Such an act of hierarchical reflection may also raise the question of the scale and degree of aggregation at which we intend to work, a question increasingly considered for its philosophical, as well as its purely technical, implications (Couclelis, 1982). The macro perspective is an old and intellectually honorable one in geography, a distancing that gives us a provocative and valuable view that disappears if all our attention is focused upon the aesthetic and emotional reactions of an individual to a landscape. Such a concern for hierarchical structure also raises the question of what might form the supporting backcloth, and what the traffic could be — an uncomfortable question that may expose the ignorance of ourselves and the official agencies who collect so much of our statistical data. We may suddenly realize, for example, that most of the census data, and most of the economic indices so assiduously collected at vast expense, are nothing but traffic with a highly redundant information content. But what are the underlying *structures*? A Nobel Prize winner in economics finally admits to the politicians ". . . a shift in structure is not anything easily accommodated in the kind of economic theories we now have" (Simon, 1980, pp. 6—7). Hardly surprising when the economists are still in the world of 19th-Century physics, where the functions of the econometricians, so exquisitely estimated for their ever-larger computer models, assume unwittingly to describe changes against a *stable* backcloth. No wonder we are in such a mess. Finally, the technical perspective should raise the question of the appropriate methodology, and the mathematical structures that underlie it; for whatever methodology we bring to bear, it will constitute an *a priori* framework that to some degree will shape our knowing. If we are prepared to stand in a genuine phenomenological tradition, and "let the data speak for themselves" (Gould, 1981), we must try to ensure that our mathematical frameworks are as unconstrained as possible. We shall always find functions if they are really there, instead of being imposed from the start, but we shall never disclose the multidimensional structures themselves if we approach our essentially descriptive task with a constrained mathematics out of classical physics. We must also be acutely aware of the way in which our mathematical languages may contain within themselves the properties about the world we think we are seeking. The existence of a potential, an analogue of the gravitational potential, demonstrates "a mathematical property, not a scientific law which needs to be discovered" (Atkin, 1977a, p. 91).

But after we have made such choices within the technical perspective, and have reflected deeply upon the appropriateness of them, we still have to give *meaning* to the structures we have created. The task of inquiry has really hardly begun, for in a sense we have created a "text", and must now employ the second perspective, the *hermeneutic,* to interpret and give meaning to it. This is not the world of definitions, but the area of patient questioning and thinking, trying to "see" what is there. Sometimes perhaps nothing is there; perhaps because we are not well prepared to see, perhaps because the structures we have defined are meaning*less*. This is disappointing, of course, but unlikely to be the fault of the algebraic language. Since we are the ones who defined the text, it may be necessary to go back to the initial technical tasks of definition. Thus, the *technical* and the *hermeneutic* traditions are not separate perspectives of inquiry, since each may well inform and shape the other. And the same is true for the third perspective, the *emancipatory;* it too is informed by, and informs, the others. For the emancipatory view requires the acknowledgement that the structures we define and interpret are, above all, *human* structures. Since these do not have the immutability that characterizes the backcloths of the physical world, but are structures we can reflect upon in the light of values that we hold, we can ask how such geometries might be changed to further goals we hold to be desirable. These goals are always shaped by historical circumstances (Scott, 1982), but in any age what *is* planning — at any scale, individual, neighborhood, urban, regional, national, or even international? Planning may be simply a matter of changing patterns of traffic — employment, income, crop yields, pollution, schooling, leisure time, alcohol consumption, oil flows, diplomatic messages ... providing, and *only providing,* the underlying geometry allows such changes under the graded t-forces we try to exert. But whatever the scale, the patterns we deem as desirable may not be attainable by the q-transmission of existing traffic, or the augmentation of current traffic levels. Then we may have to bring about *structural* change — and realize in the porcess that the search for laws (in anything approaching the sense in which the word is normally used in the physical sciences) is a very different endeavor in the human realm. For as Habermas notes: "Information about law-like connections sets off a process of reflection in the consciousness of those whom the laws are about" (Habermas, 1968, p. 310). We have the capacity to think about, and shape, the geometries that are the real multidimensional worlds we live in.

Yes, a very different perspective: one arising from the distancing that philosophical reflection and more general mathematical structures provide, and clearly a methodological stance out of the reach of the statistical tradition that has shaped so many of our inquiries over the past two decades. These certainly played their own valuable emancipatory role at one time, but their constraining nature is now apparent in the historical development of the field, not just at an unarticulated, intuitive level, but explicated in light of philosophical and mathematical reflection. Bernard Marchand (1974) once wrote that an ideal curriculum for a geographer might consist of equal parts of philosophy, mathematics and field work. There were those who considered such untraditional recommendations hyperbolic, but perhaps if they had been followed we would have had both a deeper and clearer understanding of our problems today. Of course, one would have to consider carefully the philosophical and mathematical traditions that might form part of such a curriculum. We must learn from, and grow out of, Hegel and Marx, even as we acknowledge the more bracing and relevant perspectives of algebraic topology, while acknowledging our historical debts to the traditional calculus and linear algebra. Later philosophical and mathematical perspectives become meaningful to us only as we see them in light of historical circumstance and the intellectual milieux of earlier days, even as more contemporary viewpoints throw light back upon earlier steps.

Thus, my most sincere hope is that this essay will cast some doubt upon the appropriateness of current mathematical statements in human geography, and so generate some uneasy thinking about their intellectual legitimacy. After all, we really face only two choices: either we have got it all right, that is we have already arrived at an ultimate mode of geographic expression that will be taught a hundred years from now, and presumably on down through the ages; or we still have some way to go, new forms of mathematical expression will be considered more appropriate a hundred years from now, and we still face the task of finding them. There does not seem to be very much in between these possibilities. But the fact that the editors and the publishers have the courage and good will to publish such critical thoughts, reflections, and experiences is perhaps the best sign that we may still be able to stand open to new possibilities. As Edmund Husserl once wrote (1962, p. 89): "Blindness with respect to ideas is a form of blindness of soul; one has become, through prejudice, incapable of bringing into the field of judgment what one has in the field of intuition".

Dept. of Geography
The Pennsylvania State University

BIBLIOGRAPHY

Ajo, R.: 1953, *Contributions to Social Physics,* Gleerup, Lund.
Atkin, R.: 1965, 'Abstract physics', *Il Nuevo Cimento* 38, 496–517.
Atkin, R.: 1972, 'From cohomology of observations in physics to q-connectivity in social science', *International Journal of Man-Machine Studies* 4, 139–167.
Atkin, R.: 1974, *Mathematical Structure in Human Affairs,* Heinemann Educational Books, London.
Atkin, R.: 1977a, *Q-Analysis: Theory and Practice,* University of Essex, Department of Mathematics, Research Report X, Colchester.
Atkin, R.: 1977b, *Combinatorial Connectivities in Social Systems,* Birkhäuser Verlag, Basel.
Atkin, R.: 1981, *Multidimensional Man,* Penguin Books, Harmondsworth.
Berry, B.: 1960, 'An inductive approach to the regionalization of economic development and cultural change', *Department of Geography Research Papers* 62, Chicage, 78–107.
Berry, B.: 1961, 'A method for deriving multifactor uniform regions', *Przelgad Geograficzny* 33, 263–282.
Berry, B. and W. Garrison: 1958, 'Functional bases of the central place hierarchy', *Economic Geography* 34, 145–154.
Carrothers, G.: 1956, 'An historical view of the gravity and potential concepts of human interaction', *Journal of the American Institute of Planners* 22, 94–102.
Christensen, K.: 1982, 'Geography as a human science: a philosophic critique of the positivist-humanist split', in P. Gould and G. Olsson (eds.), *A Search for Common Ground,* Pion, London.
Clark, P. and F. Evans: 1954, 'Distance to nearest neighbor as a measure of spatial relationships in populations', *Ecology* 35, 445–453.
Couclelis, H.: 1982, 'Philosophy in the construction of human reality', in P. Gould and G. Olsson (eds.), *A Search for Common Ground,* Pion, London.
Curry, L.: 1960, 'Climatic change as a random series', *Annals of the Association of American Geographers* 52, 21–31.
Curry, L.: 1962, 'The climatic factors in intensive grassland farming: The Waikato, New Zealand', *Geographical Review* 52, 174–194.
Curry, L.: 1964, 'The random spatial economy: an exploration in settlement theory', *Annals of the Association of American Geographers* 54, 138–146.
Dacey, M.: 1960, 'A note on the derivation of nearest neighbor distances', *Journal of Regional Science* 2, 81–87.
Garrison, W.: 1955, 'The spatial impact of transport media: studies of rural roads', *Papers and Proceedings of the Regional Science Association* 1, 1–14.
Gaspar, J. and P. Gould: 1981, 'The Cova da Beira: an applied structural analysis of agriculture and communication', in A. Pred (ed.), *A Festschrift for Torsten Hägerstand,* Liber, Lund.
Godlund, S.: 1956a, *Bus Service in Sweden,* Gleerup, Lund.
Godlund, S.: 1956b, *The Function and Growth of Bus Traffic within the Sphere of Urban Influence,* Gleerup, Lund.
Gould, P.: 1979, 'Geography 1957–77: the Augean period', *Annals of the Association of American Geographers* 69, 139–151.
Gould, P.: 1980, '*Q*-analysis, or a language of structure: An introduction for social

scientists, geographers and planners', *International Journal of Man-Machine Studies* 12, 169–199.

Gould, P.: 1981, 'Letting the data speak for themselves', *Annals of the Association of American Geographers* 71, 166–176.

Gould, P. 1982, 'Is it necessary to choose? Some technical, hermeneutic and emancipatory thoughts on inquiry', in P. Gould and G. Olsson (eds.), *A Search for Common Ground*, Pion, London.

Habermas, J.: 1968, *Knowledge and Human Interests*, Beacon Press, Boston.

Hägerstrand, T.: 1952, *The Propagation of Innovation Waves*, Gleerup, Lund.

Hägerstrand, T.: 1953, *Innovationsförloppet ur korologisk synpunkt*, Gleerup, Lund.

Hägerstrand, T.: 1967, 'On monte carlo simulation of diffusion', in *Quantitative Geography, Part I Economic and Cultural Topics*, Northwestern Studies in Geography 132, Evanston.

Husserl, E.: 1950, *Ideen*, Martinus Nijhoff, The Hague, translated by W. Gibson, *Ideas*, Colliers, New York, 1962.

Marchand, B.: 1974, 'Quantitative geography: Revolution or counter-revolution?', *Geoforum* 17, 15–23.

Marchand, B.: 1979, 'Dialectics and geography', in S. Gale and G. Olsson (eds.), *Philosophy in Geography*, D. Reidel, Dordrecht, pp. 237–267.

Matui, I.: 1932 'Statistical study of the distribution of scattered villages in two regions of the Tonami plain', *Japanese Journal of Geology and Geography* 9, 251–266.

McCarty, H.: 1956, 'Use of certain statistical procedures in geographical analysis', *Annals of the Association of American Geographers* 46, 263.

Misner C., K. Thorne, and J. Wheeler: 1974, *Gravitation*, W. H. Freeman, San Francisco.

Morrill, R.: 1965, *Migration and the Spread and Growth of Urban Settlement*, Gleerup, Lund.

Morrill, R. and W. Garrison: 1960, 'Projections of interregional patterns of trade in wheat and flour', *Economic Geography* 36, 116–126.

Penrose, R.: 1974, 'The role of aesthetics in pure and applied mathematical research', *Bulletin of the Institute of Mathematics and Its Applications* 10, 266–271.

Russell, B.: 1956, 'Mathematical knowledge as based on a theory of types', in R. Marsh (ed.), *Logic and Knowledge: Essays 1901–1950*, Allen and Unwin, London.

Scott, A.: 1982, 'The meaning and the social origins of discourse on the spatial foundations of society', in P. Gould and G. Olsson (eds.), *A Search for Common Ground*, Pion, London.

Simon, H.: 1980, *Items* 34, 6–7, Social Science Research Council, New York.

Steiner, G.: 1978, *Has Truth a Future?*, BBC Publications, London.

Stewart, J.: 1947 'Empirical mathematical rules concerning the distribution and equilibrium of population', *Geographical Review* 37, 461–485.

Stewart, J. and W. Warntz: 1958, 'Macrogeography and social science', *Geographical Review* 48, 167–184.

Taaffe, E.: 1958, 'A map analysis of airline competition', *Journal of Air Law and Commerce* 25, 402–427.

Thomas, E.: 1960, *Maps of Residuals from Regression*, University of Iowa Department of Geography, Iowa City.

MICHAEL F. GOODCHILD

GEOCODING AND GEOSAMPLING

1. INTRODUCTION

The purpose of this chapter is to discuss current methods and practices in two very fundamental aspects of spatial analysis. Geocoding can be defined as the process by which an entity on the earth's surface, a household, for example, is given a label identifying its location with respect to some common point or frame of reference. The section on geocoding discusses the various coordinate systems and other spatial referencing methods in common use, and their advantages and disadvantages for various kinds of applications. This leads naturally into a discussion of metrics and the measurement of distance, which again is fundamental to much of spatial analysis.

Spatial analysis creates its own problems of sampling, and far too little is known about the extent to which the results of spatial analyses are affected by sample design. The later sections of the chapter discuss various methods of sampling in space and some of their associated properties, and the accuracy of estimates from spatial samples. The related issue of spatial aggregation has attracted a great deal of attention recently and so will also be discussed. Unfortunately, it is impossible to do full justice to many of these topics in a chapter of this length, but the references provided should allow the reader to investigate further.

2. GEOCODING

2.1. *Coordinate Systems*

The most universally accepted way of specifying a location on the earth's surface is by latitude and longitude, the first being the angle formed at the earth's center between a line through the point of interest and the plane of the equator. The second is the angle between two planes through the poles, one also passing through the point and the latter passing through Greenwich, England. The poles and the equator are defined by the earth's rotation, which is certainly constant enough for most practical purposes, so it is only the choice of Greenwich which might be regarded as arbitrary. Fortunately, the

33

Gary L. Gaile and Cort J. Willmott (eds.), Spatial Statistics and Models, 33–53.
© 1984 *by D. Reidel Publishing Company.*

choice seems to have weathered all of the geopolitical changes which have occurred since it was made.

A latitude/longitude geocode consists then of a pair of angles, specified in degrees, minutes and seconds, and associated senses, either north or south of the equator for latitude, and east or west of Greenwich for longitude. A mathematically neater alternative is to express both latitude and longitude as decimal numbers, with associated signs, north and east being positive and south and west, negative.

From the point of view of precision and universality, latitude-longitude is the ideal method of geocoding the position of a point on the globe. However, there would be serious problems in any major application because of the difficulties first of determining accurate latitude and longitude for a large number of points and secondly of plotting geocoded locations on a map for display. Only a very few projections have the property that lines of constant latitude and longitude appear straight, so it is much easier in practice to use a spatial referencing system based on relationships on a flat map, despite the generality of the global referencing system.

The conventional coordinate system on a plane places the reference origin in the lower left corner. Two reference axes are drawn at right angles to each other, the first horizontally to the right and the second vertically upwards. A point's location is then specified as a distance from the origin parallel to the first axis and a second distance parallel to the second. Several aspects of this conventional Cartesian system are arbitrary, most notably the choice of the origin point and the orientation of the axes. It is usual to place the second axis in the direction of north, and the two coordinates are often referred to as easting and northing respectively, rather then x and y.

It is clearly much easier to measure the values of x and y for a point on a map than it is to calculate latitude and longitude. In practice, many applications of spatial statistics are to areas which can be shown on a single map sheet, and for which an arbitrary origin in the bottom left corner is perfectly adequate since the geocoded data will not be used in any wider context. The area covered is also sufficiently small that distortion due to projection of the globe onto a flat plane can be ignored. A more universal system may be needed for other applications, and particularly for the construction of geocoded data banks at a national scale.

Geocoding practice in the U.S. provides a good example. At the scale of individual states, projected maps of the globe are virtually distortionfree, and so it is possible for each state to develop its own system of plane coordinates for internal purposes. At the national scale, and for comparison between states, the curvature of the earth is sufficiently severe to make the use of latitude and longitude advisable, and so this is the system in which much national geocoded data are distributed. On the other hand, because of its smaller size, the U.K. is able to use a national coordinate system, the National Grid, based on Cartesian coordinates on a single projection.

The common practice in Canada is to use a series of projections for different parts of the country, so that a single geocode in this system consists of an easting and northing coupled with a projection, or zone, number. There are awkward problems with this system when the area of a study, perhaps a metropolitan area, happens to span two zones. The projection used is the Universal Transverse Mercator (UTM), which is made in effect by wrapping a sheet of paper around the poles of the earth, touching along a particular pair of lines of longitude $180°$ apart (this is in contrast to the conventional Mercator in which the paper is wrapped around the equator). These lines of longitude are called the central meridians of the projection. Since there is least distortion near this line, the zones used in the UTM grid system are narrow strips on either side of a series of central meridians.

If a location can be specified on a map as the pair (x, y) and on the globe as (ϕ, θ), then any projection can be regarded as a series of relationships between (x, y) and (ϕ, θ). A very simple example is given by

$$x = k\theta$$
$$y = k\phi$$

which defines a projection in which meridians are equally spaced and parallel to the y axis and similarly lines of constant latitude are equally spaced and parallel to x. k is the distance on the projection corresponding to one degree of either latitude or longitude. Similar, though more complex, relationships exist for every projection. A good source is Maling (1973).

From a practical point of view, the easiest way to create latitude-longitude data is first to find Cartesian coordinates on a map, and then to convert to (ϕ, θ) using the known projection characteristics of the map. Generation of large numbers of (x, y) coordinates has been made easy with the development of digitizers, devices capable of digitally encoding and recording a specified location in a defined coordinate system. Table-sized systems are now widely available.

With a variety of general and specialized coordinate systems in use, transformations from one to another are inevitable from time to time. As an example, suppose an analysis is being made of the locations of fire emergencies in a particular city. The locations have been digitized in an x, y system with arbitrary origin. Suppose it is now necessary to identify the census tabulation zones in which each emergency lies, and that the outlines of the census areas are available in latitude-longitude coordinates. Two approaches are available. If the origin, axis orientations and projection characteristics of the map from which the emergency locations were taken are all known, the transformation equations could be deduced theoretically. It is much more likely that one or more of these parameters are unknown, requiring a more pragmatic approach.

The second method is based on taking a small number of control points, in locations which are easily recognizable on a map. For these, both sets of coordinates are determined. Now let the required transformations be

$$u = f(x,y)$$
$$v = g(x,y).$$

For most applications, one is willing to assume that the transformations are linear, that is, that parallel equally spaced lines in one coordinate system would also plot as parallel and equally spaced in the other. With this assumption, the transformation equations are

$$u = a + bx + cy$$
$$v = d + ex + fy$$

which describe a wide variety of operations including any combination of origin relocation, scale change, rotation and mirror inversion. The anticlockwise angle of rotation is $\tan^{-1} (-ce/bf)^{1/2}$ and the condition for a mirror inversion is $bf < ce$.

The coefficients can now be determined from the control point data. With linear equations, a, b and c can be estimated by ordinary least squares (multiple regression) using values of x and y as independent variables and u as dependent, and similarly for d, e and f with v as dependent. Besides giving the required transformation, OLS ensures that any errors are distributed over the control points and not concentrated in a few.

The following example application is taken from a study of grocery store market penetration in London, Ontario. Locations of consumers were known in an arbitrary, digitizer-table coordinate system with an origin in the city's southwest corner. The census tract outlines were known in the national grid system, which is based on a Universal Transverse Mercator projection. In order to transform consumer (x, y) locations into the grid (u, v), twelve control points were taken at major street intersections (Table I) and coordinates determined in both systems.

The residuals from the two regressions suggested that in two cases (points 9 and 11) mistakes were made in collecting the control point data. This was confirmed when the transformations were recalibrated with the remaining nine points, giving new r^2 values of 0.998 and 0.999 respectively, and the equations shown in Table I.

TABLE I

Example of the use of control points to deduce the coefficients of a
linear transformation

Control Point	Street intersection	X	Y	UTM North	UTM East
1	Oxford and Sanitorium	2.90	9.80	4757500	472700
2	Wonderland and Southdale	4.86	5.96	4753800	476500
3	Wharncliffe and Stanley	7.32	8.56	4758200	478600
4	Oxford and Wharncliffe	7.58	9.67	4759800	478400
5	Wellington and Southdale	8.24	4.90	4754300	481500
6	Highbury and Hamilton Rd.	11.32	6.67	4758200	484100
7	Trafalgar and Clarke	13.17	7.56	4759700	486200
8	Adelaide and Dundas	9.49	8.59	4759400	481100
9	Clarke and Huron	11.48	10.62	4763700	484700
10	Highbury and Fanshawe	11.50	12.68	4765400	481500
11	Richmond and Fanshawe	9.67	12.78	4763600	476900
12	Richmond and Huron	8.28	10.73	4761500	478800

Transformations: UTM East = 4744135 + 500.95X + 1222.25Y
UTM North = 473667 + 1207.94X − 464.56Y

2.2. Alternative Methods of Geocoding

The concern in the previous section was with methods of specifying precise location. In many cases, the benefit of such precision may not justify the cost of obtaining it, and in this section we consider more approximate methods which still fall under the general heading of geocoding.

A national population census provides a good working example. In order to produce a total head count, it is not necessary that the records in a national census be geocoded in any way. However, many censuses are mandated on the need for population counts on a small area basis, often in order to provide the information on which representation in the legislative assembly is based. It is essential then to code each individual record to the smallest area for which tabulation is needed. In the U.S. and Canada, this is the block face, on one side of a residential street between two intersections. Finer coding is considered unnecessarily expensive. In order to provide a truly spatial reference, it is still necessary to establish coordinates for each block face centroid, but this is much cheaper than finding coordinates for each individual, and also need be done only once rather than at each census.

Small area data are in increasing demand for studies in marketing, site selection and urban planning. In the former context, the postal addressing system provides a useful method of geocoding consumers addresses to a level of precision which is appropriate for many market penetration studies. In Canada, the first three characters of the postal code identify an area of several thousand households. These zones, or Forward Sortation Areas, have been digitized, allowing the consumers identified on any mailing list to be mapped. A data set created by Statistics Canada identifies the correspondences between the full six character postal code (about 10^6 spatial units) and the Census enumeration area (about 10^5).

Another route to geocoding is through the street address. Although addresses are sometimes difficult to process because of spelling and format variations, it is possible in some countries to match addresses to census zones and thus to coordinate locations, and also to the postal coding system, through the use of master address data files. Political administrative units such as counties also provide a means of more approximate geocoding.

In summary, with increasing interest in spatial analyses in a number of application areas and associated development of data bases, one can anticipate a continuing trend to approximate geocoding through the standard aggregation units established by census, postal and other agencies. Some of the less desirable consequences of this are discussed in a later section of this chapter.

2.3. *Aggregation and Mapping*

Many applications of geocoded data require some form of aggregation. This is true, for example, in the tabulation of census data for statistical areas. Because of the confidentiality rules under which most surveys and national censuses are conducted, publication of results is only possible in spatially aggregated form.

If the data have been geocoded by zone, as discussed in the previous section, it is a simple matter to tabulate them by those zones, or by any larger units which respect the boundaries of those zones. Thus, many census systems will publish data for a range of areal aggregates — in Canada the region, province, census division, census subdivision, federal electoral district, census metropolitan area, etc., all of which respect the boundaries of the smallest unit for which data are published, the enumeration area, which has a mean population of a few hundred people.

Inevitably, there will be cases where statistics are needed for areas which do not respect the boundaries of the zones to which the data are geocoded. In London, Ontario, the annual assessment data, which contain records of the occupancy of every residential unit in the city, are geocoded to polling subdivisions, of which there are about 700 for a city of 250,000 people. One of the more important applications of these data are in predictions of school enrollment, yet school district boundaries do not respect those of the polling subdivisions.

In general, suppose the area of interest is divided into s source zones — each of area σ_i, $i=1, s$ — for which aggregate statistics u_i, $i=1, s$ are known. Suppose also, as in the example above, that no more precise geocode is available; in other words, statistics are not available for any smaller zones. Aggregate statistics are now needed for a set of t target zones, of area, τ_j, $j=1, t$. Consider the possibility of making estimates v_j, $j=1, t$ using a set of weights as follows:

$$v_j = \sum_i w_{ij} u_i,$$

where w_{ij} is the weight given to source zone i in estimating for target zone j. In order to ensure that every individual in each source zone is assigned to one and only one target zone, we will need

$$\sum_j w_{ij} = 1 \quad \text{for all} \quad i.$$

Now consider the possible ways of determining w_{ij}. First, one might assume that each source zone is homogeneous in density. Homogeneity is a criterion in delimiting many types of statistical and administrative areas, so the assumption will often have some validity. In that case, one can base w_{ij} on the area of intersection a_{ij} between source zone i and target zone j; in other words,

$$w_{ij} = a_{ij} / \sigma_i.$$

The estimates will be perfect if the homogeneity assumption is correct. Unfortunately, an area of intersection between two zones is not readily measured from a map, and this method is rather cumbersome to apply manually, although computer codes exist for calculating intersection areas from digitized zone outlines. There are two simpler, more approximate approaches which are much easier to carry out by hand. First, we could set w_{ij} equal for all target zones which intersect with a given source zone,

$$w_{ij} = 1/\sum_j n_{ij}$$

where $n_{ij} = 1$ if $a_{ij} > 0$. This is equivalent to an equal sharing of the source zone population among intersecting target zones. The second approach is to set w_{ij} to 1 for the target zone which has the greatest area of intersection with a given source zone.

Homogeneity of density within zones implies a view of the study area, probably a city, as a series of stepped plateaus, with sharp breaks at source zone boundaries. This is in contrast to much existing work on urban form, which has often emphasized smooth variation of such critical parameters as density. This alternative view is reflected in estimators of the form

$$w_{ij} = f(d_{ij}),$$

where d_{ij} is the distance between a control point in source zone i and a corresponding point in target zone j, and f is a decreasing function. For example, $f(d_{ij}) = e^{-\beta}d_{ij}$. It is usual in this case to ignore the constraint $\sum_j w_{ij} = 1$. Functions such as this imply a smoothly varying density, so that the value of density at a point is most like the values at neighboring points, and increasingly less like values taken from further and further away. On the other hand, the earlier approach based on area implies that density is identical to that at all points within the same source zone and unlike that at all other points. Goodchild and Lam (1980) have reviewed these methods in more detail and give an empirical comparison. An interesting variant on these methods which preserves the constraint $\sum_j w_{ij} = 1$ is given by Tobler (1979).

The third case to be considered under the heading of aggregation methods occurs when the data are geocoded to coordinates, either (x, y) or (θ, ϕ). In this case, there is no easy method of aggregation to statistical areas, but, on the other hand, the freedom exists in principle to aggregate to any choice of statistical areas with a little effort. Given a set of zones of interest, the problem here may be seen as one of identifying the zone in which each geocoded datum point lies. From the computational point of view, zones are usually represented as irregular polygons, coded as an ordered set of vertex coordinates. The problem is known, therefore, as the point-in-polygon problem, and a number of efficient codes exist. A good source for this and other standard geographical data processing problems is Baxter (1976) and an extensive catalog of computer codes has been produced by Calkins and Marble (1981).

To end this section, a brief comment will be made on the problem of mapping geocoded data. Data which have been aggregated, or geocoded to a series of zones rather than to coordinates, can be mapped in one of two ways. In a choropleth map, each zone is filled with a color or shading intensity determined by the density of points in the zone. When the shading is done by computer and output through a plotter or onto a display screen, it is possible to use a continuous range of shading intensity instead of a limited number of standard intensities. Tobler (1973) has described this recent development of interval-free choropleth maps in which the shading intensity in each zone is exactly proportional to the zone's value, thus avoiding the distorting influence of fixed intervals. However, Dobson (1973) has argued against this. He maintains that class intervals are chosen by a cartographer to help the user understand the phenomenon, and should not be regarded as mere distortion. A good review of this issue is given by Evans (1977).

The alternative method of mapping returns to the notion of a smoothly varying density surface. A control point is chosen in each polygon, usually at the centroid, which can be readily calculated from the coordinates of the polygon's vertices, as follows:

$$x_c = \frac{1}{A} \sum_{j=1}^{m} (2x_j y_j + x_j y_{j+1} + x_{j+1} y_j + 2x_{j+1} y_{j+1}) (x_{j+1} - x_j)/6$$

$$y_c = \frac{1}{A} \sum_{j=1}^{m} (y_j^2 + y_j y_{j+1} + y_{j+1}^2) (x_{j+1} - x_j)/6$$

where A is the polygon area given by

$$A = \sum_{j=1}^{m} (x_{j+1} - x_j) (y_{j+1} + y_j)/2$$

and x_i, y_i, $i = 1, m$ are the ordered pairs of polygon vertex coordinates and $x_{m+1} = x_1$, $y_{m+1} = y_1$. The polygon is assumed to have been coded in a clockwise direction in a Cartesian coordinate system.

Then the centroids are used to generate a smooth density surface, by assigning to each point in the study area a value based on those at nearby sample points.

$$z = \sum_i z_i f(d_i),$$

where d_i is the distance to the control point for polygon i and z_i is polygon i's value. The function f is a decreasing function of distance, usually negative exponential or negative power. For reviews of this and other methods of spatial interpolation see Schut (1976), Crain (1970), Lancaster and Salkaulkas (1977) and the chapter in this volume by Shepard on the SYMAP algorithm.

2.4. *Metrics*

Distance is a fundamental measure intimately related to coordinate systems. Many models of spatial interaction rely on the measurement of distance as the length of a trip, related in turn to the trip's cost or duration. One of the recurrent difficulties in this area lies in the relationship, or lack of it, between simple mathematical measures of distance and the real length of a trip by a specified mode of transport, which is determined by the transport network for that mode.

On the globe, the shortest path between two places (ϕ_1, θ_1) and (ϕ_2, θ_2) is the arc of the circle formed when a plane is passed through the two points and through the earth's center, in other words, the arc of a great circle. Its length is given by

$$R \cos^{-1} [\sin \phi_1 \sin \phi_2 + \cos \phi_1 \cos \phi_2 \cos (\theta_1 - \theta_2)],$$

where R is the radius of the earth. Since there are no projections on which all great circles plot as straight lines, it follows that this shortest path is often difficult to plot and measure from a map. And, if one insists that the earth is in fact an oblate spheroid rather than a sphere, the situation is even more complex (see for example Bomford, 1971).

On a plane, the shortest distance between two points (x_1, y_1) and (x_2, y_2) follows from Pythagoras' theorem

$$[(x_1 - x_2)^2 + (y_1 - y_2)^2]^{1/2}$$

and is the most widely used estimate of distance. In reality, it is almost always an underestimate of the true length of a trip, and so various attempts have been to improve its relationship to reality. A simple generalization leads to

$$[\,|x_1 - x_2|^p + |y_1 - y_2|^p\,]^{1/p}$$

which is known as the L_p norm or Minkowski p-metric. Its most obvious application is when $p = 1$, when it gives the distance travelled in a network of routes aligned parallel to the x and y axes. L_1 is often called the Manhattan or city-block or rectangular metric. Note, however, that unlike L_2, it is not invariant under rotation of the axes: if the available routes are not aligned with x and y the expression becomes

$$[\,|(x_1 - x_2) \cos \alpha + (y_1 - y_2) \sin \alpha|^p + $$
$$+ |(y_1 - y_2) \cos \alpha - (x_1 - x_2) \sin \alpha|^p\,]^{1/p}$$

where α is the angle of rotation between the orthogonal axes and the rectangular network of routes. Relative to straight line distance, L_1 is the same for a path parallel to one of the sets of parallel routes, but incurs a penalty of a factor of $\sqrt{2}$ at 45°.

Another simple method of increasing the accuracy of straight line distance as an estimate of trip length is by the introduction of barriers. In Figure 1,

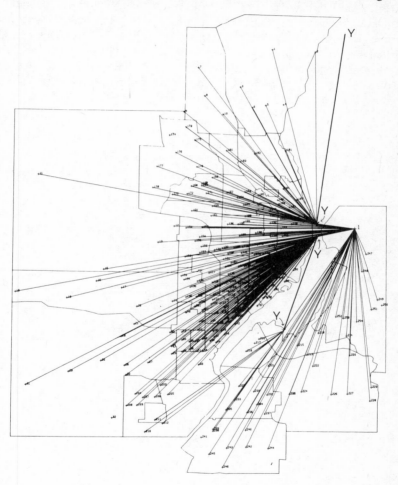

Fig. 1. Example of the use of barriers to improve the accuracy of the straight line metric, Peoria, Illinois.

a number of barriers to travel have been introduced as straight line segments for unbridged stretches of the Illinois River in Peoria, Illinois. Distances between enumeration district centroids and a hypothetical retail location have then been measured through gaps in the barrier denoting bridging points.

Ultimately, though, the most accurate way of measuring trip length is through the network itself. Figure 2 shows the network of major streets used for the purpose of routing fire emergency vehicles in London, Ontario. All traffic lights on these routes have been equipped with sensors allowing them to be reset to green by an approaching fire truck. In order to evaluate response time to a fire, it is necessary to find out and measure the fastest path from fire station to fire through this network.

Fig. 2.   Network of major streets with numbered intersections, London, Ontario.

Suppose that information is available on the time taken to traverse each link of this network under normal traffic conditions. Then the problem reduces to the standard "shortest path problem" of operations research. An efficient code suitable for applications in locational analysis can be found in Rushton *et al.* (1973). It is based on the Dijkstra (1959) algorithm which finds the shortest path from an origin node to a destination node together with the path's length.

The algorithm proceeds as follows:

1) label the origin node 'reached'.
2) Examine all 'unreached' nodes which can be reached to a single link from a 'reached' node. Find the one which can be reached with minimum total distance. Lable this node 'reached'.
3) If the destination is still 'unreached' return to Step 2.

Note that it is necessary to find the shortest paths to all nodes closer than the destination in solving for one origin-destination pair, so there is a certain economy if all distances from a particular origin have to be found.

In general, the cost of collecting detailed data on transport routes can be high, particularly for such applications as the location of social services, for which a number of modes of transport may be relevant. There has therefore been substantial interest recently in developing metrics which more accurately reflect route lengths through networks, but which can be calculated from coordinates. Love and Morris (1972, 1979) have investigated a number of complex metrics, including

$$P_1 [|x_1 - x_2|^{P_2} + |y_1 - y_2|^{P_2}]^{P_3}$$

which is a generalization of the L_p norm. From a strictly practical point of view, this is an important area and much work remains to be done.

The nest section will turn to the second subject of this chapter, which is the problem of sampling in space.

3. GEOSAMPLING

This section is divided into three parts. The first deals with sampling in space as a variation on the general sampling problem, and discusses conditions under which it is appropriate. The second part is concerned with the consequences of sampling in two areas of current interest, remote sensing and topographic mapping. Finally, the third part takes the issue of spatial aggregation within the context of sampling, and discusses some recent work in that area.

3.1. *Sampling in Space*

In the classic sampling problem, there exists a population for which information is needed. A selection of individuals is taken from this population, and statements are made about the population based on the characteristics of the selected sample. The statements will be valid as long as the sample is representative, which it will be if it was chosen randomly, in such a way that each individual had an equal chance of being chosen. If the sample was chosen by some systematic procedure, it is essential that this procedure create no bias in the resulting sample. Sampling theory, therefore, deals with two types of samples, random and systematic. A third type is often identified in those cases where it is known in advance that the population consists of diverse groups which are present in different numbers. In order to make equally confident statements about each group, it is necessary that the sample be stratified by taking equal subsamples from each group. Since the groups are not equally common, this means that the intensity of sampling must be higher among the less common groups.

Most populations from which one might want to sample in the course of a study are unevenly distributed over space. A random sample of the households in a city is not therefore a random sample of all places in the city unless the households happen to be uniformly distributed. This is unfortunate, since it is relatively easier to take a random sample of the population of all places, by taking a map and tossing darts at it. It is much more difficult to take a random sample of the households in a city because although the sampling frame for a spatial sample is readily available in the form of a map, the sampling frame for a household sample, a list of all households in the city, is much more difficult to obtain. One often resorts instead to frames such as the telephone directory, although this inevitably leads to a bias in the sample against households without telephones or with unlisted numbers.

In summary, although sampling places is relatively easy, their population, the set of all places, is rarely of interest. So although all populations are in some sense located in space, it is usually not possible to sample them by sampling locations. For example, suppose one wished to obtain a sample of households in a city. It would be tempting to think of visiting each block face in the city and selecting a random household from it. But, the result would not be a random sample of households unless each block face in the city contained exactly the same number. Similarly, it is extremely unlikely that a satisfactory sample of anything other than the set of all places can be obtained by placing a grid over a map and obtaining one case from each grid square. It appears, then, that studies in spatial analysis are unlikely to lead to unusual patterns of sampling except in the subject areas covered in the next section, where a sample of places is specifically required.

One problem of a methodological nature which seems particularly prevalent in spatial analysis is that of the 100% sample. Suppose, by way of example, that an analysis is conducted of the relationship between two census variables, say average income and the percentage of the population with postsecondary education, at the census tract scale. Because data are available for all census tracts in the city, it seems reasonable to use a 100% sample. How, then, should one interpret those aspects of the results, the significance of r^2, say, which are based on the notion that the data consist of a sample from some larger population? What is the larger population if there are no more census tracts in the city?

The question is by no means trivial, unless one accepts the answer that the larger population is simply the set of which the sample is representative. It is certainly not the set of all census tracts, since these were all chosen from one city. It is tempting to suggest that the population consists of all alternative ways of drawing the given number of census tracts in the city, but that possibility will be rejected later in this chapter. There is, in fact, no entirely satisfactory answer, and the purist would insist that the value of this kind of analysis is limited strictly to description of the city itself with no possibility of generalization to a wider context.

3.2. Samples of Space

Despite the conclusions of the previous section, there are cases where it is relevant to take samples from the set of all possible places in a study area. In the first part of this section, the problem of sampling topography in the production of topographic maps is considered. The second part discusses sampling in the context of remote sensing.

3.2.1. *Topographic Mapping.* In the traditional method of topographic mapping, a series of photographs are taken from an aircraft flying in a straight line at constant altitude. Each pair of consecutive photographs is then compared. By viewing the pair and adjusting each one to allow for parallax, it is possible to compute the relative elevations of each point on the ground, and thus to trace out contours of constant elevation. These contours are then edited by hand, additional cultural information is added and the finished map is printed.

Attempts have been made to automate this labor-intensive process at various stages. Perhaps the most ambitious is the development of the Gestalt photomapper, which takes the same pair of aerial photographs but scans them with two television cameras. The resulting images are then compared in a specially built electronic processor. The final product is a very dense regular grid of sample elevations in digital form, known as a digital terrain model (DTM) or digital elevation model (DEM). This can then be passed to a contouring algorithm or processed further.

Consider the properties of the DTM as a sample of terrain. It is systematic rather than random, since only points on the regular grid can appear in the sample. But, unless the terrain has very peculiar periodic properties, the sample will be unbiased. However, suppose that part of the study area is relatively smooth and part relatively rugged. Then, it would be more efficient to take a stratified sample with a higher density of sample points in the rugged area. In fact, the distance between sample points determines the finest level of detail the sample can reveal. A similar point applies at a very small scale, since many landscapes possess critical points, such as hilltops, and critical lines such as ridge tops and stream channels, where the slope of the landscape changes very rapidly. The final map would be much more accurate if sample points could be placed exactly on such features.

One of the critical issues in this kind of process is the payoff between increased density of sample points and map accuracy on the one hand, and volume of data and processing time and cost on the other. This clearly depends on the statistical nature of terrain, and yet very little is known in this area. One might claim that terrain is so variable and complex that no truths can exists to be discovered. But, that would seem to deny the existence of geomorphology as a science. Some progress has been made in understanding terrain as a statistical process through the concept of fractals and fractional Brownian processes (Mandelbrot, 1977), but much remains to be done in this area.

Figure 3 shows the product of an application of the Gestalt photomapper to a test area near Sudbury, Ontario. One of the more substantial difficulties in the system is in dealing with trees and tall buildings; a human operator can selectively contour the ground beneath the trees, if it is visible, but an automatic system is likely to be confused. Fortunately, the Sudbury area has very few trees because of the adverse effects of nickel smelting. Difficulties

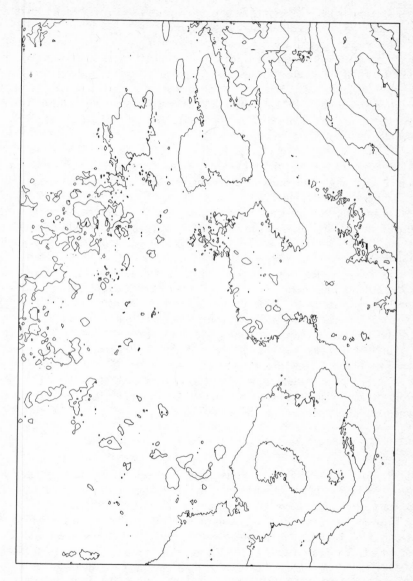

Fig. 3. Contours generated from a very dense digital terrain model of an area near Sudbury, Ontario.

are also created by lakes, which have no features to correlate, and there is an example in the top right of the area shown.

The contouring illustrates another problem with the process. Small amounts of error in elevation, caused perhaps by trees or lack of clear ground texture, result in small spurious deviations and loops in the contours, particularly in areas of substantially flat terrain. It would be useful if such spurious detail could be distinguished from real features, but to do so would require an understanding both of the statistical nature of the errors present and also of the statistical nature of real terrain.

3.2.2. *Remote Sensing.* In this section, we consider a statistical problem of spatial sampling arising in remote sensing and other areas which is relatively well understood. Suppose we are interested in determining the acreage of wheat growing in a particular area. An image of the area is obtained from an aircraft or satellite platform in the form of a regular grid of pixels, each of which is then classified as wheat or not wheat. The total acreage is then obtained by counting. Notice that this is a similar method to that used by a forester who wishes to measure an area on a map by overlaying an array of dots and counting the number falling in the area of interest. The accuracy of the area estimate clearly depends on the pixel size or density of dots, but so too does the cost of estimation. The precise relationship between them is clearly an important input to any large-scale application.

Suppose first that the area of interest occurs in very small patches, so that it is possible to assume that the probability p of a cell or dot being counted is independent of whether or not its neighbors were also counted. Then, from the binomial distribution, the standard deviation in the number counted when a total of N dots or pixels are used is

$$[Np(1-p)]^{1/2}.$$

If the total area is A, the standard deviation in the estimate of area is $[p(1-p)/N]^{1/2}A$, or in other words, the accuracy in the estimate of area depends on the total number of dots or pixels to the negative one half power.

In most cases, though, the assumption of independence will not be valid; if one pixel is classed as wheat, it is more likely that its neighbors will also be wheat, if wheat occurs in patches of more than one pixel. Frolov and Maling (1969) show that under these conditions, the dependence of accuracy on number of pixels is to the negative three fourths power, with the addition of a parameter to describe the shape of the patch. Goodchild (1980) reviewed additional literature in this area and related several of the results to the concept of fractals mentioned earlier.

3.3. *Spatial Aggregation*

This last section looks briefly at the problem of spatial representation, or to the extent to which the spatial basis for statistical data affects the results of spatial analysis. Much of the recent contribution to this area has been made in a series of papers by Openshaw (see for example 1977a, b; 1978).

We noted before in the section on sampling the difficulty of interpreting the results of computing correlations between statistics such as average income and education level for aggregate areas such as census tracts, yet the entire literature of factorial ecology (see for example Berry, 1971) is based on such relationships. The first contribution to the aggregation problem came in the mid 1950's with the recognition of the ecological fallacy — that it would be fallacious to conclude in this case those individuals with higher education enjoy higher incomes. A correlation at the aggregate or ecological level need not imply a similar correlation at the individual level.

The census tracts in the example are fairly arbitarily drawn, despite some loosely stated design criteria, and yet they clearly affect the result. It is important, then, to know to what extent the result can be affected by a redefinition of the spatial basis. Suppose one were to redraw the tracts, by reaggregating from some more basic level of smaller units. One would find in fact that the previous result was one of a very large number of possible results, each of which has a similar claim to being correct.

Openshaw argues in his papers that the range of possible results is very much greater than expected, and he shows that almost any result can be produced by suitable manipulation of zone boundaries. It is tempting to argue that the aggregation effect is much like sampling, and that we have merely observed a random sample from the population of possible results, to echo an earlier section. But, Openshaw points out that the actual boundaries have always been designed for some specific purpose using more or less clearly identified criteria, and so the analogy between zone design and sampling is false. He maintains that rather than the singular value for an observed zoning system subject to the unknown effects of a particular set of criteria, it is the entire distribution of values for all possible zoning systems which is important, or at least a measure of central tendency of the distribution. Only then can zoning be said to have a neutral effect.

This recent interest in the spatial basis of many aggregate statistics has cast doubt on much previous work and introduced an entire set of new concerns. It is clear that the issue will have to be addressed much more explicitly in future studies using this kind of data, and it is unlikely that any general answers or solutions will be found.

4. CONCLUSIONS

This chapter has covered a lot of ground in dealing with two not very related topics — geocoding and geosampling. The first is at the heart of the very technically-oriented field of geographical data processing and automated mapping, two areas of rapid growth on the borders between geography and computer science. Recent advances in the production of cheap color graphics with microcomputers ensures that this growth will continue for some time to come.

The term geosampling is not widely recognized, although the idea of sampling in space certainly creates special problems, many of which have yet to receive a satisfactory solution. Perhaps the most general point to be gathered from the discussion in this chapter is one repeated in the chapter by Daniel Griffith: that despite nearly three decades of statistical geography, we have only recently begun to develop and understand the statistics of spatial processes. Instead, it is the spatial assumptions of conventional statistics which are still too often taken as the rule, and the spatial aspects of statistical processes treated as the exception.

Dept. of Geography
The University of Western Ontario

BIBLIOGRAPHY

Baxter, R. S.: 1976, *Computer and Statistical Techniques for Planners*, Methuen, London.
Berry, B. J. L.: 1971, 'Introduction: the logic and limitations of comparative factorial ecology', *Economic Geography* 47, 209–219.
Bomford, G.: 1971, *Geodesy* (3rd edition), Clarendon, Oxford.
Calkins, K. W. and D. F. Marble: 1981, *Computer Software for Spatial Data Handling* (3 volumes), International Geographical Union, Commission on Geographical Data Sensing and Processing, Ottawa.
Crain, I.: 1970, 'Computer interpolation and contouring of two-dimensional data: a review', *Geoexploration* 8, 71–86.
Dijkstra, E. W.: 1959, 'A note on two problems in connexion with graphs', *Numerische Mathematik* 1, 269–271.

Dobson, M. W.: 1973, 'Choropleth maps without class intervals? A comment', *Geographical Analysis* 5, 358–360.

Evans, I. S.: 1977, 'The selection of class intervals', *Institute of British Geographers Transactions* 2 (NS), 98–124

Frolov, Y. S. and D. H. Maling: 1969, 'The accuracy of area measurements by point counting techniques', *Cartographic Journal* 6, 21–35.

Goodchild, M. F.: 1980, 'A fractal approach to the accuracy of geographical measures', *Mathematical Geology* 12, 85–98.

Goodchild, M. F. and N. S. Lam: 1980, 'Areal interpolation: a variant of the traditional spatial problem', *Geoprocessing* 1, 297–312.

Lancaster, P. and K. Salkaulkas: 1977, *A Survey of Curve and Surface Fitting,* University of Calgary.

Love, R. F. and J. G. Morris: 1972, 'Modelling inter city road distances by mathematical functions', *Operational Research Quarterly* 23, 61–71.

Love, R. F. and J. G. Morris: 1979, 'Mathematical models of road travel distances', *Management Science* 25, 130–139.

Maling, D. H.: 1973, *Coordinate Systems and Map Projections*, Philip, London.

Mandelbrot, B. B.: 1977, *Fractals: Form, Chance and Dimension,* Freeman, San Francisco.

Openshaw, S.: 1977a, 'A geographical solution to scale and aggregation problems in region-building, partitioning and spatial modelling', *Institute of British Geographers, Transactions* 2 (NS), 459–472.

Openshaw, S.: 1977b, 'Optimal zoning systems for spatial interaction models', *Enviroment and Planning* A 9, 169–184.

Openshaw, S.: 1978, 'An empirical study of some zone-design criteria', *Environment and Planning* A 10, 781–794.

Rushton, G., M. F. Goodchild and L. M. Ostresh Jr. (eds.): 1973, 'Computer programs for location-allocation problems', Department of Geography, University of Iowa, Monograph Number 6.

Schut, G.: 1976, 'Review of interpolation methods for digital terrain models', *Canadian Surveyor* 30, 389–412.

Tobler, W. R.: 1973, 'Choropleth maps without class intervals?' *Geographical Analysis* 5, 262–265.

Tobler, W. R.: 1979, 'Smooth pycnophylactic interpolation for geographical regions', *Journal of the American Statistical Association* 74, 519–530.

R. KEITH SEMPLE AND MILFORD B. GREEN

CLASSIFICATION IN HUMAN GEOGRAPHY

Human geography shares much methodologically with other social, physical and biological sciences. They all place emphasis on observation, classification, experimentation, and model and theory building. Classification is an important and normally early stage in the development of a discipline.

For geographers, classification has an additional aspect not encountered by other disciplines, that of regionalization.[1] It has been argued by Bunge (1966) and Grigg (1965, 1969) that regionalization can be viewed as a special case of classification. If this analogy is accepted, classification as a collection of techniques becomes of logical concern to geographers. The distinction between uniform regions and functional regions has led geographers to consider constraints upon regionalization and hence classification techniques not encountered elsewhere. The most important of these constraints being the desire for classes of regions to exhibit spatial contiguity.

Classification may be defined as the grouping of objects into classes, based on some similarity of properties, or by relationships between the objects. The object is an individual with attributes. All the individuals together form a population. To classify, one or more properties shared by all the individuals are selected as the differentiating characteristics. The population of individuals may be partitioned into one to k classes. The classes may be grouped to form a hierarchy or not depending upon the goal of the researcher.

A significant problem is the choice of the object or individual for classification. The solution is to use units of observation that are readily available and to label such individuals "Operational Taxonomic Units" (OTUs) as taxonomists have done. In geography, such OTUs are commonly spatial units.

The introduction of spatial units as OTUs brings forth the problem of location. In general, location has not been of interest as a differentiating characteristic outside of geography. The question of location is a question of contiguity. For classification of OTUs into uniform regions, contiguity is a requirement. For functional regions, it is a desirable state. Methodological solutions have been proposed by Berry (1966) and Taylor (1969). Berry suggested using contiguity as a restraining characteristic during the classification procedure while Taylor proposes contiguity as an integral part of a

55

Gary L. Gaile and Cort J. Willmott (eds.), Spatial Statistics and Models, 55–79.
© 1984 *by D. Reidel Publishing Company.*

classification algorithm. Taylor argues that the use of contiguity as a constraining characteristic has several disadvantages.

1. The use of a contiguity constraint alone makes it possible to obtain long strung-out regions whose extremes may be a relatively long distance apart.
2. It is closely related to several methods used in classes joining to form the classes of the next rank. Bunge (1966) points out that optimal regions at one scale cannot be necessarily combined at other scales.
3. It allows for individual OTUs to remain isolated well into the classification process, an undesirable feature for many problems.

If regions are to be considered as areal classes, several principles of classification become relevant as summarized by Lankford and Semple (1973).

1. Classifications should be designed for a specific purpose; they rarely serve two purposes equally well. Purpose and use must be linked.
2. The classification of any group of objects should be based upon properties which are properties of those objects; it follows that differentiating characteristics should be properties of the objects classed.
3. The differentiating characteristics must be important for the purpose of classification or else the classification is trivial.
4. Classifications are not final and must be changed as more knowledge is gained about the objects.
5. Classification should proceed at every stage and as far as possible on one principle. If this principle cannot be used for the entire classification, the properties used at the higher class must be more important than those used in lower classes.

The process of regionalization or classification normally begins by examining the characteristics or attributes of various locations or objects. It is obvious that each OTU has many characteristics. In theory, an object has an infinite number of attributes, so that if an object is conceived to exist in an n-dimensional space defined by those attributes, the space is of infinite dimension. In practice, only a selected number of the attributes are utilized in the classification process.

1. CLASSIFICATION METHODS

Considering regionalization as a special case of classification, the discussion will proceed just using the term classification. Regionalization is just the use of spatial OTU's in the classification process. Classification methods used by geographers and others may be grouped into two categories: (1) the testing of *a priori* classification, and (2) the development of a classification. The first category includes use of chi squared tests, analysis of variance, and discriminant analysis. Factor analysis and clustering algorithms form the second group. This discussion will deal only with the development of classifications.

Factor analysis (which is defined to include principal components) and clustering algorithms do not attempt to answer the fundamental question that underlies classification: What is the optimal number of groups? The procedures mentioned above rely on rules of thumb.

Procedures attempting to determine the "optimal" number of groups have been undertaken by few geographers. One such approach is by Semple *et al.* (1969).[2] The method proposes partitioning a finite set of items into an optimal number of groupings. The structure of the procedure is illustrated here with some assumptions for its correct application.

Suppose that a set of items is given, and that each item is identified by the values of a number of variables. For simplicity, measurements on only two variables are assumed for each item, but no conceptual difficulty is introduced when a larger number of variables is used. Assume that the two variables are associated with the rectangular axes of a Cartesian diagram. Then, each item is a point in the two-dimensional space and the similarity of any two items with respect to the variables involved, is measured by the distance between the two points. Hence, a cluster of points in the diagram identifies a subset of items which are more similar to one another than to other items outside of the cluster.

Grouping procedures aim at dividing a set of items into groups in such a way that the items in any one group are more similar to one another than they are to items in the other groups. These procedures, therefore, should be capable of identifying clusters of points such as were mentioned above.

The procedure outlined here aims at identifying clusters of point images and then determining which item belongs to which cluster. The method assumes that clusters of points do exist in the observation space. If the points, in fact, are distributed either randomly or uniformly in the space, then an optimal grouping becomes meaningless.

The classification procedure proposed involves the following steps:

1. The ranges of the variables are determined. Clearly, these values define the space which includes the point images of all the items. A fine rectangular grid is superimposed over this space and the number of points in each grid cell is recorded. The centers of the grid cells, therefore, can be associated with the frequencies of points in the cells. The cells which include part or all of clusters naturally will have higher

frequencies than the other cells. These frequencies can be considered as measures of a two-dimensional spatial trend with clusters corresponding to points where relative maxima of the trend occur. Thus, the problem of identifying clusters can be translated into the problem of identifying the number and location of the relative maxima of this trend.

2. The extremum points of the trend are located approximately by applying an adaptation of an algorithm developed in another paper. This algorithm determines the following:

(i) the distances from the centers of cells to each grid intersection point,

(ii) the tranformation $d = 1/(d+1)$ of these distances,

(iii) the correlation, for each grid point, between these transformed distances and the frequency values for the cells

(iv) the largest absolute value of these correlation coefficients and grid intersection to which this correlation coefficient relates. (This is taken to indicate, as a first approximation, the origin of the largest trend, and hence, the approximate location of the cluster),

(v) the regression of the cell frequencies on the transformed distances from the grid intersection identified in the previous step, and

(vi) for each cell the residual frequency resulting from this regression.

On the residual frequencies, the operations (i) through (vi) are repeated to generate successive approximations for the locations of other relative maxima of the trend. The procedure is terminated when the fraction of the total frequency variance explained by an additional iteration is smaller than a pre-determined threshold.

As a result of this second step, the number and approximate cores of the clusters are identified.

At this point, a number of grouping algorithms can be applied to assign objects to the appropriate groups. The one suggested by Semple, *et al.* (1969) is an extension of the centroid method discussed later in this paper. The procedure is as follows:

1. The point images of the items are then assigned to the nearest cluster core. Euclidean distance is used as the criterion for this assignment.

2. An optimal assignment of the items to groups is obtained by undertaking the following steps:

(i) the centroids of the point images of the items in each grouping are calculated,

(ii) all point images are assigned to the nearest centroid, so that a new grouping is obtained.

(iii)   steps (i) and (ii) are repeated until two successive iterations generate the same grouping.

3.   Artificial groups have still to be eliminated. The steps 1 through 4 above may generate artificial groups in several ways, the first of which is illustrated in Figure 1. Here, the procedure has generated a centroid related to a cluster of clusters rather than to clusters of point images.

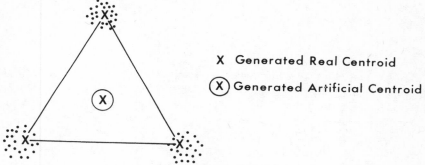

X Generated Real Centroid

(X) Generated Artificial Centroid

Fig. 1. Type one artificial group.

Four cluster centroids have been generated, three located in clusters and the fourth is an artificial one located in a central position. Artificial centroids are usually generated if the natural groupings tend toward geometrical arrangements in such a way that large negative trends are identified in the point images. For instance, in the diagram real clusters tend to have cores corresponding   to the vertices of an equilateral triangle. Consequently, the first centroid to be identified would most likely be located central to the three clusters since this would be the core of a large negative trend. This implies, of course, that the further from this core the greater becomes the frequency of point images. This situation will require special attention in the present procedure.

A second type of artificial group may appear as a result of random trends being generated in steps 1 through 4. Assume a real cluster centroid has been identified and the regression analysis has yielded residuals which are to form the terms of a second spatial frequency series. This second spatial series must contain negative residuals, and these seem to imply some sort of negative frequencies. Suppose that these negative residuals accumulate after a number of iterations. It is possible that by chance a trend may appear that is identified to be significant, in the sense that the explained variance of the trend may be within the threshold limit imposed on the analysis. This trend also is artificial and the location of the trend-maximum purely random. Consequently, items may be assigned to this random centroid but the group thus formed as undesirable. This is illustrated in Figure 2.

Fig. 2. Type two artificial group.

Assume that two real groups have been identifield with centroids located at x and y and a third significant group is identified with a centroid z located at random. Items that should be assigned to centroid x are actually closer to z and hence are assigned to z forming a third type of artificial group.

In order to identify and eliminate artificial groups a "decision rule" is defined in the following manner. An artificial group is simply a group that has more than one-half of the member items located in the outer portion of the group. For example, suppose that the most distant member of a group is thought to be located on the circumference of a circle, centered at the group core, and with radius D being the distance the member is located from the core (Figure 3). Let a second circle be defined, centered on the group core and with radius r, where $r = (R^2 /2)^{0.5}$. This defines the area of the smaller inner circle, representing the inner portion of the group, to be one-half the area of the larger circle, representing the outer portion of the group. A group is now considered artificial if more than one-half of the group members are located in the outer portion of the group.

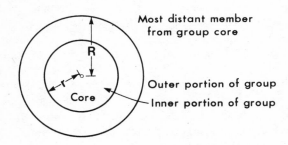

Fig. 3. Artificial group criterion

At this stage, the procedure indicates how many items have been assigned to the inner and outer portions of all groups. In this fashion, real groups are identified and retained, while artificial groups are eliminated and their members reallocated.

The result of the procedure is the partitioning of a finite set of items into an optimal number of groupings, and the simultaneous optimal assignment of the items to the groupings.

Another attempt at determining the optimal number of groups is provided by Popcock and Wishart (1969). They rejected common clustering methods in favor of their method of dense space. The method assumes the important part of a cluster is to be found in the dense part.

The first step is to select a threshold value for r, where r is a critical similarity value, and is defined to be twice the radius of a sphere containing a number of OTUs. The density of a sphere of radius $1/2\ r$ is calculated, and those spheres with values equal to or greater than a criterion value k are defined as uniform spaces.

The OTU space has a grid of spheres placed within it so every sample point lies within a sphere. The spheres with density values less than k are termed unclassifiable at this step. The remaining uniform spaces are combined if they intersect. A cluster is then defined by a set of intersecting spheres — The number of spheres is not specified *a priori*, only the criteria values are specified.

The number of clusters generated by the procedure may not serve any useful purpose other than delimiting the centers of clusters. Consequently, Popcock and Wishart (1969) direct their attention to classifying points outside of the dense spheres into clusters. Any OTU that lies within distance r from the center of a dense sphere is included in that cluster of intersecting spheres. If the OTU is found to fall between two clusters within distance r, it is allocated to the nearest sphere. Any OTU lying farther than r distance is counted as unclassifiable at this stage. These OTUs should be considered relatively remote and should only be allocated among spheres if complete classification is necessary. These remaining OTUs would be allocated to the nearest sphere.

2. CLUSTER ANALYSIS

The grouping methods as presented in the previous section are examples of cluster analysis. Cluster analysis is a general term for multivariate techniques that find groups or clusters of similar objects (OTUs) or items. The typical clustering technique uses measures of similarity (or dissimilarity) to determine if two objects should be fused into one group.

Romesburg (1979) credits clustering techniques with two advantages that make them attractive. One, the techniques in general are founded on less stringent assumptions about the population characteristics of the objects than techniques such as factor analysis. And two, they are mathematically, conceptually less difficult. Such advangages have translated themselves into making the techniques popular ones. This popularity has extended itself to only include hierarchical clustering techniques (Barker, 1976).

The basic dichotomy of clustering techniques is between hierarchical versus non-hierarchical. The hierarchical category is characterized by the consideration of an object just once, at which time it is allocated to a cluster. The allocation is irrevocable. Hierarchical procedures proceed in either an agglomerative or divisive fashion. The number of agglomerative procedures is large and a complete enumeration will not be provided here. A description of them may be found in a number of texts on cluster analysis such as those by Anderberg (1973), Duran and Odell (1974), Hartigan (1975) and Spath (1980).

Although the most common agglomerative, hierarchical techniques differ, the basic procedure for each is quite similar. The basic procedure is as follows:

1. Determine a matrix of similarity between pairs of objects. Each measurement scale has a number of similarity measures (Anderberg, 1973; Duran and Odell, 1974). The most common measure for the metric scales is the square Euclidean distance, where $d_{jk} = \Sigma_{i=1}^{n} (X_{ij} - X_{ik})^2$ with X_{ij}, X_{ik} are the data matrix values of attribute i for object j and k.

2. Find the smallest d_{jk} and combine objects j and k into the same group.

3. A new similarity matrix is constructed for the remaining groups. It is in this step that the most common procedures differ. Each has its own method of determining the new distances.

4. Search the new matrix and find the smallest distance or greatest similarity value. Combine the groups defining that distance.

5. Continue until only one group exists.

A small example is presented. Table I is a matrix of squared Euclidean distances for n number of objects O. Note that the matrix is symmetric, since clustering methods based on Euclidean distances by necessity assume that distance $d_{ij} = d_{ji}$. Suppose that the minimum distance between any

TABLE I
Initial Distance Matrix

	O_1	O_2	O_3	O_4	O_n
O_1	O				
O_2	$d_{21}{}^2$	O			
O_3	$d_{31}{}^2$	$d_{32}{}^2$	O		
O_4	$d_{41}{}^2$	$d_{42}{}^2$	$d_{43}{}^2$	O	
O_n	$d_{n1}{}^2$	$d_{n2}{}^2$	$d_{n3}{}^2$	$d_{n4}{}^2$	O

pair of objects is the distance d_{21} defined by the pair O_2 and O_1. Therefore, objects O_1 and O_2 are combined to form a group $O_1 \cup O_2$.

Table II represents the new similarity matrix. Note that the new matrix is of size $n-1$ by $n-1$. The entries in the new matrix are the same as in the old except for the first row which takes the place of the two rows representing objects O_1 and O_2. The only new distances calculated are $d_{321}, d_{421}, d_{n21}$. For computational efficiency, it is desirable to recalculate the necessary new entries, using only the distances obtained in the previous step.

TABLE II
Modified Distance Matrix

	$O_1 \cup O_2$	O_3	O_4	O_n
$O_1 \cup O_2$	O			
O_3	$d_{321}{}^2$	O		
O_4	$d_{421}{}^2$	$d_{43}{}^2$	O	
O_n	$d_{n21}{}^2$	$d_{n3}{}^2$	$d_{n4}{}^2$	O

Lance and Williams (1967) and Wishart (1969) provide a recursive scheme for the calculation of the distance matrix that depends only upon the values of the distance matrix in the previous step. Their scheme includes six common Euclidean based clustering procedures; the nearest neighbor, the furthest neighbor, the median, group average, and centroid methods. The following summary equation for calculating the necessary new distances may be found in Duran and Odell (1974). The equation is:

$$d_{hk}{}^2 = \alpha_i d_{hi}{}^2 + \alpha_j d_{hj}{}^2 + \beta d_{ij}{}^2 + \gamma |d_{hi}{}^2 - d_{hj}{}^2|$$

The value for the six common approaches are:

Nearest Neighbor $\alpha_i = \alpha_j = 1/2; \beta = 0 \gamma = -1/2$.

Furthest Neighbor $\alpha_i = \alpha_j = 1/2$; $\beta = 0$ $\gamma = 1/2$.

Median $\alpha_i = \alpha_j = 1/2$; $\beta = -1/4$; $\gamma = 0$

Group Average $\alpha_i = n_i/n_k$; $\alpha_j = n_j/n_k$; $\beta = \gamma = 0$

Centroid $\alpha_i = n_i/n_k$; $\alpha_j = n_j/n_k$; $\beta = -\alpha_i\alpha_j$; $\gamma = 0$

Ward's Method $\alpha_i = \dfrac{n_h + h_i}{n_h + n_k}$; $\alpha_j = \dfrac{n_h + n_j}{n_h + n_k}$; $\beta = \dfrac{-n_h}{= n_h + n_k}$; $\gamma = 0$

where α_i, α_j, β, are determined by the clustering process, and n_i, n_j, and n_k are the number of objects in groups i, j, and k respectively, d_{hk} is the distance between O_h and O_k, with $O_k = O_i \cup O_j$.

The methods differ only in the definition of distance between groups after the initial distance matrix has been modified. A short description of each of the methods is as follows:

1. Nearest neighbor: (also known as single linkage clustering) The distance between groups is the minimum distance between any pair of members of the two groups. This technique is prone to chaining (Lankford and Semple, 1973) — the appearance of elongated groups.

2. Furthest neighbor:[3] (also known as complete linkage clustering) the distance between groups is the distance between the most remote pair. The method generally leads to tight, hyperspherical discrete clusters. (Sneath and Sokal, 1973)

3. Centroid: the distance between two groups is the distance between their centroids. The procedure does not yield monotonic results. The procedure suffers from reversals in the joining of OTUs (clusters). A reversal occurs when an OTU joins a cluster after the cluster has formed, but joins at a higher similarity level than at which the cluster formed (Sneath and Sokal, 1973).

4. Median: (also known as the weighted pair-group centroid method) the distance between groups is the distance between the centroids, where the centroid is defined as the midway point between the centroids of the two clusters that fused to create a given cluster. This method also does not guarantee monotonic results.

5. Group average: (also known as the unweighted pair-group method using arithmetic averages) the distance between groups is the average between all pairs of the OTUs of two clusters. It is probably the most used technique.

6. Ward's method: The technique uses the within group sum of squares.

That is, the sum of squares of the distances from each cluster member to its parent cluster mean.

Evaluation of these techniques has been undertaken by a number of researchers (Blashfield, 1976; Kuiper and Fisher, 1975; Cunningham and Ogilvie, 1972). The results indicate that the single linkage method is in many instances the least desirable method. The group average and Ward's methods generally do well, but no single method is best (Everitt, 1979).

Three basic assumptions are made in using these techniques. One, it is assumed that the objects are not randomly or uniformly distributed. Second, it is assumed that the attributes (differentiating characteristics) are relevant to the question at hand. And third, it is assumed the units of measurement are valid. That is, the attributes are of the same scale (Edwards and Cavalli-Sforza, 1965). This problem is normally handled by standardization of the attributes before clustering is undertaken.

Selection of a technique from the large number available is dependent upon the problem. It may well be that no truly appropriate technique exists.

3. INFORMATION STATISTICS BASED TECHNIQUES

In an attempt to move away from a Gaussian approach to clustering, attention has been directed toward the use of information statistics (Lance and Williams, 1967, 1968; Orloci, 1969a, 1969b; Semple, 1975, 1977; Wallace and Boulton, 1968). The attraction of information statistics is that the distribution of the attributes need not be normal.

Sneath and Sokal (1973) present a discussion of information based similarity measures that may be used in clustering procedures. The basic measure of information of a distribution i is

$$H(i) = \sum_{i=1}^{N} y_1 \log_2 (1/y_i), \tag{1}$$

where N is the number of different states of an attribute and where y_i is the proportion of OTUs exhibiting state i of an attribute. Hence $\sum_{i=1}^{N} y_i = 1$ and $y_i \geq 0$. If there are m attributes of t OTUs, one can sum the separate values of $H(i)$ to yield the total information of the group

$$I = t \sum_{i=1}^{m} H(i).$$

If correlation between the attributes is considered, two additional concepts are necessary, as used by Estabrook (1967) and Orloci (1969a). For the bivariate case, joint information $I(g, i)$ is the union of the information content of the two attributes over a set of OTUs, and mutual information $I(g; i)$ is their intersection. The relation between these two quantities is

$$I(g) + I(i) - I(g, i) = I(g; i).$$

Using these concepts, Orloci (1969a, 1969b) presents a method of hierarchical clustering based on information statistics for a discrete population using frequency counts. He considers two frequency distributions X_g and X_i and calculates their relatedness by use of Rajski's coherence coefficient. Although the following discussion focuses on a pairwise approach, no difficulty is encountered in extending the approach to more attributes.

The coherence coefficient for paired comparisons is

$$R(h; i) = 1 - d^2 \, (g; i)^{.5}$$

where: $d(h; i) = 1 - I(g; i)/I(g, i)$ is called Rajski's metric and where

$$I(h; i) = \Sigma\Sigma fjk \ln fjk + N \ln N - \overset{n_g}{\underset{i=1}{\Sigma}} fgi \ln fji - \overset{n_i}{\underset{h=1}{\Sigma}} fik \ln fik \qquad (2)$$

and

$$I(g, i) = N \ln N - \Sigma\Sigma \, fjk \ln fjk. \qquad (3)$$

Table III shows the representation for the symbols in equations (2) and (3). Equation (3) is called the joint information of the two frequency distributions while equation (2) is called the mutual information.

TABLE III

Contingency Table Relating Two Frequency Distributions X_g and X_i

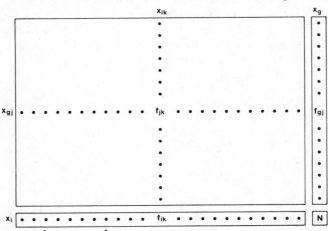

where f_{jk} is short for f_{gijk}

after Orloci (1969 pg. 152)

Orloci suggests a clustering procedure using the coherence coefficient or Rajski's metric, or the probability corresponding to the mutual information as similarity measures. A procedure similar to Euclidean distance based measures can then be used to form groups.

A somewhat different approach for classification is presented by Semple et al.[4] This clustering procedure is best explained by an examination of an example using international trade flows. The clustering procedure is based on a decomposition of an information statistic inequality measure.

For a given time period, note the dollar volume of imports (or exports) for each of a country's N largest trading partners. Calculate the fraction of total imports accounted for by each partner. Call this proportion y_i. Calculate the entropy or information content:

$$H(Y) = \sum_{i=1}^{N} y_i \log_2 (1/y_i).$$
(4)

$H(Y)$ can be regarded as a measure of equality. However, it is preferable to work with a measure of inequality, $I(Y)$. This is obtained by subtracting $H(Y)$ from its own maximum value, $\log_2 N$. Hence,

$$I(Y) = \sum_{i=1}^{N} y_i \log_2 (N y_i).$$
(5)

4. INEQUALITY BETWEEN AND WITHIN GROUPS OF PARTNERS

Suppose that trading partners are partitioned into R groups, $S_1, \ldots, S_R$, and that each partner belongs to exactly one group. We write N_r for the number of partners in S_r ($r = 1, \ldots, R$), such that

$$\sum_{r=1}^{R} N_r = N.$$

Given $H(Y)$ as in equation (4), the entropy can be written as follows:

$$H(Y) = \sum_{r=1}^{R} \left[\sum_{i \in S_r} y_i \log_2 (1/y_i) \right].$$
(6)

and the expression in brackets may be expanded to

$$\sum_{i \in S_r} y_i \log_2 (1/y_i) = Y_r \sum_{i \in S_r} (y_i/Y_r) [\log_2 (Y_r/y_i) + \log_2 (1/Y_r)],$$
(7)

where

$$Y_r = \sum_{i \in S_r} y_i \quad (r = 1, \ldots, R).$$

Y_r is the total import share of S_r. Combining (6) and (7) gives

$$H(Y) = \sum_{r=1}^{R} Y_r \log_2 (1/Y_r) + \sum_{r=1}^{R} Y_r \left[\sum_{i \in S_r} (y_i/Y_r) \log_2 (Y_r/y_i) \right]. \quad (8)$$

The first term on the right of equation (8) is the between-group entropy for imports, and the second term is the weighted average of within-group entropy. Now consider the inequality measure instead of the entropy measure. By subtracting the right-hand side of equation (8) from $\log_2 N$ and rearranging terms, it is easily verified that

$$I(Y) = \sum_{r=1}^{R} Y_r \log_2 \left(\frac{Y_r}{N_r/N} \right) + \sum_{r=1}^{R} Y_r \left[\sum_{i \in S_r} (y_i/Y_r) \log_2 \left(\frac{y_i Y_r}{1/N_r} \right) \right].$$

The first term on the right deals with between-group inequality. It takes on a value of zero when $Y_r = N_r/N$. This special case occurs when the average imports from each partner are the same regardless of its group. The second term on the right measures the within-group import inequality. It takes on a value of zero when $y_i/y_r = 1/N_r$. This occurs only when all y_i $(i=1, \ldots, N_r)$ are equal within their respective groups.

5. UNIVARIATE CLASSIFICATION

Given the import inequality measure it is now possible to operationalize a classification procedure. The most direct method would be to maximize the between-group difference in import inequality for any desired number of groups. To measure the quality of the regionalization, a statistic can be calculated which compares the maximum between-group inequality to the total possible inequality in the following manner:

$$[I_B(Y)/I(Y)] \times 100 = R_s, \quad (9)$$

where $I_B(Y)$ is the maximum between-group inequality for any given number of groups, R_s is the test statistic, and $I(Y)$ is the total inequality of equation (5).

5.1. *A Multivariate Extension*

Instead of considering each trade partner as a homogeneous import-generating unit, suppose that a decision is made to decompose the imports from the trading partner into J commodity classes. This can be taken into consideration by means of modifications to $I(Y)$ in equation (5) and $I_B(Y)$ in equation (9). The total inequality of equation (5), $I(Y)$, can be modified to

$$I(Y) = \sum_{j=1}^{J} Y_j \sum_{i=1}^{N} Y_i \log_2 NY_i,$$

where Y_j is the proportion of total imports from all trading partners accounted for by commodity class j and is expressed as

$$Y_j = \sum_{i=1}^{N} Y_{ij} \ (j = 1, \ldots, J),$$

where Y_{ij} is the proportion of total imports accounted for by commodity class j from partner i, and

$$\sum_{j=1}^{J} Y_j = 1.$$

Also, Y_i is the proportion of the imports of commodity class j derived from partner i and is expressed as

$$Y_i = u_{ij} \left| Y_j \ (i = 1, \ldots, N) \text{ and } \sum_{i=1}^{N} Y_i = 1. \right.$$

Hence, $I(Y)$ is the total import inequality weighted by the proportion of total imports accounted for by each commodity class. This takes on a minimum value of zero when $Y_i = 1/N (i=1, \ldots, N)$, and a maximum value of $\log_2 N$ when $Y_i = 1$ for some i and $Y_k = 0$ for each $k \neq i$.

The between-group inequality of equation (9), $I_B(Y)$, can be modified to

$$I_B(Y) = \sum_{j=1}^{J} Y_j \sum_{r=1}^{R} Y_{jr} \log_2 \frac{Y_{jr}}{N_r/N},$$

where

$$Y_{jr} = (\sum_{i \in S_r} Y_{ij})/Y_j$$

and is the proportion of the total imports accounted for by commodity class j in group r. All other terms retain their previous definitions. Again, the optimal multivariate grouping is achieved when $R_S = [I_B(Y)/I(Y)] \times 100$ is maximized.

On the basis of the foregoing discussion, trading partners may be grouped in such a way that each partner within each group displays a similar import (or export) commodity structure.

A number of inequality measures are available for use in the univariate classification similar to that shown by Semple *et al.* The readers attention is directed to a survey of inequality measures by Waldman (1977) and by Gaile in this volume. For the multivariate case, it appears that only information statistics may be decomposed without bias. Sneath and Sokal (1973) point out that application of information statistics to the continuous case has proven difficult, and applications to such cases are still unavailable.

6. NON-HIERARCHICAL CLUSTERING

Non-hierarchical clustering methods derive discrete clusters that all exhibit the same rank. These techniques assume that the number of groups is known, and what is required is an allocation of OTUs to the proper groups.

Barker (1976) describes the typical procedure for non-hierarchical techniques as follows.

1. Establish points at certain coordinates to act as group centers and allocate the n OTUs to these predefined groups. The allocation is normally done by considering similarity measures and allocating an object (OTU) to the center to which it is most similar.

2. An iterative procedure is then followed where group centers are redefined to represent its members. For example, the center of gravity of each group may be redefined.

3. An object is reallocated to a different group if it becomes more similar to a different group center than to the previous group center.

4. After all the objects are considered and reallocated, the group centers are redefined and the cycle repeats itself until an appropriate criterion is satisfied, such as stabilization of groups.

Several numerical criterion have been suggested for non-hierarchical clustering. The most common is the minimization of tr(W), a minimum variance partition (Everitt, 1979). W is defined in the following manner. Given an $n \times p$ data matrix X and an initial number of observations to be classed into g groups, two matrices can be found W and B such that:

$$T = X'X = W + B,$$

$$W = \sum_{i=1}^{g} \sum_{j=1}^{n_i} (X_{ij} - X_i)' (X_{ij} - X_i)$$

and

$$B = \sum_{i=1}^{g} n_i X_i 'X_i.$$

X_{ij} is the jth observation vector ($1 \times p$) in the ith cluster,
X_i is the mean vector ($1 \times p$) of the ith cluster,
n_i is the number of observations in the ith cluster, and
g is the number of clusters (McRae, 1971; Klecka, 1980).

The technique is based on MacQueen's (1967) k-means method.[5] It suffers from several disadvantages, however. First, it is transformation dependent; different results may be obtained by using raw data versus standardized data. In addition, the clusters are constrained to be hyperspherical.

If the real clusters are in some other shape misleading results may occur (Everitt, 1979). Other less popular alternative methods are discussed in Everitt (1979).

Geographers have developed a set of non-hierarchical grouping methods that are not commonly thought of as such. Location-allocation algorithms for continuous space are based on Euclidean distance minimization. Compare the following algorithm found in Rushton (1979, pp. 85–86) with Barker's description of non-hierarchical grouping. A heuristic method for location of multifacilities in continuious space can be stated as follows:

Step 1. Select starting locations for the centers;

Step 2. Form groups of demand points by allocating each demand point to it's closest center, calculate z

$$z = \sum_{i=1}^{n} \sum_{j=1}^{m} a_{ij} w_i \left[(x_i - x_j)^2 + (y_i - y_j)^2 \right]^{\frac{1}{2}}$$

where x_i, y_i are demand point coordinates $i = 1, n$,

x_j, y_j supply point coordinates $j = 1, m$; and

$a_{ij} = 1$ when demand point i is closest to supply center j— otherwise 0.

Step 3. Calculate new center locations by solving the single-facility location problem for each group of demand points:

$$x_j^* = \sum_{i=1}^{n} \frac{a_{ij} w_i x_i}{d_{ij}} \bigg/ \sum_{i=1}^{n} \frac{a_{ij} w_i}{d_{ij}} \quad y_j^* = \sum_{i=1}^{n} \frac{a_{ij} w_i y_i}{d_{ij}} \bigg/ \sum_{i=1}^{n} \frac{a_{ij} w_i}{d_{ij}}$$

where w_i is the weight that may be associated with a demand point,

x_j^* is the new X coordinate of a new group center,

y_j^* is the new Y coordinate of a new group center, and

d_{ij} is Euclidean distance between each group member and the previous group centroid.

Step 4. Go to Step 2 and repeat until there is no change in the value of z.

It should be obvious to the reader that the two approaches are not really different. Although location-allocation solution methods assume a two-dimensional space, little difficulty should be experienced in extending the methods to n-dimensional space. Only the Euclidean distance functions need be modified. Geographers thus have at their disposal an entire set of potenial non-hierarchical techniques.

7. DYADIC INTERACTION MATRICES AND CLASSIFICATION

Geographers are often interested in describing and interpreting interaction systems. Interaction is usually displayed by dyadic matrices, where each score represents a flow between an origin and destination dyad (Holmes, 1978). Such matrices can lend themselves to regionalization, which is often one of the main goals of an analysis.

Transformation of dyadic matrices are often necessary to allow for classification. Holmes divides the possible transformations into four classes.

1. Single transformations derived from attributes of rows and/or columns. Examples are association scores and hierarchization scores.
2. Matrix transformations for eliminating size differences. Examples are transaction flow analysis and biproportional analysis.
3. Matrix transformations incorporating indirect flows. Examples are graphic theoretic methods and Markov chains.
4. Ordination methods such as factor analysis, multidimensional scaling, and seriation methods.

All of the above serve to make the initial data set more tractable for research. A thorough discussion of the state of the art in dyadic interaction matrices may be found in Holmes (1978).

The set of transformations that has received the most attention as a set of classification methods are the ordination methods, in particular factor analysis. Consequently, discussion will be limited here to just ordination methods.

Factor analysis has been the only ordination method that has been consistently applied to dyadic interaction matrices, beginning with Berry (1960, 1961, 1968), Clark (1973a), and up unto the present day Davies and Musson (1978), Davies and Thompson (1980), and Nader (1981).[6]

The use of factor analysis as a regionalization technique was stimulated by the introduction of Berry's (1966, 1968) spatial field theory. He noted that the same procedures of numerical taxonomy are used to derive both formal and functional regions, and developed the field theory to relate the two regional types, using techniques of systems analysis. The field theory, operating upon a spatial system, involves places, their attributes, and the interaction among them. Choosing an appropriate portion of the earth's surface, one can develop an n-place, a-attribute, matrix. The matrix describes spatial association and variation over the n places. Berry asserts that the infinite number of attributes of n places and their variation are actually indexed by a finite number of fundamental, independent concepts. Using principal components analysis, the number of key factors underlying the total variation is identified. Each observation has a score on each factor, creating a nXs matrix of n-places and s-factors. This is the structure matrix.

A similar approach is used on interaction data. Choosing the various interactions, f's, for which data are available, and using the same n-places used above, the subset or R space is defined. For each f, we can construct an nXn matrix. Such a matrix can be "unfolded" into an $n^2 - n$ array. The arrays for each interaction type can be grouped to form a $n^2 - n$ by d matrix. Where d is the number of interaction types under consideration.

Again, the underlying factors of variation are identified. The factor scores define an $n^2 - n$ by b-factor behavior matrix.

The structure and behavior matrix are, however, not enough for formulating a field theory. There is no way to relate the matrices. Defining the similarity between the two points as the euclidean distance in s-space, an $n^2 - n$ by x matrix of place similarity of structure is developed. This similarity matrix is row-wise comparable with the dyads of the interaction matrix. It is now possible to formulate the relation between structure and behavior.

Two views could be taken: (1) dyadic behavior is a function of characteristics of places, and that changes in characteristics will affect the dyadic interaction, or (2) place characteristics are dependent upon relationships with other places, and changes in relationships would change characteristics of the places. However, as mentioned, places, their attributes, and their interaction form a system. Instead of simple cause-effect relations spatial structure and spatial behavior must be discussed as in a state of mutual equilibrium with very complex interdependencies.

Most recent work has concentrated on the analysis of single interaction matrices, with the exception of Davies and Thompson (1980), and Davies and Musson (1978) who describe the typical approach in using factor analysis for a hierarchical, functional regionalization.

1. Convert the interaction matrix into a similarity matrix, usually by the use of Pearson product-moment correlations.

2. Factor analyze the similarity matrix, using Q-mode, with origins as rows and columns as destinations. Obtain the factor loadings and factor scores.

3. The factor correlation matrix can be factor analyzed to produce a second order which represents a higher level of the structure.

4. The factor loadings are examined to determine clusters of origins that exhibit similar interaction patterns. The factor scores measure the importance of each origin as a destination for the interaction.

If a spatial structure exists, each factor will have one dominant factor score, signifying a dominant destination (Davies, 1979).

The arguments regarding the advantages and disadvantages of such a regionalization approach are too voluminous to repeat here. The reader is directed to Holmes (1978), Davies (1979), and Davies and Thompson (1980).

Multidimensional scaling as a classification technique has not been widely used in geography.[7] The technique can be used to take a similarity matrix and place the objects represented by that matrix and place them in an n-dimensional atrribute space. In a strict sense, the technique can be viewed as a conditioning technique to allow classification of objects to occur with greater ease. Once the objects are placed in the attribute space, a number of approaches ranging from visual to numerical classification techniques could be applied. Examples of this approach can be found in Slater and Winchester (1978), Johnston (1979), and Green (1981).

Seriation has been defined by Sneath and Sokal (1973) as "the reordering of rows and columns of a similarity matrix in such a way as to place the highest similarities close to the principal diagonal of the matrix with an orderly decrease in similarity values away from the diagonal." The authors are not aware of a geographic application of this technique. A description of seriation may be found in Holmes (1978) and Sneath and Sokal (1973).

8. GRAPH THEORY

The literature surrounding graph theory is quite large and will not be presented here. A concise treatment of the use of graph theory in geography may be found in Tinkler (1979). The relationship between graph theory and numerical taxonomy is well established. Most clustering algorithms can be expressed in graph theoretical equivalent. For example, single linkage clustering is analogous to a minimally connected graph, while complete linkage is analogous to a maximally connected graph (Sneath and Sokal, 1973).

Graph theory can be used to functionally regionalize a transaction matrix such as in the pioneering method of Nystuen and Dacey (1961). The connection between certain allocation models and graph theory is also well known. If we restrict our attention to just classification procedures, little input by geographers is to be found. An exception is an algorithm developed by Slater (1976) for dealing with asymmetric interaction matrices.

His procedure is a divisive hierarchical clustering algorithm. The similarity matrix is standardized by use of an iterative proportional fitting procedure (IPFP) that doubly standardizes the data. This standardization controls for unequal sizes in origins and destinations in the interaction matrix.

The entries in the matrix are each, in order of increasing, size set equal to zero. A binary matrix is then constructed after each entry has been nullified, by setting every positive entry equal to one.

The strong components of each of the digraphs can be found through matrix multiplication (Harary, 1965; Warfield, 1973). A strong component (a cluster) is said to exist if a path of directed links exists between any vertex and any other. As increasingly larger entry values are set to zero, ever larger numbers of strong components are created. Slater shows how this technique can be viewed as an hierarchical method and can be represented by a tree diagram (dendrogram). In application, this technique tends to produce contiguous groupings if applied to spatial data.

9. CONCLUSIONS

This paper has not attempted to be an exhaustive review of all of the classification techniques that have been or could be applied by geographers. The intent has been to provide a flavor of what has currently been accomplished.

The reader should be aware that different results may and do occur if different classification approaches are applied to the same data. No one technique has been demonstrated to be superior to others, although some are less useful than others. Earlier, a distinction was made between hierarchical and non-hierarchical approaches. In most instances, it would seem that increased research activity should be directed toward expansion of the non-hierarchical approaches. The hierarchical methods may well be suitable for biological and physical sciences but they are much less so for human geography.

If non-hierarchical methods are to be useful, more attention needs to be paid to the question of the optimal number of groups. The non-hierarchical methods require that the number of groups be known *a priori*. Progress was made by Semple *et al.* (1969), and Popcock and Wishart (1969), but nothing has been undertaken in human geography since their work.

Geographers have a start if application of various location-allocation models for which algorithms exist are extended to handle more than two-dimensional Euclidean distances. It may be through this approach that geographers will contribute to classification much more significantly than they have in the past.

Finally, the discipline regularly deals with a type of classification that is of little interest to others, that of regionalization. Although as spatial scientists we should be at the forefront of developing classification methods that are more applicable to regionalization, little has been attempted since

Taylor in 1969. More emphasis on including location as a discriminating characteristic is certainly in order.

Dept. of Geography
University of Saskatchewan

NOTES

[1] A discussion of the history of the concept of the region can be found in Grigg (1967).

[2] A FORTRAN program for the procedure can be found in Semple, *et al.* (1969).

[3] The furthest distance approach is available as part of the Statistical Analysis System under the procedure name CLUSTER. For further information refer to the *SAS User's Guide*, 1979 Edition, SAS Institute Inc., Post Office Box 10066, Raleigh, N. C., 27605.

[4] A FORTRAN program is available for an information statistics based classification procedure in Semple *et al.* (1972). A modified version of this procedure utilizing z values of groups can be found in Johnston and Semple (1983).

[5] A FORTRAN program for the k-means procedure may be found in Spath (1980).

[6] Dyadic interaction matrices in this context include data matrices of places (rows) by commodities (columns), places by places for an individual type of interaction, as well as matrices of places by types of interactions. The term dyadic factor analysis has been applied to analysis of places by commodities.

[7] For further information on multidimensional scaling see Kruskal and Wish (1978) and Golledge and Rushton (1972).

BIBLIOGRAPHY

Anderberg, M. R.: 1973, *Cluster Analysis for Application*, Academic Press, New York.

Barker, D.: 1976, 'Hierarchic and non-hierarchic grouping methods: An empirical comparison of two techniques', *Geografiska Annaler* 58B, 42–58.

Berry, B. J. L.: 1961, 'A method for deriving multi-factor regions', *Przeglad Geograficzny* 33, 263–279.

Berry, B. J. L.: 1966, 'Essays on commodity flows and the spatial structure of the Indian economy', *Research Paper No. 111*, Department of Geography, University of Chicago.

Berry, B. J. L.: 1960, 'An inductive approach to the regionalization of economic development', in Norton Ginsburg (ed.), *Essays on Geography and Economic Development, Research Paper No. 62*, Department of Geography, University of Chicago.

Berry, B. J. L.: 1968, 'A synthesis of formal and functional regions using a general field theory of spatial behavior', in B. J. L. Berry and D. Marble (eds.), *Spatial Analysis*, Prentice Hall, Englewood Cliffs.

Black, W. R.: 1973, 'Toward a factorial ecology of flows', *Economic Geography* 49, 59–67.

Blashfield, R. K.: 1976, 'Mixture model tests of cluster analysis: Accuracy of four agglomerative hierarchical methods', *Psychological Bulletin* 83, 377–388.

Bunge, W.: 1966, 'Gerrymandering, geography and grouping', *Geographical Review* 56, 256–263.

Casetti, E.: 1964, 'Classificatory and regional analysis by discriminant iterations', *Technical Report No. 12*, Department of Geography, Northwestern University.

Chojuicki, Z. and T. Czyz: 1973, 'Structural changes of the economic regions in Poland: A study by factor analysis of commodity flows', *Geographia Polonia* 25, 31–47.

Clark, D.: 1973a, 'The formal and functional structure of Wales', *Annals of the American Association of Geographers* 63, 71–84.

Clark, D.: 1973b, 'Urban linkage and regional structure in Wales: An analysis of change', *Transactions of the Institute of British Geographers* 58, 41–58.

Clayton, C.: 1974, 'Communication and spatial structure', *Tjidschrift voor en Economische en Sociale Geografie* 65, 221–227.

Cunningham, K. M. and J. C. Ogilvie: 1972, 'Evaluation of hierarchical grouping techniques: A preliminary study', *The Computer Journal* 15, 209–213.

Davies, W. K. D.: 1979, 'Urban connectivity in Montana', *Annals of Regional Science* 13, 29–46.

Davies, W. K. D. and T. C. Musson: 1978, 'Spatial patterns of commuting in South Wales, 1951–1971: A factor analysis definition', *Regional Studies* 14, 353–366.

Davies, W. K. D. and R. R. Thompson: 1980, 'The structure of interurban connectivity: A dyadic factor analysis of prairie commodity flows', *Regional Studies* 14, 297–311.

Duran B. S. and P. L Odell: 1974, *Cluster Analysis: A Survey*, Lecture Notes on Economics and Mathematical Systems, Springer-Verlag, Berlin.

Edwards, A. W. F. and L. L. Cavalli-Sfovza: 1965, 'A method of cluster analysis', *Biometrics* 21, 362–375.

Estabrook, G. F.: 1967, 'An information theory model for character analysis', *Taxon* 16, 86–97.

Everitt, B. S.: 1979, 'Unresolved problems in cluster analysis', *Biometrics* 35, 169–181.

Golledge, R. G. and G. Rushton: 1972, *Multidimensional Scaling: Review and Geographical Applications*, Commission on College Geography, Technical Paper No. 10, Association of American Geographers, Washington.

Gordon, A. D. and J. T. Henderson: 1977, 'An algorithm for Euclidean sum of squares classification', *Biometrics* 33, 355–362.

Green, M. B.: 1981, 'Regional preferences for interlocking directorates among the largest American corporations', *Environment and Planning A* 13, 829–839.

Grigg, D. B.: 1965. 'The logic of regional systems', *Annals of the Association of American Geographers* 55, 465–491.

Grigg, D. B.: 1969, 'Regions, models and classes', in R. J. Chorley and P. Haggett (eds.), *Models in Geography*, Methuen, London.

Harary, F., R. Z. Norman and D. Cartwright: 1965, *Structural Models: An Introduction to the Theory of Directed Graphs*, Wiley, New York.

Hartigan, J. A.: 1975, *Clustering Algorithms*, Wiley, New York.

Hirst, M. A.: 1977, 'Hierarchical aggregation procedures for interaction data: A comment', *Environment and Planning A* 9, 99–103.

Holmes, J. H.: 1978, 'Dyadic interaction matrices: A review of transformation purposes and procedures', *Progress in Human Geography* 2, 467–493.

Johnston, R. J.: 1976, *Classification in Geography*, Concepts and Techniques in Modern Geography No. 6, Geo Abstracts Ltd., Norwich.

Johnston, R. J.: 1979, 'On the characterization of urban social area', *Tijdschrift voor Economische en Sociale Geografie* 70, 232–238.

Johnston, R. J. and R. K. Semple: 1983, *Classification Using Information Statistics*, Concepts and Techniques in Modern Geography, Geo Abstracts Ltd., Norwich.

Kariel H. G. and S. L. Welling: 1977, 'A nodal structure for a set of Canadian cities using graph theory and newspaper datelines', *Canadian Geographer* 21, 142–163.

King, L. J.: 1967, 'Discriminatory analysis of urban growth patterns in Ontario and Quebec, 1951–1961', *Annals of the Association of American Geographers* 57, 566–578.

Klecka, W. R.: 1980, *Discriminant Analysis*, Sage University Paper Series on Quantitative Applications in the Social Sciences, Series No. 07–019, Sage, Beverly Hills.

Kruskal, J. B. and M. Wish: 1978, *Multidimensional Scaling*, Sage University Paper Series on Quantitative Applications in the Social Sciences, Series No. 07–011, Sage, Beverly Hills.

Kuiper, F. K. and L. Fisher: 1975, 'A Monte Carlo comparison of six clustering procedures', *Biometrics* 31, 777–783.

Lance, G. N. and W. T. Williams: 1967, 'Mixed-data classificatory Programs, 1', *Australian Computing Journal* 1, 15.

Lance, G. N. and W. T. Williams: 1968, 'Note on a new information-statistics classificatory program', *The Computer Journal* 11, 195.

Lankford, P. M.: 1969, 'Regionalization: Theory and alternative algorithms', *Geographical Analysis* 1, 196–212.

Lankford, P. M. and R. K. Semple: 1973, 'Classification and geography', *Geographia Polonica* 25, 7–30.

Leusman, C. S. and P. B. Slater: 1977, 'A functional regionalization program based on the standardization and hierarchical clustering of transactions flow tables', *Computer Applications* 4, Department of Geography, University of Nottingham, 709–777.

MacDonald, D. K. C.: 1952, 'Information theory and its application to taxonomy', *Journal of Applied Physics* 23, 529–531.

MacQueen, J.: 1967, 'Some methods for classification and analysis of multivariate observations', in L. M. Cam and J. Neyman (eds.), *Proceedings of the Fifth Berkeley Symposium on Mathematical Statistics and Probability* 1, University of California Press, Berkeley, pp. 281–297.

McRae, D. J.: 1971, 'MIKCA: A FORTRAN IV iterative K-means cluster analysis program', *Behavioral Science* 16, 423–424.

Nader, G. A.: 1981, 'The delineation of a hierarchy of nodal regions by means of higher-order factor analysis', *Regional Studies* 15, 475–492.

Nystuen, J. D. and M. F. Dacey: 1961, 'A graph theory interpretation of nodal regions', *Papers of the Regional Science Association* 7, 29–42.

Orloci, L.: 1969a, 'Information analysis of structure in biological collections', *Nature* 223, 483–484.

Orloci, L.: 1969b, 'Information theory models for hierarchic and non-hierarchic classifications', in A. J. Cole (eds.), *Numerical Taxonomy*, Academic Press, New York, pp. 148–164.

Pocock, D. C. D. and D. Wishart: 1969, 'Methods of deriving multi-factor uniform regions', *Transactions of the Institute of British Geographers* 47, 73–98.

Ray, M. D. and B. J. L. Berry: 1964, 'Multivariate socio-economic regionalization: A pilot study in central Canada', *Canadian Political Science Association Conference on Statistics*.

Rescigno, A. and G. A Maccacaro: 1960, 'The information content of biological classifications', *Symposium on Information Theory*, Butterworths, London, pp. 437–446.

Romesburg, H.: 1979, 'Use of cluster analysis in leisure research', *Journal of Leisure
Research* 11, 144–153.

Rushton, G.: 1979, *Optimal Location of Facilities*, Compress, Inc., Wentworth.

Semple, R. K., E. Casetti and L. J. King: 1969, 'The determination of the optimal
number of groupings on classification problems', *Discussion Paper No. 10*, Department of Geography, Ohio State University, Columbus.

Semple, R. K. and G. J. Demko: 1977, 'An information theoretic analysis: An application to Soviet COMECON trade flows', *Geographical Analysis* 9, 57–63.

Semple, R. K. and H. L. Gauthier: 1972, 'Spatial-temporal trends in income inequalities
in Brazil', *Geographical Analysis* 4, 169–179.

Semple, R. K. and R. G. Golledge: 1970, 'An analysis of entropy changes in a settlement
pattern over time', *Economic Geography* 46, 157–160.

Semple, R. K. and D. A. Scorrar: 1975, 'Canadian international trade', *Canadian Geo-
rapher* 19, 135–148.

Semple, R. K. and L. H. Wang: 1971, 'A geographical analysis of changing redundancy
in interurban transportation links', *Geografiska Annaler* 53B, 1–5.

Semple, R. K., C. E. Youngmann, and R. E. Zeller: 1972, 'Economic regionalization
and information theory: An Ohio example', *Discussion Paper No. 28*, Department
of Geography, Ohio State University, Columbus.

Slater, P. B.: 1976, 'A hierarchical regionalization of Japanese prefectures using 1972
interprefrectural migration flows', *Regional Studies* 10, 123–132.

Slater, P. B. and H. P. M. Winchester: 1978, 'Clustering and scaling of transaction flow
tables: A French interdepartmental migration example', *IEEE Transactions on
Systems, Man, and Cybernetics* SMC–8, 635–640.

Sneath, P. H. A. and R. R. Sokal: 1973, *Numerical Taxonomy*, W. H. Freeman, San
Francisco.

Spath, H.: 1980, *Cluster Analyses Algorithms for Data Reduction and Classification
of Objects*, Ellis Horwood, Chicester.

Stevens, B.: 1965, 'Regionalization of Pennsylvania counties for development planning',
Report submitted to Area Development Administration, U. S. Department of Commerce.

Taylor, P. J.: 1969, 'The location variable in Taxonomy', *Geographical Analysis* 1,
181–195.

Tinkler, K. J.: 1979, 'Graph Theory', *Progress in Human Geography* 3, 85–116.

Warfield, J. W.: 1973, 'Binary matrices in system modeling', *IEEE Transactions on
Systems, Man, and Cybernetics* 3, 441–449.

Waldman, L. K.: 1977, 'Types and measures of inequality', *Social Science Quarterly*
58, 229–241.

Wallace, C. S. and D. M. Boulton: 1968, 'An information measure for classification',
The Computer Journal 11, 185–194.

Wishart, D.: 1969, 'Mode analysis: A generalization of nearest neighbor which reduces
chaining effects', in A. J. Cole (eds.), *Numerical Taxonomy*, Academic Press, New
York, pp. 282–319.

ROBERT C. BALLING, JR.

CLASSIFICATION IN CLIMATOLOGY

1. INTRODUCTION

Few, if any, areas of geography rival climatology in terms of emphasis on classification. Indeed, it can be argued that far too much effort in climatology has been spent on classification exercises of questionable value (Hare, 1951; Wilcock, 1968). In 1969, Borgel listed 169 different climatic classifications that had appeared in the literature, but the general lack of Russian listings suggests that the number should have been substantially higher. Since that time, a variety of new climatic classifications of outstanding merit have been proposed. Examples include classifications based upon air mass frequencies (Oliver, 1970), satellite measurements of net radiation, vorticity, and atmospheric moisture (Barrett, 1970), energy balance terms (Terjung, 1970; Terjung and Louie, 1972), and daily insolation levels (Willmott and Vernon; 1980).

These new schemes follow a tradition that began in the 1870s when the first at least partially mathematically-based climatic classifications were introduced (de Candolle, 1874; Supan, 1879). Shortly thereafter, Wladimir Köppen (1884) published the first of many now famous papers directly addressing the problem of climatic classification. By 1928, when the still popular Köppen-Geiger wall map was issued, classification had become the central focus of climatological research. The landmark work of Thornthwaite (1948) demonstrated that Köppen's system was not adequate in many applications, and new, improved and dramatically different classifications of climate would be needed in the future.

Many of the early classification systems suffered from several fundamental shortcomings. In a paper on solar radiation regionalization, Willmott (1977b) discussed the weak theoretical underpinnings of many classification systems and the overwhelming influences of arbitrary decisions regarding (1) the number of regions; (2) the criteria used to establish boundaries between climatic types; (3) the variables chosen to characterize climate; and (4) strategies used to summarize the selected variables. However, recent advances in electronic computing, data base management, and taxonomic theory have allowed climatologists to overcome many of these fundamental classification problems.

81

Gary L. Gaile and Cort J. Willmott (eds.), Spatial Statistics and Models, 81–108.
© 1984 *by D. Reidel Publishing Company.*

It is now possible for sophisticated univariate and multivariate climatic classification systems to be generated from enormous data bases (Sokal, 1966). Earlier classifications were generally based upon one or two climatic elements, often temperature and/or precipitation, but today a much wider range of variables can be selected to represent the state of the climatic system. The ability to efficiently manipulate large matrices also allows the temporal dimension to be included in the new classification systems. Rapid advances in electronic computing have also lead to the development of new classificatory techniques that have been integrated into general climatic classification methodologies.

The primary purpose for this chapter is to examine the use of numerical taxonomic methods in climatic classification problems. The objectives and justification for classifying and/or regionalizing climatic data are presented along with the advantages of adopting numerical taxonomic procedures. The operational considerations of numerical taxonomy are discussed with attention often focused on many fundamental problems that have recently surfaced. Finally, trends in modern climatic classification are identified, and suggestions for future research are offered.

2. FUNCTIONS OF NUMERICAL CLASSIFICATION

In inductive and deductive scientific reasoning, classification serves important generalizing and synthesizing functions (Grigg, 1967). However, in the past, far too many climatologists made climatic classification an end unto itself and apparently lost sight of the ultimate objectives of their classification systems. The following interrelated objectives and justifications for climatic classification have always existed, and each one can benefit from the proper use of numerical taxonomic methods.

1) The primary objective of most classification schemes is to bring structure, order and simplicity to the complex climatic system (Harvey, 1969). The recognition of order promotes the generation of inductive hypotheses regarding the processes that create and maintain the observed order (Sokal, 1974). The hypotheses can be tested; empirical laws and generalizations may become established; existing models may be improved upon; and new theories may be constructed (Johnston, 1970; Barry and Perry, 1973). Numerical taxonomy brings objectivity and replication to classification problems, freeing the process to some degree of potential biases of the scientist (Sokal and Sneath, 1963).

2) Classification provides us with an intellectual shorthand (Abler *et al.*,

1971) in which great volumes of information can be communicated by the use of simple labels (Cline, 1949; Critchfield, 1960; Sokal, 1974). Although many modern climatologists are reluctant to integrate the Köppen classification system into their research, one may unquestionably convey a great deal of information about the climate of some location by utilizing Köppen's well-known system. Similar types of groups, or taxons, can be established using numerical taxonomic methods that maximize the efficiency of the information flow from the original data to the user.

3) In climatology, classifications are often used to identify the spatial limits, or boundaries, of a climatic type. Numerical methods can be used to assure that climatic boundaries, defined explicitly by climatic variables, show where the steepest climatic gradients occur (Steiner, 1965; McBoyle, 1971, 1972). The precise identification of spatial dimensions is crucial to understanding the physical and dynamic processes that govern the observed climatic phenomena (Gregory, 1975).

4) Climate classification serves many practical purposes along with its theoretical functions. Willmott (1977b, 1978) argued that an efficient regionalization scheme can avoid expensive redundancies in climatic data collection networks. Planners and engineers need information on the character, spatial extent, and number of climatic regimes that may be defined using a variety of "climatic resource" elements. Analyses of spatial limits of various climate types are undoubtedly useful to understanding spatial limits of phenomena that are related to food, water and energy problems. The National Climate Program Act, with its purpose "to establish a national climate program that will assist the Nation and the world to understand and respond to natural and man-induced climate processes and their implications" (National Climatic Program Advisory Committee, 1980), has certainly encouraged studies regarding the spatial dimensions of climatic phenomena (Lawson *et al.*, 1981).

It follows that climate classification systems can be designed for very general purposes or quite specific problems. Researchers should clearly state their objectives in constructing a classification system and the relationship between the problem and the classification. An investigator choosing to use numerical taxonomic methods to solve a problem should carefully consider the range and implications of procedural decisions that are made in constructing an efficient climatic classification system.

3. OPERATIONAL CONSIDERATIONS

In developing an objective classification system, climatologists are faced with a variety of subjective decisions that may significantly affect the final results (Johnston, 1968; Jackson, 1969; Lankford, 1969; Gregory, 1975; Ayoade, 1977). A researcher must select the appropriate variables for a particular problem, and develop a sampling and measurement system capable of accurately portraying selected attributes for each unit to be classified. Once the basic data are established, a researcher must choose some similarity, or dissimilarity, index to depict the association between the taxonomic units. Then, literally dozens of agglomerative or divisive schemes are available to explicitly define clusters and associated regions in the data. Finally, the researcher should select tests of the statistical validity of the classes that seem to result from the "objective" taxonomic analysis.

Accordingly, the purpose of this section is to (1) review the subjective decisions regarding numerical taxonomic strategies that have been made in climatological research; (2) evaluate the theoretical basis and validity of the choices; (3) identify recent trends in numerical taxonomy in climatology; and (4) suggest areas of potentially valuable future research.

3.1. *Basic Data*

In traditional and modern climatic classification problems, a primary goal is to arrange areas or points of the earth's surface according to some similarities found in climatic phenomena. Therefore, geographic space is the common dimension in the basic data matrices upon which climatic classifications are constructed. In univariate research, time is the other dimension, usually represented as a continuous series of daily (Willmott and Vernon, 1980), monthly (Skaggs, 1975; Willmott, 1977a) or mean annual measurements (Gregory, 1975; Ogallo, 1980). When the period of measurement is held constant, a variety of climatic indices may be represented in the basic data matrix. These indices often include long-term annual, seasonal, or monthly means of one or many climatic variables (Steiner, 1965; McBoyle, 1971; Kojima, 1973; Balling and Lawson, 1982). It is also possible to construct a numerical classification based upon changes that have occurred in climatic data between two discrete time periods (Balling, 1980).

It is fortunate for climatologists that most of their basic data are intervally scaled, and generally well-suited for statistical procedures that assume a normally distributed sample. In some studies, the data are standardized

(Lawson *et al.*, 1981) or converted to some anomaly measure (Grimmer, 1963), smoothed through time (Gregory, 1956; Lawson, 1976; Lawson *et al.*, 1981), and/or transformed to accommodate assumptions of normality (Steiner, 1965; Willmott, 1977a). However, because most numerical taxonomic procedures are robust against minor deviations from normality, researchers may justifiably elect to accept the results of classifications based upon the raw basic data (Willmott, 1978).

If an investigator seeks to develop *specific climatic regions,* a nominally scaled contiguity measure is also required. This measure is used in the clustering process to disqualify the amalgamation of noncontiguous points or areas. However, Johnston (1970, p. 295) concluded that "regionalizing with contiguity constraints over-simplifies and operates against efficient hypothesis-testing." If an investigator builds *general climatic types,* the contiguity matrix is not required. The climatic types are defined exclusively in climatic space, and the resulting clusters may or may not be associated with contiguous regions on the earth's surface.

The selection of the basic data is unquestionably the most influential step in the taxonomic procedure. The nature of the variables, the number of attributes measured, and the spatial and temporal sampling technique all profoundly and directly affect the results of the climatic classification. The decisions made at the basic data level also indirectly affect the end results by influencing other subjective decisions regarding the numerical procedures.

3.2. *Similarity Matrices*

The association between operational taxonomic units (OTUs), which in climatology are generally meteorological stations, must be quantitatively defined in a square similarity or dissimilarity matrix. Although we generally think of similarities between stations in climatic classification research, it would be equally valid and valuable to define similarities between climatic variables or discrete time units (Lund, 1963; Skaggs, 1975; Blasing, 1975, 1981).

In climatic classification studies, little use has been made of the many coefficients of association (Sokal and Sneath, 1963; Boyce, 1969; Sneath and Sokal, 1973; Clifford and Stephenson, 1975) that are available for nominally scaled variables. Because most climatic data are intervally scaled, coefficients of correlation and distance measures are widely used in defining similarities. More recently, indices associated with information theory and entropy have been effectively introduced to climatic classification problems (Johnston, 1981).

3.2.1. *Correlation Coefficients*

Coefficients of correlation have been used in numerical taxonomic research in climatology for over 50 years (e.g., Glasspoole, 1922). The Pearson product-moment correlation coefficient (r) appears frequently (Sekiguti, 1952; Gregory, 1965; Perry, 1968; Lawson *et al.*, 1981), however, the Spearman rank-order correlation coefficient may be more appropriate in cases where the raw data vary significantly from the normal distribution. These correlation coefficients are conveniently bounded by +1.0 and −1.0, and they are not affected by different metrics between variables that may introduce vastly different means and standard deviations. It is apparently assumed that highly correlated areal units have been affected by quite similar atmospheric processes.

Willmott (1978) has sharply criticized the unquestioned use of correlation coefficients, particularly in univariate climatic classification problems. He argues that the covariance coefficient (c) is a superior measure of similarity, or more correctly, dissimilarity, between stations. Unlike r, the covariance coefficient does not standardize the variances, and thus it preserves the actual magnitude of the covariance, and more accurately reflects the true spatial deviation in the data (Craddock, 1973; Richman, 1981). Willmott (1978, p. 279) suggested that the covariance coefficient "is a better measure of similarity in univariate work because it contains virtually all of r's climatologically advantageous properties and, in addition, it preserves the metric resulting in a smaller loss of information."

3.2.2. *Distance Measures*

The most common distance measure used in climatological taxonomy is the Euclidean or taxonomic distance which is defined as:

$$d_{jk}{}^2 = \sum_{m=1}^{r} (x_{km} - x_{jm})^2 \tag{1}$$

where d_{jk} is the Euclidean distance between OTUs j and k, x_{jm} and x_{km} are the locations of j and k, respectively, on each of r orthogonal (uncorrelated) dimensions (Jancey, 1966). The Euclidean distance formula is an extension of the well-known Pythagorean Theorem, $c^2 = a^2 + b^2$, in an r-dimensional space. In cases where the variables that define the Euclidean space are significantly intercorrelated, the Pythagorean Theorem must be rewritten as $c^2 = a^2 + b^2 - 2ab \cos \gamma$, where γ is the angle between segments a and b. The $\cos \gamma$ is precisely equal to the correlation between the two variables that define a and b. Yet, the climatological literature is full of numerical taxonomic studies where this assumption of orthogonality is clearly violated. Three courses of action have been taken by researchers in regard to this problem: (1) they have accepted, possibly blindly, the errors caused by intercorrelated variables; (2) they have determined the significance of intercorrelations, allowing only uncorrelated variables to be clustered (Balling, 1980); and (3) they have elected to transform their data onto orthogonal axes via principal components analysis.

3.2.3. *Principal Component Transformation*

Principal components analysis (PCA) has arisen from the large family of factor analytic techniques to become a quite popular tool in numerical taxonomy in climatology. The mathematics for PCA have been presented in a variety of places, and will not be repeated in this review (Stidd, 1967; Kutzbach, 1967; Rummel, 1970). What follows in this short subsection is a discussion of the use of PCA in transforming raw climatic data for input into taxonometric algorithms.

Before proceeding with the discussion, a clarification of the misunderstanding of the different modes of PCA is presented. Willmott (1978) showed that the climatic literature contains numerous discrepancies regarding the proper identification of the various modes of analysis. The heart of the problem was centered around the interpretation of the three general dimensions of Rummel's (1970) data cube. Following Willmott's suggestions, the "entity," "characteristic," and "occasion" dimensions may be interpreted climatologically as "climatic indices," "stations," and "time." "Climatic indices" may include statistics associated with climatic elements determined at a variety of time scales (e.g., monthly, seasonal, annual). The "stations" may be any areal units of data collection, and "time" generally refers to some continuous temporal series of measures. Accepting such an interpretation, the six modes of PCA in climatology are clearly defined (Figure 1).

Neither the S-mode or the T-mode PCA model would be appropriate in many climatic regionalization problems. Univariate research would generally focus on O-mode and P-mode approaches. If the O-mode is selected, the factor loadings would be correlations between the calculated factors and the original time intervals, and the standardized factor scores would be generated for each station. Skaggs (1975) referred to factors extracted from such a matrix as time series eigenvectors. The transpose of the O-mode matrix leads to P-mode analysis, where spatial eigenvectors are produced with factor loadings on each station and factor scores for each time unit.

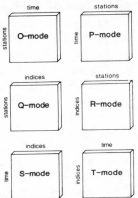

Fig. 1. Modes of factor analysis in climatic research (after Willmott, 1978).

In univariate climatic research, either the O-mode or the P-mode approach can be used to disentangle time-space dimensions. Each eigenvector is associated with both a map displaying the configuration of a dominant climatic spatial structure and a time-series plot showing how well the spatial structure is represented in each time interval. The O-mode and P-mode approaches have been used to ultimately regionalize precipitation (Dyer, 1975; Gregory, 1975; Willmott, 1977a, 1978; Ogallo, 1980), drought (Skaggs, 1975), and insolation (Willmott and Vernon, 1980) data.

Both approaches would develop a set of orthogonal composite scores that efficiently represent variance structures found in the original matrix. In clustering problems involving an O-mode analysis, an investigator may wish to weight the factor scores according to the eigenvalue (Gittus, 1964–5; McDonald, 1966; Spence, 1968; Jardine and Sibson, 1971), for the first eigenvectors will normally account for far more variance than the last few selected eigenvectors. If the factor scores are not weighted, the variance pattern strongly associated with only a few temporal units would be given equal weighting with the most important variance patterns found in many of the temporal units.

The weighting of factor scores or loadings is less theoretically sound in the remaining modes of analysis. In the *P*-mode and *R*-mode cases, the areal distribution of the station network plays a major role in determining the portion of variance explained by a given eigenvector (Johnston, 1981). Even if some test of areal distribution, such as nearest-neighbor analysis (Balling and Lawson, 1982) is applied, local clusters of stations can significantly influence the explained variance level.

In the *Q*-mode approach which has been extensively used to regionalize areal units based on long-term climatic variables (Steiner, 1965; McBoyle, 1971, 1972; Kojima, 1973; Preston-Whyte, 1974; Oliver *et al.*, 1978; Balling and Lawson, 1982) the selection and inclusion of the climatic indices may produce unreasonable eigenvalues for weighting purposes. For example, if an investigator included ten temperature-related variables and only three precipitation measures, the temperature factor would almost by definition account for more variance than some moisture component. Yet, it is quite likely that the researcher would give the two variance structures equal weighting in the clustering algorithm. Johnston (1970, p. 300) concluded that the use of eigenvalues as weights should only be used "in situations where the researcher's data closely fits his theoretical structure."

In summary, PCA is an effective and powerful tool capable of transforming the raw climatic variance patterns into a relatively small number of orthogonal dimensions. The factor scores that result from the *O*-mode and *Q*-mode approaches are particularly well-suited for climatic regionalization based upon Euclidean distance measures. Several techniques such as principal co-ordinate analysis (Gower, 1966; Russell and Moore, 1970; Mather, 1976; Austin and Yapp, 1978) and singular decomposition methods of analysis (Jalickee and Hamilton, 1977) are similar to PCA, and may prove to be valuable in a host of climatic applications.

3.2.4. *Other Similarity Measures*

Although correlation coefficients and Euclidean distance measures have been the most popular similarity indices in climatic research, other quite useful similarity measures have also been used. One non-metric coefficient, referred to as the Canberra metric, C_{jk}, is defined as:

$$C_{jk} = \sum_{i=1}^{m} \left| X'_{ij} - X'_{ik} \right| / (X'_{ij} + X'_{ik}), \qquad (2)$$

where X'_{ij} and X'_{ik} are standardized measures of m attributes at locations j and k (Williams and Lance, 1965; Russell and Moore, 1970, 1976). To avoid very small or zero values in the denominator, a constant is normally added to every standardized X value. Russell and Moore (1970) in their study of Australian homoclimates argued that the advantage of the Canberra metric lies in its relative insensitivity to extreme outliers.

Crutcher and Joiner (1977) have shown that the generalized distance statistic, D^2, of Mahalanobis (1936) can be effectively utilized in climatic taxonomic research. Although the D^2 is somewhat more difficult to compute when compared to the similarity measures described thus far, its use has several unique advantages (Rao, 1952; Berry, 1958; King, 1969). The D^2 statistic is based upon the differences between sample means and the variances within each sample. As a result, D^2 is closely related to test statistics that measure the significance of the difference between samples drawn from normally distributed populations.

Very recently, Johnston (1981) successfully introduced information-based similarity measures (Feinstein, 1958; Rajski, 1961; Estabrook, 1967; Semple and Green, 1984) to a climatic classification problem. Although in a comparative sense his results of an analysis of precipitation totals in the United Kingdom obtained by information and entropy statistics were not dramatically different than those obtained by more traditional methods, several by-products, including the secular trend analysis, appeared to be very useful. The advantages of information statistics have been argued for many years (Williams and Lance, 1965), and it seems likely that their use in climatological research is destined to increase.

3.3. *Grouping Strategies*

With the basic data and the similarity matrix established, the climatologist finds a wide range of techniques available to delineate groups within the data. Although some grouping techniques require more subjectivity than others, the decisions regarding the appropriateness of various techniques can significantly affect the final results (Johnston, 1968; Jackson, 1969; Lankford, 1969; Gregory, 1975; Ayoade, 1977). The common thread that binds all of the schemes is an attempt to define groups with the fundamental property that within-group variance is minimized while between-group variance is maximized. Three different categories of strategies commonly appear in the climatic literature: (1) correlation evaluation; (2) eigenvector interpretation; and (3) cluster analysis.

3.3.1. *Correlation Evaluation*

Possibly the simplest grouping method involves the graphical representation of the raw data coupled with some visual estimation of similarities between the plots. Climatologists have examined graphs of occurrence of extreme climatic events (Gregory, 1953), time series of running precipitation means (Gregory, 1954, 1956, 1975), and graphs of cumulative deviations (Kraus, 1955) to arrive at climatic regional structures. However, given the state of the art of numerical taxonomy, it seems likely that such subjective schemes will yield to more objective procedures in future climatic research.

A similar strategy begins with the calculation of actual correlation coefficients between OTUs. Glasspoole (1922) chose two English cities as base units and correlated annual precipitation amounts of these cities with rainfall records from surrounding stations. Although discrete regions were not established, the distance decay in correlation coefficient magnitudes strongly suggested a regional structure in temporal trends of precipitation totals. Sekiguti (1952) calculated correlations on four different climatic variables between a set of Japanese stations and subjectively developed a new "synthetical" climatic region map of Japan. Lund (1963) correlated pressure maps based on 22 data points, then used $r = 0.7$ as a critical value to establish a classification of weather types. These isocorrelate methods have been criticized on several grounds, including the initial choice of stations, the arbitrarily defined critical r values, and the possibility of non-linear relationships in the data (Barry and Perry, 1973).

3.3.2. *Eigenvector Interpretation*

Another approach for delineating climatic groups is based upon a rather direct, often subjective, interpretation of calculated eigenvectors. Using either a P-mode or R-mode model, as described earlier, each orthogonal eigenvector displays a set of factor loadings that represent the correlation between the actual climatic data from areal units and some unique variance pattern in the data. Often, these components are orthogonally rotated to simple structure to better define variance clusters in the data (Rummel, 1970). Climatic clusters may then be established based upon the relative importance of different eigenvectors at each areal unit. This procedure has been used in a number of studies of temporal trends of precipitation totals (Dyer, 1975; Gregory, 1975; Willmott, 1977a; Ogallo, 1980).

Slightly different approaches have been adopted by other investigators.

Skaggs (1975) and Iakovleva and Gurleva (1969) mapped factor scores and/or factor loadings and drew regional boundaries through areas of steepest spatial gradients. Kuipers (1970) developed a more sophisticated approach in which the loadings for each component were divided into discrete subsets, and the total variance in the array of factor loadings accounted for by the divisions was determined. When the portion of variance explained by the divisions is multiplied by the eigenvalue and divided by the total number of variables, the variance in the entire original data set explained by the eigenvector subdivision is defined. Kuipers generated a solution based upon the sub-division of factor loadings to create discrete climatological groupings. Christensen and Bryson (1966) and Blasing (1975, 1981) showed that component analysis could be an equally valuable tool in defining a classifica-tion of weather or climate types.

The direct interpretation in climatic classification problems of the eigen-vectors extracted using PCA has been sharply criticized in recent years. The following five interrelated items summarize the problems in using PCA as a method for representing climatic taxonomic structure.

1) At the heart of the argument is the fact that PCA is designed for re-ducing dimensionality, not for interpretation purposes or hypothesis testing (Kendall and Stuart, 1968; Morrison, 1976; Richman, 1981). True factor analysis, with communalities in the diagonal elements of the intercorrelation matrix, would be a superior method of analysis in studies where the factors are to be directly interpreted. The inclusion of communality values would not intersperse variance from small-scale features and local errors with variance from large-scale atmospheric systems (Richman, 1981). In their investigation of surface temperatures over the United States, Walsh and Richman (1981) have shown that PCA and true factor analysis can generate substantially different results in climatological applications.

2) In most applications, the components are orthogonally rotated to simple structure, yet true simple structure is rarely achieved (Johnston, 1981). Willmott (1978) argued that because the orthogonal rotation is affected by the position of all clusters in climatic space, the rotation may not simplify matters, but rather arrive at a more complex solution. The relaxation of the orthogonality constraint may allow obliquely rotated factors to more precisely identify variance clusters in the data (Richman, 1981), although Gregory (1975) and Ogallo (1980) were unable to discern substantial differences between precipitation regions based on orthogonally or obliquely rotated factors.

3) The interpretation of the eigenvectors remains a muddled issue. Johnston

(1981) pointed out that two stations could have the same relatively high loading of 0.7 on the same factor, and yet be uncorrelated with one another. In this hypothetical case, the two stations share slightly less than 50% of their variance with only one unique mode of variance in the original data. However, it is likely that the two stations would be placed in the same climatic cluster.

The interpretation issue is further confused by the selection of the proper number of eigenvectors to be used for interpretative purposes. Although no agreement has been reached on the superiority of the many different "cut-off" methods (Richman, 1981), the scree test used by Willmott (1977a, 1978) and many others appears to be a reasonable procedure in climatic studies. The scree test originally developed by Cattell (1966) involves a subjective examination of a plot of percent explained variance levels by individual components. The components that fall beyond the point where the tail zone of the curve flattens to some low level are eliminated from further analysis. This procedure allows climatic researchers to examine the physical nature of each component before any are blindly discarded. Willmott (1977a) reported that the scree test results in the interpretation of fewer components when compared to other cut-off methods (e.g., eliminating components with eigenvalues less than one).

4) Most PCA work utilizes the correlation coefficient, r, as the similarity coefficient. As discussed earlier in this chapter, the use of r may not be appropriate in many univariate applications.

5) A PCA solution may be biased by the spatial autocorrelation that it is attempting to disentangle. Stations close together in geographic space, and presumably close in climatic space, can force a double-weighting of a particular variance pattern. Because of the use of orthogonality constraints, all eigenvectors can be affected by such biases; and the overall PCA solution may be unstable (Richman, 1981; Horel, 1981). To guard against the influences of an ill-conditioned matrix, an investigator may wish to perturb the raw data and reapply the PCA model. A series of such tests can effectively check the stability of the original PCA solution.

It should be restated at this point that PCA is an excellent analytical tool for transforming raw data to a set of orthogonal axes. In climatic classification studies, the best use of PCA is made in preparing raw data for input into clustering algorithms that assume orthogonal structures in Euclidean space.

3.3.3. *Cluster Analysis*

Because a review of the many different clustering schemes is available in a number of places (Johnston, 1968; Jackson, 1969; Lankford, 1969; Barry and Perry, 1973; Gregory, 1975; Ayoade, 1977), including the chapter by Semple and Green (1984), no attempt will be made in this section to duplicate such a critique. Rather, the purpose of this section is to review the clustering procedures that have been adopted in climatological studies, and to develop some generalizations regarding advantages and disadvantages of the differing techniques.

All clustering in climatology is aimed at minimizing within-group variance while maximizing between-group variance. Overlapping classifications (Lance and Williams, 1967a) in which an OTU can fall into more than one discrete group have generally been avoided. Almost all classification attempts have been agglomerative as opposed to divisive. The agglomerative procedures build groups by fusing members, one at a time, often according to some selected hierarchical scheme. Divisive procedures may require less computing, but they have been shown to produce erratic, unreliable results (Sneath, 1969; Johnston, 1970). The various agglomerative strategies employed by climatologists conveniently fall into the three categories suggested by Sokal (1974): single linkage, complete linkage and average linkage clustering.

3.3.3.1. *Single linkage analysis.* The single linkage method, also referred to as elementary linkage analysis (McQuitty, 1957), allows an OTU to join a cluster when it is similar in some well defined respect to any member in the group. Although the pairwise relationship could be with any specified member of the group such as the farthest-neighbor (MacNaughton-Smith *et al.*, 1964) or the most representative member (McQuitty, 1961), most climatological studies have built linkages based upon nearest-neighbor relationships. The single linkage method has been used to group weather stations based upon inter-correlations of precipitation totals (Gregory, 1964, 1975), turbulent heat fluxes (Perry, 1969), and temperature and sunshine levels (Perry, 1968). This method minimizes computing time because a new similarity matrix is not required after each step, but "chaining effects" (Wishart, 1969) may seriously reduce the effectiveness of the clustering procedure.

3.3.3.2. *Complete linkage analysis.* An opposite approach to the single linkage method is complete linkage analysis in which an OTU can join a cluster only when it exceeds some similarity level with *every* member of the cluster. Gregory (1965, 1975) correlated precipitation records between all stations in his networks, and selected groups with the criterion that a station entered a cluster only when its correlation with every group member was higher than any correlation with ungrouped stations. Gregory referred to this procedure as simple linkage analysis, while others (McQuitty, 1966; Johnston, 1968) prefer to label the procedure as rank order typal analysis.

Cattell's ramifying linkage method (Cattell, 1944; Miller and Kahn, 1962) with its associated ρ-F analysis (Olson and Miller, 1958) is an algorithm used in climatology that also falls into the complete linkage category. Cattell's method links all OTUs that are intercorrelated above a specified magnitude such that all intercorrelations within the group exceed the critical level. However, it is possible, actually quite probable, for one OTU to be located in more than one cluster. To force OTUs into nonoverlapping groups, the ρ-F analysis locates pairs of OTUs with the reflexive property that each is more highly correlated with the other than with any other OTU. This basic pair forms the nucleus of the cluster, and the overlapping OTUs are assigned to the cluster on the basis of similarity with the basic pairs. Cattell's method with ρ-F analysis has been effectively used in climatology to determine regional structures associated with secular temperature fluctuations (Lawson *et al.*, 1972; Lawson *et al.*, 1981).

The complete linkage methods generally do not require a great deal of computing time, but they tend to result in tight, ball-shaped clusters with many outliers. However, the strict definitions used for entry into a group guarantees relatively homogeneous clusters in climatic space.

3.3.3.3. *Average linkage analysis.* Average linkage cluster analysis or hierarchical syndrome analysis (McQuitty, 1960) allows an OTU to enter a cluster based upon the *average* similarity between the OTU and the group members. Often, the average similarity is defined as the average Euclidean distance, in climatic space, between the ungrouped OTU and all OTUs in the nearby clusters. It is popular in climatology to utilize output from the factor analytical techniques in the average Euclidean distance clustering algorithm (Steiner, 1965; McBoyle, 1971, 1972; Kojima, 1973; Preston-Whyte, 1974; Oliver, Siddigi, and Goward, 1978; Balling and Lawson, 1982). In many applications, the average linkage clustering is superior to single or complete linkage procedures in producing discrete groupings that minimize within-group variance and maximize between-group variance (Williams and Lance, 1965; Johnston, 1968; Boyce, 1969).

Ward's method (Ward, 1963) uses an explicit definition of the minimization of within-group variance in the hierarchical-agglomerative grouping of OTUs. The error sum of squares, *ESS*, that is a direct measure of within-group variance, is defined as:

$$ESS = \sum_{i=1}^{K} \sum_{j=1}^{n} S_{ij}^{2},$$ (3)

where n is the number of OTUs in each of K clusters, and S_{ij} is the Euclidean distance from each OTU to its group centroid. The agglomerative procedure minimizes the jump in *ESS* at each step in the amalgamation process. The use of Ward's method has been strongly advocated by several researchers (Wishart, 1975; Willmott, 1977a, 1978; Willmott and Vernon, 1980) and adaptations of the method have been developed and effectively utilized by others (Crutcher and Joiner, 1977; Johnston, 1981).

The description presented in this section focused upon numerical classification procedures that have been widely utilized in climatology. Researchers should be aware of many other algorithms (Lance and Williams, 1967a, 1967b; Wishart, 1969; Spence and Taylor, 1970; Wolfe, 1970; Semple and Green, 1984) that may be valuably extended into climatic studies.

3.4. *Evaluating Taxonomic Structures*

The results from most of the clustering algorithms are normally presented on a dendrogram (Figure 2), more commonly referred to as a linkage tree. The investigator is then faced with a series of interrelated questions regarding the final solution to the original taxonometric problem:

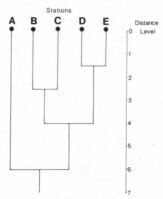

Fig. 2. Hypothetical dendrogram.

(1)   Does the dendrogram accurately represent the relationships depicted in the similarity matrix?
(2)   How many clusters should be selected?
(3)   Are the selected clusters different from one another?
(4)   How well are the original variables represented by the chosen solution?

3.4.1. Cophenetic Correlation

A cophenetic correlation coefficient (Sokal and Rohlf, 1962; Sneath, 1969) that measures distortion on a linkage tree can be calculated to effectively address the first question. This coefficient, r_c, is the Pearson product-moment correlation between the implied similarity values on a dendrogram and the actual similarities calculated in climatic space. For example, the implied distance between stations B and D on Figure 2 is 4.0 units, but the actual Euclidean distance between the two would probably not be exactly equal to 4.0. The cophenetic correlation establishes the degree of linear relationship between arrays of implied and actual distances. Sneath (1969) concluded that highest values of r_c are associated with average linkage clustering methods; however, lack of normality in the original data can significantly lower the r_c level. Balling and Lawson (1982) reported cophenetic correlations of approximately 0.9 in their study of temperature and precipitation patterns in the United States.

3.4.2. Selecting and Testing Clusters

Determining the optimum number of clusters to select remains problematic, and a number of schemes have been introduced to provide a more objective method for making the final decision. Most of these schemes are closely tied to the third question above regarding the magnitude of differences found between potential clusters.

One procedure involves the direct application of factor analytical techniques. In P-mode and R-mode analyses (Figure 1), the number of "significant" factors underlying the spatial variance would certainly suggest the number of climatic types that should be established. Willmott (1977a) and Lankford and Semple (1973) have successfully adopted such a procedure in determining their regional structure patterns.

Analysis of specific allocations of variance in the original data provides another method for choosing the proper number of groupings (Johnston,

1970). The sum of the squared distances, Σd^2, between all OTUs and a group centroid is a measure of variance, detail, or information found in the original data (Amedeo and Golledge, 1975). This total variance can be divided into two parts, within-group variance and between-group variance. All climatic detail or information is present before the clustering begins, and accordingly, the total variance equals the between-group variance. As the clustering begins, the detail lost is given by the increases in the within-group variance term. When all OTUs are contained in one large cluster, the within-group variance equals the total variance, and all detail or information is lost. The final climatic classification scheme should attempt to maximize detail (detail = between-group variance ÷ total variance) with the smallest number of discrete clusters.

Many investigators (Berry, 1961; Spence, 1968; Willmott, 1978; Willmott and Vernon, 1980; Johnston, 1981) examine the increments of change in detail associated with each step in the amalgamation procedure. The linkage tree is "broken" into discrete clusters at a step in which a large decrease in detail or information is discovered. Crutcher and Joiner (1977) suggest a more rigorous approach in which the number of clusters is determined when the variance explained by $k+1$ clusters is not statistically significantly higher than the variance explained by k clusters.

Statistical significance testing of group differences is useful in establishing both the validity and the correct number of climatic clusters (Goodall, 1966). Chi-squared tests (Clark, 1956; Zobler, 1957, 1958), analysis of variance (Godske, 1959), and tests of homogeneity (Barry and Perry, 1973) have all been suggested as appropriate testing devices. Discriminant analyses (Berry, 1958; Miller, 1962; Barry and Perry, 1973) have been used to not only determine the validity of classes, but also to reallocate OTUs once the number of classes has been selected (Steiner, 1965; Lance and Williams, 1967b; Willmott and Vernon, 1980). The procedures developed by Semple et al., (1969) and described in the chapter by Semple and Green (1984) certainly are promising tools for climatological investigation.

It has been suggested that the solution that appears to be best in a statistical sense may not be the best configuration of classes for a given problem. Williams and Dale (1965) discouraged the blind use of statistical testing claiming that inevitably, a pragmatic test by the classifier will override the first, probabilistic, test. Bunge (1966, p. 95) cautioned that "since it is obvious that no two areas on the earth's surface are identical, all regions will be significantly different in the statistical sense if a large enough sample is drawn." Willmott and Vernon (1980) very logically suggested that factors such as the previous climatic literature should also be incorporated into the final decision regarding the optimum number of climatic clusters.

3.4.3. *Canonical Correlation Approach*

It is possible, although generally lacking in the literature, to define how well each original variable is explained by the final set of clusters. Analysis of variance, or its equivalent of regression analysis with dummy variables, could be used to explicitly define the portion of variance explained in each original climatic variable by a particular cluster structure. Each variable would be tested separately using such methods. Canonical correlation analysis (Johnston, 1978; Brinkmann, 1980) is a far more powerful technique that would allow variance patterns found in the original data to be linked to variance patterns in the taxonomic structure.

To illustrate the use of canonical correlation analysis in evaluating a regional structure, long-term monthly climatic averages (1931–1978) for temperature and precipitation were established for 76 climatic divisions in the United States. A 76 × 26 matrix containing the monthly and annual temperature and precipitation data was constructed, and the well-known Köppen system was used to classify each division into a climatic type and approximate boundaries were drawn (Figure 3). Discrepancies between Figure 3 and many other published maps arise from the use of widely dispersed climatic divisions in the present illustration.

A separate 76 × 10 matrix of dummy variables portrayed the spatial variance structure of the 10 Köppen categories found in the sample. For each division, or row, a "1" appeared in the column that corresponded to that division's Köppen climatic type, and the remaining cells contained zeros. The result was a matrix of nominal variables displaying the spatial structure of the Köppen categories.

A canonical correlation analysis identified the statistical linkages between variance patterns in the matrix of climatic variables and the matrix of nominal variables. Pairs of eigenvectors called canonical functions were extracted, one eigenvector per canonical pair from each matrix, with the criterion that the square of the correlation, R_i^2, between the two must be maximized. The use of eigenvectors with matrices of nominally scaled variables has been strongly defended by Rummel (1970) and Burt (1950).

A correlation coefficient, r_{ij}, was computed to show the strength of the relationship between the jth climatic variable and the ith canonical function. The variance extracted in one set of variables by its ith canonical

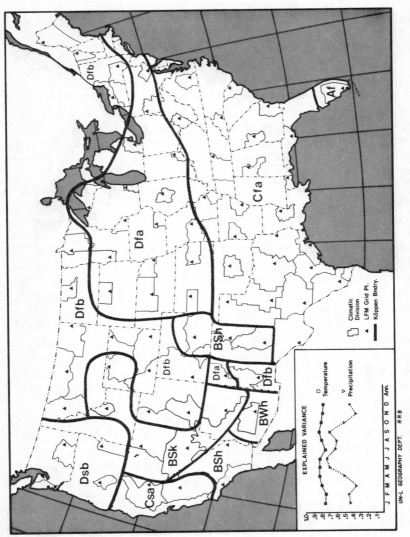

fig. 3 Köppen climatic regions with associated evaluative statistics.

function, v_i^2, is the average amount of variance accounted for in each variable. Brinkmann (1980, p. 20) reported that the "magnitude of $v_i^2 R_i^2$ is therefore a measure of the variance in one data set that is related to the variance in the other data set." Because subsequent pairs of canonical functions are uncorrelated with all preceding pairs, the values of $v_i^2 R_i^2$ may be summed to determine the total variance in one data set (climate averages) explained by the variance in another data set (climatic types). The total variance explained in any j^{th} climatic variable was estimated by evaluating $\Sigma_{i=1}^m$ $R_i^2 r_{ij}^2$, where m is the number of significant canonical pairs.

Five significant canonical pairs combined to explain 66.6% of the total variance in the 26 climatic variables. The regional structure of Köppen climatic types explains over 80% of the variance in monthly temperatures and more than 50% of the variance in high-sun monthly precipitation levels (Figure 3). However, only 36% of the spatial variance in some winter monthly precipitation variables was accounted for by the 10 climatic types.

Canonical correlation analysis can be easily integrated into the numerical taxonomical procedures described in this chapter. The results may prove to be quite valuable in determing the appropriateness of a classification in a given problem. The presentation of this example, despite its shortcomings, will hopefully encourage climatologists to specify how well their classification system represents variance in the original variables.

4. PROSPECTS OF CLIMATIC CLASSIFICATION

This chapter has focused on the taxonometric methods that have been employed relatively frequently in climatic research. Many other procedures are available that have been successfully used in other disciplines, and it seems likely that new classificatory methods will continue to appear in the climate literature. However, these new methods should be adopted because of superior intrinsic characteristics in relation to a specific problem (Barry and Perry, 1973), and not because of their availability in some easy-to-use statistical package.

More specifically, future developments in climatic classification will fall along a variety of fronts. A number of widely accepted numerical classification studies will be re-examined in light of recent challenges of the factor analytical procedures and the introduction of information theory and entropy methods to the climatic literature. Smaller-scale, hemispheric, or global scale studies may begin to appear more frequently as researchers branch away from the traditional continental scale. Dynamical and physical climatic variables, complex climatic indices, and a host of variables designed for specific problems will more commonly form the basis of future climatic classifications. A great deal of valuable research will concentrate on clustering climatic variables, map types, and time intervals instead of the usual clustering of areal units. Also, it seems very likely that more work will be done on testing the nature and validity of climatic clusters that result from numerical taxonomic procedures.

Classificatory issues concerning an abstract concept such as climate are certain to remain both complex and controversial. Climatic investigators must be well-versed in modern taxonomic methods, for many practical and theoretical problems will continue to rely on valid classifications of climatic data for their solutions.

Dept of Geography
University of Nebraska – Lincoln

BIBLIOGRAPHY

Abler, R., J. S. Adams and P. Gould: 1971, *Spatial Organization*, Prentice-Hall, Inc., Englewood Cliffs, N. J.

Amedeo, D. and R. G. Golledge: 1975, *An Introduction to Scientific Reasoning in Geography*, John Wiley, New York.

Austin, M. L. and N. Yapp: 1978, 'The definition of rainfall regions of south-eastern Australia by numerical classification methods; *Archiv für Meteorologie, Geophysik und Bioklimatologie, Ser. B.* 26, 121–142.

Ayoade, J. O.: 1977, 'On the use of multivariate techniques in climatic classification and regionalization', *Archiv für Meteorologie, Geophysik und Bioklimatologie, Ser. B.* 24, 257–267.

Balling, R. C., Jr.: 1980, 'Classification and regionalization of climatic change', *Great Plains-Rocky Mountain Geographical Journal* 9, 1–8.

Balling, R. C., Jr. and M. P. Lawson: 1982, 'Twentieth century changes in winter climatic regions', *Climatic Change* 4, 57–69.

Barrett, E. C.: 1970, 'Rethinking climatology', in C. Board, R. J. Chorley, P. Haggett, and D. R. Stoddart (eds.), *Progress in Geography*, Vol. II, Edward Arnold, London, pp. 154–205.

Barry, R. G. and A. H. Perry: 1973, *Synoptic Climatology*, Methuen, London.

Berry, B. J. L.: 1958, 'A note concerning methods of classification', *Annals of the Association of American Geographers* 48, 300–303.

Berry, B. J. L.: 1961, 'A method for deriving multi-factor uniform regions', *Przeglad Geograficzny* 33, 263–278.

Blasing, T. J.: 1975, 'A comparison of map-pattern correlation and principal component eigenvector methods for analyzing climatic anomaly patterns', *Preprint Volume,*

Fourth Conference on Probability and Statistics in Atmospheric Sciences. American Meteorological Society, Boston.

Blasing, T. J.: 1981, 'Characteristic anomaly patterns of summer sea-level pressure for the Northern Hemisphere', *Tellus* **33**, 428–437.

Borgel, G. E.: 1969, 'The nature and types of climatic classifications: an overview', M. A. Thesis, Department of Geography, UCLA.

Boyce, A. J.: 1969, 'Mapping diversity: a comparative study of some numerical methods', in A. J. Cole (ed.), *Numerical Taxonomy*, Academic Press, London, pp. 1–31.

Brinkmann, W. A. R.: 1980, 'Lake Superior area temperature variations', *Annals of the Association of American Geographers* **70**, 17–30.

Bunge, W.: 1966, *Theoretical Geography*, C. W. K. Gleerup, Lund.

Burt, C.: 1950, 'The factorial analysis of qualitative data', *British Journal of Psychology, Statistical Section* **3**, 166–185.

Candolle, A. de: 1874, *Géographie botanique raisonnée*, Genéve.

Cattell, R. B.: 1944, 'A note on correlation clusters and cluster search methods', *Psychometrika* **9**, 169–184.

Cattell, R. B.: 1966, 'The scree test for the number of factors', *Multivariate Behavioral Research* **1**, 245–276.

Christensen, W. I., Jr., and R. A. Bryson: 1966, 'An investigation of the potential of component analysis for weather classification', *Monthly Weather Review* **94**, 697–709.

Clark, P. J.: 1956, 'Grouping in spatial distributions' *Science* **123**, 373–374.

Clifford, H. T. and W. Stephenson: 1975, *An Introduction to Numerical Classification*, Academic Press, New York.

Cline, M. G.: 1949, 'Basic principles of soil classification', *Soil Science* **67**, 1–13.

Craddock, J. M.: 1973, 'Problems and prospects for eigenvector analysis in meteorology', *The Statistician* **22**, 133–145.

Critchfield, H. J.: 1960, *General Climatology*, Prentice-Hall, Englewood Cliffs, New Jersey.

Crutcher, H. L. and R. L. Joiner: 1977, 'Another look at the upper winds of the tropics', *Journal of Applied Meteorology* **16**, 462–476.

Dyer, T. G. S.: 1975, 'The assignment of rainfall stations into homogeneous groups: an application of principal components analysis', *Quarterly Journal of the Royal Meteorological Society* **101**, 1005–1013.

Estabrook, G. F.: 1967, 'A information theory model for character analysis', *Taxon* **16**, 86–97.

Feinstein, A.: 1958, *Foundations of Information Theory*, McGraw-Hill Book Co., New York.

Gittus, E.: 1964–5, 'An experiment in the identification of urban sub-areas', *Transactions of the Bartlett Society* **2**, 109–135.

Glasspoole, J.: 1922, 'A comparison of the fluctuations of annual rainfall over the British Isles', *British Rainfall* **62**, 260–266.

Godske, C. L.: 1959, 'Information, climatology, and statistics', *Geografiska Annaler* **61**, 85–93.

Goodall, D. W.: 1966, 'Hypothesis-testing in classification', *Nature* **211**, 329–330.

Gower, J. C.: 1966, 'Some distance properties of latent root and vector methods used in multivariate analysis', *Biometrika* **53**, 325–338.

Gregory, S.: 1953, 'A note on the classification of annual rainfall distribution types', *Quarterly Journal of the Royal Meteorological Society* 79, 538–543.

Gregory, S.: 1954, 'Annual rainfall areas of southern England', *Quarterly Journal of the Royal Meteorological Society* 80, 610–618.

Gregory, S.: 1956, 'Regional variations in the trend of annual rainfall over the British Isles', *Geographical Journal* 122, 346–353.

Gregory, S.: 1964, 'Climate', in J. W. Watson, and J. B. Sissons (eds.), *The British Isles: A Systematic Geography*, Nelson, London, pp. 53–73.

Gregory, S.: 1965, *Rainfall over Sierra Leone*, Department of Geography, University of Liverpool Research Paper No. 2.

Gregory, S.: 1975, 'On the delimitation of regional patterns of recent climatic fluctuations', *Weather* 30, 276–286.

Grigg, D.: 1967, 'Regions, models and classes', in R. J. Chorley and P. Haggett (eds.), *Models in Geography*, Methuen, London, pp. 461–501.

Grimmer, M.: 1963, 'The space-filtering of monthly surface temperature anomaly data in terms of pattern, using empirical orthogonal functions', *Quarterly Journal of the Royal Meteorological Society* 89, 395–408.

Hare, F. K.: 1951, 'Climatic classification' in L. D. Stamp and S. W. Wooldridge (eds.), *Essays in Geography*, Longmans, London, pp. 111–134.

Harvey, D. W.: 1969, *Explanation in Geography*, Arnold, London.

Horel, J. D.: 1981, 'A rotated principal component analysis of the interannual variability of the northern hemisphere 500 mb height field', *Monthly Weather Review* 109, 2080–2092.

Iakovleva, N. I. and K. A. Gurleva: 1969, 'Objective division into regions by expansion in terms of empirical function', *Trudy Glavnoi Geofizicheskoi Observatorii* 236, 155–164.

Jackson, D. M.: 1969, 'Comparison of classifications', in A. J. Cole (ed.), *Numerical Taxonomy*, Academic Press, London, pp. 91–111.

Jalickee, J. B. and D. R. Hamilton: 1977, 'Objective analysis and classification of oceanographic data', *Tellus* 29, 545–560.

Jancey, R. C.: 1966, 'Multidimensional group analysis', *Australian Journal of Botany* 14, 127–130.

Jardine, N. and R. Sibson: 1971, *Numerical Taxonomy*, John Wiley, London.

Johnston, R. J.: 1968, 'Choice of classification: the subjectivity of objective methods', *Annals of the Association of American Geographers* 58, 575–589.

Johnston, R. J.: 1970, 'Grouping and regionalizing: Some methodological and technical observations', *Economic Geography* 46, 293–305.

Johnston, R. J.: 1978, *Multivariate Statistical Analysis in Geography*, Longman, London.

Johnston, R. J.: 1981, 'Regarding the delimitation of regions according to climatic fluctuations', *Archiv für Meteorologie, Geophysik und Bioklimatologie, Ser. B.* 29, 215–228.

Kendall, M. G. and A. Stuart, 1968: *The Advanced Theory of Statistics*, Vol. 3, Hafner Publishers, New York.

King, L. G.: 1969, *Statistical Analysis in Geography*, Prentice-Hall, Englewood Cliffs, New Jersey.

Kojima, C.: 1973, 'Detailed climatic classification of Tohoku district by principal component analysis', *Journal of Agricultural Meteorology* 29, 165–172.

Köppen, W.: 1884, 'Die Wärmezonen der Erde, nach der Dauer der heissen, Gemässigten und kalten Zeit und nach der Wirkung der Wärme auf die organische Welt betrachtet', *Meteorologische Zeitschrift* 1, 215–226.

Köppen, W. and R. Geiger: 1928, *Klimakarte der Erde*, Justus Perthes, Gotha.

Kraus, E. G.: 1955, 'Secular changes of east-coast rainfall regimes', *Quarterly Journal of the Royal Meteorological Society* 81, 430–439.

Kuipers, W. J. A.: 1970, 'An experiment on numerical classification of scalar fields', *Idojaras* 74, 296–306.

Kutzbach, J. E.: 1967, 'Empirical eigenvectors of sea-level pressure, surface temperature and precipitation complexes over North America', *Journal of Applied Meteorology* 6, 791–802.

Lance, G. N. and W. T. Williams: 1967a, 'A general theory of classificatory sorting strategies, I.: hierarchical systems', *Computer Journal* 2, 373–380.

Lance, G. N. and W. T. Williams: 1967b, 'A general theory of classificatory sorting strategies, II: clustering systems', *Computer Journal* 10, 271–277.

Lankford, P. M.: 1969, 'Regionalization theory and alternative algorithms', *Geographical Analysis* 1, 196–212.

Lankford, P. M. and R. K. Semple: 1973, 'Classification and geography', *Geographia Polonica* 25, 7–30.

Lawson, M. P.: 1976, *The Climate of the Great American Desert*, University of Nebraska Press, Lincoln.

Lawson, M. P., R. C. Balling, Jr., A. J. Peters and D. C. Rundquist: 1981, 'Spatial analysis of secular temperature fluctuations', *Journal of Climatology* 1, 325–332.

Lawson, M. P., D. C. Rundquist, and A. J. Peters: 1972, 'Secular temperature change in the interior United States', *Great Plains-Rocky Mountain Geographical Journal* 1, 65–73.

Lund, I. A.: 1963, 'Map pattern classification by statistical methods', *Journal of Applied Meteorology* 2, 56–65.

MacNaughton-Smith, P., W. T. Williams, M. B. Dale, and L. G, Mockett: 1964, 'Dissimilarity analysis: a new technique of hierarchical subdivision', *Nature* 202, 1034–1035.

Mahalanobis, P. C.: 1936, 'On the generalized distance in statistics', *Proceedings of the National Institute of Sciences of India* 12, 49–55.

Mather, P. M.: 1976, *Computational Methods of Multivariate Analysis in Physical Geography*, John Wiley, London.

McBoyle, G. R.: 1971, 'Climatic classification of Australia by computer', *Australian Geographical Studies* 9, 1–14.

McBoyle, G. R.: 1972, 'Factor analytical approach to a climatic classification of Europe', *Climatological Bulletin No. 12*, McGill University, Montreal, pp. 273–341.

McDonald, J. R.: 1966, 'The region: its conception, design and limitations', *Annals of the Association of American Geographers* 55, 516–528.

McQuitty, L. L.: 1957, 'Elementary linkage analysis for isolating orthogonal and oblique types and typal relevancies', *Educational and Psychological Measurement* 17, 207–229.

McQuitty, L. L.: 1960, 'Hierarchical syndrome analysis', *Educational and Psychological Measurement* 20, 293–304.

McQuitty, L. L.: 1961, 'Elementary factor analysis', *Psychological Reports* 9, 71–78.

McQuitty, L. L.: 1966, 'Single and multiple classification by reciprocal pairs and rank order types', *Educational and Psychological Measurement* 26, 253–265.

Miller, R. G.: 1962, *Statistical prediction by discriminant analysis.* Meteorological Monographs, American Meteorological Society, 54 pp.

Miller, R. L. and S. S. Kahn: 1962, *Statistical Analysis in the Geological Sciences,* John Wiley, New York.

Morrison, D. F.: 1976, *Multivariate Statistical Methods,* McGraw Hill, New York.

National Climate Program Advisory Committee: 1980, *National Climate Program Five Year Plan.* NOAA, Washington.

Ogallo, L.; 1980, 'Regional classification of East African rainfall stations into homogeneous groups using the method of principal components analysis', in S. Ikeda (ed.), *Statistical Climatology,* Elsevier Scientific Publishing Company, Amsterdam, pp. 255–266.

Oliver, J. E.: 1970, 'A genetic approach to climate classification', *Annals of the Association of American Geographers* 60, 615–637.

Oliver, J. E., A. H. Siddigi, and S. N. Goward: 1978, 'Spatial patterns of climate and irrigation in Pakistan: a multivariate statistical approach', *Archiv für Meteorologie, Geophysik und Bioklimatologie, Ser. B* 25, 345–357.

Olson, E. C. and R. L. Miller: 1958, *Morphological Integration,* University of Chicago Press, Chicago.

Perry, A. H.: 1968, 'The regional variation of climatological characteristics with synoptic indices', *Weather* 23, 325–330.

Perry, A. H.: 1969, 'Sensible and latent heat transfer over the North Atlantic during some recent winter months', *Annalen der Meteorologie,* new series 4, 40–46.

Preston-Whyte, R. A.: 1974, 'Climatic classification of South Africa: a multivariate approach', *South African Geographical Journal* 65, 79–86.

Rajski, C.: 1961, 'Entropy and metric space', in Cherry C. (ed.), *Information Theory,* Butterworths, London, pp. 41–45.

Rao, C. R.: 1952, *Advanced Statistical Methods in Biometric Research,* Chapman and Hall, London.

Richman, M. B.: 1981, 'Obliquely rotated principal components: an improved meteorological map typing technique?', *Journal of Applied Meteorology* 20, 1145–1159.

Rummel, R. J.: 1970, *Applied Factor Analysis,* Northwestern University Press, Evanston.

Russell, J. S. and A. W. Moore: 1970, 'Detection of homoclimate by numerical analysis with reference to the Bigalow region (eastern Australia)', *Agricultural Meteorology* 7, 455–479.

Russell, J. S. and A. W. Moore: 1976, 'Classification of climate by pattern analysis with Australasian and Southern Africa data as an example', *Agricultural Meteorology* 16, 45–70.

Sekiguti, T.: 1952, 'Some problems of climatic classification: a new classification of climates of Japan', *Proceedings of the Eighth General Assembly and Seventeenth International Congress, International Geographical Union* (Washington), 285–290.

Semple, R. K., E. Casetti, and L. J. King: 1969, 'The determination of the optimal number of groupings in classification problems', Discussion Paper No. 10, Department of Geography, Ohio State University, 63 pp.

Semple, R. K. and M. B. Green: 1984, 'Classification in human geography', in Gaile, G. L. and C. J. Willmott (eds.), *Spatial Statistics and Models,* pp. 55–79.

Skaggs, R. H.: 1975, 'Drought in the United States, 1931–40', *Annals of the Association of American Geographers* **65**, 391–402.

Sneath, P. H. A.: 1969, 'Evaluation of clustering methods', in A. J. Cole (ed.), *Numerical Taxonomy*, Academic Press, London, pp. 257–267.

Sneath, P. H. A. and R. R. Sokal: 1973, *Numerical Taxonomy*, Freeman, San Francisco.

Sokal, R. R.: 1966, 'Numerical taxonomy', *Scientific American* **215**, 106–116.

Sokal, R. R. 1974, 'Classification purposes, principles, progress, prospects', *Science* **185**, 1115–1123.

Sokal, R. R. and F. J. Rohlf: 1962, 'The comparison of dendrograms by objective methods', *Taxon* **11**, 33–40.

Sokal, R. R. and P. H. A. Sneath: 1963, *Principles of Numerical Taxonomy*, W. H. Freeman and Company, San Francisco.

Spence, N. A.: 1968, 'A multifactor uniform regionalization of British counties on the basis of employment data for 1961', *Regional Studies* **2**, 87–104.

Spence, N. A. and P. J. Taylor: 1970, 'Quantitative methods in regional taxonomy', in Board C., R. J. Chorley, P. Haggett, and D. R. Stoddart (eds.), *Progress in Geography*, Vol. 2, Edward Arnold Ltd., London, pp. 3–64.

Steiner, D.: 1965, 'A multivariate statistical approach to climatic regionalization and classification', *Tijdschrift van het Koninklijk Nederlandsch Aardrijkskundig Genootschap* **82**, 329–347.

Stidd, C. K.: 1967, 'The use of eigenvectors for climatic estimates', *Journal of Applied Meteorology* **6**, 255–264.

Supan, A.: 1879, 'Die Temperaturzonen der Erde', *Petermann's Mittheilungen* (sic), 349–358.

Terjung, W. H.: 1970, 'Toward a climatic classification based on net radiation', *Association of American Geographers, Proceedings* **2**, 140–144.

Terjung, W. H. and S. S-F. Louie: 1972, 'Energy input-output climates of the world: a preliminary attempt', *Archiv für Meteorologie, Geophysik und Bioklimatologie, Ser. B* **20**, 129–166.

Thornthwaite, C. W.: 1948, 'An approach toward a rational classification of climate', *Geographical Review* **38**, 55–94.

Walsh, J. E. and M. B. Richman: 1981, 'Seasonality in the associations between surface temperatures over the United States and the North Pacific Ocean', *Monthly Weather Review* **109**, 767–783.

Ward, J. H. Jr.: 1963, 'Hierarchical grouping to optimize an objective function', *Journal of the American Statistical Association* **58**, 236–244.

Wilcock, A. A.: 1968, 'Köppen after fifty years', *Annals of the Association of American Geographers* **58**, 12–28.

Williams, W. T. and M. B. Dale: 1965, 'Fundamental problems in numerical taxonomy', *Advances in Botanical Research* **2**, 35–68.

Williams, W. T. and G. N. Lance: 1965, 'Logic of computer-based intrinsic classifications', *Nature* **207**, 159–161.

Willmott, C. J., 1977a: 'A component analytic approach to precipitation regionalization in California', *Archiv für Meteorologie, Geophysik und Bioklimatologie, Ser. B* **24**, 269–281.

Willmott, C. J.: 1977b, 'Toward a new climatic regionalization of the contiguous United States', Proceedings of the Second National Solar Radiation Data Workship, Huntsville,

Alabama. Johnson Environmental and Energy Center, University of Alabama, D1–D–11.

Willmott, C. J.: 1978, 'P-mode principal components analysis, grouping and precipitation regions in California', *Archiv für Meteorologie, Geophysik und Bioklimatologie, Ser. B.* **26**, 277–295.

Willmott, C. J. and M. T. Vernon: 1980, 'Solar Climates of the conterminous United States: a preliminary investigation', *Solar Energy* **24**, 295–303.

Wishart, D.: 1969, 'Mode analysis: a generalization of nearest neighbor which reduces chaining effects', in A. J. Cole (ed.), *Numerical Taxonomy*, Academic Press, London, pp. 282–308.

Wishart D.: 1975, CLUSTAN IC: User Manual. University College Computer Center, London.

Wolfe, J. H.: 1970, 'Pattern clustering by multivariate analysis', *Multivariate Behavioral Research* **5**, 329–350.

Zobler, L.: 1957, 'Statistical testing of regional boundaries', *Annals of the Association of American Geographers* **47**, 83–95.

Zobler, L.: 1958, 'Decision making in regional construction', *Annals of the Association of American Geographers* **48**, 140–148.

REAL MAPS, VIRTUAL MAPS AND INTERACTIVE CARTOGRAPHY

1. INTRODUCTION

In the last decade, numerical and analytical approaches to cartography have been growing at a rapid rate (Robinson *et al.*, 1977). This trend was recognized some time ago by Morrison (Morrison, 1974) in a perceptive article in which he discussed the changing philosophical and technical aspects of thematic cartography. The first aspect which is important here is the expansion of the definition of the concept of a map which includes the newer cartographic products and a recognition of the new strategies for mapping methodology. The second is a perception of the field of cartography as an independent scientific discipline. Many of the trends recognized by Morrison also apply to general cartography as well. One can see development taking place in numerical processing (see for example Aangeenbrug (1980)), analytical cartography (Tobler, 1979), cartographic data base development (Nyerges, 1980), geographic information systems (Tomlinson *et al.*, 1976), and cartographic systems design and operation (Aangeenbrug, 1980). These prodigious efforts, as well as many others, have resulted in a large number of new cartographic products and systems which go far beyond the conventional definition of a map. Morrison clearly recognized this need as did Riffe (1970). As this work in cartography has accelerated, so has the need for specifying an expanded model for what constitutes a map. From this need, Moellering (1980a) has developed the concepts of real and virtual maps.

This chapter is a systematic examination of this expanded notion of a cartographic map and the relationship of it to contemporary cartographic work and to some of its basic philosophical implications. Cartographic systems design is examined in light of these topics as is the expansion of these concepts into the temporal domain of dynamic cartography. Finally, working cartographic systems are examined in light of these concepts. In all cases, pertinent references will be given to provide the reader with a large body of literature which provides more detail than can be given here.

Gary L. Gaile and Cort. J. Willmott (eds.), Spatial Statistics and Models, 109–132.
© 1984 *by D. Reidel Publishing Company.*

2. REAL AND VIRTUAL MAPS

In recent years, a number of cartographic products began to appear which have many of the characteristics of conventional sheet maps, but were somehow different. Many of these kinds of maps are digital in nature. For example, it became possible to display a map-like image on the screen of a graphic CRT display terminal, to manipulate that map on the screen, and to make the map disappear with the touch of a button. It also became possible to store cartographic data in forms which could not be recognized by anyone as a map, but yet these data could easily be converted into a map image and subsequently put into some kind of hard copy form such as a printed map. This situation clearly requires an expanded definition of what constitutes a map, as was recognized by Morrison (1974). Earlier, Riffe (1970) proposed the terms of map, temporary map, and nonmap to describe conventional maps, graphic CRT images and nongraphic information. However, his effort only really dealt with products which were graphic map images in some form and clearly was not a satisfying expansion of the term map, although it was a step in the right direction. The author has been very interested in these developments in cartography and has developed the concepts of real and virtual maps (1975, 1977) to describe the situation. A real map is a cartographic product which can be handled physically and usually carried around with relative ease. Such real maps can be used directly by a map reader in a graphic two-dimensional form which directly shows the map image and from which spatial relationships are directly depicted. Examples of such maps are conventional maps, both general and thematic, globes, wall maps, plastic relief models, etc.

However, there are a host of cartographic products which contain cartographic information and may be graphic in nature, but are lacking some essential attribute of a real map. Some of these products are ephemeral in nature such as a graphic CRT terminal image or the kind of cognitive map where one has a two-dimensional cartographic image visualized in the mind, both of which can disappear in an instant. Others are hard copy in nature, such as a gazetteer or stored hologram which contain cartographic information, but yet that information is not presented in the form of a readable graphic image. Still other kinds of cartographic products exist in the data domain in the form of digital cartographic data files, or data stored in a computer system. One should note that all of these cartographic products can be straightforwardly converted into real maps. In situations where one has such cartographic products, which have many of the characteristics of real maps but yet lack some fundamental attribute of a real map, one can use the term virtual map to describe it. Although a virtual map lacks some fundamental attribute of a real map, the cartographic information in such a map can be converted into a real map. It should be noted that the terms real map and virtual map are compatible with the concept of real and virtual coordinates in computer graphics, the notion of real and virtual memory in computer science, the terms of real and virtual image in the area of image processing, and the term virtual image in optics, a fact that influenced the choice of the terms.

Moellering (1980a) in a recent article defined real and virtual maps in terms of a four part definition:

Real Map. Any cartographic product which has a directly viewable cartographic image and has a permanent tangible reality (hard copy). There is no differentiation as to whether that real map was produced by mechanical, electronic or manual means.

Virtual Map (type 1). Has a directly viewable cartographic image but only a transient reality as has a CRT map image. This is what Riffe called a temporary map. Given the direction of current scientific work, electrocognitive displays may be possible.

Virtual Map (type 2). Has a permanent tangible reality, but cannot be directly viewed as a cartographic image. These are all hard copy media, but in all cases these products must be further processed to be made viewable. It is interesting to note that the film animation adds a temporal dimension to the cartographic information.

Virtual map (type 3). Has neither of the characteristics of the earlier classes, but can be converted into a real map as readily as the other two classes of virtual maps. Computer based information in this form is usually very easily manipulated.

Note that the situation can be reduced to two central variables: direct viewability and permanent tangible reality. It turns out that from these two variables one can define four classes of real and virtual maps portrayed in a two way table as shown in Table I. In each quadrant is listed a number of cartographic products. Some have been in existence for many years like conventional maps and field notes while others, such as digital cartographic data files and laser disk storage are relatively new.

2.1. *Transformations between Real and Virtual Maps*

It is interesting to note that transformations can be defined between various classes of real and virtual maps. They are specified as $t(S_1 \rightarrow S_2)$ as signifying a transformation of cartographic information from state 1 to state 2. Most important operations in cartography can be defined by such transformations

TABLE I

Classes of real and virtual maps[a]

Directly viewable as a cartographic image

	Yes	No
Permanent tangible reality — Yes	*Real Map* Conventional Sheet Map Globe Orthophoto Map Machine Drawn Map Computer Output Microfilm Block Diagram Plastic Relief Model	*Virtual Map-Type 2* Traditional Field Data Gazetteer Anaglyph Film Animation Hologram (stored) Fourier Transform (stored) Laser Disk Data
Permanent tangible reality — No	*Virtual Map-Type 1* CRT Map Image a) refresh b) storage tube c) plasma panel Cognitive Map (two-dimensional image)	*Virtual Map-Type 3* Digital Memory (data) Magnetic Disk or Tape (data) Video Animation Digital Terrain Model Cognitive Map (relational geographic information)

[a] Reproduced with permission from the Cartographic Journal (1980), Vol. 17, part 1, pp. 12–15.

of which there are 16, as shown in Figure 1. The following are examples of these transformations: (* denotes more important transformations)

A.* $R \rightarrow R$ Real map transformations define the operation of conventional cartography. All tasks are either manual, mechanical, or photographic.

B.* $R \rightarrow V_1$ Map reading is defined by the situation where the cartographic information is extracted from the map and used to create a cognitive map in the mind of the reader.

C. $R \rightarrow V_2$ This transformation involves extracting data from a map and rendering that information into a hard copy form.

D.* $R \rightarrow V_3$ Digitizing is a very important part of modern cartography where information is converted from the graphic form of a real map into coordinates and data which are stored in a flexible digital form.

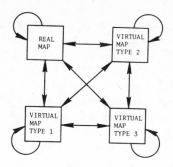

Fig. 1. Transformations between real and virtual maps.

E.* $V_1 \rightarrow R$ Making hard copies from a graphic CRT display terminal is the fundamental operation defined here. It also involves creating representations of cognitive maps stored in the mind.

F.* $V_1 \rightarrow V_1$ This transformation involves the manipulation of a graphic CTR image or the reading of a cartographic image and forming a cognitive map from that information.

G. $V_1 \rightarrow V_2$ This transformation involves converting a generated graphic CTR image to a stored form such as a hologram or film animation. Many early film animations were photographed from CRT images.

H.* $V_1 \rightarrow V_3$ This transformation involves using a graphic CRT image to modify a machine-stored cartographic data base.

I. $V_2 \rightarrow R$ Here, hard copy stored information is used to create a real map. The use of traditional field data to create a real map is an example.

J. $V_2 \rightarrow V_1$ The display of field data or laser disk data in a graphic form on a CRT display is an example of this sort of transformation.

K. $V_2 \rightarrow V_2$ Converting the form of stored hard copy cartographic information is an example of this transformation.

L.* $V_2 \rightarrow V_3$ Cartographic data editing from coding sheets to a digitized form is an example of this transformation.

M.* $V_3 \rightarrow R$ Digital plotting is an important example here. It is also possible to do three-dimensional model carving and other machine generated operations.

N.* $V_3 \rightarrow V_1$ Graphic CRT display of cartographic digital data is an essential operation in the design of any interactive cartographic system.

O. $V_3 \rightarrow V_2$ Making a hard copy product from digital cartographic data is an example of this transformation.

P.* $V_3 \rightarrow V_3$ Many mathematical operations in cartography are defined by this transformation. Tobler's (1961) notion of cartographic transformations is a part of these operations.

Since all important cartographic operations are defined by these transformations, they can be used as an aid in the design of new digital cartographic systems.

3. CARTOGRAPHIC INFORMATION AND DATA STRUCTURES

In recent years many questions have been raised concerning the nature of the cartographic information we are seeking to gather, manipulate, and digitize. One is also interested in how that information is intrinsically organized. Nyerges (1980) has identified six specific levels of cartographic information ranging from the real world to the machine code for physical devices in a computer system. The data levels are as follows:

1) Data Reality — This is essentially the real world, from which all data originates, and which contains a host of cartographic entities which have relationships between them. This includes all cartographic data which are currently collected and all information which could be collected as cartographic information. It includes everything in the real world which could be considered cartographic information.

2) Information Structure — This represents a specific structuring of cartographic information for particular sets of entities. It is a formal model that specifies the organization of cartographic information pertaining to a specific phenomenon. It includes sets of cartographic entities and the relationships between them and acts as a skeleton for the canonical structure.

3) Canonical Structure — Here one has a data model which is independent of applications and systems which process such data. It is a minimal structure which reflects the inherent organization of that set of cartographic information. It is used to bring together several information structures.

4) Data Structure — This is the level at which most cartographic data are recognized by most cartographic analysts. It is the logical data organization

designed for particular systems which includes specifying access paths and data languages which tie the structure together as a whole.

5) Storage Structure — This level is the implementation of the data structure. It includes the specification of how particular data records are stored and how pointer structures are organized which specify the explicit relationships contained in the data structure.

6) Machine Encoding — This is the physical representation of how the storage structure is contained in the physical devices of the computer system hardware.

Each of the above data levels represents a level of cartographic information which is not necessarily represented by a graphic image. The information captured in these cartographic data levels can specify many more cartographic relationships and attributes than are represented in a graphic image of a map. However, it is equally clear that these two things are intimately related to one another. Nyerges (1980) has examined this situation and applied the terms of surface and deep structure to clarify the situation. Surface structure relates to the cartographic information in the form of a cartographic image which can be read and interpreted by a map user. It is clear from the previous discussion that the surface structure image can be either a real map or a type 1 virtual map. Although the surface structure image shows the cartographic entities in the arrangement that is found in the real world, there are a host of other relationships, spatial and otherwise, which are not represented by cartographic surface structure as an image. These relationships are called deep structure, meaning that these relationships are not necessarily evident from the surface structure. Figure 2 illustrates the relationship between deep and surface structure which at the intermediate levels can be thought of as the data structure and as deep as the information structure or canonical structure. It can be seen that there are a host of relationships which carry spatial and relational information which are not evident in the surface structure. It should be pointed out that the manner in which the cartographic information structure model is conceptualized and subsequently the way in which the resulting data structure is implemented will directly affect the difficulty or ease of performing various numerical operations on the information. This applies to operations of display as well as to operations of analysis.

This discussion naturally leads into an examination of data models and data structures. It turns out that many early data structures could only be used for display purposes because they were surface level structures and had little or no deep structure to them. The data structures used in the SYMAP and CAM programs are two well known cases in point although many others

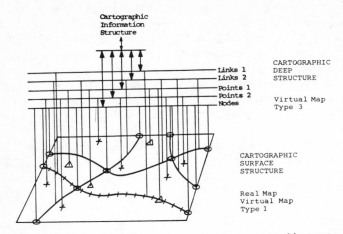

Fig. 2. The relationship between deep and surface cartographic structure.

could be cited. In more recent years it has been recognized (Peucker and Chrisman, 1975) that if the data structures had some deep structure components, such as topology (Corbett, 1979) and other relational attributes, then these structures could also be used for analytical operations in addition to straightforward display. These operations include defining neighboring polygons, polygon overlay, chaining linear segments, tracing paths through networks, point-in-polygon operations, multiple dimensional linking of cartographic objects, and many others. This move toward the inclusion of analytical processing with such data structures has lead to a deeper examination of possible alternatives for cartographic data models. This is related to the formulation and design of several kinds of data models which include hierarchical (Coleman *et al.*, 1978), relational (Vaidua *et al.*, 1982), network (Phillips, 1979), and Hypergraph-Based Data Structure (HBDS) (Bouillé, 1978). Of all these approaches to cartographic data models, the HBDS is the most general and therefore seems to offer the most potential to cartographers. However, because of its newness, more research is required before a definitive answer can be obtained. In closing, it should be noted that as a research area cartographic data models and structures offer many heretofore unanswered questions and pose a direct challenge to the creative genius of analytical cartographers.

4. CARTOGRAPHIC SYSTEMS DESIGN

The topic of cartographic systems design is one that is very rich conceptually and ripe for discussion. Cartographic information systems can be used for three very basic purposes: production, display and analysis. In any case, one must begin a five stage cycle in order to design and build such a system. The five stages of design and development are:

1) specifying the system goals,
2) specifying the system needs and feasibility,
3) logical system design and organization,
4) system implementation,
5) system testing, verification and documentation.

The fundamental approach to cartographic systems design is the same as solving any analytical problem, that is, beginning at the most general level and proceeding to more specific concerns.

4.1. *System Goals*

Specifying the system goals includes stating succinctly just what it is that the system is supposed to be able to do. The goals should be stated in terms of the fundamental operations of the system: data input, processing and analysis, and output. Each of the goals from these three, which form the basic stages of system operation, must be specified very carefully because all subsequent design decisions are based on these fundamental goals.

4.2. *System Needs and Feasibility*

The question now turns to the feasible alternatives for setting up the system such that it can operate in a rational operational and economic way. The first question concerns the data source(s) for the system. Will these data come from some already existing data stream, or will a new data collection channel have to be established? Will the data come from a statistical data source, such as the census, from a remote sensing system, or from the digitizing of maps? The mix of these data sources must be considered and analyzed very carefully. The second consideration is the fundamental theory and algorithms on which the analysis and processing are based. One basic question is whether the numerical theory exists to solve this problem. Although many advances have been made in this area in recent years, it is presumptuous to arbitrarily assume that the basic theory exists and has been adequately developed. A subsequent consideration is the expression of the theory into the form of an algorithm or set of algorithms which can be usefully integrated into such a system. The third consideration is the hardware and facilities required for the magnitude and kinds of processing envisioned. Is the system to be interactive in nature, or a conventional batch processing system? The hardware required for each alternative can be rather different and appropriate plans must be made. Is special hardware required for specific operations of the system: e.g. digitizing, image interpretation or output? These requirements must be carefully considered and specified. Finally, all of these system needs and requirements must be considered in terms of overall feasibility of the project. This question must be examined in terms of the projected costs relative to the funds available, the personnel required, as well as the facilities required. Only if all of these questions are answered positively is it feasible to proceed with the project.

4.3. *Logical System Design*

Once the feasibility of the project is established, one can proceed with the design of the system itself. The first stage is to specify the logical design of the system. Given the goals and needs of the system, the question now turns to one of how the logic of the system should be structured. To do this, one must examine four considerations: command structure, real and virtual map transformations, theory and algorithms to be used, and the data organization (Pfaff and Maderlechner, 1982; Anderson and Shapiro, 1979; Fry, 1982). These topics will be discussed individually, but in reality they constitute a whole which functions homogeneously. In order to run any cartographic system, one must be able to invoke commands which instruct the system what to do. Each command must specify a particular operation of the system which is in harmony with other system needs. In most cases, the command structure is organized in a hierarchical or partly hierarchical fashion. Each command is coordinated not only with other commands, but also with the software structure and data organization of the system. Table II shows a two level command structure by Brown and Moellering (1982) for a system which generates isarithms which represent a continuous Z surface. As one can see in the table, it is not uncommon for such systems to have several command levels built into them.

The second aspect of the logical system design is that of map transformations. In the second section, it was pointed out that transformations between various states of real and virtual maps specify most of the important operations

TABLE II
Command language for ICFITG

System prompt	Commands	Subcommands
ICFITG >	DATA	
	POINTS >	ADD
		INTERP
		DELETE
		DISZVAL
		DISALIZ
		REDRAW
		WINDOW
		RESETW
		ENDP
	TRIGRID	
	ISOLINE	
	OVRPNTS	
	OVRTRIG	
	OVRISO	
	SAVE	
	RESTORE	
	WINDOW	
	RESETW	
	ENDI	

in cartography. Therefore, it is possible to use this approach to specify the logical design of the system. Figure 3 shows a general flow chart showing the real and virtual map transformations embedded in the system. It should be

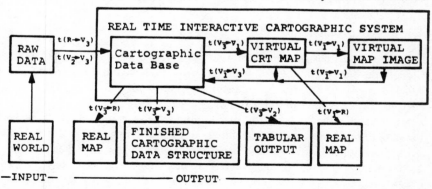

Fig. 3. Simplified design of a real time interactive cartographic system using real and virtual maps.

noted that the most important transformations used here are the $R \to V_3$, $R \to V_1$, $V_1 \to V_1$, $V_1 \to V_3$, $V_3 \to V_3$, $V_3 \to V_1$, $V_1 \to R$, and $V_3 \to R$. This particular system happens to be an interactive cartographic system which capitalizes on the use of virtual map transformations. The reason for this sort of design is that in a virtual state digital cartographic information is very easy to manipulate and analyze. One of the secrets to efficient interactive systems design is to effectively utilize these virtual map transformations of cartographic information.

Once the real and virtual map transformations have been specified, one can then take a more detailed look at the theory and algorithms involved. At this stage, the theory must be fashioned into a workable numerical procedure called an algorithm. The algorithm(s) used must be able to process and analyze the input data, or subsequently processed data, as specified by the user commands. Here, there is a direct link between the mathematical form of the algorithms and the numerical form of the information that is captured in the data structure.

The final stage of the logical design includes the data organization to be used in the system. Here, one must consider the data model to be used in the system. This refers to the information structure and canonical structure of the data, levels 2 and 3 in the Nyerges scheme. Is the data model to be used hierarchical, network, or relational, and is this the way the data to be used by the system are organized?

As noted above, all four of these aspects of the logical design relate to and interact with one another. They are discussed separately here for clarity and to facilitate understanding. However, they are, and act as, part of a whole.

4.4. *System Organization*

Once the logical design is in place, one can begin to be more specific about the system organization. Here, there are five fundamental areas of concern which have been partitioned to facilitate this discussion. The first is the communication design of the system. This deals with the way in which the person running the system, the user, communicates commands to control the operation of the system. As pointed out by Moellering (1977) this sort of communication in an interactive cartographic setting is a far richer channel of communication than ordinary cartographic communication. If one has an interactive cartographic system such as the one schematically portrayed in Figure 3, the $V_1 \to V_1$ transformations refer to man-machine communication that takes place between the system user and the CRT terminal through which the commands are flowing to the system. Through this man-machine communication channel could flow two-dimensional map displays, coordinate information from a digitizing device, the ability to point to locations of objects on the CRT screen, keyboard interaction, function buttons, audio bell signals, and other more esoteric forms of communication. It should be obvious why this provides a much richer communication channel than ordinary cartographic communication. It is the coordination of this communication with the command structure of the system which gives the system its logical processing power.

The cartographic design must be taken into account at several levels. First, the map display which appears on the CRT screen must be displayed according to the accepted principles, although the designer has considerably more flexibility than for batch systems because such CRT displays can be manipulated and changed very easily because they are in a virtual form. The second and more conventional aspect of the use of cartographic design is to organize and design the hard copy output produced by the system. Almost every cartographic information system will produce real maps in some form and in this case the principles of conventional cartographic design fully apply.

One must then turn to data structure design, level 4 in the Nyerges scheme. The data structure specifies the way in which the cartographic data are to be organized in terms of which linkages and spatial relationships are to be preserved, implemented and managed by the system. Here, the topological and relational properties of the data which are important to the system goals must be specified in an efficient manner such that the algorithms and other software can correctly use them.

Another activity which is going on concurrently is that of software design and organization. The program structure of the system must be carefully designed because it is the software side of the overall system. The standard approach is to utilize the concept of modular software design. The organization of these software modules must be compatible with the command structure of the system and the other parts of communication design and data structure design. If each command in the system has its own set of software modules, dedicated or shared, it is an easy matter to add, delete, or modify commands as it necessary during the future development of the system. The software design also includes the allocating of the proper vectors and arrays of internal memory so that the data structure can be operated efficiently.

The hardware organization configuration is also an important aspect of system organization. Earlier in the feasibility stage, it has been ascertained whether the proper hardware is available for the system. Here, the focus of the work is on configuring and coordinating the hardware with the software in order to result in a system which is truly functional and efficient. One is concerned with hardware for data input, such as digitizers or CRT terminals, processing hardware such as a large central system or smaller minicomputer systems and output devices such as CRT terminals, plotters and printers. At this level, one is also interested in the physical connection between devices to the extent that such connections will support efficient operation of the system.

Once all five of these aspects of the system design are in place and reconciled one to another, checked and carefully verified, then it is time to begin implementing the system.

4.5. System Implementation

Now begins the task of actually writing the program code for the system software. In many instances, over half of the total effort of building such a system will have already been consumed in the goals, needs and design stages. Because the system has been designed with a modular software structure, the system can be implemented in computer code the same way. Systems have a main program which serves as a subprogram command and software control center. Program commands are entered through it and it in turn calls the other logical software modules invoked during the operation of the command. Therefore, each command and associated logical modules can be developed and implemented independently from the other operations of the system. The use of modular software logic for a system can save a tremendous amount of time, effort and funds during the implementation stage.

4.6. Testing, Verification and Documentation

As each logical software module or set of modules is developed, it can be tested and verified for correct and accurate operation, one of the primary advantages of modular logic. At the same time, documentation should be defined and written which explains the operation of each module, the basic algorithm(s) involved and the calling procedures for invoking each module. As more software modules are added, one can begin to test and verify larger segments of the whole system. This is in relation to the overall logical and command structure of the system, but also in relation to the data structure design and the hardware devices. Once all of the software modules are tested and verified in place, then the entire system can be tested as a whole. If the individual modules have been carefully designed, tested, and documented, then the testing of the system can be a rather straightforward matter. However, since the number of combinations of operations is more than the square of the entire number of operations, it is usually not possible to test all combinations of all commands with all other operations. That is why careful design and implementation are crucial to the overall success of the whole system.

5. INTRODUCTION TO DYNAMIC CARTOGRAPHY

For centuries, the standard cartographic product has been the conventional real map. These maps represent some segment of the real world at one specific point in time. However, it is obvious that most phenomena in our world change through time, and cartographers have tried, within the context of conventional sheet maps, to capture such change. The most straightforward approach is to create a series of maps of the study area with one map for each period as shown in Figure 4 where each map shows the distribution of data for each time period (t). By carefully studying the map for each time period, one can deduce the change in the phenomenon through time. An alternative approach is to construct a map of change (c) between two time periods in order to emphasize the spatial components of the change more explicitly. Series of maps such as this have been constructed for point data distributions as shown and also for series of choropleth maps. If one is displaying parametric data on choropleth maps, the task of efficiently choosing a suitable set of choropleth data classes which are both informative and valid for the entire series becomes an interesting challenge. This problem has been solved by Wasilenko and Moellering (1977) by using an aggregate Z data distribution for the entire series.

However, recent developments in computer hardware and software have made it possible to generate animated sequences of maps which are truly dynamic in character, that is the cartographic representation of the data is seen to move and/or change through time in a continuous fashion in a way that symbolizes these changes and development of the cartographic phenomenon through time. Although some aspects of such animated and dynamic sequences could be generated by hand (Thrower, 1961), the possibilities for such work have greatly expanded with the development of more

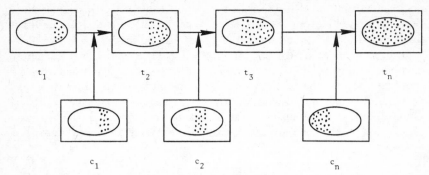

Fig. 4. A dynamic sequence in cartography with time period (t_n) and increments of change (c_n).

sophisticated computer processing and numerical data bases (Cornwell and Robinson, 1966). Hunter (1977) has shown that for almost all conventional animation techniques a numerical approach has been developed which is better and usually more efficient.

When one moves from the static real map domain over to the dynamic virtual map domain, a new range of possibilities is made available to the cartographer. As shown in the earlier figure, conventional cartography usually resorts to a series of static maps which are usually the same area and scale. Each map represents a different point in time in the sequence. The dynamic character of the Z variable is represented in the changing position of the symbols, the changing size, shape or color of the symbols, or some combination of these in the two dimensions. Modern dynamic cartography offers the possibility of displaying such information as a three dimensional surface for which the temporal changes are shown as a continuum. However, in addition to showing the changing Z surface, it is also possible to dynamically perform rotation, translation and scale change to the base as shown in Figure 5 where the Z surface is changing at the same time that the base is being rotated about its center. These possibilities have been examined in more detail by Moellering (1980b) and have resulted in three distinct display strategies being developed: real-time surface exploration, spatiotemporal data display, and linking spatial process with spatiotemporal data display. The real-time surface exploration strategy is predicated on an approach somewhat different than that discussed earlier in this section. Here, one has a fixed Z surface which is relatively complex which therefore cannot be efficiently displayed in a static setting. The fundamental notion is to "explore the surface" by moving the viewing point and also the surface such that one can move in for a closer look at more complex detail in an area or move around to get a broader view while at the same time moving the viewing point over the surface. It turns out that this capability can be most efficiently used if one carries out this activity on a real-time dynamic image generation system. This means that digital display generating will create the images at the same time that the person viewing the display changes the controls. It is not possible to fully describe such a complex phenomenon in a written article with static figures. The author has created a demonstration cartographic animation which illustrates this and the other major strategies discussed here (1978).

The second approach is that of spatiotemporal data display. Here, one has a kind of cartographic animation which is a more direct extension of temporal changes of cartographic data into the dynamic domain. Here, the change of the Z surface is portrayed as a dynamic phenomenon. One can detect nuances in the spatiotemporal dynamics which cannot easily be recognized from a series of static maps. In addition to a changing Z surface with a fixed base, it is possible to add more dynamics by moving the base to make the entire surface visible, usually by rotating it. Figure 5 is a simple example of the concept showing population change in the United States while at the same time rotating the base of the display.

The third strategy is to link spatiotemporal data display, described above, with the notion of spatial process. Here, the cartographic dynamics pictured are associated with particular stages in a spatial process. Figure 6 shows a Hagerstrand diffusion process of the spread of the innovation of farm tractors in the central part of the United States. The link between the generated display and the process is the fact that the center of the diffusion process can be clearly seen as occurring in North Dakota. Even more striking and much more subtle is the relationship played by the State of Missouri relative to that of Arkansas. As the innovation spreads out from the center and intensifies in 1940, the State of Missouri lags three of its neighboring states. However, Missouri retards the speed at which the innovation reaches Arkansas, in other words, Arkansas is in the diffusion shadow of Missouri. This situation becomes abundantly clear towards the end of the temporal sequence in 1969 when Missouri catches up with its neighboring states, while the intensification of the rate of adoption for Arkansas is right behind. It is doubtful that this shadow effect could have been detected in any other way.

These three examples illustrate the power offered by dynamic cartography. Although it is being utilized in some situations, its real potential has not really been tapped. As time proceeds, these dynamic cartographic displays, which

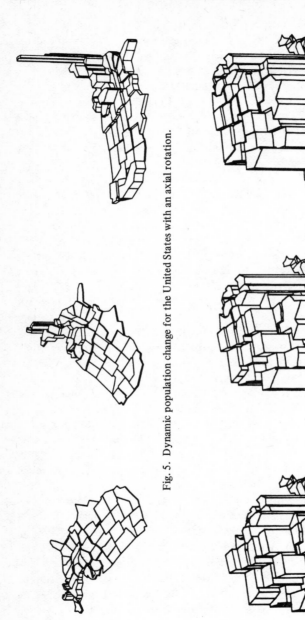

Fig. 5. Dynamic population change for the United States with an axial rotation.

1969

1954

Fig. 6. Dynamic surface of diffusion for three time periods.

1940

are currently regarded by most cartographers as being rather exotic, will become much more widely used.

6. INTERACTIVE COMPUTER-ASSISTED CARTOGRAPHIC (CAC) SYSTEMS

Interactive CAC systems are used for three basic purposes in cartography: production, data display and analysis of data. The production CAC systems are primarily oriented towards the production of conventional sheet maps. Some are large comprehensive systems involved with the entire production process, while others deal with only one of the three fundamental aspects of cartographic production: data input, processing, or output. Interactive CAC display systems concentrate on the generation of virtual type 1 CRT maps, many in color, which usually have hard copy capability, from a data base which in some cases is rather large. Many such systems can query the data base in interesting ways. The displayed maps are usually rather flashy in a visual sense. The third kind of interactive CAC system is used for analytical purposes to solve cartographic problems in a scientific sense. Such systems generally have impressive analytical capabilities coupled with a plainer kind of CRT display. Most interactive CAC systems fit into only one of the above classes, although a few are designed for a multiple purpose. Several examples are presented for each of the kinds of systems and are described below with a brief comment about each system, its goals and distinctive characteristics. This selected list only represents the tip of the iceberg as far as the total number of such systems that exist. For more extensive listings, please refer to the work by Brassel, *et al.* (1980) and two reports by the National Technical Information Service (1981a, b).

6.1. *Production*

Bathymetric Data Reduction System — BDRS (Frank *et al.*, 1981)
  BDRS is designed to be an interactive processing subsystem which handles bathymetric data from soundings, ship logs, and fathograms for Bathymetric Information System, its parent system.
Lineal Input System — LIS (Rome Air Development Center, 1975)
  LIS is an interactive data input system for digitizing map and chart information with an editing and display capability.
Digital Input-Output Display Equipment — DIODE (Shepherd, 1976)
  DIODE provides an interactive editing capability for the Automated

Cartography System. It can accept data from several source systems and is used to edit and verify those data. It is also used to preview plot files.

Wetlands Automated Mapping System — WAMS (Brooks and Neidzwiadek, 1980)

WAMS is designed as a complete system for input, processing and output for the classification, deliniation and inventory of wetlands data for the National Wetlands Inventory Project.

Computer Mapping and Graphics Subsystem — CMGS (Iler, 1981)

CMGS is a complete system for creating thematic maps based on areas such as census tracts and blocks for the City of Chicago. The system is based on the Intergraph Graphics Design System.

Applicon Graphics System — AGS (Hoinkes, 1978)

AGS is used by the Cartography Department of the Swiss Federal Institute of Technology as a complete system which has been used to product aeronautical chart overlays and base maps for the Atlas of Switzerland.

Automap (Anonymous, 1978)

Automap is a complete system with an interactive data input subsystem which has been used to produce color separated overlays for various kinds of Australian maps.

Digitizing Network System — DIGNET (Tuerke, 1976)

DIGNET is a cartographic data digitizing, input, editing and processing system for creating thematic maps in the Bundesforschungsanstalt für Landeskunde and Raumordnung in the Federal Republic of Germany.

6.2. *Display*

Domestic Information Display System — DIDS (Dalton and Billingsley, 1979)

DIDS is designed to be used with thematic data and display it in a color choroplethic format. As such, it is a very slick and flashy system with video projection output.

Spatial Data Management System — SDMS (Donelson, 1978)

SDMS is a very innovative and visionary graphics display system which is controlled by the operator in a "media room" who controls the system with two digital joysticks and a touch sensitive screen on a video montor. Output is by video projection, quadraphonic sound and video monitors.

Interactive Urban Mapping System — INTURMAP (Clement, 1973)

INTURMAP is designed to create map displays of information which has been extracted from a data base by an innovative query language which has been designed specifically for the information contained in the system.

Interactive Choropleth Mapping System — ICMS (Turner and Moellering, 1979)

ICMS is designed to provide the viewer with a full range of design, classing and display options for creating shaded choropleth maps.

Automated Radar Video Mapping Program — ARVMP (Feldman, 1981)

ARVMAP produces maps to overlay radar display screens at air control towers to aid in the display of constantly changing locations of aircraft in the navigation control area.

Interactive Contouring from an Irregular Triangular Grid — ICFITG (Brown and Moellering, 1982)

ICFITG is designed to interactively create and edit isarithmic Z surface representations of parametric data.

6.3. *Analysis*

Geo-Data Analysis and display system — GADS (Carlson *et al*., 1974)

GADS has been designed for the analysis of urban data zones which can be displayed as both maps and graphs.

Demonstration Image Processing System — DEMONS (Schrock, 1980)

DEMONS is a system for use in digital image processing in terms of both photointerpretation and mapping.

Transit Planning — TRANPLAN (Moellering *et al*., 1977)

TRANPLAN can be used to design transit systems with disaggregated individual modal choice data as the basis of the analysis and product maps of the designed system.

Interactive Graphic Transit Design System — IGTDS (White and Cousineau, 1980)

IGTDS can be used to analyze aggregate modal choice data associated with the use of several kinds of transportation and display that information as both graphs and skeletal system maps.

The above listings are intended to whet the curiosity and intellectual appetite of the reader. For the realities of transferring and installing software systems, see Baxter (1980).

Dept. of Geography
The Ohio State University

BIBLIOGRAPHY

Aangeenbrug, R. (ed.): 1980, *Proceedings of the International Symposium on Computer Assisted Cartography IV*, American Congress on Surveying and Mapping, Falls Church.

Anderson, R. and N. Shapiro: 1979, *Design Considerations for Computer-Based Interactive Map Display Systems*, DARPA Report #R–23–82.

Anonymous: 1978, 'Australian automated mapmaking system boosts production capacity', *ACSM Bulletin* 62, 11–13.

Baxter, R.: 1980, 'The transfer of software systems for map data processing', in H. Freeman and G. Pieroni (eds.), *Map Data Processing*, Academic Press, New York, pp. 223–246.

Bouillé. F.: 1978, 'Structuring cartographic data and spatial processes with the Hypergraph-Based Data Structure', in G. Dutton (ed.), *Harvard Papers on Geographic Information Systems* 5, Harvard University Press, Cambridge.

Brassel, K., M. Wasilenko and D. Marble: 1980, *Cartography and Graphics*, Computer Software for Spatial Data Handling 3, IGU Commission on Geographical Data Sensing and Processing, Ottawa.

Brooks, W. and H. Neidzwiadek: 1980, 'The wetlands analytical mapping system production environment', *Technical Papers of the American Congress on Surveying and Mapping, 40th Annual Meeting*, 308–314.

Brown, R. and H. Moellering: 1982, 'ICFITG: A program for interactive contouring from an irregular triangular grid', *Proceedings, 42nd Annual Meeting of the American Congress on Surveying and Mapping*, 1–15.

Carlson, E., J. Bennett, G. Giddings, and P. Mantey: 1974, *The Design and Evaluation of an Interactive Geo-Data Analysis and Display System*, IBM Research Report RJ 1342.

Clement, A.: 1973, *Report on INTURMAP: The Interactive Urban Mapping System*, University of British Columbia, Vancouver.

Coleman, P., R. Durfee, and R. Edwards: 1978, 'Applications of a hierarchical polygonal structure in spatial analysis and cartographic display', *Harvard Papers on Geographical Information Systems* 3, Harvard University Press, Cambridge.

Corbett, J.: 1979, *Topological Principles in Cartography*, Technical Paper No. 48, U.S. Bureau of the Census, Washington.

Cornwell, B. and A. H. Robinson: 1966, 'Possibilities for computer animated films in cartography', *Cartographic Journal* 3(1), 79–82.

Dalton, J. and J. Billingsley: 1979, 'Interactive mapping software of the domestic information display system', *Proceedings of the International Symposium on Computer-Assisted Cartography IV* 1, 119–126.

Donelson, W.: 1978, 'Spatial management of information', *Computer Graphics* 12(3), 203–209.

Feldman, A.: 1981, 'The National Ocean Survey's aeronautical radar video map: A unique cartographic product', *Technical Papers of the American Congress on Surveying and Mapping, 41st Annual Meeting*, 443–454.

Frank, G., J. Moran and Lanier: 1981, 'Bathymetric data reduction subsystem', *Proceedings of the 41st Annual Meeting of the American Congress on Surveying and Mapping*, 549–570.

Fry, M.: 1982, 'Real-time graphics in command/control situation displays', *Computer* 15(4), 9–17.

Hoinkes, C.: 1978, 'Usefulness and limitations of a small computer graphics system in map production', Paper presented at the IX International Conference on Cartography, College Park, Maryland.

Hunter, G.: 1977, 'Computer animation survey', *Computers and Graphics* **2**(4), 225–229.

Iler, W.: 'The use of computer mapping in planning and public works management: The case of Chicago', *American Cartographer* **8**(2), 115–125.

Moellering, H.: 1975, 'Interactive cartography', *Proceedings of the International Symposium on Computer-Assisted Cartography*, AUTO-CARTO II, 415–421.

Moellering, H.: 1977, 'Interactive cartographic design', *Proceedings of the 37th American Congress on Surveying and Mapping*, 516–530.

Moellering, H.: 1978, *A Demonstration of the Real-Time Display of Three Dimensional Cartographic Objects*, Computer animated videotape, Department of Geography, Ohio State University, Columbus.

Moellering, H.: 1980a, 'Strategies of real-time cartography', *Cartographic Journal* **17**(1), 12–15.

Moellering, H.: 1980b, 'The real-time animation of three dimensional maps', *American Cartographer* **7**(1), 67–75.

Moellering, H., H. Gauthier, and J. Osleeb: 1977, 'An interactive graphic transit planning system based on individuals', *Urban Systems* **2**, 93–103.

Morrison, J.: 1974, 'Changing philosophical-technical aspects of thematic cartography', *American Cartographer* **1**(1), 5–14.

National Technical Information Service: 1981a, *Computer Aided Mapping: 1976 – January, 1981* (Citations from the NTIS data base).

National Technical Information Service: 1982a, *Computer-Aided Mapping: 1970 – January, 1981* (Citations from the Engineering Index data base).

Nyerges, T.: 1980, *Modeling the Structure of Cartographic Information for Query Processing*, Unpublished Ph.D. dissertation, Department of Geography, Ohio State University, Columbus.

Peucker, T. and N. Chrisman: 1975, 'Cartographic data structures', *American Cartographer* **2**(1), 55–69.

Pfaff, G. and G. Maderlechner: 1982, 'Tools for configuring interactive picture processing systems', *IEEE Computer Graphics and Applications* **2**(5), 35–49.

Phillips, R.: 1979, 'A query language for a network data base with graphical entities', *Computer Graphics* **11**(2), 179–185.

Riffe, P.: 1970, 'Conventional map, real map or nonmap?', *International Yearbook of Cartography* **10**, 95–103.

Robinson, A. H., J. Morrison, and P. Muehrcke: 1977, 'Cartography 1950 – 2000', *Transactions of the Institute of British Geographers* New series **2**(1), 3–18.

Rome Air Development Center: 1975, *Lineal Input System*, Final Technical Report, RADC-TR-75-11.

Schrock, B.: 1980, 'Applications of digital displays in photointerpretation and digital mapping', *Technical Papers of the American Society of Photogrammetry, 46th Annual Meeting*, 201–212.

Shepherd, W.: 1976, 'Editing of Digital Data in the Automated Cargography System at the U.S. Army Engineering Topographic Laboratories', *Computer Graphics* **10**, 35–56.

Thrower, H.: 1961, 'Animated cartography in the United States', *International Yearbook of Cartography* **1**, 20–29.

Tobler, W.: 1961, *Map Transformations of Geographic Space*, Unpublished Ph.D. dissertation, Department of Geography, University of Washington, Seattle.

Tobler, W.: 1979, 'A transformational view of cartography', *American Cartographer* 6(2), 101–106.

Tomlinson, R., H. Calkins and D. Marble: 1976, *Computer Handling of Geographical Data*, UNESCO Press, Geneva.

Tuerke, K.: 1976, 'A system for interactive acquisition and administration of geometric data for thematic map production', *Computer Graphics* 10(2), 154–162.

Turner, S. and H. Moellering: 1979, 'ICMS: An interactive choropleth mapping system', *Proceedings of the American Congress on Surveying and Mapping, 39th Annual Meeting*, 225–268.

Vaidua, P., L. Shapiro, R. Haralick, and G. Minden: 1982, 'An experimental relational database system for cartographic applications', *Proceedings of the 48th Annual Meeting of the American Society of Photogrammetry*, 133–142.

Wasilenko, M. and H. Moellering: 1977, *An Information Theoretic Model for the Derivation of Choropleth Classes*, Discussion Paper No. 56, Department of Geography, Ohio State University, Columbus.

White, R. and R. Cousineau: 1980, 'Application of the interactive graphic transit design system (IGTDS) in van pooling service design', *Proceedings of the Inaugural Conference of the National Computer Graphics Association*, 127–142.

DONALD S. SHEPARD

COMPUTER MAPPING: THE SYMAP
INTERPOLATION ALGORITHM

1. INTRODUCTION

A major application of computer mapping is to display levels of some dependent variable over a geographical area. In general, this dependent variable is known only at a limited number of specified locations, henceforth termed "data points," and must be interpolated for other locations. The need for an interpolation algorithm arises in a great variety of applications. In city, regional and geographical planning, social and economic characteristics (e.g., population density) are known only at the centers of data collection zones (e.g., towns or census tracts). In meteorology and air pollution analysis, atmospheric conditions and pollution concentration are known only at monitoring stations. In geology and oceanography, depths are known only where soundings have been made. In epidemiology, the death rates are known only for some representative point (or as an overall average) for the state or county over which vital statistics have been calculated. The values of the dependent variable to be mapped (subsequently denoted by Z) form a surface over a geographical area in the same way that a relief map represents a topographic surface.

If an investigator has control over the location of data points, he can array them in a regular lattice or grid, with a uniform spacing between points. In that case, interpolation can be accomplished easily by a number of established methods. Available methods for interpolating from a rectangular grid include fitting a hyperbolic paraboloid to each four data points by double linear interpolation (Switzer *et al.*, 1964) and fitting a polynomial to up to 25 surrounding data points by Newton's divided difference formula (Steffensen, 1927, Berezin and Zhidkov, 1965) or bicubic spline interpolation (deBoor, 1962). For a triangular grid, a plane can easily be fit to every group of three adjacent points.

For most applications mentioned above, the location of data points is beyond the control of the map maker and does not correspond to any geometric pattern. In these cases, an investigator must cope with irregularly spaced data points. Sometimes, the surface to be mapped need not fit the data points exactly. That is, the mapped surface need not attain the exact

133

Gary L. Gaile and Cort J. Willmott (eds.), Spatial Statistics and Models, 133–145.
© 1984 *by D. Reidel Publishing Company.*

value of the dependent variable specified at the data point. Then, the irregular location of data points does not present a serious complication. A trend surface (e.g., a polynominal of specified order) can be fit to the data by regression (Krumbein, 1959).

For the surface to fit the data points exactly, however, only cumbersome interpolation procedures were available prior to the SYMAP interpolation algorithm. These methods required the user to group data points manually into triangles or quadrilaterals (Bengtsson and Nordbeck, 1964). The SYMAP interpolation algorithm was developed by the author at the Harvard University Laboratory for Computer Graphics and Spatial Analysis and reported in 1968 (Shepard, 1968a, b). It represented a major convenience, as it provides a method to generate automatically a smooth (continuously differentiable) surface which passes through all data points and was readily programmable for computer mapping.

2. DESCRIPTION OF THE ALGORITHM

The SYMAP program produces a computer map on a standard line printer with detail equal to the width of a print character using symbols to indicate the interpolated values. Interpolated values are shown by contour lines and shading, where darker symbols generally denote higher values of the dependent variable. Interpolated values can also be transferred to other programs for other displays or analyses. The coordinates (x, y) corresponding to the center of a symbol are termed character locations. These are points, P, for which a value must be interpolated. The method of calculation is a weighted average of slopes and values from nearby data points. As the weights are based on the inverses of the distances to data points, the interpolation algorithm is termed a gravity model with some embellishments. This simple, intuitive idea has provided the basis for a practical interpolation algorithm. The basic gravity model is explained first, and then the embellishments are discussed.

2.1. *The Basic Model*

According to the basic gravity model, the computed value at a point P, Z_p, is a weighted average of the values at data points $1, 2, \ldots n$, with the weight based on the inverse square of the distance. The exponent of two (square) was chosen because squared distance is particularly easy and fast to compute using the familiar formula for the hypotenuse of a right triangle, and because the resulting spacing of contour lines was intuitively appealing. In mathematical notation, let Z_1 be the value of the dependent variable to be mapped (e.g. pollution concentration) at data point 1, let Z_2 be the value at data point 2, let $\overline{P1}$ be the distance from P to data point 1, and let $\overline{P2}$ be the distance from P to data point 2, etc. Then,

$$Z_p = \frac{\sum_{i=1}^{n} \frac{1}{(\overline{Pi})^2} Z_i}{\sum_{i=1}^{n} \frac{1}{(\overline{Pi})^2}}$$

If the point P is very near data point 1, for example, then $\overline{P1}$ is small compared to $\overline{P2}, \ldots, \overline{Pn}$, so that the weight $(1/\overline{P1})^2$ is large compared to $(1/\overline{P2})^2$, $\ldots, (1/\overline{Pn})^2$.

Therefore, as the distance $\overline{P1}$ tends to zero, the value at P is the limit of

$$\frac{(1/\overline{P1})^2}{(1/\overline{P1})^2} = Z_1.$$

Thus, for points near data point 1, the computed value is near the value Z_1.

It can be shown that by computing such a value Z_p for every point P over the map area, one obtains a "smooth" surface. However, this simple method contains several shortcomings:

(1) As the number of data points becomes large (hundreds or thousands), this method for calculating Z_p becomes long and inefficient.

(2) Direction from data points to the point P is not considered, giving interpolated values that are implausible in some situations. Under this simple method, the computed value at P depends only on the distances to the data points $1, 2, \ldots n$, but not on their location relative to P. For example, assuming $\overline{P1}$ and $\overline{P2}$ are held fixed in length, the following configurations of data points give *identical* values at P:

+	+	+		+	+	+
1	P	2		P	2	1

(3) Because of the inverse square weight, the surface is level at every data point (i.e., the derivative is zero) regardless of the location of that data point or its data value.

As the method of weighted averages was well suited to computer application and satisfied the basic criteria, it was retained as the basis for the SYMAP program, but several important embellishments were added to correct the shortcomings above and increase the flexibility of the program.

2.2. *Search Radius*

The amount of computation was limited by computing Z_p from only the "nearby" data points. Based on the number of data points and the area over which they extend, the algorithm sets an initial search radius, R. It is computed so that on the average, 7 data points will be within this radius of every location P on the map. If, in fact, more than 10 data points (the specified maximum) are found, the furthest are eliminated by contracting the search radius until only 10 data points remain. If fewer than 4 data points (the specified *minimum*) number are found within the initial search radius, the search radius expands until 4 points are reached or it equals the user-specified maximum, or until no further points can be found.* The radius, R, that is finally used is termed the final search radius, R'. In effect, data points beyond the final search radius receive a weight of 0.

A finite search radius could create discontinuities in the interpolated surface between two adjacent character locations where a data point lies just inside the final search radius at the first location and just outside at the second. To avoid this problem, the weighting function was modified somewhat by defining an inverse distance function, S_j, for each data point, P_j. The function S_j is calculated as the pure inverse of the distance $\overline{P_j}$ (not yet squared) for data points j within the distance $R'/3$. For points between distances $R'/3$ and R', however the final weight S_j is a quadratic function of distance. Its coefficients are specified (uniquely) so that it is tangent to the inverse distance when $\overline{P_j}$ equals $R'/3$, and tangent to the abscissa when $\overline{P_j}$ equals R'. This modified function, S_j, gives weights that increase smoothly from 0 to infinity as one moves from character locations P far away from a data point to ones coincident upon it.

2.3. *Direction*

Intuitively, it was felt that several data points close to one another should be given smaller weights than a single isolated data point. That is, the effects of nearby data points should shadow one another. This concept requires that the weight for a data point be based on its direction, as well as its distance,

---

* Various user options allow departures from the default procedure above.

from a character location. To accomplish this a "directional isolation", T_i, of data point i is found by the sum

$$T_i = \sum_{j \neq i} S_j \left[1 - \cos (i P_j)\right],$$

where the points j are all other data points within the final search radius R', and iPj is the angle at point P subtended by data points i and j. In the SYMAP computer program, these cosines are easily computed by scalar products. If the other data points $(1, 2, \ldots, n)$ lie in about the same direction from P as point i does, then the angles $iP1$, $iP2$, iPn are small; thus, the quantities $1 - \cos(iPj)$ are also small, and the sum T_i is also close to zero. The total weighting of data point i is

$$W_i = (S_i)^2 \times (H + T_i), \tag{1}$$

where

$$H = \sum_{j=1}^{n} S_j$$

is a normalizing term added to limit the maximum effect of "directional isolation" to a doubling of the weight based on distance. Overall, the greater a data point's "directional isolation" and the smaller its distance, the greater is its weight and influence in determining the interpolated value.

2.4. Slopes

To prevent the occurrence of a level surface at data points, a "slope" or two-dimensional gradient is estimated at each data point i by taking a weighted average of the slopes of secant planes to surrounding data points, j. The weights are the variables W_j defined in (1). Each secant plane is oriented so that it contains the points P and so that the line from P to i is the line of steepest slope in that plane. The gradient at point i, calculated as the average of the slopes of these planes, is represented by the partial derivatives in the x and y directions at point i,

$$\frac{\partial z}{\partial x}\bigg|_i \quad \text{and} \quad \frac{\partial z}{\partial y}\bigg|_i.$$

These slopes are used to calculate adjustments to the values of the dependent variable at each data point,

ΔZ_i, defined by

$$\Delta Z_i = \left(\frac{\partial z}{\partial x}\bigg|_i \Delta X + \frac{\partial z}{\partial y}\bigg|_i \Delta y \right) K_i.$$

Here Δx and Δy are the x and y distances, respectively, of character location P from i. The factor, $K_i = a/(a + \overline{Pi})$, is inserted to limit the effect of slope in extrapolating beyond the range of actual data values. The parameter a is chosen so that even if i were the data point with the steepest slope, ΔZ would still be less in magnitude than one tenth of the total range of Z. (This fraction was chosen because ten levels of symbols are commonly used. The fraction can be changed by the program user.)

Using the adjustments ΔZ_i, the final interpolated value Z at point P is defined by

$$Z_i = \frac{\Sigma W_i (Z_i + \Delta Z_i)}{\Sigma W_i}.$$

If a data point i is higher than the surrounding data points, the slope at point i will not be zero unless the weighted slopes of the secant planes exactly cancel. Otherwise, the surface will continue to rise in the direction indicated by the pattern of surrounding points as a whole. As a consequence, relative maxima and minima often do not occur at data points. Unless requested otherwise by the user, the program separately restricts interpolated values to the range of the input data values.

The interpolation algorithm gives reasonable results when extrapolating beyond the study area. As the distance increases all the nearest data points have roughly the same distance and direction, resulting in approximately equal weightings. Thus, the values will tend towards a limit near the average of the closest data points.

2.5. Refinements for Speed and Accuracy

To increase computational speed, the full (primary) interpolation algorithm is normally used only at regular grid points representing one sixth of the total character locations (every third horizontal and every second vertical location). Simple linear interpolation is used for the intervening points. To avoid truncation and round-off errors, the value at a grid location is set equal to that of a data point within the distance of 1 1/2 character locations.

Data points were indexed by location to simplify the search for nearby data points.

2.6. *Refinements for Flexibility*

Finally, several refinements were introduced to increase the flexibility of the program. A capability of barriers was created to force the interpolation to detour around or not cross at all designated bodies of water, geological faults, highways, mountain ranges, or other physical features in calculating distance to data points.

Another user option allows the program to create Thiessen polygons (termed proximal maps). In a proximal map, the "interpolated" value is the value of the single nearest data point. Each data point is surrounded by a polygonal zone with constant value, a Thiessen polygon. This type of map is created by limiting the search to the single nearest data point.

3. ILLUSTRATION AND CHARACTERISTICS

3.1. *Profile for Co-linear Data Points*

To describe the performance of the interpolation algorithm in a simple situation, a hypothetical data set was constructed with three data points placed along a straight line (Figure 1). Taking the center point (Point B) as the origin, point A was placed 5 units to the left and point C 2 units to the right. The heights (values of the dependent variable, Z) were set at 7 for A, 0 for B, and 6 for C. Figure 1 is a plot of a section (vertical slice) through the interpolated surface along the axis from A to B to C. Notice that the

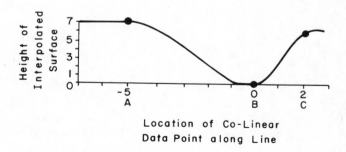

Fig. 1. Section of interpolated surface from three data points.

interpolated surface reproduces the values of the data points exactly at points
A, *B*, and *C*. As one follows the interpolated surface from point *B* to *C*, the
surface continues to rise to the right of point *C*. To the left of points *A* and
B, the surface is flat. This pattern arises because the slope feature of the
interpolation would have created a value more extreme than the range of the
given values of the dependent variables (from 0 to 7). The value would have
been higher than 7 to the left of *A*, and lower than 0 to the left of *B*. Cen-
soring the interpolated values at the range of the original data results in a flat
surface at the maximum and minimum values of the data range to the left
of points *A* and *B*, respectively. The plot also indicates that outside of these
flat spots, the slope of the surface changes continuously.

Figure 2 shows the surface interpolated from these same data points in
three dimensions with five levels of symbolism. The range of the dependent
variable from 0 to 7 has been divided into 5 equal intervals. The bunching
of contours shows that the surface is steepest roughly midway between points
A and *B* and *B* and *C*. The absence of contour lines in the immediate vicinity
of each of the data points indicates that the slope is relatively small there.
The presence of the symbol "0" along the top center border of the map
shows that the interpolated value is near the average of the three data values
(0, 6, and 7) in this area. At character locations distant from all data points,

Fig. 2. Contour map produced by SYMAP program from three co-linear data points.

where one data point does not shadow another, the interpolated value is near the average of all data values. The numbers 1 and 5 in the interior of the map show the location and level of symbolism of the data points.

3.2. *Representative Example*

Figure 3 illustrates some of the SYMAP capabilities in an application to air pollution. The map shows ambient concentrations of sulfur dioxide on a

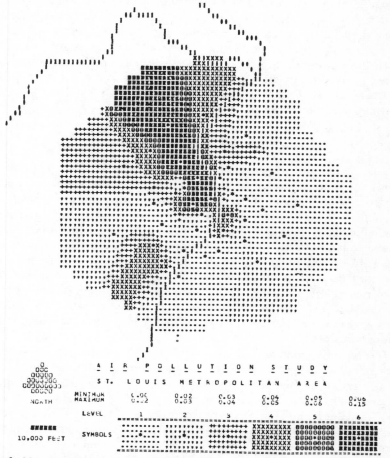

Fig. 3. Map of ambient concentrations of sulfur dioxide (parts per million) produced by SYMAP program.

winter day with moderate southerly winds (January 22, 1965) for the metropolitan area around St. Louis, Missouri. As the symbol key indicates, darker symbols denote higher levels of pollution, and wide value ranges were assigned the extreme symbols in order to provide greater detail in the middle range. Furthermore, by using an option in the program, interpolation was restricted to a maximum distance of 25,000 feet (3 km) from any data point to indicate that concentrations could not be meaningfully interpolated beyond this distance. Areas for which interpolated values could not be computed were left blank. The border of this blank area is somewhat irregular because the primary interpolation was not performed at every data point. Asterisks denote the locations of the 40 irregular data points from which the map was drawn. Finally, the Mississippi and Missouri Rivers are shown by the program using a legends elective. This map of actual pollution levels, and others of simulated levels, proved useful in a simulation study of air pollution control (Shepard, 1970).

4. ACCURACY OF INTERPOLATION

In general, any interpolated surface will be perfectly accurate only at data points. At other character locations, accuracy depends on the agreement between the assumptions in the interpolation algorithm and the behavior of the surface being mapped, and on the distance between adjacent points relative to the scale in the data being mapped (the minimum distance over which substantial variations in the data occur). The interpolated surface based on SYMAP or any other algorithm is valid only where the distance between adjacent data points is finer than the scale of the data. As a general purpose interpolation algorithm, the SYMAP interpolation algorithm is not based on mathematical analysis of a particular type of surface, but rather on intuitive ideas about a smooth surface as would be applied in fitting a curve or drawing contours by eye.

One would expect that the accuracy of the interpolation would increase with additional data points. To examine the accuracy quantitatively, a complex reference surface was constructed with 3840 character locations (a rectangle of 60 X 64 positions). The reference surface was constructed with the SYMAP program as an arbitrary theoretical surface with 4 local internal maxima (peaks) and 6 internal minima (pits) from 635 data points. Increasing numbers (N) of data points were sampled from the reference surface according to a uniform rectangular grid. The interpolation algorithm attempted to reconstruct the original surface by interpolating from the sample points as data points. At each character location on the reference surface, the difference between the reference and interpolated values were computed. Then the mean, variance, and mean square difference (mean squared plus variance) were computed for the surface as a whole for each collection of sample points. All three statistics tend towards zero as the number of sampled points increases from 4 to 272. The relationship was studied systematically by plotting on log-log scale the relative root mean square of differences against the number of sampled points. The relative root mean square (Rel) is a dimensionless quantity (a pure number) indicating relative error.

The plot and fitted line based on ordinary least squares (in logarithms) in Figure 4 indicates an excellent linear relationship:

$$Rel = 2.83 \, N^{-0.56}. \tag{2}$$

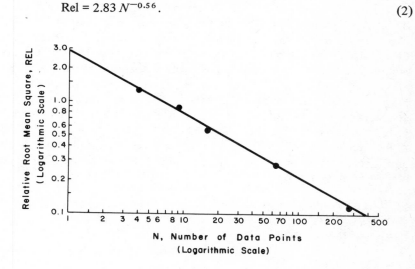

Fig. 4. Plot of relative error against number of data points

The proportion of variance explained (r^2) is 99.7%. According to this fitted curve, the relative error appears to be on the order of 100% when the number of data points is approximately the same as the number of extreme points (local peaks and pits) on the reference surface. The empirical exponent in (2), −0.56, is close to the inverse square root relationship (exponent of −0.50) that pervades estimates of error under independent samples from a normal distribution.

Approximating the exponent by −0.5 and rewriting (2) gives

$$(1/\text{Rel})^2 \simeq k\,(1/n) \tag{3}$$

where k is a constant. The left side of (3), the inverse square of the relative error, indicates the precision of the interpolated map. The expression $1/n$ on the right side indicates the density of data points. Thus, (3) shows that the precision of an interpolated map is proportional to its density of data points.

5. CONCLUSIONS

As the interpolation algorithm was designed to produce an interpolated surface that the author considered intuitively reasonable, it may not be theoretically optimal for interpolating where the underiying surface has a known mathematical structure. It has, however, been highly practical. Since the SYMAP interpolation algorithm was first written in 1967 at the Laboratory for Computer Graphics and Spatial Analysis, Harvard Graduate School of Design, the procedure has proved to be a reliable and flexible program for mapping quantitative data by computer. Under the SYMAP program, the interpolated surface can be displayed as a contour map (as in Figure 2 and 3) or used to produce a perspective surface (with the SYMVU or ASPEX programs). As of 1980, the program has been installed at 528 user organizations in several countries and applied to thousands of mapping projects (*Lab-log 1980*).

Institute for Health Research
Harvard School of Public Health and
Veterans Administration Outpatient Clinic

BIBLIOGRAPHY

Bengsson, B. E. and S. Nordbeck: 1964, *Construction of Isarithms and Isarithmic Maps by Computers,* Report BIT 4, University of Lund, Lund, pp. 87–105.

Berezin, I. S. and N. P. Zhidkov: 1965, *Computing Methods,* Vol. 1, Chapter 2, Addison-Wesley, Reading, Mass.

DeBoor, C.: 1962, 'Bicubic spline interpolation', *Journal of Mathematical Physics* **41,** 212–218.

Krumbein, W. C.: 1959, 'Trend surface analysis of contour-type maps with irregular control point spacing', *Journal of Geophysical Research* **64,** 823–834.

Lab-log 1980: 1980, Laboratory for Computer Graphics and Spatial Analysis, Harvard Graduate School of Design, Cambridge, Mass.

Shepard, D. S.: 1968a, 'A two-dimensional interpolation function for computer mapping of irregularly spaced data', *Harvard Theoretical Geography Papers* No. 15, Laboratory for Computer Graphics, Harvard University Graduate School of Design, Cambridge, Mass.

Shepard, D. S.: 1968b, 'A two-dimensional interpolation function for irregularly spaced data [revised]', *Proceedings of the 23rd National Conference of the Association for Computing Machinery*, Brandon/Systems Press, Inc., Princeton, N.J.

Shepard, D. S.: 1970, 'A load shifting model for air pollution control in the electric power industry', *Journal of the Air Pollution Control Association* 20 (11), 756–761.

Steffensen, J. F.: 1927, *Interpolation*, Williams and Wilkins, Baltimore, Chapter 19.

Switzer, P., C. M. Mohn, and R. E. Heitman: 1964, *Statistical Analyses of Ocean Terrain and Contour Plotting Procedures*, Project Trident Report No. 1440464, Arthur D. Little, Inc., Cambridge, Mass.

FRITS P. AGTERBERG

TREND SURFACE ANALYSIS

1. INTRODUCTION

The method of trend surface analysis was originally introduced into the earth sciences by Oldham and Sutherland (1955), Miller (1956), Krumbein (1956, 1959), Grant (1957) and Whitten (1959). These authors used the method for the analysis of gravity maps, stratigraphic maps (facies maps), isopach maps and maps representing specific attributes of sedimentary and igneous rocks.

In the course of time, the number of applications has increased significantly and the method itself has been refined and generalized. Recent studies in which trend surface analysis was used as the primary tool for arriving at geological conclusions include Gannicott *et al.* (1979) and Jakeman (1980). The theory of the technique has been documented in a number of textbooks. (Krumbein and Graybill, 1965; Harbaugh and Meriam, 1968; Koch and Link, 1971; Davis, 1973; Agterberg, 1974a; Dobrin, 1976; and Ripley, 1981). Computer programs for trend surface analysis also are widely available (see Agterberg and Chung, 1975) or can be readily prepared by modifying existing subroutines at most computing centers. The reader is referred to the extensive literature on the topic for a more comprehensive treatment of theoretical aspects and numerous other applications.

This article contains a brief description of the basic model used and case history studies in stratigraphy, petrology and economic geology. Trend surface analysis is a relatively simple technique which is useful when (1) the trend and the residuals (observed values minus trend values) can be interpreted from a spatial point of view, and (2) the number of observations is limited so that rather extensive interpolations must be based on relatively few data.

In practical applications, care should be taken not to rely too heavily on the statistical significance tests which have been developed to decide on the degree of a trend surface (analysis of variance) and to check residuals for "outliers" (*t*-test), or on confidence belts which can be calculated for the trend surfaces. These statistical tests produce exact results only if the residuals are stochastically independent. In reality, the residuals from a trend

147

Gary L. Gaile and Cort J. Willmott (eds.), Spatial Statistics and Models, 147–171.
© 1984 *by D. Reidel Publishing Company.*

surface frequently are subject to significant spatial autocorrelation. In that situation, the test statistics based on the model of uncorrelated residuals may be severely biased (Agterberg, 1964; Watson, 1971). However, even biased test statistics can provide useful information. Moreover, in some applications, the spatial autocorrelation of residuals can be modeled by using a homogeneous, random-process model. Examples of the latter type of approach also will be given in this article.

2. BASIC THEORY AND APPLICATIONS

In trend surface analysis, the trend in observational data which are areally distributed is described by means of a two-dimensional polynomial equation of the first, second or a higher degree. Two methods closely related to polynomial trend surface analysis but not to be discussed here are the method which uses two-dimensional Fourier series instead of polynomials (Davis, 1973) and the method of spatial filtering (Robinson and Merriam, 1980). Suppose that the geographic co-ordinates of a point are written as u and v for the east-west and north-sourth directions, respectively. An observation made at a point k can be written as $Y_k = Y(u_k, v_k)$ to indicate that it represents a specific value assumed by the variable $Y(u, v)$. In trend surface analysis, it is assumed that

$$Y_k = T_k + R_k$$

where $T_k = T(u_k, v_k)$ represents the trend and R_k is the residual at point k. T_k is a specific value of the variable $T(u, v)$ with

$$T(u, v) = b_{00} + b_{10}u + b_{01}v + b_{20}u^2 + b_{11}uv + \ldots + b_{pq}u^p v^q. \qquad (1)$$

In general, u and v form a rectangular co-ordinate system. However, latitudes and longitudes also have been used (cf. Vistelius and Hurst, 1964).

In specific applications, $p+q \leqslant r$ where r denotes the degree of the trend surface. Depending on the value of r, a trend surface is called linear ($r=1$), quadratic ($r=2$), cubic ($r=3$), quartic ($r=4$) or quintic ($r=5$). Higher degree surfaces also have been used. For example, Whitten (1970) employed octic ($r=8$) surfaces. Coons et al. (1967) fitted polynomial surfaces of the 13th degree. A trend surface of degree r has $m = \frac{1}{2}(r+1)(r+2)$ coefficients b_{pq}. These can be calculated only if the number of observation points (n) satisfies the condition $n \geqslant m$. If $n = m$, a special type of surface is fitted with the property $T_k = Y_k$ and no residuals. In most applications of trend surface analysis, n is several times larger than the number of coefficients (m).

Trend surfaces are fitted to data by using the method of least squares which is also used in multiple regression analysis. This means that for any degree, ΣR_k^2 representing the sum of squares of the residuals at all observation points $k=1, \ldots, n$ has the smallest possible value for all possible surfaces of that degree. This principle uniquely determines the coefficients b_{pq} of equation (1).

Matrix algebra commonly is used to represent the calculations which are laborious and performed by using a digital computer. Suppose that the n observations Y_k are represented as a column vector $\mathbf{Y}$ and that the information on geographical co-ordinates is written as a matrix $\mathbf{X}$ with

$$
\mathbf{X} =
\begin{bmatrix}
1 & u_1 & v_1 & u_1^2 & \ldots & u_1^p v_1^q \\
1 & u_2 & v_2 & u_2^2 & \ldots & u_2^p v_2^q \\
\cdot & \cdot & \cdot & \cdot & & \cdot \\
\cdot & \cdot & \cdot & \cdot & & \cdot \\
\cdot & \cdot & \cdot & \cdot & & \cdot \\
1 & u_k & v_k & u_k^2 & \ldots & u_k^p v_k^q \\
\cdot & \cdot & \cdot & \cdot & & \cdot \\
\cdot & \cdot & \cdot & \cdot & & \cdot \\
\cdot & \cdot & \cdot & \cdot & & \cdot \\
1 & u_n & v_n & u_n^2 & \ldots & u_n^p v_n^q
\end{bmatrix}
$$

Then the column vector $\mathbf{B}$ for all coefficients $(b_{00}, b_{10}, \ldots, b_{pq})$ satisfies

$$
\mathbf{B} = \mathbf{X}(\mathbf{X}^T\mathbf{X})^{-1}\mathbf{X}^T\mathbf{Y} \tag{2}
$$

where $\mathbf{X}^T$ is the transpose matrix of $\mathbf{X}$. The locations of the observation points may be irregularly spaced. If they are regularly spaced, the calculations can be simplified.

Although equation (2) is valid in general, it is well known to practitioners of trend surface analysis that the matrix $\mathbf{X}^T\mathbf{X}$ may turn out to be singular so that the inverse $(\mathbf{X}^T\mathbf{X})^{-1}$ does not exist, or it may be nearly singular so that it is difficult to invert it because the precision of the calculations on any digital computer is limited. Many methods have been developed to circumvent these special problems. An inversion problem does not arise when Whitten's (1970) method of orthogonal polynomials for irregularly spaced data points is used. As discussed in more detail by Ripley (1981, Section 4.1), it is not necessary to use orthogonal polynomials if an orthogonal matrix **Q** (with n rows and n columns) and a matrix **R** (with m rows and n columns) can be determined with **QX** = **R**. The matrix **R** has the property that its first m rows form a triangular matrix **P**. In modern algorithms for multiple regression, the m coefficients follow from **B** = **P**$^{-1}$**C** where **C** is a vector consisting of the first m elements of the vector **QY**.

A typical example of trend surface analysis is shown in Figure 1 (after

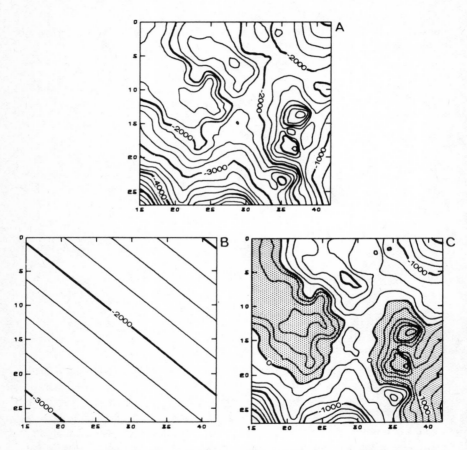

Fig. 1. Top of Arbuckle Formation in central Kansas. Contours are in feet below sea level. Geographic co-ordinates are in arbitrary units (Area shown measures 320 km on a side). A. Contour map of original data; B. Linear trend surface; C. Residuals from linear trend surface (after Davis, 1973).

Davis, 1973). Figure 1A gives the contours (in feet below sea level) of the top of Ordovician rocks (Arbuckle Formation) in central Kansas. The linear trend surface is shown in Figure 1B and the corresponding residuals in Figure 1C. The sum of the values R_k contoured in Figure 1C and the values T_k (Figure 1B) gives the original pattern (Figure 1A).

Some problems of trend surface analysis can be illustrated by the fitting of curves to data collected along a line. An example is shown in Figure 2

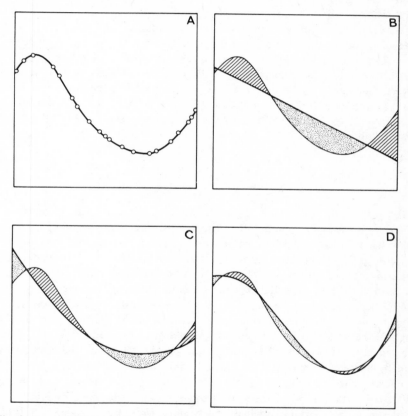

Fig. 2. Concept of trend illustrated by means of two-dimensional graphs (after Davis, 1973). Value (vertical scale) is plotted against distance (horizontal scale). A. Collection of original data points and smooth curve on which they lie; B. Straight-line trend fitted to the observations; C. Parabolic (quadratic) trend; D. Cubic trend. Shadings represent positive and negative residuals from the trends.

(after Davis, 1973). The observations fall on a smooth curve which, however, is not a low-degree polynomial curve. The magnitudes of the residuals decrease when the degree of the polynomial is increased. The example of Figure 2 is artificial but it illustrates two important points:

(1) A good fit is not necessarily the object of trend analysis. Instead of this, the aim usually is to divide the data into a regional trend component and local residuals which can be linked to separate spatial processes of regional and local significance, respectively. Examples of the interpretation of trends and residuals will be given later in this article.

(2) Each curve-fitting of Figure 2 yields residuals that from a continuous curve. Adjoining residuals along a line therefore are not statistically independent like a succession of values drawn at random from a statistical population. Instead of this, the residuals are spatially autocorrelated. During the past 20 years, much progress has been made in the analysis of spatially autocorrelated data (Matheron, 1965; Cliff and Ord, 1973; Delphiner, 1976; Schwarzacher, 1980). This topic also will be considered later in this article and elsewhere in this volume.

3. TREND SURFACE ANALYSIS OF MINERALOGICAL DATA, MOUNT ALBERT PERIDOTITE INTRUSION

The outline of the Mount Albert peridotite intrusion, Gaspé Peninsula, Quebec, is shown in Figure 3. The rocks consisting of olivine and pyroxenes have been serpentinized to a variable extent with a corresponding decrease in specific gravity from about 3.2 for unaltered peridotite to 2.5 for serpentinite. The magnesium content of olivine and orthopyroxene varies across the intrusion according to patterns which resemble that of the specific gravity (Agterberg, 1964 and 1974a). The Mg-content of orthopyroxene was determined for 174 samples of which the locations are shown in Figure 3. The optical method used for this purpose (MacGregor and Smith, 1963) is subject to a measurement error of approximately 1% Mg. Moreover, there are many small, short-range changes in the Mg-content of orthopyroxene.

A sequence of trend surfaces was computed (see Agterberg and Chung, 1975). The ratio (R^2) of the sum of squares due to the trend divided by the sum of squares of the original observations (R^2 also is called "multiple correlation coefficient squared") provides a measure of the relative strength of the trends. For different degrees, R^2 increases from 0.217 ($r=1$), 0.389 ($r=2$), 0.490 ($r=3$), 0.519 ($r=4$) to 0.536 ($r=5$). After cubic fit ($r=3$), R^2 starts leveling off. The higher degree surfaces ($r \geqslant 3$) resemble each other

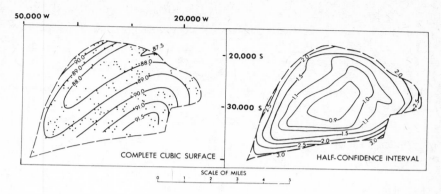

Fig. 3. Outline of Mount Albert peridotite intrusion. Cubic trend-surface and its 95% half-condicence interval for Mg-content of orthopyroxene. Dots indicate locations of specimens. Co-ordinate system is in feet (after Agterberg, 1964).

very closely suggesting that the "trend" has been found. The residuals are essentially uncorrelated in this application.

The technique of analysis of variance can be helpful to select the degree of the trend surface to be used. Table I shows results of F-tests for the steps from degree 2 to 3 and from degree 3 to 4, respectively. If the residuals for a trend surface of degree r are uncorrelated and normally distributed, the F-ratio calculated for the improvement of fit obtained when proceeding from degree r to degree $r+1$ is a value close to 1.0. In Table IA, $F=17.53$ which is much greater than 1.0 but in Table IB, $F=1.93$. Statistical tables for the F-distribution can be consulted to check whether or not the improvement in fit is statistically significant for a given level of significance α. Setting $\alpha=0.05$, the first value ($F=17.53$) is signifcant but the second value ($F=1.93$) is not, indicating that the cubic trend surface (see Figure 3, left side) is probably the best choice that can be made.

Polynomial trend surfaces can be represented as maps consisting of symbols produced on the printer of a digital computer. Figure 4 shows output of the computer program TREND (Agterberg and Chung, 1975) for the cubic trend surface of Figure 3. This program also prints a map for the half-confidence interval of each trend surface. The formulae used for calculating confidence intervals on trend surfaces can be found in Krumbein and Graybill (1965) and Agterberg (1974a). A contoured version of the 95% half-confidence of the cubic trend surface is shown in Figure 3 (right side).

The interpretation of the half-confidence interval is as follows. Suppose

TABLE I[a]

Mg-content (in percent) of orthopyroxene, Mount Albert peridotite intrusion

Source of variation	Sum of squares	Degrees of freedom	Mean square	F-ratio
A. Quadratic	210.53	5		
Cubic-quadratic	54.65	4	13.66	17.53
Residual (cubic)	275.65	164	1.68	
Total	540.83	173		
B. Cubic	265.18	9		
Quartic-cubic	15.75	5	3.15	1.93
Residual (quartic)	259.90	159	1.63	
Total	540.83	173		

[a] Analysis of variance tables to test statistical significance of steps (A) from quadratic to cubic, and (B) from cubic to quartic trend surface, respectively. Mean square is sum of squares divided by degrees of freedom. F-ratio is between mean squares for step to next degree and residuals. Uncorrelated, normally distributed residuals would yield an F-ratio close to one. Statistical tables can be consulted to test the F-ratios computed. The value 1.93 (in B) is not significant with a probability of 95% (α=0.05). The reader who is unfamiliar with this type of analysis of variance table is referred to Davis (1973) for more detailed definitions.

that the values on the trend surface (Figure 3, left side) are called T_i and the corresponding values on the 95% half-confidence interval (right side) are called C_i. The 95% confidence interval for the trend surface T_i then is given by $T_i \pm C_i$ placed around the calculated surface T_i. A confidence interval can be readily computed as a companion to any fitted trend surface. However, it is only meaningful if the conditions of stochastical independence and normal distribution for the residuals are at least approximately satisfied.

In Figure 3, the width of the half-confidence interval is nearly constant at points i which are located within the cluster of observation points. However, it widens rapidly near the edges of this cluster indicating that a computed trend value T_i can not be very precise unless the point i is on all sides sur- rounded by observation points. This so-called edge effect becomes more serious when the degree of the trend surface increases. It may be a good reason for approximating the trend in a region by a larger number of low-degree

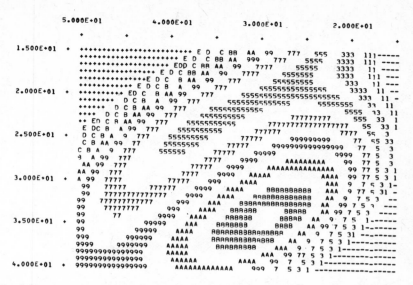

Fig. 4. Output of program TREND (Agterberg and Chung, 1975) for cubic trend surface show by means of contours in Figure 3. Co-ordinate system is in thousands of feet. Calculated value (see Figure 3) = $\frac{1}{2}$ (Printed value + 170); $A=11$, $B=13$, $C=14$, etc.; plus signs indicate values equal to 21 and greater; minus signs indicate negative values.

trend surfaces (e.g., $r=2$) calculated for overlapping clusters of observation points rather than by a single high-degree trend surface which may be very imprecise near the edges or within gaps in the cluster of observation points (cf. Agterberg, 1974a).

Practitioners of trend surface analysis should develop an appreciation of the relationship between a polynomial trend surface and the geometrical configuration of the cluster of observation points on which this surface is based. An interesting experiment consists of constructing a low-degree trend surface from data for a relatively small number of observation points. One of the points then is moved away from the cluster of observation points. It will be seen that the relative effect of the value at this point on the shape of the entire trend surface increases with distance. There also is a tendency for the trend surface to pass almost exactly through the value at the outlying point. In fact, the residual value at this point decreases to zero when the distance increases. For a quantitative assessment of this effect, the reader is referred to Agterberg and Chung (1975).

4. TREND ANALYSIS OF SPECIFIC GRAVITY DATA, MOUNT ALBERT PERIDOTITE INTRUSION

Figure 5A shows the locations of points at which 359 samples were taken for which the specific gravity was determined. The spatial variability of these data is illustrated in Figure 5B for a profile across the intrusion. The quintic trend surface ($r=5$) provides a good description of the specific gravity trend. A profile across the quintic trend surface is shown in Figure 5E. Arithmetic averages for sets of values falling between successive vertical lines in Figure 5B also are shown in Figure 5E. These averages are well described by the quintic curve for the profile indicating that the relatively simple method of constructing a running average produces the same result as a trend surface when the number of observations is large. The running average method consists of calculating the arithmetic average of all values contained in a square or circle which is moved across the map area and contouring the results. This method can be used only when many data are available.

The topographic relief of Mount Albert is shown in Figure 5A. Because the samples were taken at points with different elevations, it is possible to fit a three-dimensional polynomial trend to the data by adding terms in w (elevation above sea level) to those in u and v. Figure 5C and 5D represent horizontal intersections of the best fitting three-dimensional cubic solution obtained by setting w equal to 3000 ft. (Figure 5C) and 2000 ft. (Figure 5D), respectively. These patterns suggest that there is a significant trend in the vertical direction in addition to the changes in mean specific gravity in the horizontal directions. Two of the three rivers originating on Mount Albert follow zones of relatively low mean specific gravity (zones of maximum serpentinization) at the 3000 ft. level rather than at the 2000 ft. level. A further comparison with the contour map of the topographic surface (Figure 5A) suggests that present-day topography was controlled by the distribution of less resistant rocks at higher levels.

5. SPATIAL AUTOCORRELATION OF RESIDUALS

It has been pointed out that the residuals in Figure 1 and 2 form continuous patterns. On the other hand, the residuals in the examples of Figures 3 and 5 are nearly uncorrelated. In other applications, the residuals are partly stochastically independent and partly continuous. Then it may be useful to define a trend-signal-noise model instead of the trend-residuals model used before. This means that each residual R is regarded as the sum of a value S

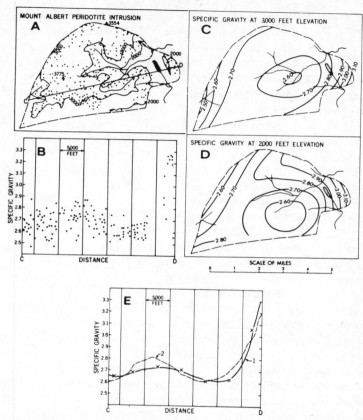

Fig. 5A. Schematic contour map of Mount Albert peridotite intrusion; elevations are in feet above sea level: B. Variations of specific gravity along section CD (see A for location). All values within 2500 ft from section line were perpendicularly projected to it; C. and D. Cubic trend surfaces for 3000 ft and 2000 ft levels obtained by contouring three-dimensional cubic trend in two horizontal planes. In most of the area, today's topography resembles the 3000 ft pattern more closely than the 2000 ft pattern; E. Crosses represent averages for values within blocks measuring 500 ft on a side (see B). Curve 1 is intersection of quintic trend surface with profile CD; curve 2 represents variation of three-dimensional cubic trend along topographic surface (from Agterberg, 1964).

which is part of a continuous random function (signal) and a stochastically independent component N (noise). The terms "signal" and "noise" have been adopted from the statistical theory of communication (e.g. Lee, 1960) and time series analysis (e.g. Parzen, 1967).

An example of this type of statistical modeling is shown in Figure 6. The original data (from De Wijs, 1951) consist of 118 zinc concentration values for samples taken at regular intervals along a sphalerite vein near Pulacayo, Bolivia. The best-fitting straight line turns out to be nearly horizontal suggesting that there is no trend. On the other hand, successive values are not stochastically independent. For example, the first autocorrelation coefficient $r(1)$ obtained by correlating the first 117 values of Figure 6A to their neighbors on the right amounts to 0.453. Further autocorrelation coefficients are $r(2)=0.290$, $r(3)=0.302$, $r(4)=0.180$, etc. Agterberg (1974a) fitted an exponential function to these values with $r(d)=0.5157 \exp(-0.1892d)$ where d represents distance (or "lag") expressed in sampling intervals. For short distances $(d \rightarrow 0)$, $r(d)$ approaches 0.5157. The value 1.0 would be obtained only if the spatial variability is continuous (as e.g. the residuals in Figure 2). In the signal-noise model of Figure 5, 0.5157 or 52% of the spatial variability is regarded as belonging to a continuous signal and $(1-0.5157=)$ 48% is interpreted as purely random, white noise. The basic assumption in a signal-noise model is that the signal can be characterized by a homogeneous autocorrelation function that is independent of location (a "stationarity" assumption). By using the experimental function fitted to the autocorrelation coefficients, it is possible to filter out the noise from the data in order to extract the signal (see Figure 5B).

The method for filtering in Figure 5 makes use of Fourier transforms (cf. Agterberg, 1974a). The signal is more commonly extracted by a method of matrix inversion (Kriging) that will be explained in more detail later in this section. During the late 1960's, there was a considerable amount of discussion among earth scientists and geostatisticians regarding the question of which technique is better; Trend surface analysis, or Kriging (see e.g., Matheron, 1967)? The technique of Kriging (named after the South African geostatistician D. G. Krige) also is based on the assumption of a homogeneous spatial autocorrelation function. As a contribution to this discussion, Agterberg (1970) performed the following experiment.

A set of 200 elevation data for the top of the Arbuckle Formation in Kansas (cf. Figure 1) was randomly divided into three samples: two "control" samples (No. 1 and No. 2) each consisting of 75 data and a test sample (No. 3) of 50 data. Three different techniques were applied to samples No. 1 and No. 2 and the results used to make predictions of the elevations at the top of the Arbuckle Formation at the 50 points of sample No. 3. These three techniques were (1) Trend surface analysis; (2) Kriging; and (3) Trend surface analysis and Kriging of residuals.

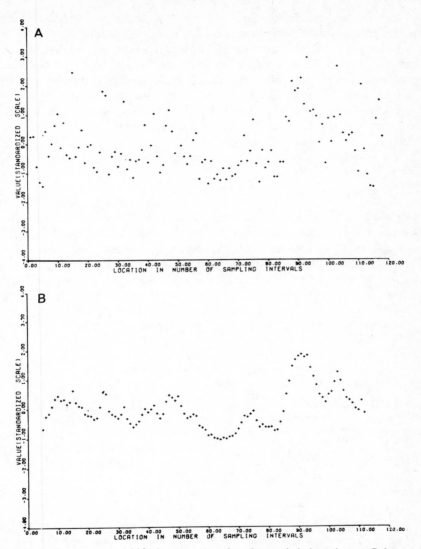

Fig. 6. A. Space series of 118 zinc per cent values from sphalerite vein near Pulacayo, Bolivia (original data from De Wijs, 1951); B. "Signal" retained after removal of "white noise" component. Scale invertical direction is for standardized zinc values obtained by subtracting the mean (=15.16%) from the original data and dividing by their standard deviation (=8.01%) in both diagrams: sampling interval is 2 m (after Agterberg, 1974a).

A theoretical autocorrelation function was determined for deviations from the mean (for Kriging of original data) and also for residuals from each fitted trend (for Kriging of residuals). The resulting two-dimensional function can be used to obtain the autocorrelation coefficient for any pair of two points which are a given distance apart in a given direction. The Kriging value at a particular point is obtained by calculating the best moving average of all (n) known values contained within a predetermined neighborhood around that point. This method of Kriging is explained in more detail in Agterberg (1970) and Agterberg and Chung (1973).

The known values receive different weights that can be written as a column vector W with

$$W = R_1^{-1} R_0,$$

where R_1 is an ($n \times n$) matrix consisting of autocorrelation coefficients for all possible pairs of the n known values in the neighborhood, and R_0 is a column vector of autocorrelation coefficients for distances between the locations of the n known values and the point at which the Kriging value is to be estimated. In a different version of this technique, it is required that the sum of the weights of the known values is unity (see e.g. Agterberg and Chung, 1973).

The results summarized in Table II show that for this experiment, Kriging

TABLE II[a]

Elevation of top of Arbuckle formation in Kansas

	Without Kriging		With Kriging	
	Sample No. 1	Sample No. 2	Sample No. 1	Sample No. 2
No trend	0.0	0.0	76.7	53.6
Linear	30.2	34.2	53.5	61.4
Quadratic	73.8	68.5	80.9	79.5
Cubic	60.3	74.6	68.9	82.6
Quartic	76.5	72.6	81.3	78.3

[a] Test of predicted values for Sample No. 3 made by different techniques applied to Samples No. 1 and No. 2, respectively. Tabulated value is percentage of total sum of squares of original data (corrected for mean) explained by predicted values. In order to calculate this value, the predicted values were subtracted from the observed values of Sample No. 3. The sum of squares of the differences was divided by the total sum of squares with respect to the mean. This ratio was subtracted from one and the result multiplied by 100.

as a predictive tool performed as well as trend surface analysis. The best results were obtained when Kriging was applied to the residuals of the polynomial trend surfaces. The choice of a theoretical model for the spatial autocorrelation function is somewhat subjective. It is possible that the Kriging predictions of the experiment could be further improved by modifying the model that was used (also see Tukey, 1970). However, it was clearly demonstrated that the results of trend surface analysis occasionally can be improved by adopting a trend-signal-noise model instead of the usual trend-residual model. This type of model was later used by Agterberg and Chung (1973) in a study of the spatial variability of sulphur in coal seams in the Lingan Mine, Nova Scotia. It also will be employed in the case history study to be described in the next section.

It is noted that an elegant modification of the Kriging method for calculating the moving average of values in a neighborhood in the presence of trends has been developed in geostatistics (Delphiner, 1976). However, the aim of the latter method is to obtain optimum interpolation values and not to separately estimate both trends and residuals.

6. TREND-SIGNAL-NOISE MODEL APPLIED TO DRILL-HOLE DATA FROM THE ELLIOT LAKE AREA, ONTARIO

In the Elliot Lake area (Figure 7), the Archean basement rocks of the Canadian Shield are unconformably overlain by Proterozoic rocks which have been subjected to folding. This yielded the Quirke Syncline (trough-shaped fold) of which the axial plane is shown as the trace in Figure 7. The bottom of the Matinenda Formation which contains uraniferous conglomerates coincides with the top of the Archean basement except in some places where it is separated from it by a sequence of earlier Proterozoic volcanic rocks of variable thickness. Locations of boreholes are shown in Figure 7 where the squares indicate boreholes in which significant uranium mineralization was encountered and the triangles represent other boreholes. The bottom of the Matinenda Formation in feet above or below sea level was available for all boreholes of Figure 7. Quadratic trend surfaces were fitted to these data from overlapping clusters of observation points (see Figure 8).

Robertson (1966) has attempted to reconstruct the topography of the top of the Archean basement as it was before the later structural deformation. According to Robertson and other geologists familiar with the area, the uraniferous conglomerates in the Matinenda Formation would have been deposited in topographical depressions in the top of the basement. This

Fig. 7. "Signal" for bottom of Matinenda Formation, Elliot Lake area, obtained by contouring Kriging values (in feet) computed at points on grid with 1 km-spacing. Archean basement rocks shown by pattern. Trace of axial plane of Quirke Syncline is shown also. Squares and triangles represent locations of drill-holes with and without significant uranium mineralization, respectively. Universal Transverse Mercator grid locations of corner points of map area are shown in km.

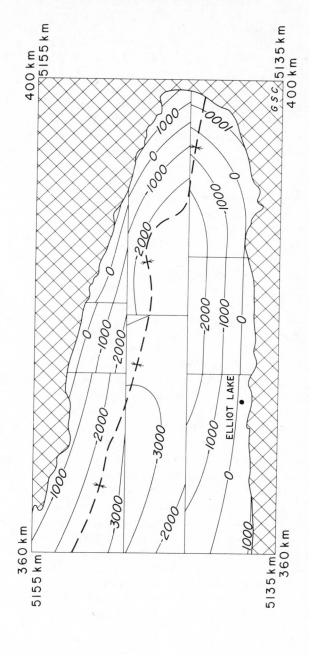

Fig. 8. Contours (in feet above sealevel) of parts of eight quadratic trend surfaces fitted to bottom of Matinenda Formation, Elliot Lake area.

geological model provides a good reason for the application of a trend-signal-noise model similar to the statistical model used in the preceding section. Ideally, the trend in this model would represent the structural deformation and the signal would represent the original topographical surface on which the Matinenda Formation was deposited. Thus, it would be meaningful to extract the signal from the data by elimination of (1) the trend, and (2) the noise representing irregular local variability which is unpredictable on the scale at which the sampling (by drilling) was carried out. Although the concepts of "trend" (deterministic polynomial equation), "signal" (homogeneous autocorrelation function), and stochastically independent "noise" have different statistical connotations, the differences between the features they represent usually are less distinct. It will be seen that some of the signal in the present example represents structural deformation. It also is known that these concepts depend on the sampling density. In general, if more measurements are performed, some of the signal becomes trend and some of the noise becomes signal.

Although it can be assumed that the major uranium-producing conglomerates in the Elliot Lake area have been deposited in channels, the geometrical pattern of the channels remains a subject of speculation, at least in places removed from the mining areas. Bain (1960) assumed a single "uraniferous river channel" (see also Stanton, 1972, Figures 16–12) winding its way through the basin so that it fits the approximately NW trending channels at the Quirke, Nordic and Pronto mineralized zones. On the other hand, Derry (1960) assumed separate, subparallel channels. It will be seen than the results obtained by the trend-signal-noise model fit in with Derry's pattern and not with Bain's pattern.

The following procedure was followed to obtain a two-dimensional auto-correlation function for residuals from the trend of Figure 8. By using polar co-ordinates, distances between pairs of boreholes were grouped according to (1) distance (1-km spacing), and (2) direction of connecting line (45°-wide segments). This yields domains of different sizes. The autocorrelation coefficients for pairs of values grouped according to this method are shown in Figure 10. These values were assigned to the centers of gravity of their domains. A two-dimensional quadratic exponential (Gaussian) function with superimposed noise component was fitted by trend surface analysis of logarithmically transformed positive autocorrelation coefficients obtained from the grouped data. Both the input pattern of autocorrelation coefficients and the fitted function are symmetrical with respect to the origin where $r(0)=1$. A profile through the origin across the quadratic trend surface fitted

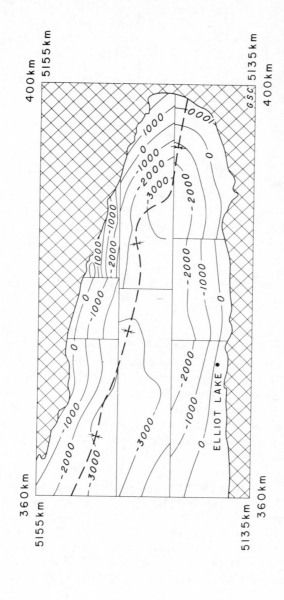

Fig. 9. Sum of trend (see Figure 8) and signal (see Figure 7) for bottom of Matinenda Formation. Note strong resemblance between patterns of Figure 8 and 9 illustrating that the fluctuations (signal) contoured in Figure 7 have relatively small magnitudes.

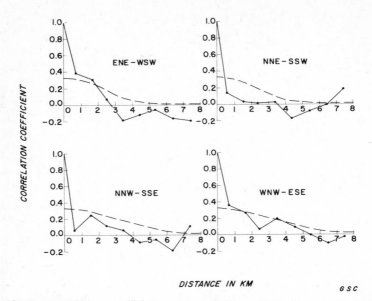

GSC

Fig. 10. Autocorrelation coefficients computed for residuals from quadratic trend surfaces (see text for method used) computed with profiles (broken lines) across theoretical two-dimensional model used for Kriging.

to log $r(d)$ therefore is a parabola with its maximum at the origin. Each parabola becomes a Gaussian curve when the antilog is taken. Four profiles across the fitted function are shown in Figure 10. The maximum of the fitted function fell at 0.325 indicating that only 32½% of the variance of the residuals is explained by the signal versus 67% by the noise. The function has elliptical contours which are elongated in approximately the NW-SE direction. This directional anisotropy would indicate that the actual topographical features (channels?) which constitute the signal are elongated in the NW-SE direction.

The signal was extracted from the residuals by using the theoretical autocorrelation function. The Kriging method was used to estimate the values of the signal at the intersection points of a grid (UTM-grid) with 1 km-spacing. Every Kriging value was estimated from all observations falling within the ellipse described by the 0.01 contour of the theoretical Gaussian autocorrelation function. This ellipse is approximately 13 km long and about 7 km wide. The estimated Kriging values on the 1-km grid defined a relatively smooth pattern which was contoured yielding the pattern of Figure 7.

The pattern of Figure 7 shows a number of minima and maxima. The amplitudes of these fluctuations are very small in comparison with the variations described by the trend (Figure 8) as can be seen in Figure 9 — representing the sum of trend and signal. Ideally, the signal would correspond to depressions and uplifts in the Archean basement, as it seems to do in most of the southern part of the area. However, other features of the estimated signal can be interpreted as belonging to the later structural deformation pattern. The lack of a clearly developed negative anomaly at Quirke Lake in the northern part of the area where significant uranium mineralization occurs may be caused by the fact that the channel direction is approximately parallel to the structural trend in this part of the area. This would make it hard and perhaps impossible to discriminate between the two patterns by means of the present statistical model.

As a concluding remark, it is noted that the statistical analysis described in this section was performed in 1976. During the past few years additional borehole data have become available for the Elliot Lake area but these have not been considered for the present case history study.

7. LOGISTIC TREND SURFACE ANALYSIS

Trend surface analysis can be regarded as an application of the general linear model of the least squares. The term "linear" in this context applies to the coefficients b_{pq} which occur only in linear form in the polynomial equation. An advantage of the linear model is that the unknown coefficients are solved through the inversion of a single matrix (see before). It is more cumbersome to obtain solutions for nonlinear functions of the coefficients because then an iterative process with many inversions may have to be used. An example is provided by logistic trend surface analysis.

The logistic model can be used for the estimation of probabilities of the occurrence of a discrete event. Applications of this model have been made in geography (Wrigley, 1976 and 1977) as well as in geology (Agterberg, 1974b; Chung, 1978; Chung and Agterberg, 1980).

From trend surface analysis, the logistic model can be written in the form

$$L(u, v) = (1 + e^{-T(u, v)})^{-1}, \tag{3}$$

where $T(u, v)$ is as in equation (1). Although $T(u, v)$ can assume any value depending on location and on the values of its coefficients, $L(u, v)$ only can assume values in the interval between 0.0 and 1.0. It cannot be negative or greater than 1.0 and, for this reason, can be used to represent the probability of occurrence of a discrete event.

Figure 11 shows the island of Newfoundland subdivided into square cells

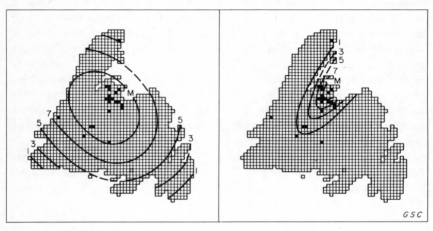

Fig. 11. Island of Newfoundland. Trend surface analysis of occurrence of massive sulphide deposits in cells measuring 10 km on a side. Calculated values for cells were subjected to the transformation 9(value-MIN) / (MAX-MIN) where MIN and MAX represent smallest and largest calculated value. Transformed values were contoured (M=8.5); A. Contours of quadratic trend surface; MIN=−0.0733, MAX=0.0741; B. Contours of logistic quadratic trend surface. Solution obtained after 13 iterations for level of convergence equal to 0.001 (see Chung, 1978); MIN=0.0000; MAX=0.2188.

measuring 10 km on a side. Cells known to contain one or more massive sulphide deposits are indicated by means of a pattern. Occurrence of massive sulphide deposits in a cell is an event for which the probability of occurrence can be estimated. In Figure 11, the results of two methods of trend surface analysis are shown. In both situations, the vector **Y** of observed values consisted of elements equal to 1.0 for the 21 cells with deposits and elements equal to 0.0 for the 1388 cells without deposits. First, $T(u, v)$ was fitted directly to the data for the second degree (r=2). The result is shown in Figure 11A. Next $L(u, v)$ of equation (3) was fitted with $T(u, v)$ of the second degree (see Figure 11B). The general linear model of least squares frequently can be used to estimate probabilities of discrete events (Agterberg, 1974a and 1974b). However, in the example of Figure 11, the pattern for the logistic model (Figure 11b) is obviously more meaningful than the pattern of the corresponding linear model (Figure 11A), if the contours are to be interpreted as indicative of the chances that a cell contains massive sulphide deposits. The main reason that $L(u, v)$ is more suitable than $T(u, v)$ in this type of application is related to the fact that $T(u, v)$ in Figure 11A is an elliptic paraboloid. It means that any vertical intersection of the pattern of Figure 11A is a parabola without inflection points at either side of its maximum value. The many 0.0 values for empty cells then result in small positive values for areas with known deposits and small negative values for areas without known deposits. The pattern of Figure 11B on the other hand, is positive everywhere, with small positive values in the areas without known deposits. This is because the logistic trend surface model of Figure 11B is more flexible than the ordinary trend surface model of Figure 11A. Both patterns of Figure 11 were obtained by using a system for interactive graphic computer programs for multivariate statistical analysis of geological data (SIMSAG) developed by Chung (1979).

8. CONCLUDING REMARKS

In this chapter, it has been attempted not only to present the basic model used in trend surface analysis which is very simple but also to illustrate the approach by means of various case history studies. It should be kept in mind that trend surface analysis is probably most useful when trend and residuals can be linked to separate spatial processes which were operative on a regional scale and a local scale, respectively.

Geomathematics Section
Geologic Survey of Canada

ACKNOWLEDGEMENTS

Thanks are due to C. F. Chung, Geological Survey of Canada, for his collaboration during the studies resulting in Figures 7–11, and to V. Ruzicka, Geological Survey of Canada, for providing the drill-hole data from the Elliot Lake area. I am grateful to G. Bonham-Carter, Geological Survey of Canada, for critical reading of the manuscript.

BIBLIOGRAPHY

Agterberg, F. P.: 1964, 'Methods of trend surface analysis', *Quarterly Colorado School of Mines* **59**, 111–130.

Agterberg, F. P.: 1970, 'Autocorrelation functions in geology', in D. F. Merriam (ed.), *Geostatistics*, Plenum, New York, pp. 113–142.

Agterberg, F. P.: 1974a, *Geomathematics*, Elsevier, Amsterdam.

Agterberg, F. P.: 1974b, 'Automatic contouring of geological maps to detect target areas for mineral exploration', *Journal of Mathematical Geology* 6, 373–394.

Agterberg, F. P. and C. F. Chung: 1973, 'Geomathematical prediction of sulphur in coal, new Lingian Mine area, Sydney coal field', *Canadian Mineralogy and Metallurgical Bulletin* October, 85–96.

Agterberg, F. P. and C. F. Chung: 1975, 'A computer program for polynomial trend-surface analysis', *Geological Survey of Canada Papers* 75(21), 51 p.

Bain, G. W.: 1960, 'Patterns to ores in layered rocks', *Economic Geology* 55, 695–731.

Chung, C. F.: 1978, 'Computer program for the logistic model to estimate the probability of occurrence of discrete events', *Geological Survey of Canada Papers* 78(11), 23 p.

Chung, C. F.: 1979, 'A system of interactive graphic programs for multivariate statistical analysis for geological data', *Proceedings of the 12th Symposium on Interface Computer Science and Statistics*, University of Waterloo, pp. 452–456.

Chung, C. F. and F. P. Agterberg: 1980, 'Regression models for estimating mineral resources from geological map data', *Journal of Mathematical Geology* 12, 473–488.

Cliff, A. D. and J. K. Ord: 1973, *Spatial Autocorrelation*, Pion, London.

Coons, R. L., G. P. Woolard, and G. Hershery: 1967, 'Structural significance and analysis of Mid-Continent Gravity High', *Bulletin of the American Association of Petroleum Geologists* 51, 2381–2399.

Davis, J. C.: 1973, *Statistics and Data Analysis in Geology*, Wiley, New York.

Delphiner, P.: 1976, 'Linear estimation of nonstationary spatial phenomena', in M. Guarascio, M. David, and C. Huigbregts (eds.), *Advanced Geostatistics in the Mining Industry*, Reidel, Dordrecht, pp. 49–68.

De Wijs, H. J.: 1951, 'Statistics of ore distribution', *Geol. Mijnbouw* 30, 365–375.

Derry, D. R.: 1960, 'Evidence of the origin of the Blind River uranium deposits', *Economic Geology* 55, 906–927.

Dobrin, M. B.: 1976, *Introduction to Geophysical Prospecting* 3rd ed., McGraw-Hill, New York.

Gannicott, R. A., G. A. Armbrust, and F. P. Agterberg: 1979, 'Use of trend surface analysis to delimit hydrothermal alteration of patterns', *Canadian Mineralogy and Metallurgical Bulletin* June, 82–89.

Grant, F. A.: 1957, 'A problem in the analysis of geophysical data', *Geophysics* 22, 309–344.

Harbaugh, J. W. and D. F. Merriam: 1968, *Computer Applications in Stratigraphic Analysis*, Wiley, New York.

Jakeman, B. L.: 1980, 'The relation between formation structure and thickness in the Permo-Triassic succession of the Southern Coalfield, Sydney Basin, New South Wales, Australia', *Journal of Mathematical Geology* 12, 185–212.

Koch, Jr., G. S. and R. F. Link: 1971, *Statistical Analysis of Geological Data*, Vol. 2, Wiley, New York.

Krumbein, W. C.: 1956, 'Regional and local components in facies maps', *Bulletin of the American Association of Petroleum Geologists* 40, 2163–2194.

Krumbein, W. C.: 1959, 'Trend-surface analysis of contour type maps with irregular control-point spacing', *Journal of Geophysical Research* **64**, 823–834.

Krumbein, W. C. and F. A. Graybill: 1965, *An Introduction to Statistical Models in Geology*, McGraw-Hill, New York.

Lee, Y. W.: 1960, *Statistical Theory of Communication*, Wiley, New York.

MacGregor, I. D. and C. H. Smith: 1963, 'The use of chrome spinels in petrographic studies of ultramafic intrusions', *Canadian Mineralogist* **7**, 403–412.

Matheron, G.: 1956, Les variables régionalisées et leur estimation, Masson, Paris.

Matheron, G.: 1967, 'Kriging or polynomial interpolation procedures?', *Transactions of the Canadian Institute of Mineralogy and Metallurgy* **70**, 240–244.

Miller, R. L.: 1956, 'Trend surfaces: Their application to analysis and description of environments of sedimentation', *Journal of Geology* **64**, 425–446.

Oldham, C. H. G. and D. B. Sutherland: 1955, 'Orthogonal polynomials: Their use in estimating the regional effect', *Geophysics* **20**, 295–306.

Parzen, E.: 1967, 'Time series analysis for models of signal plus white noise', in *Spectral Analysis of Time Series*, Wiley, New York.

Ripley, B. D.: 1981, *Spatial Statistics*, Wiley, New York.

Robertson, J. A.: 1966, 'The relationship of mineralization to stratigraphy in the Blind River area, Ontario', *Geological Association of Canada Special Paper* **3**, 121–136.

Robinson, J. E. and D. F. Merriam: 1980, 'Recognition of subtle features in geological maps', in A. D. Miall (ed.), *Facts and Principles of World Petroleum Occurrence*, Canadian Society of Petroleum Geologists Mem. 6, pp. 269–282.

Schwarzacher, W.: 1980, 'Models for the theory of stratigraphic correlation', *Journal of Mathematical Geology* **12**, 213–234.

Stanton, R. L.: 1972, *Ore Petrology*, McGraw-Hill, New York.

Tukey, J. W.: 1970, 'Some further inputs', in D. F. Merriam (ed.), *Geostatistics*, Plenum, New York, pp. 163–174.

Vistelius, A. B. and V. J. Hurst: 1964, 'Phosphorus in granitic rocks of North America', *Geological Society of America Bulletin* **75**, 1055–1092.

Watson, G. S.: 1971, 'Trend-surface analysis', *Journal of Mathematical Geology* **3**, 215–226.

Whitten, E. H. T.: 1959, 'Composite trends in a granite: Modal variation and ghost stratigraphy in part of the Donegal Granite, Eire', *Journal of Geophysical Research* **64**, 835–848.

Whitten, E. H. T.: 1970, 'Orthogonal polynomial trend surfaces for irregularly spaced data', *Journal of Mathematical Geology* **2**, 141–152.

Wrigley, N.: 1976, *Introduction to the Use of Logistic Models in Geography*, Concepts and Techniques in Modern Geography No. 10, Geo Abstracts, Norwich.

Wrigley, N.: 1977, *Probability Surface Mapping: An Introduction with Examples and FORTRAN Programmes*, Concepts and Techniques in Modern Geography No. 16, Geo Abstracts, Norwich.

JAMES E. BURT

NONLINEAR MODELS AND METHODS

1. INTRODUCTION

In a mathematical model the attributes or characteristics of the system being modeled appear as parameters. A model of groundwater flow, for example, would very likely use hydraulic conductivity to characterize the soil or rock medium. Similarly, social science gravity models usually contain distance raised to some power which is interpreted as the "friction of distance" or some other property of space. Clearly, for a model to be used in simulation, parameter values must be assigned. When this is done, a correspondence is established between the model and a particular physical setting or social/ economic situation. This paper is concerned with methods by which this correspondence can be established for one class of models. Another paper (Willmott, this volume) discusses ways to analyze the degree of correspondence between a model and the phenomena it purports to represent.

The assignment of parameters is a step in model building termed calibration, where a model is tuned to a particular situation. The most direct means of calibrating a model is to simply specify the conditions under which a simuation is to take place. Alternatively, one might measure the properties represented by the parameters and use the measured values in a simulation. Unfortunately, the direct approach is very often not available. In many cases, theory is not sufficiently developed to allow one to proceed logically from specification of a simulation situation to parameter values. That is, the interpretation of the model parameters in terms of system characteristics may be too vague to permit values to be assigned just by knowing the system characteristics. Air pollution models, for example, often contain one or more eddy diffusivities which accout for the action of turbulent swirls in the dispersion of a pollutant. One would expect that the diffusion parameters should be related in some way to wind speed, terrain roughness, etc., but because no comprehensive theory of turbulence exists, it isn't possible to deduce a value for the eddy diffusivity from the physical characteristics of the problem. Social science modelers also often face theoretical deficiencies when attempting to assign parameter values. Even in those cases where model parameters are related in a straightforward way to system

173

Gary L. Gaile and Cort J. Willmott (eds.), Spatial Statistics and Models, 173–190.
© 1984 *by D. Reidel Publishing Company.*

characteristics, it may be that measurements of the appropriate characteristics do not exist.

For these reasons researchers are often forced to use some indirect method- of assigning parameter values. The most common method is as follows. Measurements are taken on the variables present in the model. If the model is structurally correct, there must exist some combination of parameter values which will reproduce the measurements on the variables. The idea in indirect calibration is to choose parameter values consistent with the observations. Notice that this approach is indirect in the sense that observations are taken on the variables, not on the parameters. The parameters must be identified on the basis of aggregate model behavior.

Linear regression may be seen as a very simple example of the identification problem. The variables x and y are taken to be related by the parameters b_1 and b_2 according to

$$y = b_1 + b_2 x + a,$$

where a is an error or disturbance term. Observations of x and y are taken, and the parameters are assigned values consistent with the observations. In regression analysis, the phrase "consistent with observations" usually means that computed values of y deviate as little as possible in a least squares sense from observed values of y. In other words, the procedure is to minimize

$$f = \sum_{i=1}^{m} (\hat{y}_i - y_i)^2, \tag{1}$$

where $\hat{y}_i$ is an observed value of y, y_i is a value computed from x_i and m is the number of observations. Recall that for fixed observations f is a function of the parameters only, $f = f(b_1, b_2)$, thus the problem is one of solving the linear system of equations

$$g_1 = \frac{\partial f(b_1, b_2)}{\partial b_1} = 0,$$

$$g_2 = \frac{\partial f(b_1, b_2)}{\partial b_2} = 0. \tag{2}$$

The fact that (2) is a linear system greatly simplifies solution of the pro- blem, of course. In fact, if equations analogous to (2) are not linear one cannot be certain that a single minimum exists, and there is no foolproof way of locating a minimum in the event it does exist.

This paper is concerned with parameter estimation in nonlinear situations. The objective is to provide an introduction to nonlinear problems and to the concepts upon which commonly used solution methods are based. Many of these are available in the form of commercial computer routines, thus the discussion is intended to put the reader in a position to select intelligently among them. A minimum of mathematical expertise is assumed here: a familiarity with calculus through Taylor series and applied statistics through multiple regression. Those having broader training are encouraged to consult one or more of the excellent texts treating nonlinear problems (e.g., Luenberger, 1973; Rosen *et al.*, 1970; Ortega and Rheingoldt, 1970; Ralston and Rabinowitz, 1978, Rao, 1979; Murray, 1972; Gill and Murray, 1974; Denn, 1969; Mangasarian *et al.*, 1975).

This presentation is motivated from the viewpoint of parameter estimation, but the reader should understand that the need to solve nonlinear equations arises in many other contexts as well, such as dynamic programming, variational problems, and the numerical integration of nonlinear differential equations.

2. NOTATION

In the notational system used here, scalars appear in normal type face, vectors are depicted by lower case bold face, and matrices are denoted by upper case bold type (e.g., f, $\mathbf{b}$, $\mathbf{X}$).

Consider a typical problem where a single dependent variable is used as a calibration variable. The observations consist of an m by 1 vector $\mathbf{y}$ representing the dependent variable and an m by l matrix $\mathbf{X}$ representing the l independent variables. The parameters appear as a vector of length n. If the parameter vector is $\mathbf{b}$, we have

$$\mathbf{y} = \mathbf{q}\,(\mathbf{b}, \mathbf{X}),$$

where q denotes the action of the model in assigning values of y. In curve fitting problems, the model is likely to be a relatively simple analytical function. In other applications, q may be much more complicated; it could, for example, represent the integration of a set of differential equations. The essential point is that $\mathbf{b}$ is to be selected in such a way that computed values of y agree as closely as possible with the observations. The notion of agreement with observations is made explicit by specifying an objective function f which measures disagreement between computed and observed values. By choosing **b** such that the objective function is minimized, the model is fit to the observations.

In least squares, for example, the objective function is given by (1). Notice that f is a scalar depending only on the unknown parameter vector. If the derivatives of f with respect to the elements of **b** exist, they must vanish at the minimum. That is

$$g(\mathbf{b}^*) = \left[\frac{\partial f(\mathbf{b}^*)}{\partial b_1}, \frac{\partial f(\mathbf{b}^*)}{\partial b_2}, \ldots \frac{\partial f(\mathbf{b}^*)}{\partial b_n} \right]^T = 0, \qquad (3)$$

where **b*** is the value of **b** minimizing f. Equation (3) is analogous to (2), except that the component equations are now nonlinear and require special methods. The nonlinearities arise because the objective function is not a quadratic in **b**. This in turn might arise because the model is nonlinear in **b** or because a least squares criterion is not being used, or both.

All the methods discussed here assume that the first derivatives of f exist and some require the existence of second derivatives as well. If f is even moderately complicated, the programming required to compute these will be laborious and error-prone. In such cases it may be preferable to use finite difference approximations to the derivatives. For example, a common approximation to **g** is the forward difference

$$g_j(\mathbf{b}) = \frac{\partial f(\mathbf{b})}{\partial b_j} \approx \frac{f(\mathbf{b} + h_j) - f(\mathbf{b})}{h_j},$$

where h_j is a small change in b_j. We see that all n components of **g** can be obtained at a cost of $n+1$ evaluations of f plus some arithmetic. (Higher order derivatives can be approximated in an analogous manner). A more accurate approximation is the central difference

$$g_j(\mathbf{b}) \approx \frac{f(\mathbf{b} + h_j) - f(\mathbf{b} - h_j)}{2h_j}$$

This increase in accuracy comes at the expense of an increase in the number of function evaluations required ($2n$).

Many routines approximate the required derivatives using formulas similar to those above. In the discussion below, no notational distinction will be made between a derivative and its approximation. There is, of course, a numerical distinction between them and it is important to realize that routines which seem advantageous because they do not require the user to supply derivatives most likely are approximating them internally. This will increase the computational costs both directly in the approximation process, and indirectly in that the performance of the method will degrade somewhat owing to error present in the approximation.

3. SOME PARTICULAR NONLINEAR METHODS

3.1. *Preliminaries*

From the above discussion it is seen that the problem of fitting a model to data may be viewed as one of minimizing f or as solving the nonlinear system (3). In general, it is preferable to attack the minimization problem directly rather than applying general-purpose algorithms for solving nonlinear equations. In choosing methods developed specifically for minimization, it is possible to exploit mathematical advantages appearing in minimization that do not occur in general nonlinear problems.

The function f maps from R^n to R^1, thus it is a hypersurface defined over an n-dimensional domain. In minimizing f it is necessary to search this surface for its lowest value. (Maximization problems are treated by multiplying f by minus one.) Computational limitations rule out an exhaustive search for the minimum when n is even moderately large (e.g., greater than 2). The secret to successfully minimizing f is to search the surface intelligently. The most obvious ingredient in an intelligent search is that f should decrease with each successive step in the search procedure. That is, if b^k is the present value of b, we should require that $f(b^{k+1}) < f(b^k)$. If the inequality is not observed, another value of b^{k+1} should be chosen, or else the search should be terminated on the grounds that either the minimum has been reached or the method has failed.

All nonlinear methods generate a sequence of b which cause f to decrease from iteration to iteration. They differ greatly, however, in the rate at which f decreases, or equivalently, in the rate of convergence to a minimum. The rate of convergence may be specified by the "quotient order" of convergence. A method is said to converge at order p if there exists some number c between zero and unity such that

$$\left| b^{k+1} - b^* \right| \leqslant c \left| b^k - b^* \right|^p$$

for increasing k. As the order of convergence (p) increases, the rate of convergence increases. The methods below all possess one of 3 convergence orders. If p is unity, the method will possess linear convergence. If the convergence rate is linear, yet c changes with k such that c approaches zero as k approaches infinity, the metod will possess superlinear convergence. Finally, for p equal to 2, quadratic convergence exists.

3.2. *Steepest Descent Method*

This method, also known as Cauchy's method, is based on the idea that if one wishes to find the lowest point on a surface, one should head in the direction that the surface decreases fastest. This direction is, of course, normal to the contours of f. It is an elementary problem in the calculus of several variables to show that this gradient direction is defined by a vector given by

$$g(\mathbf{b}) = \left[\frac{\partial f(\mathbf{b})}{\partial b_1}, \frac{\partial f(\mathbf{b})}{\partial b_2}, \cdots \frac{\partial f(\mathbf{b})}{\partial b_n}\right]^T. \tag{4}$$

This suggests that $\mathbf{b}^{k+1}$ should lie in a direction from $\mathbf{b}^k$ computed by (4) evaluated at $\mathbf{b}^k$. Furthermore, one should move as far as possible in the gradient direction before f begins to increase. Given $\mathbf{b}^k$ the next value is

$$\mathbf{b}^{k+1} = \mathbf{b}^k - d\, \mathbf{g}(\mathbf{b}^k),$$

where d is a scalar step size controlling how far to move. The step size must itself be found by a search method, but this is a search in only one dimension and there is no need to find this minimum to extreme accuracy. A convenient method is to approximate $f(\mathbf{b}^{k+1})$ using a quadratic constructed from 3 values of d. The value of d minimizing the quadratic may be found anlytically and used as the optimum d.

As an example of the steepest descent method, consider the problem presented by Huff (this volume). The problem is to maximize

$$f(\mathbf{b}) = \prod_{j=1}^{1} \frac{\exp(-b_1 X_{2j} - b_2 X_{2j})}{\prod\limits_{k=1}^{p} \exp(-b_1 X_{1k} - b_2 X_{2k})}$$

Figure 1 shows contours of constant f for values of b_1 ranging from -0.1 to 0.9 and b_2 ranging from -0.4 to 0.6. Also shown is the path followed by the steepest descent method from a starting value of $b_1 = b_2 = 0$. It can be seen that in 2-space the search moves normal to a contour line until it becomes tangent to a new contour line. At that point it moves off in a new direction, normal to the old direction, again stopping when tangent to a contour line. Also note that the step size is at first very large, but becomes progressively smaller as the extremum is approached.

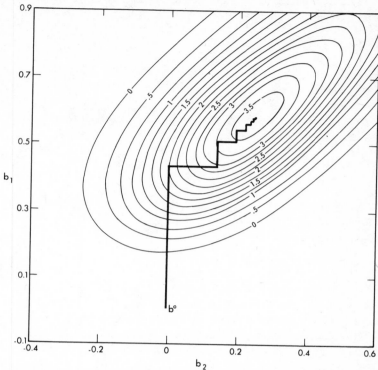

Fig 1. The path followed by the steepest descent method applied to Huff's maximum likelihood function. The contours are level curves of f as a function of the parameters b_1 and b_2. The search path consists of a set of orthogonal steps, each beginning normal to a contour and terminating at contour tangency. For more than two parameters each step is orthogonal to the previous step, but a group of steps do not form a mutually orthogonal set.

The principal advantages of the steepest descent method are its simplicity and the fact that it will always ultimately converge on a point where the gradient vanishes. The method works best on problems similar to the example, where the contours are not excessively elongated. As another example, consider Figure 2. This is a least squares surface corresponding to 1000 observations generated from the model

$$y = b_2 \, e^{b_1} + a \, ,$$

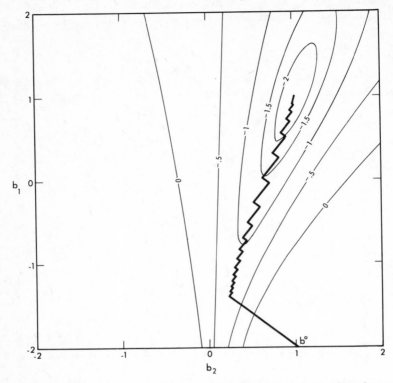

Fig. 2. The method of steepest descent applied to a least squares function of two parameters. The objective function is contoured in powers of ten. The method quickly finds the central valley, but progress is slow because the valley curves slightly as the minimum is approached.

where a is a normally distributed error term. In the example both b_1 and b_2 are unity, thus the surface takes on its minimum at $(1, 1)$. Note that because the error term is additive, the model cannot be linearized by taking logarithms. (In fact, if logarithms are taken and used in a linear regression procedure, the 95% confidence intervals obtained for b_1 and b_2 will not contain the true values.) The figure shows the path of the steepest descent method through a narrow valley. Because the valley curves slightly, the method is forced to wind its way slowly toward the minimum in numerous short steps.

Another disadvantage of the steepest descent method is that although progress is usually rapid far from the solution, convergence near the extremum is often very slow. In fact, convergence is only linear, and methods having higher orders of convergence are generally preferred.

3.3. Newton's Method and the Gauss-Newton Method

Both of these methods are based on linearization of the problem and are quadratically convergent. In Newton's method the gradient vector is linearized by expanding in a Taylor's series:

$$g(b^{k+1}) = g(b^k) + H(b^k)(b^{k+1} - b^k). \tag{5}$$

Here $H(b^k)$ is the n by n matrix of first partial derivatives of g. In terms of the function to be minimized, this matrix (called the Hessian of f) is

$$H(b^k)_{ij} = \frac{\partial^2 f(b^k)}{\partial b_i \, \partial b_j}.$$

The Hessian matrix is symmetric and it is positive definite near the minimum. Both of these properties can be exploited in computing or approximating H. Because (5) is linear it can be solved for a value of b^{k+1} which causes g to vanish:

$$b^{k+1} = b^k - H(b^k)^{-1} g(b^k).$$

When g is evaluated at b^{k+1} it will not be zero because (5) is only an approximation. If g is unacceptably large, H is recomputed at the new point and (5) is solved with the new values. There is of course no need to explicitly invert H; from a computational standpoint it is cheaper to solve $H(b^k)(b^{k+1} - b^k) = -g(b^k)$ for $(b^{k+1} - b^k)$. Adding this to b^k gives the new point.

The Gauss-Newton method was developed for least squares problems and is very similar to Newton's method. The difference is that the model q is linearized rather than the gradient. That is, we write

$$q(b^{k+1}, X) = q(b^k, X) + J(b^k)(b^{k+1} - b^k),$$

where $J(b^k)$ is the m by n Jacobian matrix of partial derivatives $\partial q(b^k, X_i)/\partial b_j$. A value of $(b^{k+1} - b^k)$ is sought which minimizes the sum of squares

$$\Sigma \, [\hat{y} - q(b^k, X) - J(b^k)(b^{k+1} - b^k)]^2$$

This is a problem in linear regression with solution

$$(b^{k+1} - b^k) = [J(b^k)^T J(b^k)]^{-1} J(b^k)^T [\hat{y} - q(b^k, X)]$$

Again, in paractice the inverse would not be computed explicitly; instead the following linear system is solved:

$$[J(b^k)^T \, J(b^k)] \, (b^{k+1} - b^k) = J(b^k)^T \, [\hat{y} - q \, (b^k, X) \qquad (6)$$

Both of these methods replace the original problem with a linear approximation and then solve the approximate problem exactly. They therefore perform well in regions where the linear approximation is a good one. This is often the case near the minimum of f. Far from the minimum the linear representation may be very poor with the result that the algorithm will actually diverge. Consider the example shown in Figure 3. This is another

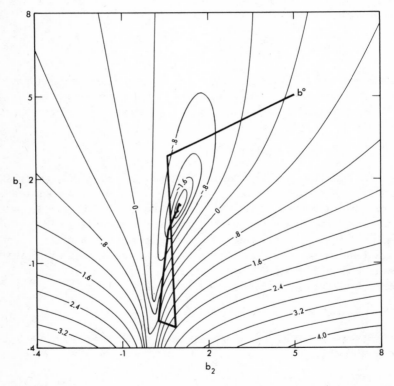

Fig. 3. The Gauss-Newton path on the least squares surface of Figure 2. The algorithm shows a tendency for divergence on the second step, but then recovers and converges to the minimum. Note that the narrow valley is negotiated without the difficulties of the steepest descent method.

section of the least squares surface used previously. It is seen that near the minimum, at the point (1, 1), the contours are approximately elliptical, indicating that q is not too different than linear in this neighborhood. The figure also shows the path followed by the Gauss-Newton method, beginning at the point (5, 5). The first step is an improvement, but for the next step the method moves far beyond the central hollow. In this case the method ultimately converges, but only because it works its way back into a region of approximate linearity. Notice that the search moves rapidly through the same general area that the steepest descent method advanced only slowly (Figure 2).

In general, these methods will converge rapidly given good starting values, but may converge slowly or not at all from poor locations. Another problem with these methods is that the linear system may be poorly conditioned to the extent that solution is not possible using even sophisticated methods. For these reasons (divergence and poor conditioning) some modifications to the basic methods are usually required.

3.4. *Marquardt's Method*

This method (Marquardt, 1963) treats the divergence and conditioning issues simultaneously for least squares problems. Marquardt noted that the search direction given by the steepest descent and Gauss-Newton methods are not usually the same. His method amounts to searching in a direction somewhere between the two. When the linear approximation is a good one, the search direction is near the Gauss-Newton direction. Otherwise a direction closer to the gradient of f is chosen. This interpolation between the two directions is accomplished by adding a small positive constant d to the diagonal of $\mathbf{J}^T\mathbf{J}$ so that one solves

$$[\mathbf{J}(\mathbf{b}^k)^T \, \mathbf{J}(\mathbf{b}^k) + d\mathbf{I}] \, (\mathbf{b}^{k+1} - \mathbf{b}^k) = \mathbf{J}(\mathbf{b}^k)^T \, [\hat{\mathbf{y}} - \mathbf{q}(\mathbf{b}^k, \mathbf{X})] \, , \quad (7)$$

where $\mathbf{I}$ is the identity matrix. The value of d controls the direction moved and is critical to the performance of the algorithm. As d increases, the search direction approaches the gradient direction so that a steepest descent step is taken. If d vanishes, equation (7) degrades to the Gauss-Newton equation (6). Implementations of Marquardt's method vary d during the course of the search, decreasing d in those regions where $\mathbf{q}$ is nearly linear. Notice that d also conditions the system to be solved thereby assuring good numerical properties.

Figure 4 illustrates the performance of Marquardt's method on the least

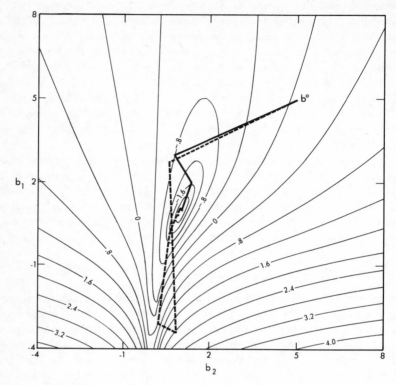

Fig. 4. Marquardt's (solid line) and the Gauss-Newton (dashed line) methods applied to the surface of Figure 3. The first Marquardt step is very near the Gauss-Newton step, terminating in a region where the linear approximation is poor. The next step is thus caused to be roughly midway between the Gauss-Newton and gradient directions. No tendency to diverge is observed.

squares problem of Figure 3. (The Gauss-Newton path is shown again for comparison.) For the first step, the algorithm takes what is very nearly a Gauss-Newton step. At the new point, d is increased so that the second step is about halfway between the Gauss-Newton and steepest descent directions. The method thereby avoids the overshoot of the unmodified Gauss-Newton search and converges on the minimum very quickly.

Marquardt's method is preferred over both the steepest descent and unmodified Gauss-Newton methods (Bard, 1974). It is available as a stand-alone procedure in the SAS and SPSS packages and as a Fortran subroutine in the IMSL library. The BMD package also contains a nonlinear least squares procedure, but uses another modification of the Gauss-Newton method called partial sweeping. Here a stepwise procedure is used to select a linearly independent subset of partical derivatives of q, so that the linear system will be well-conditioned.

3.5. Newton-like (Modified Newton) and Quasi-Newton Methods

These methods are modifications to Newton's method for general minimization (not just least squares problems). The Newton-like methods perturb the Hessian matrix (or a finite difference approximation to $\mathbf{H}$) to improve its numerical properties. Letting $\mathbf{D}^k$ be a diagonal matrix, one solves

$$[\mathbf{H}(\mathbf{b}^k) + \mathbf{D}^k] \, (\mathbf{b}^{k+1} - \mathbf{b}^k) = - \mathbf{g}(\mathbf{b}^k) . \tag{8}$$

Some implementations (e.g., the NAG library) factor the matrix in brackets before solving the system and thus do not operate on $\mathbf{H}$ directly. The effect, however, is as if (8) were solved. Other modifications to Newton's method are concerned with efficiency, not just the stability of Equation (8). They typically achieve their advantage by requiring fewer function evaluations to compute $\mathbf{H}$ or they may compute $\mathbf{H}$ less than once every iteration. Obviously, this latter approach will work well in regions where $\mathbf{H}$ is nearly constant.

Quasi-Newton methods take a different tack. In these methods an approximation to $\mathbf{H}(\mathbf{b}^k)$ is computed by updating the approximation at the previous step, $\mathbf{H}(\mathbf{b}^{k-1})$. This is in contrast to the modified Newton methods that approximate $\mathbf{H}(\mathbf{b}^k)$ by finite differencing f at $\mathbf{b}^k$. The advantage once again is efficiency, with fewer function evaluations to approximate $\mathbf{H}$ and fewer arithmetic operations to solve the linear system (Gill and Murray, 1972). Quasi-Newton methods are available in the NAG and IMSL libraries.

Figure 5 shows a quasi-Newton path on Huff's problem treated earlier by steepest descent. It can be seen that the method retains rapid convergence without problems of divergence. Actually, the updating of $\mathbf{H}$ causes the method to lose the quadratic convergence of Newton's method, but it does converge superlinearly and can therefore be expected to perform much better than the steepest descent method.

3.6. Conjugate Direction Methods

The steepest descent method operates by generating a sequence of search directions that are normal to the contours of f. This amounts to a sequence

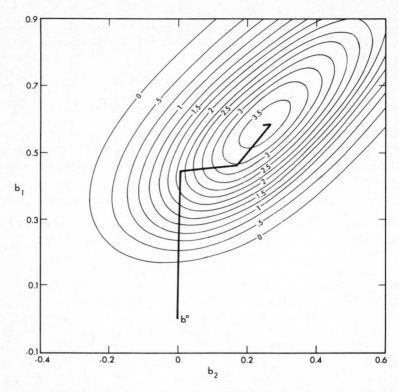

Fig. 5. A quasi-Newton path on the surface of Firure 1. The superior convergence
properties of this method are indicated by the small number of steps required.

of steps that are also normal to one another from step to step, as is clear from
the figures that were presented earlier. Conjugate direction methods impose
a different condition on the relationship between search directions – they
must be mutually conjugate. Consider the Hessian of f. If two search direc-
tions $\mathbf{u}$ and $\mathbf{v}$ are conjugate with respect to $\mathbf{H}$, then $\mathbf{u}^T\mathbf{H}\mathbf{v}$ is zero. (In the
special case where $\mathbf{H}$ is a diagonal matrix with constant values, $\mathbf{u}$ and $\mathbf{v}$ will
also be orthogonal.) The advantage of searching in conjugate directions over
orthogonal gradient directions is convergence speed. In fact, any method
using conjugate directions will locate the minimum of a quadratic function
in a finite number of steps (Wismer and Chattergy, 1978).

     There are a variety of ways to generate conjugate search directions, each leading to a different minimization algorithm. For example, the Fletcher-Reeves method (1964) is able to generate such directions without computing H explicitly, thus no second derivatives (or second derivative approximations) are required. Another variant is Powell's (1977) restart method. Here, conjugate directions are found without using even first derivative information from the previous iteration. This is advantageous because there is no need to store any matrices from iteration to iteration. The method is therefore able to attack large problems (n greater than 100) with minimal computer memory requirements while maintaining good convergence properties. (There is some loss in computational speed owing to the need to restart, thus one would not prefer this method for small n.) Powell's method is implementated in the IMSL library.

4. STOPPING RULES AND SCALING

The performance of most algorithms depends upon the scale of b and f (an exception is the unmodified Newton method). For example, if the parameters are scaled so that the contours of f are circular, the steepest descent method will reach the minimum in one step. Generally, it is desirable to have all the elements of b nearly the same size and also have their influence on f be similar (i.e., nearly equal values in $g(b)$). If an algorithm is performing poorly on a problem one should determine if either or both of these properties are severely violated and attempt to mitigate against them by rescaling b. Similarly, it may be helpful to rescale f. The solution point is not modified by linear transformations on f, thus one can multiply by or add any constant to f without changing the minimum obtained. It is good practice to scale f so that it is on the order of unity and to remove and purely additive constants in f. Failure to do this can sometimes cause roundoff errors to unduly influence computed values of f and its derivatives.

The question of when to terminate the search is not trivial and is obviously related to the scale of f and b. Ideally at least three conditions should be met: the gradient vector should be near zero, the parameter vector should be changing very little from iteration to iteration, and f should be nearly constant from trial to trial. Most routines monitor their progress using one or more of these criteria as determined by the user. One might, for example, instruct a routine to terminate when no member of b is changing by more than one part in five. An error condition will often indicate whether or not convergence has been achieved, but it is prudent to examine the gradient vector as well as f to verify that a minimum has been found. It must be realized that if f can be computed to only a few digits of accuracy it is fruitless to demand extreme accuracy in the location of the minimum.

One must also be aware that a user's definition of a successful search may be at odds with what a routine considers a success. Because the gradient is a nonlinear function of b, it may have more than one root. When this is true, f may possess multiple local minima. It may be that one of these local depressions is lower than any other (a global minimum) or several may have the same value. The methods described above locate local minima only. There is no guarantee that the point found is the true minimum of f; a successful search implies only that the point found is lower than any other in the immediate neighborhood. Attempts can be made to find a global minimum and/or detect multiple minima by starting searches from a variety of widely spaced points. If all searches reach the same minimum, one has more confidence that it is, in fact, a global minimum. Another approach is to evaluate f on a grid of b-values, thereby allowing slices of f to be at least crudely contoured as in Figures 1 through 5 (see Aird and Rice, 1977). A search using one of the methods described above would then be used, starting from the lowest point on the contour maps. This method is practical only for small n, of course.

5. CLOSURE

Selecting a minimization method for a particular problem can be difficult because unless much is known about the objective function, it is not easy to predict how a method will perform. There are, however, several general guide-lines which can be given. Perhaps most important is to match the advantages of the method chosen with the properties of the problem. For example, if evaluation of the objective function is expensive a quasi-Newton method might be appropriate. If f is cheap to evaluate, one might trade more evaluations for less arithmetic in solving for the next point. Similarly, Powell's method is preferred when n is large or computer memory is restricted. If f is a least squares function, methods designed specifically for least squares should be considered first. These will take advantage of the fact that $2\mathbf{J}(\mathbf{b})^T\mathbf{J}(\mathbf{b})$ is often a good approximation to $\mathbf{H}(\mathbf{b})$, thereby avoiding the need to compute second derivatives of f. (As an added benefit, confidence intervals for $\mathbf{b}$ will be provided automatically in most cases, whereas the user would need to compute them separately if a general minimizer is used.) The derivatives of f are also a consideration. Many routines approximate required derivatives internally, but at a cost of one or two function evaluations per derivative.

If the derivatives can be coded analytically without much difficulty then they should be supplied to the routine along with the objective function.

Another point to make in this context is that there is no substitute for information about f. This is useful both in selecting a method and in evaluating results obtained from the routine selected. A preliminary investigation of f may well be worth the effort, particularly if f is inexpensive to evaluate.

Finally, the discussion here has been confined to unconstrained minimization — b has not been limited in any way. Very often, of course, some values of b are not admissible (e.g., negative population density). If no local minima exist in the inadmissable region (and f exists there) then the problem may be solved as if it were unconstrained. When this is not the case some modification to the unconstrained approach is required.

The first approach to investigate is a transformation of f so that it becomes unconstrained. Rosenbrock (1960), shows how f can be increased near the edges of the feasible region using quadratic multipliers of the parameters. (Other of these so-called "penalty" function methods are described in the references). Failing this, a routine designed for constrained problems must be used. Many of these use straightforward extensions of unconstrained methods. The BMD package, for example, uses partial sweeping to preclude the possiblity of changing a parameter beyond its feasible range. The NAG library uses an active set strategy for bounded parameters. When a boundary is encountered, the unconstrained search direction is modified so that it has not component in the direction of the bounded variable. Changes in the free directions are not restricted. Other types of constraints such as linear or nonlinear constraints require more complicated approaches and will not be discussed here. The reader is again referred to advanced texts for theoretical development of constrained methods. A variety of algorithms may be found in the NAG library.

Dept. of Geography
University of Wisconsin-Madison

BIBLIOGRAPHY

Aird, T. J. and J. R. Rice: 1977, 'Systematic search in high dimensional sets', *SIAM Journ. Numer. Anal.* **14**, 296–312.

Bard, Y.: 1974, *Nonlinear Parameter Estimation*, Academic Press, New York.

Denn, M. M.: 1969, *Optimization by Variational Methods*, McGraw-Hill, New York.

Gill, P. E. and W. Murray: 1972, 'Quasi-Newton methods for unconstrained minimization', *Journ. Inst. Math. Appl.* **9**, 505–536.

Gill, P. E. and W. Murray (eds.): 1974, *Numerical Methods for Constrained Optimization*, Academic Press, New York.

Flectcher, R. and C. M. Reeves: 1964, 'Function minimization by conjugate gradients', *Computer Journal* 7, 149–154.

Luenberger, D. G.: 1973, *An Introduction to Linear and Nonlinear Programming*, Addison-Wesley, Reading, Mass.

Mangasarian, O. L., R. R. Meyer, and S. M. Robinson (eds.): 1975, *Nonlinear Programming 2*, Academic Press, New York.

Marquardt, D. W.: 1963, 'An algorithm for least squares estimation of nonlinear parameters', *SIAM Journ.* 11, 431–441.

Murray, W. (ed.): 1972, *Numerical Methods for Unconstrained Optimization*, Academic Press, New York.

Ortega, J. M. and W. C. Rheinboldt: 1970, *Iterative Solution of Nonlinear Equations in Several Variables*, Academic Press, New York.

Powell, M. J. D.: 1977, 'Restart procedures for the conjugate gradient method', *Math. Prog.* 12, 241–254.

Ralston, A. and P. Rabinowitz: 1978, *A First Course in Numerical Analysis*, McGraw-Hill, New York.

Rao, S. S.: 1979, *Optimization: Theory and Applications*, Wiley Eastern, New Delhi.

Rosen, J. B., O. T. Mangasarian O. L., and R. Ritter: 1970, *Nonlinear Programming*, Academic Press, New York.

Rosenbrock, M. M.: 1960, 'An automatic method for finding the greatest or least value of a function', *Computer Journal.* 3, 175–184.

Wisner, D. A. and R. Chattergy: 1978, *Introduction to Non-linear Optimization*, North-Holland, New York.

DAVID M. MARK

SOME PROBLEMS WITH THE USE OF REGRESSION ANALYSIS IN GEOGRAPHY

1. INTRODUCTION

Many of the fundamental questions in science concern relations among two or more variables. "Are these variables related?" "What is the nature of the relationship?" "Can the value of one variable be predicted, given the values of some others?" "Does the relationship conform to some theoretically-derived one?" "Do two samples conform to the same relationship?" Geographers have at times used regression analysis to provide answers to all of these questions, often with little realization of the assumptions of the technique or of alternative statistical procedures for addressing these questions.

This paper will discuss some problems associated with the use of linear regression analysis in geography. Attention will focus on the critical differences among the questions listed above, on the implications of these differences, and on alternative methods for estimating linear relationships. In the bulk of the paper, discussion will be restricted to the bivariate situation; additional problems and difficulties presented by multivariate analysis will then be sketched.

1.1. *Some Assumptions*

Poole and O'Farrell (1971) discussed the assumptions of linear regression analysis. The relative importance of these depends on the question being asked, and some will be discussed further below.

One critical assumption is that of *linearity*. Essentially, the underlying relationships between the dependent (y) variable and each of the independent (x) variables must follow a linear equation, that is, be a straight line. It is important to note, however, that the variables actually involved in the regression equation may represent non-linear tranformations of the variables originally measured. Ideally, the transformations of the variables should be selected on the basis of a theoretically-derived concept of the expected form of the relationship. For example, as noted by Church and Mark (1980), there are good *a priori* reasons for expecting that relationships between many

Gary L. Gaile and Cort J. Willmott (eds.), Spatial Statistics and Models, 191–199.
© 1984 *by D. Reidel Publishing Company.*

geomorphometric variables will be *power functions* of the form $y = ax^b$. It is well-known that such equations can be linearized by taking the logarithms of both variables. Of course, there are exceptions: some downstream changes along streams are best represented by the negative exponential distribution, but if one were forced to perform a regression on geomorphometric variables without an opportunity to test for linearity, it is recommended that logarithms of all variables be taken before entering them in the analysis.

Perhaps the most useful test of the linearity assumption is a visual inspection of a bivariate graphical plot or scattergram. With the advent of computer programs and machine-readable data sets, all too many statistical analyses are performed without the researcher "seeing" the data. Since one or two outlying points may greatly influence a regression coefficient or a correlation value, it is dangerous to simply interpret such coefficients as unbiased estimates of population values.

If there is no theoretical basis for choosing data transformations, or for retaining the original variables, a scattergram may aid in selecting the best transformations. Another approach involves fitting the four possible relationships which can be formed from the original and logarithmically-transformed variables, and choosing the one which maximizes the squared correlation coefficient. Once again, such an approach can be misleading, and visual inspection is recommended.

Another key assumption is that of *homoscedasticity*. This simply means that the amount of scatter about the fitted line (the residual variance) is constant and does not change with the independent variable. This might also be achieved through transformations of the data, and if observations are subject to a similar percentage or relative error, the logarithmic transformation will again be appropriate. A linear relationship with an intercept of zero can be represented either as a linear or power function relationship. The preferred choice between these alternatives would then be the version which produces the most even distribution of scatter.

A third general assumption listed by Poole and O'Farrell (1971) is that of *bivariate normality*. This assumption is more critical for the testing of hypotheses concerning correlation or regression coefficients than for the estimation of the coefficients themselves. Since a great many geomorphic (Gardner, 1973) and other geographic variables have lognormal distributions, a logarithmic transformation of the variables will often achieve approximate bivariate normality, linearity, and homoscedasticity simultaneously. In the following discussion, it will be assumed that all three of these conditions have been met or adequately approximated.

2. REGRESSION ANALYSIS AND GEOGRAPHICAL QUESTIONS

2.1. *Are These Variables Related?*

If this question is to be answered from observed data, we are concerned with the *probability* that the variables are linearly related. This is clearly a question of *correlation*, and yet one frequently finds examples in the geographical literature in which regression analysis results are presented in answer to this question. (This was pointed out in an unpublished manuscript by Stephenson, 1972.) The standard tests of whether the correlation is zero ($r = 0$) and whether the regression coefficient is zero ($b = 0$) both lead to identical probability estimates. This form of misuse of regression does not lead to difficulties of interpretation, other than perhaps to reduce reader confidence in other aspects of the statistical procedures used in a study. It almost certainly results from the availability of computer programs for regression analysis, which often represent the most simple way to compute correlation coefficients. However, regression is subject to more assumptions than correlation, and the gratuitous presentation of biased regression equations, when the question is simply one of correlation, may lead to more serious difficulties when other researchers attempt to use the results.

2.2. *What is the Nature of the Relationship?*

This question is somewhat vague. If the purpose of the analysis is simply to describe, one might be tempted to conclude that assumptions are not important. However, if coefficients or fitted lines are published, other researchers may later attempt to make inductive generalizations, or to compare the results to some theoretical postulates not considered in the original study. If science is to progress, it is of paramount importance that such simple descriptive relations be unbiased estimates of population parameters. It is thus recommended that the same care should be taken to avoid bias in simple descriptive studies as must be used in testing hypotheses about coefficients; as will be discussed below, regression analysis is frequently biased and thus inappropriate for such applications.

2.3. *Can the Value of One Variable be Predicted, Given the Values of Some Others?*

The question of prediction is one of the most clear-cut in the area of curve fitting. If the assumptions listed in the introduction of this paper are met, the least squares regression equation produces the "best" predictive equation. This result is subject to the additional assumption that the new independent variable values from which predictions are to be made are drawn from the same population as were the original values of those variables upon which the equation was based. The predictions are "best" in the sense that they are the most probable estimates, conditional on the values of the independent variables, and that their standard error of estimate is the minimum possible. In predictive situations, it is obvious that the variable to be predicted must be placed in the position of the dependent variable, regardless of the causal linkages involved. It is inappropriate and often incorrect to solve such an equation algebraically for another variable.

While there is little if any disagreement over the appropriateness of regression analysis for prediction, such prediction is only rarely the chief objective of geographical curve fitting. If prediction is used in a temporal sense, involving estimation of future values of some variable, one can rarely state with confidence that future independent variables will be drawn from the same population as were past values, or in fact that the coefficients themselves are stable over time. When a time perspective is not involved, the only situation in which prediction is actually objective would be where a population of x-values can be divided into two sub-sets, with associated values of an independent variable available for one subset and desired for another. While regression analysis is entirely appropriate here, such situations are indeed rare in geography.

2.4. *Does the Relationship Conform to Some Theoretically-Derived One?*

This is, or at least should be, the most important question about bivariate relationships in geography. The science of geography will advance most rapidly if precise, testable hypotheses about such relationships can be derived deductively from basic axioms and theoretical principles. If such hypotheses can be stated as equations complete with coefficients and parameters, then verifying and falsifying these parameters becomes of critical importance. Given paired observations of the variables, it is necessary to determine from the data unbiased estimates of population parameters, together with their standard errors. Then, the sample estimates of parameters can be compared with the theoretical ones. While regression analysis has frequently been used in this context, it is actually inappropriate, and produces unbiased estimates only occasionally and by chance (Lindley, 1947; Kendall and Stuart, 1965;

Mark and Church, 1977; Mark and Peucker, 1978; Jones, 1979). Generally, the alternative statistical procedure termed *functional* or structural analysis, should be used.

Details of this technique may be found in the aforementioned publications, and only the implications will be outlined here. Basically, given a bivariate data set which conforms to the assumptions listed in the introduction, functional analysis estimates the two parameters of the linear relationship. Unlike regression analysis, however, functional analysis requires one additional parameter: an estimate of the ratio of the error variance of y to the error variance of x. If this ratio is denoted by λ, then it is possible (Mark and Church, 1977, p. 67) to estimate the unbiased slope, b_f, given only the regression slope (b_r) and the correlation coefficient (r):

$$b_f = [(b_r^2/r^2 - \lambda) + \{(b_r^2/r^2 - \lambda)^2 + 4\lambda b_r^2\}^{1/2}]/2b_r.$$

If the independent variable, x, is free of error, then λ goes to infinity, and the functional slope becomes equal to the regression slope. In this special case, regression and functional analysis produce identical slope estimates. Thus, while technically regression analysis should never be used to estimate equation parameters, it can be used to answer such questions in the special case when x is free of error. Poole and O'Farrell's (1971, p. 148) statement that "x free or error" is an assumption of regression and it can be viewed as a condition for equivalence of the methods in which regression produces unbiased estimates.

When y is free of error, λ is zero. In this case, the slope is the same as the one obtained by regressing x on y, and then solving for y. This is equivalent to $b_f = b_r/r^2$. The two regression lines are the extreme values of the functional slope, the limiting cases. Note that b_f is minimized when λ goes to infinity; unless x is indeed free of error, the regression slope is a biased estimate which always underestimates the true slope.

When neither variable is free of error, the functional relation (which, like the regression line, must pass through the bivariate mean) will lie between the two regression lines. Two other special cases of functional analysis are of interest. When the error variances of the variables are equal ($\lambda = 1$), the line becomes the principal axis. This is the bivariate version of the principal components method, and is the line which minimizes the sum of the squared distances from the points measured perpendicular to the line. The *reduced major axis* (Kermack and Haldane, 1950; see also Dent, 1935) is another special case which implicity assumes that λ can be approximated by the ratio of the total variances of y and x. This is equivalent to the principal axis relating standardized versions of the variables. While Lindley (1947) showed that this solution is biased, it probably represents the best *a priori* estimate if nothing is known about the true error distribution in the model. It is generally much less reasonable to assume that all the error or residual scatter is attributable to one of the variables.

What is meant by the term "error"? While there has been some discussion of this question, it seems clear that it must include all reasons for departure from a perfect linear relationship, including measurement error, sampling error, effects of variables not in the analysis, other aspects of model mis-specification, and any stochastic component in a probabilistic model. While it may be possible to determine the measurement and sampling errors, the quantities and attributes of the remaining unexplained variance are much more problematical. While the estimation of λ may be difficult, especially in human geography, the assumption that λ is either zero or infinite, which is implicit in the application of regression analysis, can rarely be justified.

Of course, in hypothesis testing, the formulation of an appropriate null hypothesis or theoretical value is extremely important. In biology and geomorphology, concepts of dimensional balance can lead to the form of isometric relationships in which shape or form is independent of size (Gould, 1966; Church and Mark, 1980). If the isometry hypothesis can be rejected, one then must look for those aspects of function or process which force this scale distortion. It is thus of key importance to provide an unbiased test of empirically-derived parameters against the isometric ones. Theoretical or quasi-theoretical values of coefficients or exponents are available in many other areas of physical and human geography.

2.5. *Do Two Samples Conform to the Same Relationship?*

Although the deductive approach discussed in the preceding section is highly desirable, precise theories are lacking in much of geography. In such cases, empirical estimates of parameters may contribute to inductive generalizations leading to theory construction. Again, it is essential that such empirical parameters be unbiased, and thus functional analysis must be used. If correlations vary and if both variables are subject to error, samples having identical underlying distributions will nevertheless have different regression slopes, subject to different degrees of underestimation and bias. Misapplication of regression may mask similarities and inhibit subsequent generalization.

3. SOME COMMENTS ON MULTIPLE REGRESSION

In multiple regression analysis, one variable is considered to be a linear function of two or more independent variables. As noted by Poole and O'Farrell (1971), multiple regression is subject to all of the assumptions of bivariate regression, plus another: the independent variables must be statistically independent of each other. Inattention to this assumption can seriously influence results and interpretations.

Frequently, multiple regression is used in a stepwise manner. In the first step, the independent variable having the highest simple correlation coefficient is entered into the equation, while in subsequent steps, the variable having the highest partial correlation (strongest correlation with the residuals) is added. It is not unusual to find studies which interpret this order of entry, with the first being assumed to be most important (e.g., see Amerson, 1975, and Hecht, 1974). However, if independent variables are mutually correlated, the order of entry will be strongly influenced by the correlation structure (see Hauser, 1974). Wong (1963) has described procedures for dealing with data having multicollinearity. His procedure involved a principal components analysis of the independent variables to produce a set of orthogonal variables. The dependent variable was then regressed on these in the usual way.

When the objective of the analysis is prediction, multiple regression is once again a robust procedure, and is little influenced by departures from assumptions. On the other hand, theoretical statements which specify coefficients in a multivariate linear relationship are rare; while the author does not know of any applications, the functional analysis procedure generalizes to the multivariate situation, and would require a value λ_i for each independent variable. If each x_i is multipled by $1/\lambda_i$, the result is a set of variables all (including y) with the same error variance. A principal components analysis would then lead to the multivariate functional relationship.

4. FINAL COMMENTS

If one general comment on the use of statistical methods in geography were to be made, it would be that all statistical techniques make assumptions about the data. If these assumptions are not appropriate, the results may be misleading and perhaps biased. It is thus imperative for geographers using statistical methods to become familiar with the assumptions of their techniques, and to test whether the data conform to these assumptions. If they do not conform, it may be possible to transform data in such a way that the assumptions are more appropriate. If the transformed data do not satisfy the necessary assumptions, alternative procedures, perhaps non-parametric ones, should be used, or the analysis abandoned.

Interestingly, the assumptions of statistical techniques are seldom emphasized in statistics courses or books. Nevertheless, the information is available in the statistical literature, and many of the techniques have been discussed critically in the geographical literature as well.

While regression analysis is perhaps the most widely used statistical procedure in geography, it is likely also the most often misused. This paper has outlined many of the assumptions of regression, and shown how their neglect may lead to biased results. If other techniques are subjected to similar critical analyses, it may be possible to improve the ability of statistical geography to support the development and verification of geographical theories.

Dept. of Geography
State University of New York at Buffalo

BIBLIOGRAPHY

Amerson, A. B., Jr.: 1975, 'Species richness on the nondisturbed north-western Hawaiian Islands', *Ecology* 56, 435–444.

Church, M. and D. M. Mark: 1980, 'On size and scale in geomorphology', *Progress in Physical Geography* 4, 342–390.

Dent, B. M.: 1935, 'On observations of points connected by a linear relation', *Proc. Physical Soc. London* 47, pf 1, 92–108.

Gardner, V.: 1973, 'Univariate distributional characteristics of some morphometric variables', *Geografiska Annaler Ser. A* 54, 147–154.

Gould, S. J.: 1966, 'Allometry and size in ontogeny and phylogeny', *Biological Review* 41, 587–640.

Hauser, D. P.: 1974, 'Some problems in the use of stepwise regression techniques in geographical research', *Canadian Geographer* 18, 148–158.

Hecht, A.: 1974, 'The journey-to-work distance in relation to the socioeconomic characteristics of workers', *Canadian Geographer* 18, 367–378.

Jones, T. A.: 1979, 'Fitting straight lines when both variables are subject to error: I. Maximum likelihood and least-squares estimation', *Mathematical Geology* 11, 1–25.

Kendall, M. G. and A. Stuart: 1965, *The Advanced Theory of Statistics*, vol. 2, Hafner, New York.

Kermack, K. A. and J. B. S. Haldane: 1950, 'Organic correlation and allometry', *Biometrika* 37, 30–41.

Lindley, D. V.: 1947, 'Regression lines and the linear functional relationship', *Journal of the Royal Statistical Society, Suppl.* 9, 218–244.

Mark, D. M. and M. Church: 1977, 'On the misuse of regression in Earth Science', *Mathematical Geology* 9, 63–75.

Mark, D. M. and T. K. Peucker: 1978, 'Regression analysis and geographic models', *Canadian Geographer* 22, 51–64.

Poole, M. A. and P. N. O'Farrell: 1971, 'The assumptions of the linear regression model', *Transactions, Institute of British Geographers,* 52, 145–156.

Stephenson, L. K.: 1972, 'A note on the use of correlation and regression', Unpublished paper presented to the Ohio Academy of Sciences, April, 1972.

Wong, S. T.: 1963, 'A multivariate statistical model for predicting mean annual flood in New England', *Annals, Association of American Geographers* 53, 298–311.

JOHN MIRON

SPATIAL AUTOCORRELATION IN REGRESSION ANALYSIS: A BEGINNER'S GUIDE

Since about 1960, there has been a rapidly increasing technical literature on the concept of spatial autocorrelation and its implications for statistical estimation in geography. Because this literature has tended, of necessity, to be theoretical and difficult to follow, many potential users have either shied away from it or misunderstood its usefulness and its limitations. This is unfortunate. Many empirical geographers could beneficially use the techniques developed in this area, especially in regression analysis with zonal data. Further, this literature identifies a number of fundamental conceptual issues in geographic research of which every geographer should be aware. It is with these concerns in mind that I have written this paper. The purpose of the paper is to provide a relatively non-technical introduction to spatial atuo-correlation and its implications for regression analysis.

A sample problem is described in the first section of this paper; the problem having to do with house price variations within a city. In this example, the autocorrelation is argued to be arising from an omitted variable. The implications of this for the regression intercept and slope coefficients as well as t-values are assessed. In this section, autocorrelation is seen as a manifestation of another category of problems, not as a problem in and of itself. This discussion is entirely non-mathematical and requires of the reader only a basic familiarity with the concept of multiple regression.

It is argued in Section 2 that spatial autocorrelation is an important part of the discovery process by which one improves on a current base of knowledge. This differs sharply from a commonly held view that spatial autocorrelation is a nuisance against which empirical grographers must be prepared. Instead, we should use a finding of spatial autocorrelation to tell us how and when to better define a process under study. As in the first section, this discussion is entirely non-mathematical.

Sections 3 to 5 are concerned with some of the technical aspects of the identification, estimation and resolution of spatial autocorrelation in regression analysis. Here, some prior knowledge of matrices, eigenvalues, least squares and maximum likelihood estimation methods, and random variables is assumed. A small numerical example is introduced in Section 3 and most of the methods introduced through Section 5 are applied to this example. The intention here

201

Gary L. Gaile and Cort J. Willmott (eds.), Spatial Statistics and Models, 201–222.
© 1984 *by D. Reidel Publishing Company.*

is to give the uninitiated reader worked examples which illustrate how each method operates.

This paper is intended to be a beginner's guide and not an overall survey. Selected topics in autocorrelation have been deleted altogether in order to make this guide brief and yet systematic. There is, for example, no general discussion of different spatial autocorrelation measures or test statistics. Technical aspects of hypothesis-testing have also been omitted. In addition, this paper focuses exclusively on a simple form of first-order linear spatial autocorrelation. Readers who are interested in pursuing these omitted topics are referred to Hepple (1976), Cliff and Ord (1973), Hordijk (1974), Ord (1975), and Sen (1976).

1. A PROBLEM SCENARIO

Suppose we are interested in the determinants of owner-occupied house price variations within an urban area. To analyze these spatial variations, we begin by partitioning the city into zones. Of course, there may be any number of different configurations or sizes of zones and this creates problems which are discussed later in this paper. For the sake of argument, assume that 100 such zones (subscripted as $i = 1, 2, \ldots 100$) have already been defined, each of which contains roughly the same number of owner-occupied houses. Suppose further that we have taken a proportional random sample of owner-occupied households from each of these zones.[1] For each zone "i", we compute the average current expected selling price (P_i). We find that P_i varies from one zone to the next, being highest in zone 27, say, and lowest in zone 81. It is these variations in P_i that we seek to explain.

After some initial thought, we decide that zones such as 27 have a high average price partly because they typically contain larger, more luxurious dwellings. We want to quantify size-of-dwelling to measure its impact on P_i but recognize that there are many measures of size: floor area, number of rooms, lot size, and the presence or number of particular kinds of spaces such as finished basements, garage spaces, bathrooms, and so on. Suppose that we have chosen two of these, floor area and lot size, as the most important. For each of the 100 zonal samples, we calculate the mean floor area (F_i) and the mean lot size (L_i) in square meters.

To unravel the effects of these two variables on P_i, we decide to use Ordinary Least Squares (OLS) linear regression. With P_i as the dependent variable and F_i and L_i as the independents, we estimate an equation such as the following.

$$P_i = 10\,000 + 350F_i + 175L_i + e_i$$
$$(4.20) \quad (5.11)$$

$$N = 100 \qquad r^2 = 0.355 \tag{1}$$

where the intercept and slope coefficient values (10 000, 350 and 175), the t-values for the slope coefficients (4.20 and 5.11), and the coefficient of determination (0.355) are here given hypothetical values. The e_i terms are the observed residuals from the regression analysis.

These empirical results are contingent upon the samples data used. If we were to draw another similar random sample from the same urban area, calculate P_i, F_i, and L_i, and re-estimate the regression results described in (1) above, different empirical values would be obtained. In other words, the slope coefficient of F_i, to take just one example, might be something larger or smaller than 350. The t-test value for each slope coefficient gives an idea of the sampling variability attached to that slope estimate.

To fix our ideas more clearly, let us hypothesize that P_i is some linear function of F_i and L_i, i.e.,

$$P_i = \beta_0 + \beta_1 F_i + \beta_2 L_i + u_i , \tag{2}$$

where β_0, β_1, and β_2 are unobserved parameters and u_i is an unobserved random error term. The Gauss-Markov Theorem provides some assurance that the intercept and slope values in (1) are "good" estimates of β_0, β_1, and β_2. That Theorem asserts that, under certain assumptions, these OLS estimates are unbiased and relatively efficient. Crudely put, this means that an OLS estimate, such as 350 for the slope of F_i, comes relatively close to the correct value (β_1 in this case) more often than could other estimates based on the same sample data. Furthermore, the OLS estimate does not tend to be systematically smaller or larger than the correct value. [2]

The Gauss-Markov Theorem holds in this particular case only if certain assumptions are met. One of these is the assumption of a linear model such as (2) above. Other necessary assumptions are discussed below. If these assumptions are all met, the regression results in (1) above are a powerful tool for measuring the impacts of lot size and floor area on house prices. Consider two zones "i" and "j" in which the average lot sizes are equal ($L_i = L_j$) but in which in average floor area in "i" is 1 square meter more than in "j". From

(1), the average house price in "i" should tend to be about $350 higher than that in "j". In this specific sense, a figure around $350 per square meter is the marginal effect of average floor area on average house price between zones. Similarly, a figure around $175 per square meter is the marginal effect of average lot size on average house price between zones.

Let us now throw a wrench into the analysis to this point. Most observers of urban housing markets would agree that at least one important explanatory variable is missing in (1) and (2) above; some measure either of location *vis-à-vis* the central part of the city or of the general accessibility of that zone to work, shopping or other facilities. In general, housing which is closer to the CBD or is more accessible to work, shopping or other amenities will be more expensive than more remote or less accessible housing, other things being equal. If one were to use the intercept and slope coefficients in (1) to estimate average house prices, one would tend to systematically understimate in central, more accessible zones and overestimate in more remote zones. One way of looking at this problem is to say "so what?". The estimates in (1) are in some sense averaged over the entire urban area and therefore should be expected to show local variations. Just as any summary statistic can be misleading, it can also be helpful in certain situations.

However, the missing variable problem is more insidious than this in two respects. First, the exclusion of D_i, where D_i is a measure of accessibility of place i, may well be biasing the slope coefficients for F_i and L_i in (1). Why? Suppose in this urban area that more-accessible zones typically contain smaller dwellings and that less-accessible zones contain larger dwellings. In other words, suppose D_i is negatively related to F_i and L_i. In that case, the slope coefficients of F_i and L_i and (1) are each a confounding of the effects of both size-of-dwelling and location. In simple terms, some of the impact which D_i, the missing variable, has on average price has been "loaded" onto F_i and L_i to the extent that they are intercorrelated. Thus, the marginal effect of, say, F_i may be much larger than $350 even when averaged over the entire urban area. The true marginal effect (β_1) of this variable is being systematically underestimated because a larger dwelling is typically found in a less-accessible location where prices are correspondingly lower. In general, the biasing effect on either F_i or L_i may be positive, negative, or zero depending on the extent and direction of intercorrelation among these and the excluded D_i.

The second respect in which the missing variable problem is insidious is subtle but no less important. Let us suppose that the missing variable D_i is not perfectly correlated with F_i and L_i. In that case, part of the effect of D_i on P_i will show up in (2) via the random error, u_i which represents the combined effects of all excluded variables. Because D_i has an effect on P_i and because part of this effect cannot be "loaded" onto F_i or L_i, it appears along with any number of other similar effects in the term. Usually in practice, a general accessibility measure does not change quickly from one zone to its neighbor. If i and j are adjacent, D_i and D_j often are quite similar compared to the differences between central and fringe zones. Thus, the excluded variable D_i could impart a spatial dependence to u_i, if it dominates the remaining excluded variable effects. This spatial dependence of the unobserved errors on other nearby errors is called spatial autocorrelation.

The effect of dependence among the u_i terms is twofold. First, it makes OLS estimates of the t-test values unreliable. In other words, the t-values of 4.20 and 5.11 in (1) no longer tell us whether or not F_i or L_i respectively has a significant effect on average house price. We thus cannot assess how much sampling variability should be attached to slope estimates such as 350 and 175 in (1). Secondly, it is no longer true that OLS estimates are relatively efficient: i.e., have a small sampling variability associated with them. Instead, it can be shown that a different kind of estimate, based on Generalized Least Squares (GLS), is also unbiased but more efficient and thus preferable.

Thus, the exclusion of an important independent variable makes it difficult to interpret the results of an OLS regression analysis. It is not clear whether OLS gives an unbiased measure of the marginal effect of an independent variable on the dependent variable. Further, to the extent that the excluded variable imparts a spatial dependence to the unobserved random error term in the hypothesized model (2), it makes the t-tests and an assessment of sampling variability unreliable. In a worst-case scenario, we end up with biased slope estimates whose significance cannot be tested.

The same problems in regression analysis apply in two other cases besides the missing variables case. One case is that of an improper structural form. Suppose, for example, that P_i is a log-linear, not a linear, function of F_i and L_i. By improperly using a linear structural form, we mis-estimate the marginal effects of the independent variables. Also, the use of a linear form effectively "warps" the original log-linear form error terms creating the possibility of either spatial or some other dependency among them. The second case concerns systematic measurement errors in the dependent variable. Suppose for example that house prices are consistently under-estimated in one part of the urban area compared to the rest. To the extent that F_i or L_i are either consistently high or low in this part of the city, the

OLS slope coefficients will be biased. Also, this measurement error may well be reflected in the random error terms which could thus be spatially dependent.

2. WHAT DOES SPATIAL AUTOCORRELATION TELL US?

The above introduction to spatial autocorrelation may appear round-about compared with standard introductions to the topic. Most papers on spatial autocorrelation in regression analysis begin directly by defining the problem as one of spatial dependence without referring to the missing variable, improper structural form, or measurement error problem. They propose Generalized Least Squares or some variant as a computational method for "solving" the spatial autocorrelation problem. Such solution techniques are discussed in Section 5 below. In this paper, spatial autocorrelation is not treated as a problem to be solved in and of itself. Rather, it is portrayed as a manifestation of the missing variable, improper structural form, or measurement error problems.

The approach taken here has three advantages:

(1) It makes clear just why spatial autocorrelation exists. Spatial auto-correlation is neither a magical phenomenon nor a statistical nuisance against which empirical geographers must be prepared. It is a specific consequence of the failure to accurately measure or specify variables or relationships.

(2) It suggests how spatial autocorrelation might be corrected. As in any scientific enquiry, one should ask why spatial autocorrelation is occurring. Having clarified that a missing variable, improper structural form, or measurement error is the problem, one should move to redress the problem with new data collection or estimation. In this process, the detection of spatial autocorrelation becomes an important part of the discovery process in research whereby one extends and improves upon a current base of knowledge.

(3) It suggests that to look at spatial autocorrelation as merely a statistical nuisance to be corrected can be dangerous. A missing variable, an improper structural form, or measurement error can also bias the estimated marginal effects of included independent variables. Computational approaches such as GLS which can correct for the spatial dependency problem cannot identify these potential biases.

To some empirical geographers, these stern admonitions are a cold comfort. Having undertaken an extensive regression analysis, they are reminded at the end of the ever-present "danger" of spatial autocorrelation. They apply one of the techniques to be described in Section 4 below for its identification and, to their consternation, detect its presence. However, at that stage, there is little inclination to set out on a new process of discovery to extend their current knowledge. They want the quick fix.

I do not mean to be overly critical here. At times, any empiricist can get caught in such a situation and I would, upon reflection, include myself here. The computational methods discussed in Section 5 below do provide some immediate relief from spatial autocorrelation. However, these are relief from a symptom of a problem not a cure for the problem itself.

With this caution in mind, let us turn to three questions. How do we formally model autocorrelation? How do we identify when spatial auto-correlation is present? How do we "correct" for it? These three questions are the subjects of the next three sections respectively.

Before turning to these topics, however, let us note two important features of spatial autocorrelation: the scale effect and process dependency. To an empirical geographer, these features can be both frustrating and the source of much richness. Let us illustrate them by two examples.

Example A: You are studying the yield per hectare of a certain type of wheat to the application rate of a certain type of fertilizer. Your data are zonal average yields and average application rates. You suspect that a second independent variable affecting yield is weather. This omitted variable should vary systematically over space being similar for adjacent locations. Is the missing weather variable the cause of an observed spatial autocorrelation problem?

Example B: You are studying the adoption of a new farming technology within a region. You hypothesize that because the new technology is costly, it will be adopted quickly in affluent farming areas and more slowly, if at all, in others. You think that a second (omitted) independent variable affecting adoption on one farm is the successful adoption of the technology by its neighbors: a "show and tell" or contagion effect. Is this missing contagion effect the cause of the observed spatial autocorrelation?

The answer to both of the above questions is "perhaps". In Example A, the geographic size of a zone is important. If the zones are so small that the entire study area is within one localized weather region, the spatial variability of weather may be negligible and thus not contribute to spatial

autocorrelation. At the other extreme, the zones may be so large that correlation between average weather conditions in adjacent zones is small.
Presumably, somewhere in between are geographic scales (i.e., sizes of zone)
where there is substantial spatial variability in weather between zones and yet
a substantial correlation between patterns in adjacent zones.

In Example B, the contagion effect may well be different depending
on how long the innovation has been around. In the early days of the spread
of the innovation, the contagion effect would be quite strong if there are
many potential users who are merely awaiting some display of, or local
comment on, the new technology. Later, after the technology has been
widely adopted, the contagion effect may be quite small in that the remaining
non-adopters have had opportunities to see the innovation in place but have
not implemented it. Such non-adoptors may not be easily converted simply
by the proximity of numerous adopters. If the contagion variable were
omitted, one might thus expect spatial autocorrelation whose intensity
or nature changes with the maturation of the innovation diffusion. In general,
the nature of the spatial autocorrelation present changes with the process
being studied.

These two examples illustrate an important point. Other researchers
may find a spatial autocorrelation problem when they regress, say, yield
against fertilizer application. However, you may not find a similar result in
your own work if you are dealing with a different geographic scale or a
different process or phase of a process. Such complexities may seem confusing.
They should not. Most geographical processes are rich in detail and complexity. An analysis of spatial autocorrelation can help us to understand more
fully how and why these processes operate.

3. THE IDENTIFICATION OF SPATIAL AUTOCORRELATION

Suppose we wish to estimate a linear model such as (2) above and want to
know if the u_i terms are spatially dependent. How would we detect spatial
autocorrelation? This question really poses two problems. First, we cannot
observe the u_i terms directly. If we cannot observe them, how can we tell
whether or not they are spatially dependent? The answer is that we must
develop estimates of the u_i's. Some estimation procedures and their limitations
are discussed in Section 3.1. Secondly, we must use these estimates of the
u_i terms to measure the extent of autocorrelation. How do we do this?
Some approaches are discussed in Section 3.2.

3.1 Estimation of Unobserved Random Errors

Let us begin here by specifying a linear model in matrix form. As is well-known, any linear model such as (2) above can be written as

$$Y = X\beta + u,$$

(3)

where Y and u are $n \times 1$ matrices, β is a $k \times 1$ matrix, X is $n \times k$, n is the number of observations, and k is the number of independent variables plus one (for the intercept). The first column of X is a unit vector and each succeeding column is a vector of n observations, one column per independent variable.

Consider as a working example, the data presented in the first three columns of Table I. There are $n = 10$ observations. $X1$ and $X2$ are the in-

TABLE I Some hypothetical data

Observation	Y	X1	X2	Contiguity matrix
A	2.5	3.8	2.2	0 0 1 0 0 0 0 0 0 0
B	1.9	4.0	2.0	0 0 1 0 0 0 0 0 1 0
C	1.4	3.8	2.1	1 1 0 1 0 0 0 0 0 0
D	2.0	3.7	1.8	0 0 1 0 1 0 1 0 0 0
E	1.6	3.6	1.7	0 0 0 1 0 1 1 1 0 1
F	3.6	3.3	1.6	0 0 0 0 1 0 0 0 0 1
G	2.1	3.8	1.7	0 0 0 1 1 0 0 1 1 1
H	2.1	3.9	1.6	0 0 0 0 1 0 1 0 1 1
I	3.6	4.2	1.8	0 1 0 0 0 0 1 1 0 0
J	2.4	3.6	1.4	0 0 0 0 1 1 1 1 0 0

dependent variables so $k = 3$. The X matrix is given by

$$X = \begin{bmatrix} 1 & 3.8 & 2.2 \\ 1 & 4.0 & 2.0 \\ 1 & 3.8 & 2.1 \\ 1 & 3.7 & 1.8 \\ 1 & 3.6 & 1.7 \\ 1 & 3.3 & 1.6 \\ 1 & 3.8 & 1.7 \\ 1 & 3.9 & 1.6 \\ 1 & 4.2 & 1.8 \\ 1 & 3.6 & 1.4 \end{bmatrix}$$

and $\mathbf{Y}$ is a 10×1 matrix composed of the left column of numbers in Table I. The β and $\mathbf{u}$ matrices are, of course, unobservable.

In Ordinary Least Squares (OLS), β is approximated by $\hat{\beta}$ where

$$\hat{\beta} = (\mathbf{X'X})^{-1} \mathbf{X'Y}. \tag{4}$$

For the sample data in Table I, one would obtain[3]

$$(\mathbf{X'X})^{-1} = \begin{bmatrix} 26.5386 & -6.7274 & -0.6014 \\ -6.7274 & 2.1967 & -0.8683 \\ -0.6014 & -0.8683 & 2.1647 \end{bmatrix} \quad \mathbf{X'Y} = \begin{bmatrix} 23.2 \\ 87.39 \\ 41.09 \end{bmatrix} \text{ and } \hat{\beta} = \begin{bmatrix} 3.0812 \\ 0.2177 \\ -0.8839 \end{bmatrix}. \tag{5}$$

The observed regression residuals matrix, $\mathbf{e}$, is formed by $\mathbf{e} = \mathbf{Y} - \mathbf{X}\hat{\beta}$ which after substitution from (4) yields, alternatively,

$$\mathbf{e} = \mathbf{MY}, \tag{6}$$

where $\mathbf{M} = \mathbf{I} - \mathbf{X}(\mathbf{X'X})^{-1} \mathbf{X'}$ and $\mathbf{I}$ is an $n \times n$ identity matrix.

For the sample data, one obtains

$$\mathbf{M} = \begin{bmatrix} 5555 & -2142 & -3584 & -1289 & -718 & -727 & -138 & 1014 & 161 & 1867 \\ -2142 & 7722 & -1887 & -799 & -222 & 1002 & -867 & -935 & -2414 & 543 \\ -3584 & -1887 & 7061 & -1207 & -765 & -730 & -359 & 490 & -190 & 1170 \\ -1289 & -799 & -1207 & 8878 & -1202 & -1607 & -877 & -632 & -310 & -955 \\ -718 & -222 & -765 & -1202 & 8456 & -2478 & -954 & -706 & 274 & -1686 \\ -727 & 1002 & -730 & -1607 & -2478 & 4917 & -743 & 122 & 2730 & -2487 \\ -138 & -867 & -359 & -877 & -954 & -743 & 8758 & -1607 & -1597 & -1617 \\ 1014 & -935 & 490 & -632 & -706 & 122 & -1607 & 7418 & -2885 & -2278 \\ 161 & -2414 & -190 & -310 & 274 & 2730 & -1597 & -2885 & 5011 & -781 \\ 1867 & 543 & 1170 & -955 & -1686 & -2487 & -1617 & -2278 & -781 & 6224 \end{bmatrix} \quad \mathbf{e} = \begin{bmatrix} 5359 \\ -2485 \\ -6525 \\ -2959 \\ -7625 \\ 12144 \\ -3061 \\ -4162 \\ 11952 \\ -2277 \end{bmatrix} \tag{7}$$

where the entries have been multiplied by $10\,000$ for ease of presentation.

The Gauss-Markov Theorem asserts that $\hat{\beta}$ is a Best Linear Unbiased (BLU) estimator of β, if the following assumptions are met:

(i) $E(\mathbf{u}) = \emptyset$
(ii) $\mathrm{Cov}(\mathbf{u}) = \sigma_u^2 \mathbf{I}$
(iii) $\mathbf{X}$ is of rank k
(iv) $\mathbf{X}$ is nonrandom.

Let us focus here on assumptions (i) and (ii). Assumption (i) asserts that the unobserved random errors have a zero expected value. This is innocuous enough. Assumption (ii) states that the random error terms are homoscedastic and independent. If spatial autocorrelation is present, it is this assumption which is violated.

Since one cannot observe $\mathbf{u}$ directly, a common practice is to use $\mathbf{e}$ as an estimate. Much the same as $\hat\beta$ estimates β, it is argued that e estimates u. But, are the observed regression residuals "good" approximations to unobserved error terms? If one takes (6) and substitutes in (3), one gets

$$e = Mu.$$

Taking the expected value of both sides and invoking assumptions (i) and (iv) yields

$$E(e) = \emptyset$$

so that e, like u, has a zero expected value. Thus, e is unbiased. In this sense, the two are similar. However, the covariance matrix of e under assumptions (i) to (iv) is given by

$$Cov(e) = E(ee') = \sigma_u^2 M. \tag{8}$$

Unlike u, e does not have a scalar covariance matrix ($\sigma_u^2\ I$). In other words, even when the unobserved random errors are homoscedastic and independent, the observed errors will not tend to be so. For example, the covariance between the error terms for observations C and J; $E(u_3 u_{10})$, is zero by assumption (ii) but $E(e_3 e_{10}) = 0.1170\ \sigma_u^2$ from (6) and (7). Because of this, observing a dependence among OLS regression residuals does not necessarily imply a dependence among the unobserved random errors.

It should be remembered here that the covariance matrix in (8) represents expected values. It is the average of a large number of different samples of ee' matrices when assumptions (i) to (iv) hold. Because of sampling variability, the ee' matrix for any one sample may deviate from $\sigma_u^2\ M$. In our numerical example, for instance, ee' is computed from (7) as the following:

$$
ee' = \begin{bmatrix}
2871 & -1524 & -3497 & -1586 & -4086 & 6508 & -1640 & -2230 & 6405 & -1220 \\
-1524 & 809 & 1856 & 842 & 2169 & -3455 & 871 & 1184 & -3400 & 648 \\
-3497 & 1856 & 4258 & 1931 & 4976 & -7924 & 1997 & 2716 & -7799 & 1486 \\
-1586 & 842 & 1931 & 876 & 2256 & -3594 & 906 & 1232 & -3537 & 674 \\
-4086 & 2169 & 4976 & 2256 & 5815 & -9260 & 2334 & 3174 & -9114 & 1736 \\
6508 & -3455 & -7924 & -3594 & -9260 & 14748 & -3717 & -5055 & 14515 & -2765 \\
-1640 & 871 & 1997 & 906 & 2334 & -3717 & 937 & 1274 & -3658 & 697 \\
-2230 & 1184 & 2716 & 1232 & 3174 & -5055 & 1274 & 1733 & -4975 & 948 \\
6405 & -3400 & -7799 & -3537 & -9114 & 14515 & -3658 & -4975 & 14285 & -2721 \\
-1220 & 648 & 1486 & 674 & 1736 & -2765 & 697 & 948 & -2721 & 518
\end{bmatrix} \tag{9}
$$

As in (7), each entry has been multipled by 10000 for ease of presentation.

The route pursued by almost all spatial autocorrelation analysts is to ask whether a sample ee' such as (9) is likely to be drawn from a parent of $\sigma_u^2\ M$. If it is unlikely, the conclusion is that $Cov(e) \neq \sigma_u^2\ M$. However, this implies that at least one of the assumptions of the Gauss-Markov Theorem does not hold, otherwise the Cov(**e**) would have to be σ_u^2 **M**. Spatial autocorrelation tests, in particular, investigate the failure of assumption (ii) as is explained below in Sections 4 and 5.

Recently Cliff and Ord (1973; pp. 97–99) and Brandsma and Ketellapper (1979) have proposed an alternative route. Rather than using OLS residuals, they suggest, following the econometric work of Theil, using Linear Unbiased Scalar-covariance (LUS) residuals. LUS estimators are a class of residual estimates which have a scalar covariance matrix not unlike σ_u^2 **I** for **u**. There are several different LUS estimators currently in use, each based on a different criterion and each producing a different set of residuals from the same set of sample data. Brandsma and Ketellapper (1979; p. 117) discuss two of these.

The main shortcoming of the LUS approach is that not all error terms can be estimated simultaneously. If there are n observations and k parameters (intercept plus slope coefficients), only up to n-k residuals can be independently estimated. Further, the LUS residual estimate for an observation varies depending on which other k observations have been excluded. In our above example, where $k = 3$, the LUS residual estimate for observation D when A, B, and C are excluded will be different, for example, from that obtained when A, G, and J are excluded. This necessitates a decision rule for deciding which k observations are to be excluded. In spatial analysis, no conventions have arisen to date in this regard although Brandsma and Ketellapper (1979, p. 117) do offer some suggestions.

3.2. *The Representation of Spatial Autocorrelation*

To begin our discussion, consider the random error term u_i for observation i. Suppose that autocorrelation is arising because of a missing variable Z which takes on a value of z_i for observation i.[4] Further, let us assume that u_i is a linear combination of z_i and an independent random component, v_i; that is,

$$u_i = \gamma z_i + v_i \qquad\qquad i = 1, 2, \ldots, n, \qquad\qquad (10)$$

where γ is a parameter measuring the marginal expected effect of z_i on the dependent variable. Taking (10) for two observations, i and j, yields

$$E(u_i u_j) = \gamma^2 z_i z_j$$

Thus, the spatial autocorrelation of u_i is linked to the spatial covariance of the omitted variable Z and to γ.

It is not always, or even often, the case that we can identify the source of the autocorrelation well enough to specify a model such as (10). Virtually all spatial autocorrelation analysts begin with a somewhat different formulation. As in (10), they argue that each u_i is the sum of two components; one that varies systematically across space and one that is an independent random component. The latter, the v_i term, is effectively a random error within a random error. Unlike (10), the spatially systematic component is related to the random errors for nearby observations.

$$u_i = f(u_1, u_2, \ldots, u_n) + v_i \qquad i = 1, 2, \ldots, n. \tag{11}$$

In (11), "f" is the systematic spatial component and v_i is, as before, the independent random component. Typically, it is assumed that $E(\mathbf{V}) = \mathbf{0}$ and $\text{Cov}(\mathbf{V}) = \sigma_v^2 \mathbf{I}$ where $\mathbf{V}$ is the $n \times 1$ matrix of v_i terms.

While they may disagree on methods of estimation or other issues, analysts have universally accepted the paradigm of (11). However, it is not clear that (11) is necessarily a good way of characterizing the problem. It may commit us to a causal mechanism which was never intended. Reconsider the wheat yield problem in Example A above and suppose that spatial autocorrelation is present because of the missing variable "weather". Suppose further that there are other missing variables as well but these engender no dependence and thus are included in v_i. Suppose that one of these other variables is the application of a new irrigation technique. In zone "i", this new technique is applied, leading to a higher yield than might otherwise be expected. In our model, this means a larger v_i, u_i, and thus y_i. However, the values of u (and thus y) will also change for other zones because error terms in (11) are in part dependent on u_i. If the only spatial mechanism present is the similarity of weather in adjacent zones, this change in v_i should not affect any other u_j. In this case, (11) is inappropriate. The widespread use of (11) does not discharge one of the responsibility of carefully considering the implications of using it in the specific context of one's own research problems.

Most of the work on spatial autocorrelation has assumed a special case of (11). In this special case, "f" reduces to a linear function:

$$\mathbf{U} = \rho \mathbf{A} \mathbf{U} + \mathbf{V}, \tag{12}$$

where $\mathbf{A}$ is an $n \times n$ matrix whose typical element, a_{ij}, gives the marginal direct effect of u_j on u_i and where ρ is a scalar. The elements of $\mathbf{A}$ may be defined in any fashion but the following rules are often observed:

(i) $a_{ij} = 0$ if "i" and "j" are not adjacent or if $i = j$

(ii) $a_{ij} > 0$ if "i" and "j" are adjacent

(iii) $\sum_j a_{ij} = 1$.

Rules (i) and (ii) are used where the hypothesized autocorrelation is of "first-order", i.e., the direct dependency is between adjacent neighbors only. Where the direct dependency is not thought to be of this kind, some other rules should be defined. Rule (iii) merely normalizes the **A** matrix so that each row sums to unity. Henceforth, it is assumed that these three rules hold whenever **A** is used.

In a linear formulation such as (11), it is easy to show explicitly the direct and indirect effects of an error term v_i as just noted. In (11), v_i directly affects u_i. It indirectly affects the u_j term for each zone j which is contiguous to i. Further, it also indirectly affects zones further away by a series of chain reactions where v_i affects u_i which affects u_j which affects u_1 and so on. The full set of direct and indirect effects are given by

$$U = (I - \rho A)^{-1} \, V \tag{13}$$

where $(I - \rho A)^{-1}$ exists. The typical element of $(I - \rho A)^{-1}$ shows the marginal direct and indirect effect of v_i on u_j.

In (12) and (13), it is sometimes helpful to distinguish between the structure and the intensity of the spatial autocorrelation process. The structure is the **A** matrix and the intensity is ρ. The structure indicates where the first-order connections are on the map and how important these are relative to one another. The intensity indicates how important the autocorrelation component is relative to the independent random error, v_i, in determining u_i.

There are situations where one might want to use the sample data to estimate both the structure and the intensity of the autocorrelation. This is not usually possible if there are only n observations: one per zone. After estimating k parameters, at most $n - k$ autocorrelation estimates are possible. If no restrictions are put on **A**, there are n^2 coefficients of the form a_{ij} and one ρ to be estimated. Clearly, $n^2 + 1 > n - k$. Even if one invokes rules (i) to (iii), there are still $n(k_1 - 1) + 1$ autocorrelation coefficients to be estimated where k_1 is the average number of neighbors per zone.

Basically, three kinds of solutions to this problem have been proposed. One is to pool cross-sectional and time series data. If one has data on n zones for each of t time periods, there may be enough data to estimate ρ, **A**, and β together. Arora and Brown (1977) discuss such an approach. The second is to reduce the number of coefficients in **A** to be estimated. This is achieved by assuming some additional rules about the a_{ij}'s. For example, one might assume that $a_{ij} = \gamma_i d_{ij}^\delta$ where d_{ij} is a measurable centroid-to-centroid distance, γ_i is a scalar to ensure rule (iii) is achieved and δ is a parameter to be estimated.[5] In this case, there are just two autocorrelation parameters, ρ and δ, to be estimated. The third approach is to arbitrarily assume an **A** matrix; i.e., specify the structure of the autocorrelation process *a priori*. In this last approach, just one coefficient, ρ, need be estimated from the sample data.

This latter approach is the one typically used. Its principal advantage is that it adds just one parameter (ρ) to be estimated. A variety of methods can be used to estimate ρ either alone or in conjunction with the β matrix of intercept and slope coefficients. Its principal disadvantage is that one must pre-specify the **A** matrix. If **A** is not correctly specified, the estimate of ρ may of course be meaningless. With this important reservation in mind, let us look next at methods of estimating the intensity of spatial autocorrelation given an *a priori* structure.

4. THE ESTIMATION OF AUTOCORRELATION INTENSITY

Let us reconsider the sample data in Table I above. The right-hand side of that table gives a contiguity matrix for the observations with entries of unity where i and j are contiguous observations and zero elsewhere. Observation J, for example, is contiguous to four others; E, F, G, and H. For each observation, let k_i be the number of contiguous zones (e.g., $k_J = 4$). Let $a_{ij} = 1/k_i$, if i and j are contiguous and zero otherwise. This defines one simple **A** matrix which satisfies rules (i) to (iii) above. Suppose that we want to estimate the intensity of autocorrelation given this **A** matrix.

There are basically two approaches to this estimation. One is to use some kind of two-stage estimation procedure. In a first stage, the intercept and slope coefficients are estimated. In the second stage, an estimate of intensity is derived based on these earlier estimates. The second kind of procedure simultaneously estimates both the β matrix and ρ. Let us consider each of these in turn.

4.1. *Two-Stage Estimation*

Suppose that you have already undertaken an OLS regression with the data from Table I and obtained the results as described in (5) and (7). Looking at the residuals in (7) and at the contiguity matrix in Table I, you wonder if there is a spatial autocorrelation problem.

A method of analysis is suggested by the following reworking of (12).

$$U = \rho U^* + V, \qquad \text{where } U^* = AU \qquad (14)$$

The typical element, u_i^*, of U^* is a weighted average for zone "i" of the unobserved errors in contiguous zones if rules (i) to (iii) are followed in defining A. Thus, (14) suggests that u_i is linearly related to u_i^*. Suppose we calculate an $e^* = Ae$ as the weighted averages of the observed residuals in contiguous observations. One could then estimate ρ in (14) by regressing e_i against e_i^* while constraining the intercept to zero.

In this method, one would estimate ρ as follows:

$$\hat{\rho} = (e'e^*)\,/\,(e^{*\prime}e^*) = (e'Ae)\,/\,(e'A'Ae). \qquad (15)$$

For our sample data, for example,

$$e^* = \begin{bmatrix} -.6525 \\ .2713 \\ -.0148 \\ -.5737 \\ -.0063 \\ -.4951 \\ -.1014 \\ -.0253 \\ -.3356 \\ -.0676 \end{bmatrix} \qquad \begin{array}{l} e'e^* = -1.1880 \\[2em] e^{*\prime}e^* = 1.2021 \end{array} \qquad \hat{\rho} = -0.988$$

Is $\hat{\rho}$ an unbiased estimator of ρ? In other words, would repeated samplings give an average $\hat{\rho}$ which tends towards ρ? This is a difficult question which has not been fully resolved, to my knowledge, in the literature. It appears that $\hat{\rho}$ will in general be biased and that the magnitude of the bias will depend on sample size, ρ, A, and X. However, just how large or small the bias is in absolute value is unclear in general.

It is possible to estimate ρ using a maximum likelihood (ML) method instead of OLS. Given the linear model (3) and the first-order linear spatial autocorrelation in (12), the log-likelihood function, L, can be written as

$$L = -(n/2)\ln(2\pi) - (n/2)\ln\sigma^2 + \ln|I - pA|$$
$$- (1/(2\sigma^2))\,((Y - X\beta)^1\,(I - \rho A)^{-1}\,(I - \rho A)\,(Y - X\beta)) \qquad (16)$$

In (16), $|\mathbf{I} - \rho\mathbf{A}|$ is the jacobian of the transformation between $\mathbf{U}$ and $\mathbf{V}$. Hepple (1976) and Ord (1975) assert that $|\mathbf{I} - \rho\mathbf{A}| = \pi_{i=1}^{n}\,(1 - \rho\lambda_i)$ where λ_i is the ith eigenvalue of $\mathbf{A}$. Therefore

$$\ln|\mathbf{I} - \rho\mathbf{A}| = \sum_{i=1}^{n} \ln\,(1 - \rho\lambda_i). \tag{17}$$

To maximize L, differentiate (16) with respect to ρ. This gives, using (17),

$$\frac{\delta L}{\delta\rho} = -\sum_{i=1}^{n} \frac{\lambda_i}{1-\rho\lambda_i} - \frac{1}{\sigma^2}\,(-\mathbf{Z'AZ} + \mathbf{Z'A'AZ}\rho) = 0 \tag{18}$$

where $\mathbf{Z} = \mathbf{Y} - \mathbf{X}\beta$.

Given $\hat{\beta} = (\mathbf{X'X})^{-1}\,\mathbf{X'Y}$ as an approximation to β, $\mathbf{e}$ as an estimate of $\mathbf{Z}$, and $\bar{\sigma}^2 = (\mathbf{e'e})\,/\,n$ as an estimate of σ^2, one can numerically solve (18) for the Maximum Likelihood estimate of ρ.

For the sample data in Table I, the 10 eigenvalues of $\mathbf{A}$ are

$$\begin{array}{ccccc}
1.0000 & 0.7539 & 0.4333 & -0.8365 & 0.1849 \\
0.0257 & -0.5885 & -0.4428 & -0.3083 & 0.2217.
\end{array}$$

Further $\mathbf{e'e} = 4.685$, $\mathbf{e'Ae} = -1.1880$, and $\mathbf{e'A'Ae} = 1.2021$. The value of $\bar{\rho}$, found numerically from (16), is -0.433.

$\bar{\rho}$ is absolutely smaller than $\hat{\rho}$. If the left hand term of (18), $-\Sigma_{i=1}^{n}\,\lambda_i\,/\,(1 - \rho\lambda_i)$ were zero, then (18) would reduce to (15) and $\bar{\rho} = \hat{\rho}$. However, this left-hand term is not typically zero but instead acts to "penalize" larger ρ estimates. Because of this, the ML $\bar{\rho}$ tends to be smaller than the OLS $\hat{\rho}$.

Is $\bar{\rho}$ preferable to $\hat{\rho}$? Ord (1975; pp. 121–122) argues in favor of Maximum Likelihood estimators because their variability is smaller for large sample sizes *vis-à-vis* the least squares estimators. However, like $\hat{\rho}$, $\bar{\rho}$ is not unbiased so that there is little to choose between them especially when dealing with smaller sample sizes.

4.2. *Simultaneous Estimation*

The methods discussed above are typically employed when one has already undertaken a regression analysis and has a set of regression residuals in hand. One typically is asking "Are these residuals evidence of spatial autocorrelation?". There is an alternative approach. One might begin earlier with an observed $\mathbf{Y}$ and an observed $\mathbf{X}$ matrix and ask "How can we jointly estimate all of the parameters of the following model?"

$$\mathbf{Y} = \mathbf{X}\beta + \mathbf{U} \qquad \mathbf{U} = \rho\mathbf{AU} + \mathbf{V} \qquad E(\mathbf{V}) = \emptyset \qquad \text{Cov}(\mathbf{V}) = \sigma^2\mathbf{I}$$

These parameters are β, ρ, and σ^2.

Let us illustrate this approach using the method of maximum likelihood. The log-likelihood function has been given already in (16). To maximize L, we differentiate first with respect to σ^2 and β.

$$\frac{\delta L}{\delta \sigma^2} = 0 \qquad \text{yields} \qquad \sigma^2 = (1/n)\, \mathbf{Z}'\, \mathbf{V}^{-1}\, \mathbf{Z} \qquad (19)$$

and

$$\frac{\delta L}{\delta \beta} = 0 \qquad \text{yields} \qquad \beta = (\mathbf{X}'\, \mathbf{V}^{-1}\, \mathbf{X})^{-1}\, \mathbf{X}'\, \mathbf{V}^{-1}\, \mathbf{Y} \qquad (20)$$

Next, substitute these into (16) to yield a "concentrated" log-likelihood function, L^*.

$$L^* = -(n/2)(1 + \ln 2\pi) - (n/2)\log \sigma^2 + \sum_{i=1}^{n} \ln(1 - \rho\lambda_i).$$

Maximizing L^* with respect to ρ yields the following first-order condition:

$$-\frac{n}{\sigma^2}\left(-\mathbf{Z}'\, \mathbf{AZ} + \mathbf{Z}'\, \mathbf{A}'\, \mathbf{AZ}\rho\right) - \sum_{i=1}^{n} \frac{\lambda_i}{1 - \rho\lambda_i} = 0. \qquad (21)$$

This condition differs from the earlier two-stage Maximum Likelihood estimator (18) in two important respects. First, it must be solved simultaneously with (19) and (20) unlike (18) wherein β (and therefore $\mathbf{Z}$) and σ^2 are estimated first using OLS. Secondly, an "n" appears which is not present in (18). For large sample sizes, the term in parentheses on the left of (21) comes to dominate. In other words, when n is large,

$$\bar{\rho} \simeq (\mathbf{Z}'\, \mathbf{AZ}) / (\mathbf{Z}'\, \mathbf{A}'\, \mathbf{AZ}). \qquad (22)$$

While keeping in mind the first distinction, (22) is similar to (15) suggesting the convergence of OLS and ML estimators at large sample sizes.

To derive these ML estimates, the following procedure is recommended:

1. Try an initial estimate of $\bar{\rho}_0$
2. Create $\mathbf{I} - \rho\mathbf{A}$ and $\mathbf{V}^{-1} = (\mathbf{I} - \rho\mathbf{A})'\,(\mathbf{I} - \rho\mathbf{A})$
3. Estimate β using (20)
4. Estimate $\mathbf{Z} = \mathbf{Y} - \mathbf{X}\beta$
5. Estimate σ^2 using (19)
6. Numerically solve (21) for $\bar{\rho}$. Call this estimate $\bar{\rho}_1$
7. Compare $\bar{\rho}_0$ in 1 with $\bar{\rho}_1$ in 6
   If same, stop.
   If different, set $\bar{\rho}_0 = \bar{\rho}_1$. Go to 2.

This procedure was applied to the sample data from Table I. Initially, $\bar{\rho}_0$ was set at zero. The procedure converged to $\bar{\rho} = -1.135$ after 4 iterations. A summary of the results at each iteration is presented in Table II.

TABLE II

Iteration values in simultaneous estimation via maximum likelihood using sample data from Table I

Iteration	$\bar{\rho}_0$	$\bar{\beta}_1$	$\bar{\beta}_2$	$\bar{\beta}_3$	Z' A' AZ	Z' AZ	$\bar{\sigma}^2$	$\bar{\rho}_1$
1	0.000	3.0812	0.2177	−0.8839	1.2021	−1.1880	0.4685	−0.851
2	−0.851	2.1337	0.5815	−1.1736	0.8203	−1.3678	0.3113	−1.118
3	−1.118	1.8607	0.6768	−1.2301	0.7705	−1.3788	0.2796	−1.135
4	−1.135	1.8441	0.6825	−1.2334	0.7677	−1.3792	0.2779	−1.135

Note: Convergence of procedure after four iterations (i.e., $\bar{\rho}_0 = \bar{\rho}_1$)

It is also possible, of course, to do simultaneous estimation using a least squares, rather than maximum likelihood, criterion, Here, the objective is to minimize

$$(\mathbf{Y} - \mathbf{X}\beta)' \, \mathbf{V}^{-1} \, (\mathbf{Y} - \mathbf{X}\beta), \tag{23}$$

where $\mathbf{V}^{-1} = (\mathbf{I} - \rho\mathbf{A})' \, (\mathbf{I} - \rho\mathbf{A})$.
Maximizing (23) with respect to β and ρ yields

$$\hat{\beta} = (\mathbf{X}' \, \mathbf{V}^{-1} \, \mathbf{X})^{-1} \, \mathbf{X}' \, \mathbf{V}^{-1} \, \mathbf{Y},$$
$$\hat{\rho} = (\mathbf{Z}' \, \mathbf{AZ}) \, / \, (\mathbf{Z}' \, \mathbf{A}' \, \mathbf{AZ}),$$

where $\mathbf{Z} = \mathbf{Y} - \mathbf{X}\beta$. Again, these estimates must be found iteratively following a procedure like that for the ML estimates above.

As noted at the outset of this paper, the issue of significance testing for the β and ρ estimates under either ML or OLS using either two-stage or simultaneous estimation are not extensively discussed here. The interested reader is referred to Hepple (1976) or Ord (1975) in the case of the ML method. In the case of least squares, the covariance matrix for $\hat{\beta}$ is $\sigma^2 \, (\mathbf{X}' \, \mathbf{V}^{-1} \, \mathbf{X})^{-1}$. The variance of an intercept or slope coefficient is given by the appropriate diagonal elements of this matrix. These variances can be contrasted with the OLS estimator which is given by $\sigma^2 \, (\mathbf{X}'\mathbf{X})^{-1}$.

5. CORRECTING FOR SPATIAL AUTOCORRELATION

As in Sections 3 and 4, let us continue to assume that the structure of autocorrelation, $\mathbf{A}$, is known *a priori*. One can then "correct" for spatial autocorrelation under two different circumstances: (i) ρ known and (ii) ρ unknown. Presumably, the second is the more common circumstance but by considering the "ρ known" case first, some important conceptual points can be made which are relevant to either case.

5.1 ρ Known

If ρ is known, the problem is simply to find a relatively efficient estimator for β (and σ^2). Using either a least squares or maximum likelihood criterion, one derives the same estimator for β namely

$$\hat{\beta} = \tilde{\beta} = (\mathbf{X}' \, \mathbf{V}^{-1} \, \mathbf{X})^{-1} \, \mathbf{X}' \, \mathbf{V}^{-1} \, \mathbf{Y}. \tag{24}$$

In least squares, this is usually called a Generalized Least Squares (GLS) estimator to differentiate it from the OLS estimator. $\hat{\beta} = (\mathbf{X}' \, \mathbf{X})^{-1} \, \mathbf{X}' \, \mathbf{Y}$.[6] The ML and GLS estimators for σ^2, $\tilde{\sigma}^2$ and $\hat{\sigma}^2$ respectively, are somewhat different, i.e.,

$$\tilde{\sigma}^2 = (1 \, / \, n) \, \mathbf{e}' \, \mathbf{V}^{-1} \, \mathbf{e} \quad \text{and} \quad \hat{\sigma}^2 = (1 \, / \, (n{-}k)) \, \mathbf{e}' \, \mathbf{V}^{-1} \, \mathbf{e}.$$

The ML and GLS estimator for β in (24) can be shown to be unbiased. This is also true however of the OLS estimator. The advantage of (24) is that it has a smaller variance. In other words, the values for β given by (24) are more likely to come closer to the true values more often than does the OLS estimator.

Let us not forget here, though, the argument of Sections 1 and 2 above. Spatial autocorrelation should not be viewed as a problem in and of itself. It is more correctly seen as a manifestation of the omitted variable, improper structural form, or measurement error problem. Typically, these problems create both spatial dependencies and biases. Correcting for spatial auto-correlation relieves the first but not the second. An estimator such as (24) may well give different numerical answers compared to OLS but these different answers will be no less biased.

To illustrate this last point, consider again the data in Table II. The OLS estimator (4) for our sample data gives, from (5).

$$\text{OLS: } \hat{\beta} = (\mathbf{X}' \, \mathbf{X})^{-1} \, \mathbf{X}' \, \mathbf{Y} = \begin{bmatrix} 3.0812 \\ 0.2177 \\ -0.8839 \end{bmatrix}.$$

Suppose $\rho = -1.135$ in fact. The GLS estimator is given by the bottom row in Table II, namely,

$$\text{GLS: } \hat{\beta} = (\mathbf{X}' \, \mathbf{V}^{-1} \, \mathbf{X})^{-1} \, \mathbf{X}' \, \mathbf{V}^{-1} \, \mathbf{Y} = \begin{bmatrix} 1.8441 \\ 0.6825 \\ -1.2334 \end{bmatrix}$$

assuming $\rho = -1.135$. These numerical estimates are different. However, both are unbiased estimators of β if spatial dependency is our only "problem". At the same time, if our problem is really an omitted variable, an improper structural form, or a measurement error which manifests itself in a spatial dependency, then there may also be a bias problem present in both the OLS and GLS estimators.

5.2. *Unknown* ρ

How do we "correct" for the effects of autocorrelation when its intensity is unknown? The problem here is to estimate ρ and correct for its effect on the OLS estimator. This, however, is what has been described already in Section 4.2. The procedures described there allow one to derive ρ and β estimates simultaneously. In this sense, our question has already been answered.

In this paper, issues relating to significance testing have been omitted. It should be remembered, however, from Section 5.1 above, that the principal advantage of these procedures is that they result in smaller variances; i.e., more reliable estimates. The reader is referred to the closing discussion of Section 4.2 for more information on variance calculations and significance testing.

6. CONCLUSION

While it is very difficult to provide a beginner's guide to spatial autocorrelation in regression analysis, such a guide is indispensable; not only has spatial autocorrelation much to offer empirical geographers in their everyday work, but also the "problem" of spatial autocorrelation has often been misunderstood. Specifically, I have forwarded the idea here that spatial autocorrelation is a manifestation of a "problem", not the problem itself. Further, it has been illustrated that the "problem" being manifested is not some magical phenomenon or statistical quirk. Rather, the "problem" which creates spatial autocorrelation is our imperfect understanding and measurement of the process we are studying.

Center for Urban and Community Studies
University of Toronto

NOTES

[1] These assumptions ensure a similar sample size from each zone.
[2] Specifically the OLS estimates have the lowest variance of any linear estimator. See Judge *et al.* (1980, pp. 15–16).
[3] Four decimal places are maintained in all data presented.
[4] It is assumed that z_i is expressed as a deviation from its mean.
[5] Arora and Brown (1977) discuss some other possibilities wherein the random error term for zone i has a regional and a local component.
[6] See, for example, Judge *et al.* (1980, pp. 261–267).

BIBLIOGRAPHY

Arora, S. S. and M. Brown: 1977, 'Alternative approaches to spatial autocorrelation: An improvement over current practice', *International Regional Science Review* 2 (1), 67–78.

Brandsma, A. S. and R. H. Ketellapper: 1979, 'Further evidence on alternative procedures for testing of spatial autocorrelation among regression disturbances', in C. P. A. Bartels and R. H. Ketellapper (eds.), *Exploratory and Explanatory Statistical Analysis of Spatial Data*, Martinus Nijhoff, The Hauge, pp. 113–135.

Cliff, A. D. and J. K. Ord: 1973, *Spatial Autocorrelation*, Pion, London.

Hepple, L. W.: 1976, 'A maximum likelihood model for econometric estimation with spatial series', in I. Masser (ed.), *Theory and Practice in Regional Science*, Pion, London.

Hordijk, L.: 1974, 'Spatial correlation in the disturbances of a linear interregional model', *Regional and Urban Economics* 4, 117–140.

Judge, G. G. *et al.*: 1980, *The Theory and Practice of Econometrics*, Wiley, New York.

Ord, K.: 1975, 'Estimation methods for models of spatial interaction', *Journal of the American Statistical Association* 70, 120–126.

Sen, A.: 1976, 'Large sample-size distributions of statistics used in testing for spatial autocorrelation', *Geographical Analysis* 9, 175–184.

GARY L. GAILE

MEASURES OF SPATIAL EQUALITY

1. INTRODUCTION

There has been an inequality of concern throughout history about equality as a social issue. This varying concern serves, in part, to explain the exclusion of equality in many theoretical contexts. Equality did have its moments in the intellectual sun under the pens of Aristotle, Hobbes, Rousseau, Marx and Mill. Yet, with the rise of capitalism, inequality came to be accepted as a transitional economic reality necessary for the engine of economic progress. Indeed, Kant decreed that inequality among men was a rich source of much that was evil, but also of everything that was good. Over time inequalities were to slowly decrease as economic systems matured.

Whether societal inequalities will be reduced in the long run remains an issue of speculation. *Spatial* inequality, however, has raised new issues. It, too, was ignored by most early spatial analysts. Planners generally assumed spatial inequalities would dissolve as nations became progressively integrated as transport costs were reduced. In the early 1960s, however, planners began to realize that increased national growth did not necessarily equate with national goals when that growth was unequally spatially distributed. Further, it was realized that trade-offs between growth goals of efficiency and distribution goals of equality were often required in planning (Gaile, 1977). To accurately predict the dual results of policy in terms of efficiency and equality requires the use of techniques to objectively measure spatial equality. These techniques are also useful in a wide range of contexts where distribution is a consideration.

2. CONSIDERATIONS IN THE MEASUREMENT OF EQUALITY

2.1. *Spatial versus Socio-Spatial Equality*

Spatial analysts often weigh each region equally when measuring equality. Thus, they measure simple spatial equality. If this approach is used as a method of measurement, planning for optimization might lead to investment in less-populated as well as less-developed regions. In human spatial

223

Gary L. Gaile and Cort J. Willmott (eds.), Spatial Statistics and Models, 223–233.
© 1984 *by D. Reidel Publishing Company.*

analysis, equality is socially as well as spatially conceived. Human spatial analysts thus face a more complex measurement problem than their colleagues in the physical sciences. When people are a factor in the equality measured, it is desirable to weight each region by its population share. The result is termed a measure of "socio-spatial equality". In the measures presented in this work, both "spatial equality" measures in which the regions are weighted equally and "socio-spatial equality" measures in which regions are weighted by population will be given.

2.2. *Scale Specification and Aggregation*

Moreso than many statistical techniques, the measurement of equality is sensitive to scale specification and aggregation. Ecological fallacy must be guarded against since distributional measures of which equality measures are a part are highly dependent on aggregation. Thus, in the measurement and use of equality measures, scale and level of aggregation must be explicitly specified and inferences and substantive analyses from measurements must be restricted to the scale used.

2.3. *Absolute versus Relative Equality*

Measures of absolute equality are dependent on the number of cases being measured. Thus the maximum and minimum values the measurement can obtain depend on the number of cases. A relative equality measure is independent of the number of cases measured, and its maximum and minimum values are fixed (Theil, 1967). To illustrate, compare the equality in a group of two cases versus a group of a thousand cases when one case has all of the variable being measured and the rest have none of it. In a measure of relative equality, the results are the same in both instances. In a measure of absolute equality, equality is less in the large group in which so many more have nothing, than in the group with only two cases. Waldman (1977) further disaggregates the classification of absolute and relative equality measures depending on how the measures treat null categories.

3. SIMPLE MEASURES OF EQUALITY

Several simple measures of equality have been proposed. While most of these are straightforward and easily understandable, they generally have mathematical properties which diminish their utility.

Perhaps the simplest measure in this group is a function of the range

$$SE_1 = (\text{maximum } x_i - \text{minimum } x_i) \, / \, \Sigma x_i,$$

where SE_1 is the first measurement of "spatial equality" presented, x_i is the measure of the variable for the ith region, and $\Sigma x_i = \Sigma_{i=1}^n x_i$, where n is the number of regions. This shorthand notation for summation will be used in all further equations unless Σ is otherwise scripted. The "socio-spatial equality" (SSE) version of this measure is

$$SSE_1 = \{\text{maximum } (x_i N_i) - \text{minimum } (x_i N_i)\} \, / \, \Sigma(x_i N_i)$$

where N_i is the population of the ith region. SE_1 and SSE_1 are the crudest of the equality measures, both being scale dependent (i.e., absolute) and insensitive to all variations other than at the extremes.

Another simple measure of spatial equality is the mean deviation

$$SE_2 = (\Sigma \, |x_i - \bar{x}|) \, / \, n,$$

where $\bar{x}$ is the arithmetic mean. The socio-spatial equality version of the mean deviation is

$$SSE_2 = \frac{\Sigma\{N_i \, | \, x_i - [\Sigma(x_i N_i) \, / \, \Sigma N_i] \, |\}}{\Sigma N_i}.$$

While SE_2 and SSE_2 are relatively easy to interpret, they are both absolute measures and are difficult to understand from a theoretical perspective. Equality measures should be sensitive to changes in rank and distribution. If there is a transfer of the variable measured from a higher to a lower ranked case (e.g., from rich to poor in the case of income), then an equality measure should shift towards equality. A disadvantage in SE_2 and SSE_2 is that they are not affected by transfers on the same side of the mean.

The standard deviation (SE_3) of a population is also often used as a measure of spatial equality

$$SE_3 = [\Sigma(x_i - \bar{x})^2 \, / \, n]^{1/2}.$$

The socio-spatial equality version (SSE_3) of the standard deviation is

$$SSE_3 = \{\Sigma \, [N_i(x_i - \bar{x}_p)^2] \, / \, \Sigma N_i\}^{1/2},$$

where $\bar{x}_p$ is the population mean. These measures require either assumptions of normality or transformation of the data in order to make them inferentially useful. Further, the measures are scale dependent, i.e., absolute. In terms of transfers within the distribution, a drawback of the standard deviation measures is that they weight transfers at the lower end of the distribution more heavily.

A modified version of SE_3 and SSE_3 can be attained by employing Pearson's coefficient of variation (SE_4) in which

$$SE_4 = 100 \, (SE_3 / \bar{x})$$

or its socio-spatial equality version

$$SSE_4 = 100 \, (SSE_3 / \bar{x}_p).$$

The coefficient of variation measures are highly affected by the value of the mean and share the distributional problems of the standard deviation. Further, in a hypothetical comparison of measures by Waldman (1977), the coefficient of variation measures yielded the highest maximum value (above 1.0) and thus may be construed as difficult to interpret. The square of this index has been used as another measure and Niehans (1950) has used a further modification.

The variance of the logarithms (SE_5) is yet another commonly used index

$$SE_5 = [\Sigma \, (\log x_i - \log \bar{x}_g)^2] \, / \, n = \Sigma \, [\log (x_i / \bar{x}_g)]^2 \, / \, n,$$

where $\bar{x}_g$ is the geometric mean calculated

$$\log \bar{x}_g = \Sigma \log x_i \, / \, n.$$

The socio-spatial equality version is

$$SSE_5 = \Sigma \, \{N_i \, [\log x_i - (\Sigma (\log x_i \cdot N_i) \, / \, \Sigma N_i)]^2 \}.$$

This measure is regarded as not as "convenient" as those using an arithmetic mean and is disadvantaged in being the "second-moment extension of the geometric mean" (Theil, 1967, p. 124).

The Herfindahl (1950) index (SE_6) was derived by squaring an index developed by Hirschman (1945). The index was used as a measure of industrial concentration and has been used by Britton (1967) and Hauser and Keeble (1971) who referred to it as the "I-index". The spatial equality measure is

$$SE_6 = \Sigma \, (x_i / \, \Sigma x_i)^2$$

and the socio-spatial equality measure is

$$SE_6 = \Sigma \{ [N_i (x_i / \Sigma x_i)^2] / \Sigma N_i \}.$$

The Herfindahl index is size-dependent (absolute) and it and related indices have been dismissed by Hart as "superfluous because they can be derived from the parameters of the underlying size distribution" (1971, p. 78).

Pareto (1897) proposed a universal law of income distribution which contained within it a measure of equality. According to Pareto, regardless of time, ideology, institutions or the type of society, income distributions tended to be described by

$$\log N_x = K - \alpha \log x,$$

where N_x is the size of the population with an income equal to or greater than x and K and α are constants. The absolute value of α is Pareto's index of equality. Soltow (1971) shows the statistical relationship in Pareto's law to be that of a straight line income distribution (after the axes have been transformed logarithmically) where α is a negative slope when N_x is a function of x. The spatial equality measure (SE_7) based on Pareto's law is calculated

$$SE_7 = \frac{\Sigma (\log R_i\, x_i) - (\Sigma \log x_i)\,(\Sigma \log R_i)}{\Sigma (\log x_i)^2 - (\Sigma \log x_i)^2},$$

where R_i is the rank of the ith case. The socio-spatial equality version is

$$SSE_7 = \frac{n\, \Sigma (\log Y_i - \log x_i) - (\Sigma \log x_i)\,(\Sigma \log Y_i)}{n\, \Sigma (\log x_i)^2 - (\Sigma \log x_i)^2},$$

where $Y_i = \Sigma N_i - \Sigma_{j>i}^n N_j$. Ross (1969) has challenged the universality of Pareto's law, thus the distributional basis of the measure has been questioned. Further, both SE_7 and SSE_7 have been found by Kravis (1962) to emphasize the higher values in the distribution.

4. LORENZ CURVE MEASURES

The Lorenz (1905) curve is the paramount graphical representation of equality. This diagrammatical tool allows for the visual and quantitative comparison of the cumulative relationship between two variables. The Lorenz curve can be defined mathematically as the curve whose ordinate and abscissa are Φ and F, such that

$$F(x) = \int_{-\infty}^{x} f(x)dx,$$

$$\Phi(x) = \frac{1}{\mu} \int_{-\infty}^{x} xf(x)dx,$$

where μ is the population mean of x. Convexity to the F-axis is a necessary condition for all Lorenz curves.

The commonest equality measure is the Gini (1913–14) coefficient which is a direct function of the Lorenz curve. It can be shown mathematically, following Kendall and Stuart (1958, p. 49) that the Gini coefficient is equal to twice the area between the line $F = \Phi$ and the Lorenz curve:

$$2 \text{ (area of concentration)} = \int_{0}^{1} F d\Phi - \int_{0}^{1} \Phi dF$$

and therefore

$$2\mu(\text{area}) = \int_{-\infty}^{\infty} F(x) \, x \, dF(x) - \mu \int_{-\infty}^{\infty} \Phi(x) dF(x)$$

$$= \int_{-\infty}^{\infty} x \, dF(x) \int_{-\infty}^{x} dF(y) - \int_{-\infty}^{\infty} dF(x) \int_{-\infty}^{x} y \, dF(y)$$

$$= \int_{-\infty}^{\infty} \int_{-\infty}^{x} (x - y) \, dF(x) \, dF(y).$$

Given $\int_{-\infty}^{\infty} \int_{-\infty}^{x} (x - y) \, dF(x) \, dF(y) = 0$, therefore

$$2\mu(\text{area}) = \frac{1}{2} \left[\int_{-\infty}^{\infty} \int_{-\infty}^{x} (x - y) \, dF(x) \, dF(y) + \right.$$

$$\left. \int_{-\infty}^{\infty} \int_{x}^{\infty} (y - x) \, dF(x) \, dF(y) \right]$$

$$= \frac{1}{2} \int_{-\infty}^{\infty} \int_{-\infty}^{\infty} |x - y| \, dF(x) \, dF(y)$$

$$= \frac{1}{2} \Delta_1.$$

The Gini coefficient is defined as

$$SE_8 = \frac{\Delta_1}{2\mu}.$$

A large class of distributions generate symmetrical Lorenz curves (Kendall, 1956, p. 185). Symmetrical Lorenz curves yield Gini coefficients which reflect skewness and kurtosis as well as dispersion (Hart, 1971, p. 74). A major difficulty of the Gini coefficient is its difficulty of measurement. Its use as a precise measure is severely limited by its "mathematical intractability" (*ibid*.). That geographers have consistently made errors in the formulation or calculation of the Gini coefficient is evidenced in King (1969, pp. 115–116), Smith (1975), Coates *et al.* (1977, p. 20) and Chu (1982). Smith (1982, pp. 364–365) demonstrates a method for calculation which is cumbersome and relies on graphics. There are simple approximations to the statistic (e.g., Morgan, 1962), but the correct Gini measure of socio-spatial equality is

$$SSE_8 = \tfrac{1}{2} \sum_{i=1}^{n} \sum_{j=1}^{n} \left| x_i y_j - x_j y_i \right| = \tfrac{1}{2} \sum_{i=1}^{n} \sum_{j=1}^{n} x_i x_j \left| (y_i/x_i) - (y_j/x_j) \right|.$$

The Gini coefficient does not allow for within and between set decomposition and is unduly influenced by values at the upper end of the Lorenz curve.

Schutz (1951) developed a simpler index which is also based on the Lorenz curve, but which is much simpler to calculate than the Gini coefficient. The Schutz index and scale modifications of it are often incorrectly labeled as Gini coefficient measures. The Schutz index of spatial equality is

$$SE_9 = \Sigma \left| (100 \, x_i \, / \, \Sigma x_i) - (100 \, / \, n) \right|$$

and its socio-spatial equality version is

$$SSE_9 = \Sigma \left| (100 \, x_i N_i \, / \, \Sigma x_i N_i) - (100 \, N_i \, / \, \Sigma N_i) \right|.$$

This index varies from 0 (at equality) to 200. It is the sum of deviations of the slope of the Lorenz curve from the diagonal. Vandenvries (1974) and Kuznets (1963) have used the index and it is sometimes termed the "Kuznets index".

Hall and Tideman (1967), Rosenbluth (1961) and Tress (1938) have proposed other Lorenz curve measures, but they are not preferable to the original Gini coefficient or the simpler Schutz index.

All Lorenz curve measures are based on ranked variables and are functions of the mean, thus implying some assumptions about the measure of equality used. Various Lorenz-based equality measures will rank equality differently if compared Lorenz curves intersect, largely because of different weightings in the situation of a transfer. The Schutz index is unaffected by transfers on the same side of the mean and the Gini coefficient weighs mid-distribution transfers more heavily than other transfers.

5. RELATIVE ENTROPY EQUALITY MEASURES

The last measure of equality to be reviewed is based on Shannon's (1948) measure of statistical entropy. This measure is a purely statistical index which can be derived through probability theory (Georgescu-Roegen, 1971). The measure is closely linked in the literature with the Second Law of Thermodynamics (Wilson, 1970). As a "social physics" analog, an entropy measure has several advantages (see Gaile, 1977). Yet the links between the statistical measure of entropy and the Second Law of Thermodynamics are convoluted. The late William Krumbein once remarked that it was unfortunate that these two very important concepts shared the same name.

A general relative entropic measure of spatial equality is

$$SE_{10} = \Sigma \left[(x_i / \Sigma x_i) \log_2 (x_i / \Sigma x_i) \right] / \log_2 n$$

and the socio-spatial equality measure is

$$SSE_{10} = \Sigma \left[N_i (x_i / \Sigma N_i x_i) \log_2 (x_i / \Sigma N_i x_i) \right] / \log_2 \Sigma N_i.$$

These two measures are part of a family of similar entropy measures which have been proposed. These measures are refinements on the general measure which allow for within and between set decompositions (Theil, 1972; Semple and Green, 1984), a completely sampled population (Walsh and Webber, 1977), considering the size of the regions explicitly (Batty, 1974) and comparing prior and posterior distributions (Kullback, 1959; Walsh and O'Kelley, 1979).

The general equality measure SSE_{10} is relative, thus varying from 0 to 1.0 (equality). The measure can be subtracted from 1.0 to yield a measure of inequality which lends itself more readily to disaggregation. The relationship between an inequality measure $(1.0 - SSE_{10})$ and a Lorenz curve is that the measure is a weighted average of the logs of the estimated slope of the Lorenz curve at each x_i (Hart, 1971).

The entropic measures are reasonably tractable and are not unduly affected by extreme values. They are, however, non-linear and somewhat difficult to interpret given that index values tend to be concentrated near one extreme of the range of possible values. A fuller discussion of the versatility and limitations of entropic equality measures can be found in Walsh and O'Kelley (1979).

6. CONCLUSION

Alonso's plea for "a simple and intuitively satisfactory measure of equality" (1969, p. 10) has yet to be fully answered. The best simple index — the Schutz index — has several statistical limitations. The entropic measures just are not that simple. The Gini coefficient has a history of misapplication along with its statistical limitations. As Sartre noted, attempting to attain equality is analogous to attempting to attain an understanding of the deity — noble, but impossible. Perhaps the same is true of a perfect measure of equality.

Dept. of Geography
University of Connecticut

BIBLIOGRAPHY

Alonso, W.: 1969, 'Urban and regional imbalances in economic development', *Economic Development and Cultural Change* 17, 1–14.
Batty, M.: 1974, 'Spatial entropy', *Geographical Analysis* 6, 1–32.
Britton, J. H.: 1967, *Regional Analysis and Economic Geography*, Bell, London.
Chu, D.K.Y.: 1982, 'Some analyses of recent Chinese provincial data', *Professional Geographer* 34(4), 431–437.
Coates, B. E., R. J. Johnston, and P. L. Knox: 1977, *Geography and Inequality*, Oxford, Oxford.
Gaile, G. L.: 1977, 'Effiquity: A comparison of a measure of efficiency with an entropic measure of the equality of discrete spatial distributions', *Economic Geography* 53(3), 265–282.
Georgescu-Roegen, N.: 1971, *The Entropy Law and the Economic Process*, Harvard, Cambridge.
Gini, C.: 1913–14, 'Sulla misura dell concentrazione e della variabilita dei caraterri', *Atti del Reale Instituto Veneto di Scienze, Lettere ed Arti* 53 (2).
Hall, M. and N. Tideman: 1967, 'Measures of concentration', *Journal of the American Statistical Association* 62, 162–168.
Hart, P. E.: 1971, 'Entropy and other measures of concentration', *Journal of the Royal Statistical Society* 134, 162–168.

Hauser, D. P. and D. E. Keeble: 1971, 'Manufacturing growth in Outer South-East England, Part 1', *Regional Studies* 5, 215–232.

Herfindahl, O. C.: 1950, *Concentration in the Steel Industry*, Unpublished Ph.D. Dissertation, Columbia University, New York.

Hirschman, A. O.: 1945, *National Power and the Structure of Foreign Trade*, University of California Press, Berkeley.

Kendall, M. G.: 1956, 'Discussion on Hart-Price', *Journal of the Royal Statistical Society* 119, 183–186.

Kendall, M. G. and A. Stuart: 1958, *The Advanced Theory of Statistics*, vol. I, *Distribution Theory*, Hafner, New York.

King, L. J.: 1969, *Statistical Analysis in Geography*, Prentice Hall, Englewood Cliffs.

Kravis, I. B.: 1962, *The Structure of Income: Some Quantitative Essays*, University of Pennsylvania Press, Philadelphia.

Kullback, S.: 1959, *Information Theory and Statistics*, Wiley, New York.

Kuznets, S.: 1963, 'Quantitative aspects of the economic growth of nations: VIII, distribution of income by size', *Economic Development and Cultural Change* 11, 245–276.

Lorenz, M. C.: 1905, 'Methods of measuring the concentration of wealth', *Publications of the American Statistical Association* 9 new series, 209–219.

Morgan, J.: 1962, 'The anatomy of income distribution', *Review of Economics and Statistics* 64, 270–283.

Niehans, J.: 1950, 'An index of the size of industrial establishments', *International Economic Papers* 8, 122–132.

Pareto, V.: 1897, *Cours d'economie politique*, vol. 2, Rouge, Lausanne.

Rosenbluth, G.: 1961, 'Round table – Gesprach über Messung der industriellen Konzentration', in S. Arndt (ed.), *Die Konzentration in der Wirtschaft*, Kuncker and Humboldt, Berlin.

Ross, M. H.: 1969, *Income: Analysis and Policy*, 2nd ed., McGraw-Hill, New York.

Schutz, R. R.: 1951, 'On the measurement of income inequality', *American Economic Review* 41, 107–122.

Semple, R. K. and M. Green: 1984, 'Classification in human geography', in G. L. Gaile and C. J. Willmott (eds.), *Spatial Statistics and Models*, 55–79.

Shannon, C. E.: 1948, 'A mathematical theory of communicating', *Bell System Technical Journal* 27, 379–423 and 623–656.

Smith, D. M.: 1975, *Patterns in Human Geography*, Crane Russak, New York.

Smith, D. M.: 1982, *Where the Grass is Greener: Living in an Unequal World*, Johns Hopkins, Baltimore.

Soltow, L.: 1971, 'An index of the poor and rich of Scotland 1861–1961', *Scottish Journal of Political Economy* 18, 49–68.

Theil, H.: 1967, *Economics and Information Theory*, North-Holland, Amsterdam.

Theil, H.: 1972, *Statistical Decomposition Analysis*, North-Holland, Amsterdam.

Tress, R. C.: 1938, 'Unemployment diversification of industry', *Manchester Scholar* 9, 73–86.

Vandenvries, R.: 1974, 'Income distribution in Peru after World War II', *The Journal of Developing Areas* 8, 409–420.

Waldman, L. K.: 1977, 'Types and measures of inequality', *Social Science Quarterly* 58, 229–241.

Walsh, J. A. and M. O'Kelley: 1979, 'An information theoretical approach to measurement of spatial inequality', *Economic and Social Review* **10**(4), 267–286.

Walsh, J. A. and M. J. Webber: 1977, 'Information theory: Some concepts and measures', *Environment and Planning A* **9**, 395–417.

Wilson, A. G.: 1970, *Entropy in Urban and Regional Modelling*, Pion, London.

ADVANCES IN THE ANALYSIS OF SPATIAL TIME SERIES

1. INTRODUCTION

Spatial time series is an expression coined to describe the dynamic relationships within and between points or regions distributed across space. The most comprehensive representation of such relationships is based on a form of systems structure developed by Bennett and Chorley (1978) and Bennett (1979) given in question (1):

$$
\begin{bmatrix} Y_{t1}^1 \\ \vdots \\ Y_{t1}^m \\ \cdots \\ \vdots \\ \cdots \\ Y_{tN}^1 \\ \vdots \\ Y_{tN}^m \end{bmatrix}
=
\begin{bmatrix}
S_{11}^{11} & S_{11}^{12} & \ldots & S_{11}^{1n_1} & \ldots & S_{1n}^{11} & S_{1N}^{12} & \ldots & S_{1N}^{1n_N} \\
\vdots & \vdots & \ddots & \vdots & & \vdots & \vdots & \ddots & \vdots \\
S_{11}^{m_1 1} & S_{11}^{m_1 2} & \ldots & S_{11}^{m_1 n_1} & & S_{1N}^{m_1 2} & S_{1N}^{m_1 2} & \ldots & S_{1N}^{m_1 n_2} \\
\cdots & & & & & & & & \\
\vdots & & & & \ddots & & & & \vdots \\
\cdots & & & & & & & & \\
S_{N1}^{11} & S_{N1}^{12} & \ldots & S_{N1}^{1n_N} & & S_{NN}^{11} & S_{NN}^{12} & \ldots & S_{NN}^{1n_N} \\
\vdots & \vdots & \ddots & \vdots & & \vdots & \vdots & \ddots & \vdots \\
S_{N1}^{m_N 1} & S_{N1}^{m_N 2} & \ldots & S_{N1}^{m_N n_N} & \ldots & S_{NN}^{m_N 1} & S_{NN}^{m_N 2} & \ldots & S_{NN}^{m_N n_N}
\end{bmatrix}
\begin{bmatrix} X_{t1}^1 \\ \vdots \\ X_{t1}^{n_1} \\ \vdots \\ X_{tN}^1 \\ \vdots \\ X_{tN}^{n_N} \end{bmatrix}
, \quad (1)
$$

where,

$$
X_t = \begin{bmatrix} X_{t1}^1 \\ X_{t1}^2 \\ \vdots \\ X_{t1}^{n_1} \\ \vdots \\ X_{tN}^1 \end{bmatrix} ; \qquad Y_t = \begin{bmatrix} Y_{t1}^1 \\ Y_{t1}^2 \\ \vdots \\ Y_{t1}^m{}_1 \\ \vdots \\ Y_{tN}^1 \end{bmatrix}
$$

$(n_1 + \ldots + n_N) \times 1$

$(m_1 + \ldots + m_N) \times 1$

235

Gary L. Gaile and Cort J. Willmott (eds.), Spatial Statistics and Models, 235–251.
© 1984 by D. Reidel Publishing Company.

and where S_{ij}^{kl} is the set of regression parameters relating endogenous and exogenous variables. These coefficients represent the interaction between exogenous variable k and endogenous variable l between any region i and region j. The diagonal elements give the interregional interactions between regions. There are N regions, each with m_j exogenous variables and n_i endogenous variables, and there may be different numbers of exogenous and endogenous variables in each region.

The spatial system structure of equation (1) is a very general representation; however, it is also very complex. As a result, various alternative approaches have been developed for special cases. The most important of these is the *leading indicator model*, where change in one variable in one region is used to forecast or extrapolate to another region (i.e. only one pairwise interaction in (1) is studied at any one time (King *et al.*, 1969); Haggett, 1971; Haggett *et al.*, 1977)); the *weights matrix model* is a development of the leading indicator approach where instead of using a single region, a weighted sum of changes in several regions is used to forecast in the region of interest (Cliff and Ord, 1973, 1980; Cliff *et al.*, 1975). *Purely spatial models* are a further approach where temporal pattern is suppressed and it is desired to model interactions on the plane, e.g., to extrapolate map pattern. The advantage of the system model (1) is that it allows simultaneous estimation methods to be applied directly. Hence, a substantial body of estimation theory can be applied directly to spatial time series problems, thus offering the major advantage that no new statistical sampling theory is required. However, a major disadvantage of representations such as (1) is the large dimension of the resulting estimation problem. It is for this reason that many practical applications are made with alternative models. However, equation (1) gives the more general approach which allows the more ready development of mathematical and statistical theory.

Considerable developments have been made over recent years with each of the representations of spatial time series and this review can only highlight the major lines of research which have emerged. The chapter attempts to review these developments in four main sections: (1) developments in identification and estimation; (2) models of changing parameters; (3) forecasting and control, and (4) research priorities.

2. DEVELOPMENTS IN IDENTIFICATION AND ESTIMATION

Identification is the term usually applied to specifying or defining the structure of models such as equation (1), whilst estimation applies to the determination of the values of their coefficients. It is the solution of these two issues to which considerable attention has been directed in the analysis of spatial time series. These problems are discussed here within their various subcategories.

2.1. Representation and Map Pattern

A major hurdle in the way of practical application and interpretation of both spatial time series and other spatial models is the specificity of each practical situation: the spatial arrangement, size, shape and organization of the spatial cells or lattice for which data are derived affects the spatial processes which can be identified and the parameters which can be estimated, i.e., model structure is not independent of the spatial data base adopted: the so-called 'Curry effect' (see Curry, 1972; Sheppard, 1979). This problem is of lesser importance if the data base is stable and it is not sought to make comparative studies. However, if the data bases are not compatible and require interpolation, or if comparative quantitative study is undertaken, then the results may be invalid. This results from the convolution of data *structure* with spatial time series *process*.

There are several separate but interacting issues involved in these effects to which considerable attention has been directed. First, there is *map pattern*: that the results of any finite sample analysis depends on the specifics of the sample structure of the data set (Curry, 1972; Johnston, 1973). The second issue is *spatial autocorrelation*: that any spatial structure in exogenous variables will seriously bias inferences that can be drawn as to relations with endogenous variables (Curry, 1972; Cliff and Ord, 1973; Cliff *et al.*, 1974, 1975, 1976; Curry *et al.*, 1975, 1976; Bennett, 1979; Sheppard, 1979). The third issue is that of *areal units*. Where aggregated data, such as those from the Census, are employed the individual objects of study cannot be accessed directly. For any set of individuals, there is a wide range of possible ways of aggregating and each will produce different results when statistical methods are applied to the resulting aggregated data. This problem, which has been extensively recognized in statistics (Gehlke and Biehl, 1934; Kendall and Yule, 1950), has only recently been approached by geographers (see Openshaw and Taylor, 1981), but there are now extensive simulation results available which demonstrate the effects of different zoning systems (Openshaw, 1977; Openshaw and Taylor, 1979, 1981). However, there is still no general theory which allows either the relation of aggregate data to individual data, or data affected by map pattern to generating process and this is a difficulty of which future research must be aware.

2.2. *Spatial Autocorrelation*

The theory of test statistics for the presence of a particular pattern of spatial autocorrelation has been one of the main developments of the late 1960s and early 1970s, especially deriving from the work by Cliff and Ord (1973, 1980) generalizing the Moran and Geary statistics. More recently, concern with spatial autocorrelation has shifted from one mainly of detection to one of model calibration and estimation with respect to underlying spatial process. This shift in attention is well-illustrated by Haining (1981b) who distinguishes two levels of conception of spatial realizations. At a first level is *spatial process* which requires mathematical statements about variables and their parameters, defining a system state with all possible values of variables spanning a state space. Spatial process is then conceived as the rule governing the temporal trajectory of the system as a chain of changes in state through time. *Spatial pattern* is the second level of information: the map of a single realization of the underlying spatial process. It is this second level which constitutes the data available for empirical analysis. For stochastic systems, this two-level conception is extended to a three-level one in which the under-lying process is stochastic giving a second level of the spatial probability distribution (random field) which is then observed as one map surface at a third level.

Considerable developments have now been made with statistical methods which seek to infer the structure of the underlying spatial processes from outcome data based on deductive theory of the underlying spatial process. Early work in statistics by Whittle (1954, 1963) extended by Besag (1972, 1974) has now been extensively developed by Haining for purely spatial cases. This work includes the development of significance tests for the Whittle r statistic and determination of whether underlying processes are autogressive or moving-average (Haining, 1977a, 1977b, 1978a); whether processes are unilateral or multilateral (Haining, 1977b); and estimating parameters in spatial process models (Haining, 1978a). These methods have been extended to central place populations (Haining, 1980), interaction models (Haining, 1978b, 1978c), and population distribution (Haining, 1981a, 1981b). Other recent work on this problem is that by Getis and Boots (1978) and Getis (1982) extending Ripley's (1977) work on spatial models and point pattern evolution. Burridge (1981) has sought a common factor approach to asymptotic tests for spatial autoregressive processes which defines conditions where models can be reduced to non-spatial processes with spatially auto-correlated disturbances.

Together with these developments of spatial process models, developments have also been made to refining and extending the spatial autocorrelation test statistics of Cliff and Ord. Hubert, *et al.* (1981) developed a generalized procedure for evaluating spatial autocorrelation, Besag and Diggle (1977) and Brandsma and Ketallapper (1979) developed simulation methods. The properties of spatial autocorrelation tests have been further developed in a wide range of sources of which the most important are Cliff and Ord (1980), Hubert (1978), Sen (1976), Sen and Sööt (1977), Shapiro and Hubert (1979), Sokal (1979) and Guptill (1975).

2.3. Identification and Estimation

As impressive as the developments with spatial autocorrelation are, few of these consider the relation of spatial pattern to spatial process and the way in which spatial time series can be used to reveal the latter. Major developments in the understanding of the properties of space-time correlation functions have been given by Griffith (1976, 1980, 1981) and by Hewings (see White and Hewings, 1980; Hooper and Hewings, 1981). These now allow a wider description of the properties, sample size characteristics, and wider applications of spatial autocorrelation and partial autocorrelation statistics applied as diagnostics of space-time processes.

Considerable developments in both identification and estimation theory have also been made by extending multivariate statistical estimation theory to space-time processes. As outlined in the introduction (1), this is one of the most important properties of the spatial systems representation adopted here. Early generalizations of multivariate estimation theory were those by Hepple (1976), Hordijk and Nijkamp (1977), Arora and Brown (1978) and Bennett (1979, Chapters 6 and 7). This work has now been extensively developed by Hordijk (1979), Otter (1978a) and Hepple (1979) to include most major examples of the general linear model for space-time systems (e.g., 2SLS, 3SLS, FIML, etc.) and Bayesian inference. The Bayesian method is particularly important since it indicates a means of overcoming many of the problems of statistical research which have been so widely castigated as positivism. These criticisms are particularly aptly applied to statistical inference using Neyman-Pearson theory. Bayesian approaches offer considerably improved alternatives to this classical approach since the intention is to explicitly use prior theory and information, it does not require repeatability of experiments and, instead of a decision as to acceptance or rejection, leads to the alternative of a confidence statement of degree of belief. Despite an early suggestion for Bayesian work (e.g., Curry, 1968), this has been largely neglected until the efforts of Otter, Hepple and more recently Wilson and Bennett (1984) to widen the range of methodological approaches which can be applied to analysis of spatial time series. This extension to Bayesian approaches should hold much for future research.

As well as developments in theory and methodology, there has also been considerable development of the applications literature of identification and estimation. Marchand (1981a, 1981b) develops one of the first attempts at use of maximum-entropy spectral analysis, whilst Jeffrey and Adams (1980) have extended the work of King *et al.* (1972) on applying factor analysis to spatial time series. Labor market applications with employment, unemployment and wage data remain one of the main areas of application, however. Major applications are Bartels (1979), Cook and Falchi (1981), Dunn (1981) and Martin (1981).

2.4. *Boundaries and Missing Data*

Despite their rather specific characteristics, these two issues raise considerable difficulties in the way of analysis of spatial time series which, like the map pattern problem, have often been conveniently ignored and this has led to considerable inadequacy in results. Most finite sample models are relatively sensitive to boundary conditions. Haggett (1980, 1981) summarizes the effect of internal and external boundary effects on models of trend surfaces, point patterns and distance distributions. Haggett suggests that in space-time problems such boundary effects can be modeled by catastrophe and bifurcation theory, although the solutions are by no means simple. More recently, simulation methods have been applied by Haining *et al.* (1983) to the assessment of the effect of missing data on model estimates. These results extend to the case of missing data at the boundary of the system of interest. Using the results of the statistical theory of Orchard and Woodbury (1972), Haining *et al.* demonstrate that missing data have considerable effects on model estimates. Alternatively, turning the problem around, they demonstrate that missing data (either internal or at the boundary) can be estimated optimally using the spatial process models discussed earlier.

3. MODELS OF CHANGING PARAMETERS

Ten years ago the notion of adaptation and change over time in the structure of models estimated for spatial data was barely perceived and little discussed.

Since the mid-1970's, however, various evolving parameter structures have been hypothesized for spatial time series applications and considerable advances have been made in both statistical technique and mathematical theory. Some of the earliest developments of changing-parameter models for spatial time series are those by Bennett (1975, 1976, 1978, 1979) and Martin (1978), using Kalman filtering and related methods. Much of the spirit of thinking of these developments has been applied to the developments by Cliff *et al.* (1980) who have combined Kalman filtering with the weights matrix model of spatial time series. This has been employed extensively for forecasting and simulating the spatial passage of epidemics with the main area of application being measles in Iceland. Subsequent work by Martin (1979, 1981) has extended the Kalman structure to applications with reduced form estimations of spatial patterns of wage inflation linked to developments of the Phillips-curve model.

One of the perennial problems with this area of work has been that of determining if patterns of parameter change which have been detected reflect significant and real shifts or are a purely random pattern arising from mis-specification or corruption from data errors or other instances of noise. Early applications of the methods to spatial time series used the Quandt likelihood ratio test to assess significance of shifts between two parameter regimes (Bennett, 1976) and this has been subsequently extended to the use of cumulative sum tests on the residuals (Bennett, 1979) using the results of Brown *et al.* (1978). This approach has now been extensively applied to unemployment time series by Dunn (1981, 1982) who has also developed a number of both *ad hoc* diagnostics of parameter changes and tests based on serial correlation of heteroscedasticity of the residuals. These tests derive from the statistical theory developed by Garbade (1977), Harvey and Collier (1977), Harvey and Phillips (1974, 1977) and Phillips and Harvey (1974). Results with each of these developments are extremely encouraging and should stimulate a wide range of further applications and developments of these methods in the future.

The development of changing-parameter models has been stimulated primarily by the availability of recursive estimators of both univariate and multivariate systems. Although most developments have relied on recursive forms of least-squares estimation, the theoretical developments which have been most stimulating have flowed from the use of Kalman filtering. Interestingly, this is a most general approach which does not depend solely on least-squares properties; indeed the results for Kalman recursive estimation can be derived by Bayesian, orthogonal projections and a number of other theoretical stances.

The Bayesian approach is particularly important in suggesting ways out of the methodological dilemmas of Neyman-Pearson theory and has been now given a considerable airing in the context of spatial time series by Hepple (1979) and Otter (1978a, 1978b).

A further development of changing-parameter models has been by use of two groups of techniques developed at the Department of Statistics, UMIST: evolutionary spectral analysis, and threshold autoregression. Evolutionary spectral analysis, due originally to Priestley (1965), has now been applied successfully to a number of spatial time series phenomena ranging from stream channels (Bennett, 1976) to air pollution (Bennett et al., 1976). Threshold autoregression and more general threshold models are the result of the work mainly of Tong (see Tong and Lim, 1980; Tong, 1980c) who has extended the theory to a wide class of phenomena and transformations. Particularly stimulating of future research and application in spatial time series is the suggestion of the close link of nonstationary parameter models with catastrophe theory. Speculated upon by Bennett and Chorley (1978), Tong (1980a, 1980b) has developed the more formal theory linking the canonical cusp catastrophe and threshold autoregressive models. This is developed for applications to sunspot and predator-prey models.

It is now becoming clear that catastrophe and bifurcation theory is likely to provide increasing stimulus to the development of adaptive spatial time series models over the next few years. Important early work with catastrophe theory of Amson (1972a, 1972b) has been developed by Wilson (1978) and his coworkers, to include developments also of more general dynamical systems in which bifurcation theory provides the main focus. Depending as it does on analysis of points of singularity in systems of related differential or difference equations, it is likely that bifurcation theory will prove to be an important stimulus to spatial time series. It is in such problems that the complex coupling of regional and dynamical behavior in highly interdependent systems gives rise to many complex singularities in manifolds of coefficient and control spaces (see Wilson and Bennett, 1984). Early developments of this work are encouraging for model choice models (Wilson, 1976, 1978), speed flow curves (Dendrinos, 1978a), central place studies (Casti and Swain, 1975; Mees, 1975), housing stock location models (Dendrinos, 1977, 1978b), and retailing location (e.g., Wilson, 1981; Harris and Wilson, 1978; Wilson and Clark, 1979).

4. FORECASTING AND CONTROL

Spatial time series models have been highly stimulative of development of both forecasting and control; perhaps, indeed more than any other statistical theoretical development in spatial analysis, spatial time series had led to a greater awareness of the potential and the difficulties of interfacing quantitative analysis with policy choices and planning. Major development of the spatial location aspects of control work has derived from the interfacing of traditional location-allocation models with dynamic equations of spatial evolution. Important theoretical and practical developments of this work have been made by Williams and Wilson (1976), Coelho and Wilson (1976) and Phiri (1979), with the main practical application being the allocation of retail and other stock in urban systems. Taking the stimulus of control applications to macro-economics (see, e.g., Chow, 1975; Pindyck, 1973), there have now been a wide range of applications of control theory approaches to large scale spatial problems. The largest scale of these are to management of river, estuarine and air pollution (Nijkamp, 1975, 1979; Nijkamp and Verhage, 1976) but there are also smaller scale studies with sediment movement, hydrology, plant growth and irrigation management (Bennett and Chorley, 1978; Lai, 1979).

More recently, however, there has been considerable attention devoted to two particular applications of optimal control to spatial time series. In the first of these, that of controlling growth in a national system of settlements, migration and job mobility have been determined as optimal instruments of control to achieve given objectives of regional concentration or regional balance (see MacKinnon, 1975; Evtushevko and MacKinnon, 1976; MacKinnon and Rogerson, 1981; Tan, 1979). The second area of application has been to financial resource allocation through systems of intergovernmental grants. In this case, the system dynamic is a model of changing needs and local tax resources, and the control instruments are local tax rates and higher-level government grants. Tan (1979), Bennett and Tan (1979a, 1979b, 1981), Bennett (1981, 1982), and Tan and Bennett (1984) develop a hierarchical control solution to this problem using a new set of algorithms in which state and/or control variables are subject to linear equality and inequality constraints.

Two major research problems in applications of spatial time series models to forecasting and control concern the relation of control to the underlying statistics of the system under study (see Chorley and Bennett, 1981). A first difficulty is that the system model is not usually known with certainty but is identified and estimated from time series data. This has important implications since it is usually not the case that a separation principle holds between attempts at estimation and control. Separate treatment of the two problems usually does not lead to attainment of a global minimum for control or an unbiased estimate for estimation (Åstrom and Wittenmark, 1971). The properties of solutions to this difficulty using either the self-tuning regulator, suggested by Åstrom and Wittenmark, or the learning algorithm suggested by Chow (1975), are not known for spatial time series and experience needs to be accumulated with both methods of approach.

The second research problem concerns the difficulty of identifying and estimating spatial systems which have been operating under policy feedback: so-called identification in the closed-loop. The problem is that when policy feedback is optimal, then forecasts and data on system endogenous variables are fed back to affect the values of system exogenous variables. As a result, the distinction of exogenous and endogenous variables break down and the model may become underidentified. The consequence is that the operation of the open-loop system (uncontrolled) may become undetectable. This problem has been discussed by Bennett (1978) and further theoretical work has been developed by Otter (1979a, 1979b). Solutions to the difficulty normally result in the necessity of using reduced form and other special estimators.

5. CONCLUSION: RESEARCH PRIORITIES

Since the central concern of spatial time series methods is with dynamics and change over space, this has directed attention away from problems which are ones mainly of spatial pattern and towards studies of spatial process. As a result, the research priorties for developments in the future can be expected to be ones which continue the development of process study. This has profound implicatons at all levels of study. At the methodological level, it suggests that increased attention should be directed at developing understanding of the generating process behind spatial pattern. This may lead, on the one hand, to the need to develop Bayesian methods which to date have been accorded only a relatively small place in the analysis of spatial time series, and on the other hand, to the need to develop better theory and solutions to interface behavioral models of process and pattern. One thrust of this interfacing must certainly come from better relations between micro and macro models. A further implication of process-oriented study is the need to more clearly understand the mediation of spatial process by the spatial structure of data. Although now widely recognized as a difficulty, there is still an absence of real theory to suggest how structure mediates process, and a complete absence of transformations to transfer from one level of discussion to another. These are priorities not just for spatial time series, but for the whole of spatial analysis.

Dept. of Geography
University of Cambridge

REFERENCES

Amson, J. C.: 1972a, 'The dependence of population distribution on location costs', *Environment and Planning* 4, 163–181.

Amson, J. C.: 1972b, 'Equilibrium models of cities: 1. An axiomatic theory', *Environment and Planning* 4, 429–444.

Arora, S. S. and M. Brown: 1979, 'Alternative approaches to spatial autocorrelation: an improvement over current practice', *International Regional Science Review* 2, 67–78.

Åstrom, K. J. and B. Wittenmark: 1971, 'Problems of identification and control', *Journal of Mathematics and its Applications* 34, 90–113.

Bartels, C. A. P.: 1979, 'Operational statistical methods for analysing spatial data, in C. A. P. Bartels and R. H. Ketellapper (eds.), *Exploratory and explanatory statistical analysis of spatial data*, Nijhoff, Leiden.

Bennett, R. J.: 1975, 'Dynamic systems modelling of the North West Region: 3. Adaptive-parameter policy model', *Environment and Planning A* 7, 617–636.

Bennett, R. J.: 1976, 'Adaptive adjustments of channel geometry', *Earth Surface Processes* 1, 131–150.

Bennett, R. J.: 1978, 'Forecasting in Urban and Regional Planning closed loops: the examples of road and air traffic forecasts', *Environment and Planning* A 10, 145–162.

Bennett, R. J.: 1979, *Spatial Time Series: Analysis – forecasting – control*. Pion, London.

Bennett, R. J.: 1981, 'A hierarchical control solution to allocation of the British Rate Support Grant', *Geographical Analysis* 13, 300–314.

Bennett, R. J.: 1982, 'A hierarchical control solution to allocation of the Rate Support Grant using representative needs as targets', *Transactions Institute of British Geographers N.S.* 7, 163–186.

Bennett, R. J., W. J. Campbell, and R. A. Maughan: 1976, 'Changes in Atmospheric Pollution concentrations', in C. A. Brebbia (ed.), *Mathematical Models for Environmental Problems*, Pentach, London.

Bennett, R. J. and R. J. Chorley: 1978, *Environmental Systems: philosophy analysis and control*, Methuen, London.

Bennett, R. J. and K. C. Tan: 1979a, 'Stochastic control of regional economies', in C. A. P. Bartels and R. H. Ketellapper (eds.), *Exploratory and Explanatory Statistical Analysis of Spatial Data*, Nijhoff, Leiden.

Bennett, R. J. and K. C. Tan: 1979b, 'Allocation of the U.K. Rate Support Grant by use of the methods of optimal control', *Environment and Planning* A 11, 1011–1027.

Bennett, R. J. and K. C. Tan: 1981, 'Space-time models of financial resource allocation', in D. A. Griffith and R. D. MacKinnon (eds.), *Dynamic Spatial Models*, NATO ASI, Sijthoff-Noordhoff, Alphen aan den Rijn.

Besag, J. E.: 1972, 'On the correlation structure of two-dimensional stationary processes', *Biometrika* 59, 43–48.

Besag, J. E.: 1974, 'Spatial interaction and the statistical analysis of lattice systems', *Journal Royal Statistical Society* B 36, 192–325.

Besag, J. E. and P. J. Diggle: 1977, 'Simple Monte Carlo tests for spatial pattern', *Applied Statistics* 26, 327–333.

Brandsma, A. S. and R. H. Ketallapper: 1979, 'A Biparametric approach to spatial autocorrelation', *Environment and Planning* A 11, 51–58.

Brown, R. L., J. Durbin, J. M. Evans: 1978, 'Techniques for testing the constancy of regression relationships over time', *Journal Royal Statistical Society* B 37, 149–192.

Burridge, P.: 1981, 'Testing for a common factor in a spatial autoregression model', *Environment and Planning* A 13, 795–800.

Casti, J. and H. Swain: 1975, 'Catastrophic theory and urban processes', IIASA. Report RM–75–14, Laxenburg.

Chorley, R. J. and R. J. Bennett: 1981, 'Optimization: Control models', in N. Wrigley and R. J. Bennett (eds.), *Quantitative Geography: a British view*, Routledge, London.

Chow, K. C.: 1975, *Analysis and Control of Dynamic Economic Systems*, Wiley, New York.

Cliff, A. D., P. Haggett, J. K. Ord, K. Bassett, and R. Davies: 1975, *Elements of Spatial Structure*, University Press, Cambridge.

Cliff, A. D., R. L. Martin, J. K. Ord: 1978, 'Evaluating the friction of distance parameters in gravity models', *Regional Studies* 8, 281–6.

Cliff, A. D., R. L. Martin, and J. K. Ord: 1975, 'Map pattern and friction of distance parameters: reply to comments by R. J. Johnston and by L. Curry, D. A. Griffith and E. S. Sheppard', *Regional Studies* 9, 285–8.

Cliff, A. D., R. L. Martin, and J. K. Ord: 1976, 'A reply to the final comment', *Regional Studies* 10, 341–2.

Cliff, A. D. and J. K. Ord: 1973, *Spatial Autocorrelation*, Pion, London.

Cliff, A. D. and J. K. Ord: 1980, *Spatial Processes: Theory and Applications*, Pion, London.

Coelho, J. D. and A. G. Wilson: 1976, 'The optimum location and size of shopping centres', *Regional Studies* 10, 413–421.

Cook, T. and P. Falchi: 1981, 'Time series modelling in a regional economy: an exposition of Box-Jenkins technique', *Environment and Planning* A 13, 635–644.

Curry, L.: 1968, 'Seasonal programming and Bayesian assessment of atmospheric resources', in W. R. D. Sewell (ed.), *Human Dimensions of Weather Modification*, University of Chicago, Dept. of Geography, Research Paper 105.

Curry, L.: 1972, 'A spatial analysis of gravity flows', *Regional Studies* 6, 131–47.

Curry, L., D. A. Griffith, and E. S. Sheppard: 1975, 'Those gravity parameters again', *Regional Studies* 9, 289–96.

Dendrinos, D. S.: 1977, 'Slums in capitalist urban setting: some insights from catastrophe theory', *Geographica Polonica* 42, 63–75.

Dendrinos, D. S.: 1978a, 'Operating speeds and volume to capacity ratios: the observed relationship and the fold catastrophe', *Transportation Research* 12, 191–4.

Dendrinos, D. S.: 1978b, 'Urban dynamics and urban cycles', *Environment and Planning A* **10**, 43–9.

Dunn, R.: 1981a, *Time Series Analysis in a Spatial Context*, unpublished Ph.D., University of Bristol.

Dunn, R.: 1982, 'Parameter instability in models of local unemployment responses', *Environment and Planning A*, 75–94.

Evtushenko, Y. and R. D. MacKinnon: 1976, 'Nonlinear programming approach to optimal settlement system planning', *Environment and Planning A* **8**, 637–654.

Garbade, K.: 1977, 'Two methods for examining the stability of regression coefficients', *Journal of the American Statistical Association* **72**, 54–63.

Gehlke, C. E. and K. Biehl: 1934, 'Certain effects of grouping upon the size of the correlation coefficient in Census tract material', *Journal of the American Statistical Association* **29**, 169–70.

Getis, A. and B. Boots: 1978, *Models of Spatial Processes: An approach to the study of point, line and area patterns*, University Press, Cambridge.

Getis, A.: 1982, 'Pattern change and distance variation in the square', *Geographical Analysis* **14**, 72–78.

Griffith, D. A.: 1976, 'Spatial structure and spatial interaction: A review', *Environment and Planning A* **8**, 731–740.

Griffith, D. A.: 1980, 'Towards a theory of spatial statistics', *Geographical Analysis* **12**, 325–339.

Griffith, D. A.: 1981, 'Interdependence in space and time: numerical and interpretative considerations', in D. A. Griffith and R.D. MacKinnon (eds.), *Dynamic Spatial Models* NATO ASI, Sijthoff-Noordhoff, Alphen aan den Rijn.

Guptill, S. C.: 1975, *Spatial Filtering of Normal Data: an Explanation.* Unpublished Ph.D., University of Michigan, Ann Arbor.

Haggett, P.: 1971, 'Leeds and lags in inter-regional systems: a study of the cyclic fluctuations in the south west economy', in M. Chisholm and G. Manners (eds.), *Spatial Policy Problems of the British Economy*, University Press, Cambridge.

Haggett, P.: 1980: 'Boundary problems in quantitative geography', in H. Kishimoto (ed), *Die Bedeutung von Grenzen in der Geographie*, Kimmerley and Frey, Zürich.

Haggett, P.: 1981, 'The edges of space', in R. J. Bennett (ed.), *European Progress in Spatial Analysis*, Pion, London.

Haggett, P., A. D. Cliff, and A. Frey: 1977, *Locational Analysis in Human Geography*, Arnold, London.

Haining, R. P.: 1977a, 'Model specification in stationary random fields', *Geographical Analysis* **9**, 107–129.

Haining, R. P.: 1977b, 'The moving average model of dependences for a rectangular plane lattice', *Transactions of the Institute of British Geographers N.S.* **3**, 202–225.

Haining, R. P.: 1978a, *Specification and estimation problems in models of spatial dependence.* Northwestern Studies in Geography No. 12. Northwestern University Press, Evanston.

Haining, R. P.: 1978b, 'Interaction modelling of central place lattices', *Journal of Regional Science* **18**, 217–228.

Haining, R. P.: 1978c, 'Estimating spatial interaction models', *Environment and Planning A* **10**, 305–320.

Haining, R. P.: 1980, 'Intraregional estimation of central place population parameters', *Journal of Regional Science*, 365–375.

Haining, R. P.: 1981a, 'Spatial interdependence in population distributions: a study in univariate map analysis. 1. Rural population densities; 2. Urban population densities', *Environment and Planning* A 13, 65–84, 85–96.

Haining, R. P.: 1981b, 'Analysing univariate maps', *Progress in Human Geography* 5, 58–78.

Haining, R. P., D. A. Griffith, and R. J. Bennett: 1983, 'Simulating two dimensional autocorrelated surfaces', *Geographical Analysis* 15, 247–255.

Harris, B. and A. G. Wilson: 1978, 'Equilibrium values and dynamics of attractiveness terms in production-considered spatial interaction models', *Environment and Planning* A 10, 371–398.

Harvey, A. C. and P. Collier: 1977, 'Testing for functional misspecification in regression analysis', *Journal of Econometrics* 6, 103–119.

Harvey, A. C. and G. D. S. Phillips: 1974, 'A comparison of the power of some tests for heteroscedasticity in the general linear model', *Journal of Econometrics* 2, 307–316.

Harvey, A. C. and G. D. A. Phillips: 1977, *Testing for Stochastic Parameters in Regression Models*. University of Kent, Dept. of Quantitative Social Science.

Hepple, L. W.: 1976, 'A maximum likelihood model for econometric estimation with spatial series', in I. Masser (ed.), *Theory and Practice in Regional Science*, Pion, London.

Hepple, L. W.: 1978, 'Forecasting the economic recession in Britain's depressed regions', in R. L. Martin, N. Thrift, and R. J. Bennett (eds.), *Towards the Dynamic Analysis of Spatial Systems*, Pion, London.

Hepple, L. W.: 1979, 'Bayesian analysis of the linear model with spatial dependence', in C. A. P. Bartels and R. H. Ketellapper (eds.), *Exploratory and Explanatory Statistical Analysis of Spatial Data*, Nijhoff, Leiden.

Hopper, P. M. and A. J. D. Hewings: 1981, 'Some properties of space-time processes', *Geographical Analysis* 13, 203–223.

Hordijk, L.: 1979, 'Problems in estimating econometric relations in space', *Papers, Regional Science Association* 42, 99–115.

Hordijk, L. and P. Nijkamp: 1977, 'Dynamic models for spatial autocorrelation', *Environment and Planning* A 9, 505–519.

Hubert, L. J.: 1979, 'Nonparametric tests for patterns in geographic variation: possible generalizations', *Geographical Analysis* 10, 86–88.

Hubert, L. J., R. G. Golledge, and C. M. Costanzo: 1981, 'Generalized procedures for evaluating spatial autocorrelation', *Geographical Analysis* 13, 224–233.

Jeffrey, D. and J. C. Adams: 1980, 'Spatial-sectoral patterns of employment growth in Yorkshire and Humberside, 1963–1975: A time series factor analytic approach', *Regional Studies* 14, 441–453.

Johnston, R. J.: 1973, 'On frictions of distace and regression coefficients', *Area* 5, 187–191.

Kendall, M. G. and G. U. Yule: 1950, *An Introduction to the Theory of Statistics*, Griffin, London.

King, L. J., E. Casetti, and D. Jeffrey: 1969, 'Economic impulses in a regional system of cities: a study of spatial interaction', *Regional Studies* 3, 213–218.

King, L. J., E. Casetti, and D. Jeffrey: 1972, 'Cyclical fluctuations in unemployment levels in US metropolitan areas', *Tijdschrift economische en social geographie* **63**, 345–352.

Lai, P. W.: 1979, *A Transfer Function Approach to Short Term Stochastic Models for Soil Tensions in a Sandy Soil*, unpublished Ph.D. thesis, University of London.

MacKinnon, R. D.: 1975, 'Controlling interregional migration processes of a Markovian type', *Environment and Planning* A **7**, 781–792.

MacKinnon, R. D. and P. Rogerson: 1981, 'Information sensitive migration models', in D. A. Griffith and R. D. MacKinnon (eds.), *Dynamic Spatial Models*, NATO ASI, Sijthoff-Noordhoff, Alphen aan den Rijn.

Marchand, C.: 1981a, 'Maximum entropy spectra and the spatial and temporal dimensions of economic fluctuations in an urban system', *Geographical Analysis* **13**, 95–116.

Marchand, C.: 1981b, 'Maximum entropy spectral and cross spectral analysis of economic time series in a multiregional context', in D. A. Griffith and R. D. MacKinnon (eds.), *Dynamic Spatial Models* Sijthoff-Noordhoff, Alphen aan den Rijn.

Martin, R. L.: 1978, 'Kalman filter modelling of time-varying processes in urban and regional analysis', in R. L. Martin, N. Thrift, and R. J. Bennett (eds.), *Towards the Dynamic Analysis of Spatial Systems*, Pion, London.

Martin, R. L.: 1979, 'Subregional Philips curves, inflationary expectations, and the intermarket relative wage structure: substance and methodology', in N. Wrigley (ed.), *Statistical Application in the Spatial Sciences*, Pion, London.

Martin, R. L. (ed.): 1981, *Regional Wage Inflation and Unemployment*, Pion, London.

Mees, A. I.: 1975, 'The renewal of cities in medieval Europe – an application of catastrophe theory', *Regional Science and Urban Economics* **5**, 403–426.

Nijkamp, P.: 1975, 'Spatial interdependencies and environmental effects', in A. Karlqvist, L. Lundqvist, and F. Snickars (eds.), *Dynamic Allocation of Urban Space*, Saxon House, Farnborough.

Nijkamp, P.: 1979, *Multidimensional spatial data and decision analysis*, Wiley, Chichester.

Nijkamp, P. and C. Verhage: 1976, 'Cost benefit analysis and optimal control theory for environmental decisions: a case study of the Dollard estuary', in M. Chatterji and P. von Rompuy (eds.), *Environment Regional Science and Interregional Modelling*, Springer, Berlin.

Openshaw, S.: 1977, 'Optimal zoning systems for spatial interaction models', *Environment and Planning* A **9**, 169–184.

Openshaw, S. and P. J. Taylor: 1979, 'A million or so correlation coefficients: three experiments on the modifiable areal unit problem', in N. Wrigley (ed.), *Statistical Applications in the Spatial Sciences* Pion, London.

Openshaw, S. and P. J. Taylor: 1981, 'The modifiable areal unit problem', in N. Wrigley and R. J. Bennett (eds.), *Quantitative Geography: A British View*, Routledge, London.

Orchard, T. and M. A. Woodbury: 1972, 'A missing information principle: theory and application', *Proceedings of 6th Berkeley Symposium, Mathematical Statistics and Probability* **1**, 697–715.

Otter, P. W.: 1978a, 'The discrete Kalman filter applied to linear regression models: statistical considerations and an application', *Statistica Neerlandica* **32**, 41–56.

Otter, P. W.: 1978b, *Kalman Filtering in Time-Series Analysis Compared with the Box-Jenkins Approach and Exponential Smoothing*, University of Groningen, Econometric Institute.

Otter, P. W.: 1979, *Identification and Estimation of Linear (Economic) Systems*, Operating under Linear Closed-Loop Control, University of Groningen, Econometric Institute.

Phillips, D. A. and A. C. Harvey: 1974, 'A simple test for serial correlation in regression analysis', *Journal of the American Statistical Association* 69, 935–939.

Phiri, P. A.: 1979, *Equilibrium Points and Control Problems in Dynamic Urban Modelling*, unpublished Ph.D. thesis, University of Leeds.

Pindyck, R.: 1973, *Optimal Planning for Economic Stabilisation*, North-Holland, Amsterdam.

Priestley, M. B. 1965, 'Evolutionary spectra and nonstationary processes', *Journal Royal Statistical Society* B 27, 204–237.

Ripley, B. D. 1977, 'Modelling spatial patterns', *Journal of the Royal Statistical Society* B 39, 172–212.

Sen, A. K.: 1976, 'Large sample-size distribution of statistics used in testing for spatial autocorrelation', *Geographical Analysis* 8, 175–184.

Sen, A. K. and S. Sööt: 1977, 'Some tests for spatial correlation', *Environment and Planning* A 9, 897–903.

Shapiro, C. P. and L. Hubert: 1979, 'Asymptotic normality of permutation statistics derived from weighted sums of univariate functions', *The Annals of Statistics* 4, 788–784.

Sheppard, E. S.: 1979, 'Gravity parameter estimation', *Geographical Analysis* 11, 120–132.

Sokal, R. R.: 1979, 'Testing statistical significances of geographical variation patterns', *Systematic Zoology* 28, 227–232.

Tan, K. C.: 1979, 'Optimal control of linear econometric systems with linear equality constraints on the control variables', *International Economic Review* 20, 253–258.

Tan, K. C. and R. J. Bennett: 1983, *Optimal Control of Spatial Systems*, Allen and Unwin, London.

Tong, H.: 1980a, *On the Structure of Threshold Time Series Models*, University of Manchester Institute of Science and Technology, Technical Report No. 134.

Tong, H.: 1980b, *Catastrophe Theory and Threshold Autoregressive Modelling*, University of Manchester Institute of Science and Technology, Technical Report No. 125.

Tong, H.: 1980c, *A Note on the Connection Between Threshold Autoregressive Models and Catastrophe Theory*. University of Manchester Institute of Science and Technology, Technical Report No. 129.

Tong, H. and K. S. Lim: 1980, 'Threshold autoregression, limit cycles and cyclical data', *Journal Royal Statistical Society* B 42, 244–254.

White, E. N. and G. J. D. Hewings: 1980, *Space-time Employment Modelling: Some Results Using Seemingly Unrelated Regression Estimates*, Mimeo, University of Illinois, Urbana.

Whittle, P.: 1954, 'On stationary processes in the plane', *Biometrika* 41, 434–449.

Whittle, P.: 1963: 'Stochastic processes in several dimensions', *Bulletin of the International Statistical Institute* 34, 974–993.

Wilson, A. G.: 1976, 'Catastrophe theory and urban modelling: an application to modal choice', *Environment and Planning* A 8, 351–356.

Wilson, A. G.: 1978, 'Towards models of evolution and gensis of urban structure', in

R. L. Martin, N. Thrift, and R. J. Bennett (eds.), *Towards the Dynamic Analysis of Spatial Systems*, Pion, London.

Wilson, A. G.: 1983, *Catastrophe Theory and Bifurcation*, Croom Helm, London.

Wilson, A. G. and R. J. Bennett: 1983, *Human Geography and Planning: A Guidebook to Mathematical Theory*. Wiley, London.

Wilson, A. G. and M. Clark: 1979, 'Some illustrations of catastrophe theory applied to urban retailing structure', in M. Breheny (ed.), *London Papers in Regional Science*, Pion, London.

JOHN H. SCHUENEMEYER

DIRECTIONAL DATA ANALYSIS

1. INTRODUCTION

Directional observations are common in the earth sciences. They include wind and ocean currents, solar radiation, fabric measurements, crystal orientation, movement of continental ice sheets, paleocurrents, B-axial lineations, faults, and orientation of pebbles. The interpretation of orientation data increases our understanding of the earth.

Directional data often are divided into directed and undirected line segments.

1. The directed line segments are sometimes called circular data or lines with a sense. Examples include wind and paleomagnetic measurements.
2. Undirected line segments are referred to as axial data or lines without a sense. For undirected data, it is not possible to distinguish between an angle θ and $\theta + 180°$. Examples include pebble orientations, B-axis lineations, and fold axes.

Satisfactory statistical theory has been developed for many directed line segment problems. Some of the associated techniques have been adapted to solve undirected line problems, however, further research is needed in this area.

Directional data are measured in two or three dimensions. Planar or two-dimensional measurements often include pebble orientations and wind measurements. Measurements of the directions of solar radiation and fault lines usually require a three-dimensional representation.

Many of the distributions and procedures used to analyze data in two dimensions are special cases of those for three and higher dimensions. For example, Watson and Williams (1956) derived a distribution which in two dimensions is the von Mises distribution and is the Fisher distribution in three dimensions. However, for the purpose of illustration, some of the two-dimensional procedures are considered separately.

All those who analyze directional data owe a great debt to K. V. Mardia and G. S. Watson. Mardia (1972) has written an important statistical text book in this area and reviewed (1975) more recent developments. The applications of directional data analysis in geology are discussed by Watson (1966, 1970), Koch and Link (1971, section 10.7), Agterberg (1974, Ch. 14) and

Gary L. Gaile and Cort J. Willmott (eds.), Spatial Statistics and Models, 253–270.
© 1984 *by D. Reidel Publishing Company.*

others. The interest in directional data analysis dates back at least to the mathematicians and astronomers of the 18th century. However, a major roadblock to advancements in this area has been computational complexity. Even today, many such problems require complex calculations which must be solved numerically using a computer. A large number of useful tables and graphs have been reproduced in Mardia (1972).

This paper will concentrate on the analysis of directional data. Many of these problems are similar to those in linear analysis, such as investigation of the form of the distribution, parameter estimation, and comparison of samples from several populations. Many of the statistical techniques are also similar to those in linear analysis. No attempt is made to present a comprehensive treatment of problems associated with directional data. Topics such as regression, trend surface analysis, experimental design, and sampling are not discussed. Agterberg (1974) and Mardia (1972) discuss some of these.

One note of caution regarding sampling — it is difficult to obtain a random sample in the real world, although often samples are representative and statistical techniques robust, so results are reasonable. Random samples of directional data are more difficult to obtain, thus probability statements based on samples should be interpreted cautiously. Measurements of directional data in geology such as folds, for example, are made only on exposed surfaces. Often, an unstated and sometimes questionable assumption is that these measurements are representative of the unseen phenomenon. Other vectors such as air currents, vary over space and time which complicates the task of obtaining a random sample.

2. ANALYSIS OF PLANAR DATA

The analysis of orientation data should begin like any other data analysis — by graphically looking at the data. For planar data, this presentation often takes the form of a rose diagram which is obtained by plotting a frequency distribution on polar graph paper. Unlike the histogram in linear analysis, the rose diagram, obtained by plotting the frequency as a distance from the center of the circle, does not preserve the proportional relationship between frequency and area. An "equal area" rose diagram, however, can be constructed by plotting the square root of the frequency. For axial data, the rose diagram between 180° and 360° is a reflection through the origin of the diagram in 0° to 180°. Thus, two clusters are defined by the rose diagram when only one exists. Krumbein (1939) suggested doubling the angles so that the data will define a single cluster, however, this procedure doubles the dispersion.

The form of the distribution as displayed in a rose diagram serves as a guide to the next step in data analysis. One often observes (see Figure 1) either a) no preferred orientations, b) a unique preferred orientation, c) multiple modes or clusters, or d) a unique preferred orientation for undirected data. Of course, the distinction between these categories is not always apparent from inspection of graphical displays.

For unimodal data, the location and dispersion usually are estimated. The observed distribution may be compared to theoretical models using either conventional chi-square goodness of fit or nonparametric tests. If multiple modes exist, one can choose between fitting multimodal distributions and

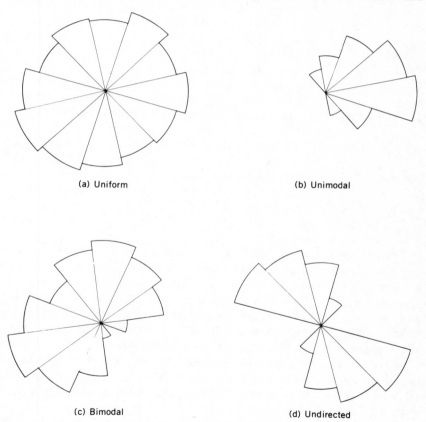

(a) Uniform   (b) Unimodal

(c) Bimodal   (d) Undirected

Fig. 1. Rose diagrams of directional data.

using a clustering procedure to partition the data. When no clear preferred orientation appears to exist or the dispersion is large, a test of uniformity is appropriate.

2.1. *Measures of Location and Scale*

For a simple random sample of directional data, $\theta_1, \theta_2, \ldots, \theta_N$ the mean $\bar{x}_0$ and variance s_0^2 are obtained from the following computations. The mean resultant length $(\bar{R})$ is first computed from

$$\bar{C} = \frac{1}{N} \sum_{i=1}^{N} \cos \theta_i,$$

$$\bar{S} = \frac{1}{N} \sum_{i=1}^{N} \sin \theta_i$$

and

$$\bar{R} = (\bar{C}^2 + \bar{S}^2)^{\frac{1}{2}}.$$

The mean direction $\bar{x}_0$ of $(\theta_1, \theta_2, \ldots, \theta_N)$ subsequently is the solution to

$$\bar{x}_0 = \begin{cases} \bar{x}_0' \text{ if } \bar{S} > 0, \bar{C} > 0 \\ \bar{x}_0' + \pi \text{ if } \bar{C} < 0 \\ \bar{x}_0' + 2\pi \text{ if } \bar{S} < 0, \bar{C} > 0. \end{cases}$$

where $\bar{C} = \bar{R} \cos \bar{x}_0$, $\bar{S} = \bar{R} \sin \bar{x}_0$ and $\bar{x}_0' = \tan^{-1}(\bar{S}/\bar{C})$.

The sample circular variance is $s_0^2 = 1 - \bar{R}$ although it is generally more convenient to work with R or $\bar{R}$.

For undirected data the angles are doubled and the calculations proceed as in the directed data case. The sample mean $\bar{x}_a = \bar{x}_0/2$ and the sample variance $s_a^2 = 1 - (1 - s_0^2)^{\frac{1}{4}}$.

Other measures of location and scale commonly used in linear statistical analysis are the median and interquartile range. For directional data, the order statistics from a sample are defined by the largest gap in the data. For example, consider the measurements (in degrees): 18, 21, 30, 45, 67, 129, 352. The largest gap occurs between 129 and 352. Thus, 352 can be considered the first order statistic and the median is 30. Clearly, the median is not necessarily unique, however, for unimodal distributions the population median is unique.

The outlier problem is somewhat different for directional data because data values are bounded between $0°$ and $360°$. If the data are dispersed, i.e.

if the variance is large, it is difficult to recognize outliers. If data are concentrated, outliers can often be recognized from data plots. The influence of extreme points can be determined by a jackknife method, that is, recomputing estimates of location and scale with each point removed. Recently, Lenth (1981) discussed some robust measures of location for directional data.

2.2. *The von Mises Distribution*

Much of the theory of directional data analysis has focused upon the von Mises distribution which plays a role somewhat analogous to that of the normal distribution in linear analysis. The density function for the von Mises distribution is

$$f(\theta; \mu_0, \kappa) = \exp[\kappa(\cos(\theta - \mu_0))]/(2\pi I_0(\kappa))$$

where $I_0(\kappa)$ is the modified Bessel function of the first kind and order zero. The mean direction is μ_0 and κ is the concentration parameter, a measure of variability. Density functions for various concentrations are displayed in Figure 2. When $\kappa = 0$ the von Mises distribution becomes the circular uniform

$$f(\theta; \mu_0, 0) = 1/2\pi$$

since $I_0(0) = 1$. Other distributions, similar in shape to the von Mises include the cardioid, wrapped Cauchy, and wrapped normal which are described in Mardia (1972).

If $(\theta_1, \theta_2, \ldots, \theta_N)$ is a random sample from a von Mises distribution $M(\mu_0, \kappa)$, then the maximum likelihood (and moment) estimates are

$$\hat{\mu}_0 = \bar{x}_0$$

and

$$\hat{\kappa} = A^{-1}(\bar{R})$$

when μ_0 is unknown. $A_d(\kappa) = (I_{d/2}(\kappa)/I_{d/2-1}(\kappa))$ and $d = 2$ for the von Mises distribution. If μ_0 is known, $\hat{\kappa} = A_2^{-1}(\bar{C})$. This expression must be evaluated numerically, however, Mardia (1972, Appendix 2.3) presents a table for $\hat{\kappa}$ given $\bar{R}$. The distributions of $\bar{x}_0$ and R are not independent. Thus, the estimate of μ_0 is conditioned upon R and the estimate of κ is conditioned upon $\bar{x}_0$. Maximum likelihood estimates have the desirable

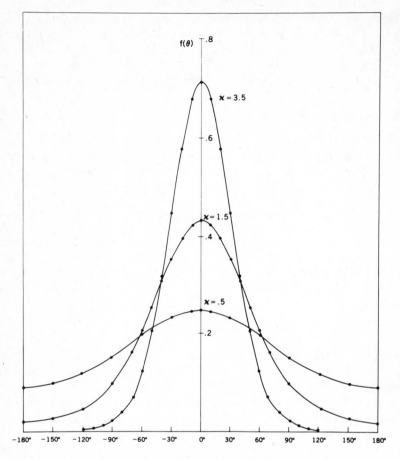

Fig. 2. The von Mises density functions for $\kappa = 0.5, 1.5,$ and 3.5.

property of having minimum variance, however, they are often biased. This lead Schou (1978) to propose an alternate to the maximum likelihood estimate of κ. His estimate $\bar{\kappa}$, is zero if $0 \leqslant R \leqslant \sqrt{N}$ and is the unique positive solution to $NA_d(\kappa) = RA_d(\kappa R)$ if $\sqrt{N} < R < N$. Simulation studies show a considerable reduction of bias for $\bar{\kappa}$ when compared with $\hat{\kappa}$.

For axial data the angles are doubled and analysis proceeds in the usual way. The magnitude of the concentration parameter κ reflects the increase in dispersion caused by doubling the angles.

2.3. *Goodness of Fit Tests*

The appropriate test to compare an empirical with a theoretical distribution depends, as in linear analysis, on the alternatives and the sample size.

If the null hypothesis is uniformity and the alternative, the von Mises distribution, with the mean μ_0 and concentration parameter κ both unknown, the Rayleigh test is the uniformily most powerful invariant test. This test of uniformity is valid for other alternatives but is not optimal. For this test, the mean direction $\bar{R}$ is used as the test statistic and critical values may be obtained from Mardia (1972, Appendix 2.5). For large $N(N \geqslant 20)$, $2N\bar{R}^2 \sim \chi^2$ (Mardia, 1972). If the null hypothesis is rejected, a goodness of fit test to von Mises distribution may be used. This and many other important tests are based upon the results of Watson and Williams (1956).

The use of the chi-square goodness of fit test is analogous to its use in linear analysis and will not be discussed further. A Kolmogorov type nonparametric test has been derived by Kuiper (1960). Kuiper's test involves finding both

$$D_N^+ = \max_\theta (S_N(\theta) - F(\theta))$$

and

$$D_N^- = \max_\theta (F(\theta) - S_N(\theta))$$

where $S = i/N$, $\theta_i \leqslant \theta < \theta_{i+1}$, $i = 1, 2, \ldots, N-1$ is the empirical distribution and $F(\theta)$ is the theoretical distribution under the null hypothesis; in this case, the von Mises distribution. Kuiper's test statistic is

$$V_N = D_N^+ + D_N^-$$

which is rotationally invariant. Percentage points for the distribution of V_N are given by Kuiper (1960). To test for uniformity, $F(\theta) = \theta/2\pi$, $0 < \theta \leqslant 2\pi$, Mardia (1972, Section 7.2.6) summarizes the performance of several tests of uniformity and concludes that, at least for small sample sizes, Kuiper's test is preferable. For undirected or axial data, angles are doubled and then the procedures previously described apply. In general, if $\theta_1, \theta_2, \ldots, \theta_N$ represents observations from a population concentrated on $(0, 2\pi/a)$ make the transformation $\theta_i' = a\theta_i$. Then the θ_i' are concentrated on $(0, 2\pi)$. The chi-square and other tests of uniformity do not differentiate between a random sample from a uniform population and a regular or evenly spaced pattern, nor can they be expected to do so. Of course, it is possible to derive a statistic to test for any specific regular pattern against an alternative of randomness.

2.4. *Multi-Modal Distributions*

Multi-modal distributions may be viewed as coming from a single population or as mixtures of several unimodal distributions. From a practical standpoint, a distribution having more than two modes should be treated as a mixture of unimodal distributions. A numerical solution for the bimodal von Mises distribution concentrated on $(0, 2\pi)$ which has five parameters has been given by Jones and James (1969). Spurr (1981) gives two additional methods for estimating the parameters of a bimodal von Mises distribution concentrated on $(0, \pi)$. Mixtures of more than two populations are not readily separable for two-dimensional data. Mardia and Spurr (1973) discuss procedures to partition multi-modal data, however, such partitioning is not very precise.

One approach, although not rationally invariant, is to partition the circle into even arc increments and fit "clustering" distributions such as the negative binomial to the count data.

3. THREE-DIMENSIONAL DIRECTIONAL DATA

The graphical representation of three-dimensional data often takes the form of points on a unit sphere. The coordinates of a point in three-space are often expressed in spherical coordinates. The observed direction is specified by direction cosines (l, m, n), where

$$l = \cos \phi \cos \theta,$$
$$m = \cos \phi \sin \theta$$

and

$$n = \sin \phi$$

and where θ represents a direction in the horizontal plane, and ϕ an angle in the direction away from the plane. The orientation of these angles (θ, ϕ) is shown in Figure 3. The coordinate system conventions are those frequently used in geology and geography. In geography, ϕ is the latitude, $-90° \leqslant \phi \leqslant 90°$, with $90°$ being the north pole, $0°$ the equator, and $-90°$ the south pole. The longitude is measured from $0°$ (prime meridian) to $360°$

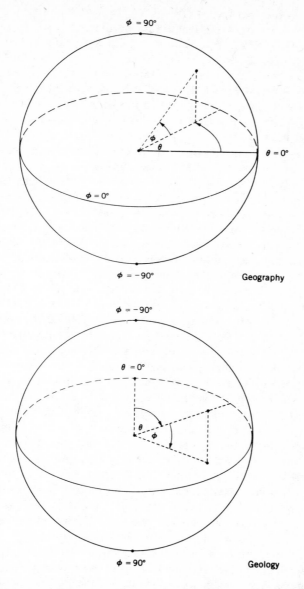

Fig. 3. Commonly used coordinate systems in geography and geology.

eastwards (counter clockwise). This is a right hand coordinate system with the positive direction upwards (toward the north pole).

In geology (θ, ϕ) are the azimuth and dip (or inclination), respectively. The azimuth $0° \leq \theta < 360°$, increases in a clockwise manner with $0°$ representing north (x), $90°$ east (y), $180°$ south, and $270°$ west. The dip $-90° \leq \phi \leq 90°$ is the angle from the horizontal, with positive angles downward (z). For example, a dip of $30°$ is a vertical angle $30°$ below the horizontal. This convention also is a right handed coordinate system but with positive downward.

In geology, the distribution of beds or other plane surfaces may be important. They can be studied with the same methodology used to study lines since the normal to a plane is a point on a sphere. Axial data can be represented by points on a hemisphere. Data on a hemisphere can be projected onto a circular area. Two commonly used projections are the Wulff net and the Lambert equal area projection, called the Schmidt net by geologists. The Wulff net preserves angles. The Schmidt net is most useful since our interest is in the distribution of points. For this projection, the dip ϕ is converted to a distance $p = \sqrt{2} V \sin (45° - |\phi|/2)$ from the center of the projected circle, where V is the radius of the sphere. Thus, point (θ, ϕ) on the sphere maps into a point (θ, p) on the primitive circle. For example, the point $(68°, 25°)$ on the unit sphere is plotted as $(68°, 0.76)$ on polar graph paper. The point $(0°, 90°)$ plots as a point in the center of the projection circle. Points on a sphere may of course be plotted on a single primitive circle by choosing different plotting symbols for each hemisphere. Distributions of points near the equator should be rotated prior to being plotted, else they will be projected at the perimeter of the projection circle. Further information on projection systems may be found in Turner and Weiss (1963, pp. 58–64), Vistelius (1966), or other books on structural geology.

The investigation of specific conjectures is usually guided by a stereographic projection plot of the data. Questions of interest are: Are the points randomly distributed? Are outliers present? Can data be represented by some well-known distribution? Stereographic projection plots are shown in Figure 4 for several patterns of practical interest. For purposes of illustration, these patterns are more pronounced than one might observe in nature. The open circle (Figure 4) denotes points from the unseen hemisphere.

The *uniform* distribution is one where points are generated randomly with no preferred orientation. A *unimodal* distribution occurs when points are concentrated about a unique mode — Fisher's is the most important unimodal distribution. A special case of a *bimodal* distribution, called the *bipolar*

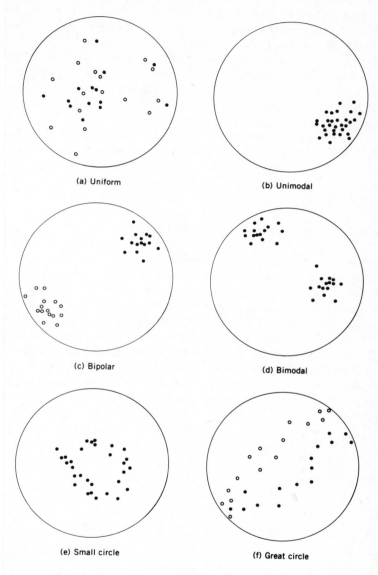

(a) Uniform

(b) Unimodal

(c) Bipolar

(d) Bimodal

(e) Small circle

(f) Great circle

Fig. 4. Equal area projections of directional data.

distribution, occurs when the distribution is rotationally symmetric about the axis joining the modes and the axis joining the antimodes. For a *girdle* distribution, points are concentrated on a great circle of the sphere. Another important distribution is represented by the concentration of points on a *small circle*. A *multi-modal* distribution or *cluster of points* is not uncommon.

Important works on spherical distributions include those by Fisher (1953), Watson (1956a), Watson and Williams (1956), Bingham (1964), and Bingham and Mardia (1978) Undirected data presents a more difficult problem because the number of observations that would be plotted on a hemisphere to represent a certain direction are twice the number that would be plotted on a sphere. However, some of the methods for the analysis of spherical data work reasonably well when applied to undirected data.

3.1. *A Test of Uniformity*

In three dimensions, the resultant length R is derived from

$$R^2 = (\Sigma\, l_i)^2 + (\Sigma\, m_i)^2 + (\Sigma\, n_i)^2,$$

where l_i, m_i, and n_i are the direction cosines of (θ_i, ϕ_i). Watson (1956b, c) proposed a test of randomness based upon the length R, which will be small if the points are randomly distributed. For $N \geqslant 20$, R is approximately distributed as $\sqrt{N\, \chi^2\, (3)\, /\, 3}$. For $5 \leqslant N \leqslant 20$, significant points of R are given by Watson (1956c) for 1 and 5%. For two dimensions, this test reduces to the Rayleigh test of uniformity. Watson's test is optimal when the alternative is the Fisher's distribution but it can be used for other alternatives. If the hypothesis of randomness is rejected and the distribution is unimodal, meaningful estimates of the azimuth and dip can be obtained from the following calculations. Let

$$\bar{l} = \Sigma\, l_i/N$$
$$\bar{m} = \Sigma\, m_i/N$$
$$\bar{n} = \Sigma\, n_i/N;$$

then,

$$\hat{\theta} = \tan^{-1}\, (\bar{m}/\bar{l}) \text{ (four quadrant)}$$

and

$$\hat{\phi} = \sin^{-1}\, (\bar{n}).$$

3.2. *The Fisher Distribution*

The most important unimodal spherical distribution was derived by Arnold (1941) and independently derived and developed by Fisher (1953). It has the following density function:

$$f(l, m, n) = c(k) \exp[\kappa (l\lambda + m\mu + n\nu)],$$

where $c(k) = \kappa/(4\pi\sinh \kappa)$ and and $\lambda = \cos \phi \cos \theta$, $\mu = \cos \phi \sin \theta$, and $\nu = \sin \phi$. The mode is at (λ, μ, ν) and the antimode at $(-\lambda, -\mu, -\nu)$. When $\phi = 0$, this density function reduces to $M(\mu_0, \kappa) = c(k) \exp[\kappa(l\lambda + m\mu)]$ which is the von Mises distribution. The maximum likelihood estimate of the precision κ is the solution to

$$\coth \hat{\kappa} - (1/\hat{\kappa}) = \bar{R}.$$

Tables for $\hat{\kappa}$ given $\bar{R}$ are given in Mardia (1972, Appendix 3.2). Fisher (1953) showed that a $(1 - \alpha) 100\%$ cone of confidence from the semivertical angle A can be obtained from $\cos A = 1 + ((N - R)/(NR)) \log_e \alpha$ for $\kappa \geqslant 3$. A Fortran computer program to compute the basic cluster statistics including R, $\hat{\theta}$, $\hat{\phi}$, $\hat{\kappa}$ and A was developed by Schuenemeyer, *et al.* (1972).

3.3. *Distributions on a Hemisphere*

Arnold (1941) derived a unimodal hemispherical distribution

$$h(l, m, n) = \frac{\sinh \kappa}{e^{-\kappa} - 1} \cdot f(l, m, n)$$

where $f(l, m, n)$ is the Fisher spherical distribution, however, the statistical theory for this distribution has not been developed. When the points are highly concentrated, an estimate of κ for Fisher's distribution can be used.

The Bingham distribution (1964) described by Mardia (1972) — is an important axial distribution. It can assume the form of the uniform, girdle, or bimodal distribution where the girdle and bimodal forms can be asymmetric. The density function for the Bingham distribution is

$$f(x; \mu, \kappa) = (4\pi d(\kappa))^{-1} \exp(\kappa_1(x'\mu_1)^2 + \kappa_2(x'\mu_2)^2 + \kappa_3(x'\mu)^2)$$

where $\kappa = \operatorname{diag}(\kappa_1, \kappa_2, \kappa_3)$, μ_1, μ_2, μ_3 are three orthogonal normalized vectors, $d(\kappa)$ is a constant which depends only on κ_1, κ_2, and κ_3, and $x' = (l, m, n)$ a vector of direction cosines. This distribution has the Dimroth-Watson distribution (see Watson, 1956a) as a special case. The Dimroth-Watson can be either a symmetric girdle or bipolar distribution.

Bingham and Mardia (1978) have also proposed a distribution to model measurements which cluster about a small circle on a sphere. This distribution has the Fisher and the Dimroth-Watson distributions as special cases.

3.4. *Diagnostic Tools for Determining the Distributional Form*

Watson (1966, 1970) suggests using the eigenvalues of the matrix of cross products of the directions cosines as a diagnostic tool to help identify the form of the spherical distribution. Let

$$\mathbf{T} = \begin{bmatrix} \Sigma\, l_i^2 & & \\ \Sigma\, l_i m_i & \Sigma\, m_i^2 & \\ \Sigma\, l_i n_i & \Sigma\, l_i m_i & \Sigma n_i^2 \end{bmatrix}$$

be such a matrix with eigenvalues τ_1, τ_2, τ_3 and corresponding eigenvectors $\mathbf{t}_1, \mathbf{t}_2, \mathbf{t}_3$. The relative sizes of τ_1, τ_2, τ_3 and R yield information about the form of the spherical distribution. When comparisons of relative sizes of eigenvalues are made across populations, it is useful to view the eigenvalues as a fraction of their total variance because $\Sigma_{i=1}^{3}\, \tau_i = \Sigma l_i^2 + \Sigma m_i^2 + \Sigma n_i^2 = N$. The fractions $\tau_i' = \tau_i/N$ are eigenvalues normalized by the sample size N. Also, the resultant mean lengths, $\bar{R}$'s, would be compared instead of the R's when sample sizes differed among populations.

The eigenvalues are divided into three cases by their relative sizes. The form of the associated distribution can be described as follows:

Case 1. When the eigenvalues are approximately equal a uniform distribution is indicated. Also R is small. There is no preferred orientation.

Case 2. When two eigenvalues are small, and one is large, the observations lie either in one or two clusters. A large R indicates a unimodal distribution, otherwise bimodality is indicated. If the two small eigenvalues are approximately equal the distribution is bipolar. An estimate of the direction of a single cluster or two antipodal clusters for τ_3 large is

$$\hat{\theta} = \tan^{-1}\,(t_{32}/t_{31})$$

and

$$\hat{\phi} = \sin^{-1}\,(t_{33}),$$

where $t_3' = (t_{31}, t_{32}, t_{33})$. A candidate for the bipolar form is the Dimroth-Watson distribution (1956c). Often it is difficult to distinguish between a unimodal and small circle distribution on the basis of the eigenvalues and the length R.

Case 3. When one eigenvalue is small and the other two are large, the distribution may be girdle. If τ_1 is small, the girdle plane is spanned by t_2, t_3. If τ_2 and τ_3 are approximately equal, the girdle distribution has rotational symmetry about t_1. The direction of the line perpendicular to the girdle is

$$\hat{\theta} = \tan^{-1}(t_{12}/t_{11})$$

and

$$\hat{\phi} = \sin^{-1}(t_{13})$$

where $t_1' = (t_{11}, t_{12}, t_{13})$. Two large eigenvalues can also occur when the distribution is bimodal, if the modes are substantially less than $180°$ apart.

Clearly in a diagnostic situation, words like approximately equal, small, and large are not precisely defined. Table I presents eigenvalues of the direction cosine cross product matrix and the length R for the distributions in

TABLE I

Diagnostic information for spherical distributions

Form of the distribution	Eigenvalues			R
a) Uniform	4.68	7.58	17.73	1.86
b) Unimodal	0.72	28.06	1.23	29.00
c) Bipolar	0.73	28.38	0.89	2.04
d) Bimodial	14.84	0.72	14.44	20.54
e) Small circle	3.41	4.62	21.98	25.61
f) Great circle	0.52	15.48	14.00	0.85

Figure 4. Each of these distributions consists of a sample of size 30. Points in the southern hemisphere are plotted with closed circles and points in the northern hemisphere with open circles. These results are rotationally invariant, although the order of the eigenvalues may change as points are rotated. They illustrate the need to properly apply statistical tests as well as graph the data. The critical region for rejecting the null hypothesis of uniformity at the 5% significance level is $R \geqslant 8.84$ using Watson's test. The

hypothesis of uniformity would clearly be accepted for the data in Figure 4a since $R = 1.86$. This result appears to be reasonable even though the eigenvalues differ in size from each other. However, the hypothesis of uniformity would also be accepted for the bipolar distribution (Figure 4c). This occurs because the test is not optimal against a bipolar distribution and illustrates the need to plot the data and look at the eigenvalues of the direction cosine cross product matrix. Note, that the eigenvalues of the bimodal distribution are similar in magnitude to the great circle distribution (Figure 4f), however, R is large in the bimodal case indicating concentration while it is small, 0.85, for the great circle distribution.

The user can gain insight into the diagnostic process by plotting distributions of points on a beach ball or globe and computing the eigenvalues of the cross product matrix of direction cosines. The program by Schuenemeyer, Koch, and Link (1972) computes these and other cluster statistics.

3.5. *Cell Methods to Test for Preferred Orientation*

The procedures described in the previous section have been rotationally invariant. Another set of procedures which lack this property but are computationally simpler have been suggested by Dudley *et al.* (1975). Their procedures are applicable to data which can be represented on a hemisphere. The hemisphere is divided into units of equal area. The partitioned hemisphere and directional measurements are projected onto the primitive circle using Lambert's equal area projection and the distribution of points in the cells is investigated. In particular, they look at the number of points in a single cell. If a cell was chosen prior to collecting the data, a binomial model would imply uniformity since the probability that at least k points are in this cell of area A on a sphere with unit surface area is $\Sigma_{x=k}^{N} b(x; p = A, N)$. However, if the cell was chosen to contain the most or the fewest points, other distributions which have been tabulated by Dudley *et al.* (1975) would be required since the selection process changes the probabilities. To attempt to reject uniformity using their procedure, one would find the cell containing the largest number of points. This is called the N_{max} test. To test for a girdle distribution one finds the cell containing the minimum number of points which may occur near the pole of the distribution; this is called the N_{min} and empty cell test. The N_{max} and N_{min} tests of course yield insight into the form of the distribution if it is non-uniform; the chi-square test does not.

Mahtab *et al.* (1972) use the cell method to identify clusters on a hemisphere. A Poisson model is used to recognize clusters and a computer program is provided.

4. TESTS AMONG SEVERAL POPULATIONS

Many of the multiple sample tests are derived in Watson and Williams (1956) and are described by Irving (1964) and Mardia (1972). One of the most useful is a test to determine whether two or more clusters have the same mean direction. Watson and Williams (1956) suggest the statistic

$$\frac{\Sigma R_i - R}{\Sigma N_i - \Sigma R_i} \cdot \frac{\Sigma N_i - k}{k - 1}$$

which has an F-distribution with $(p - 1)(k - 1)$ and $(p - 1)(\Sigma N_i - k)$ degrees of freedom, where p is the dimensionality of the data, k is the number of populations, N_i is the number of measurements in the ith population, R_i is the resultant length for the ith population, and R is the overall resultant length.

Dept. of Mathematical Sciences
University of Delaware

BIBLIOGRAPHY

Agterberg, F. P.: 1974, *Geomathematics*, Elsevier, New York.

Arnold, K. J.: 1941, *On Spherical Probability Distribution*, Unpublished Ph.D. Dissertation, MIT, Cambridge.

Bingham, C.: 1964, *Distributions on the Sphere and on the Projective Plane*, Unpublished Ph.D. Dissertation, Yale University, New Haven.

Bingham, C. and K. V. Mardia: 1978, 'A small circle distribution on the sphere', *Biometrika* 65, 379–389.

Dudley, R. M., P. C. Perkins, and E. Gine M.: 1975, 'Statistical tests for preferred orientations', *Journal of Geology* 83, 685–705.

Fisher, R. A.: 1953, 'Dispersion on a sphere', *Proceedings of the Royal Society London* A217, 295–305.

Irving, E.: 1964, *Paleomagnetism*, John Wiley, New York.

Jones, T. A. and W. R. James: 1969, 'Analysis of bimodal orientation data', *Mathematical Geology* 1, 129–135.

Koch, G. S. Jr. and R. F. Link: 1971, *Statistical Analysis of Geological Data, Vol. II*, John Wiley, New York.

Krumbein, W. C.: 1939, 'Preferred orientation of pebbles in sedimentary deposits', *Journal of Geology* 47, 673–706.

Kuiper, N. H.: 1960, 'Tests concerning random points on a circle', *Ned. Akad. Wet. Proc.* A63, 38–47.

Lenth, R. V.: 1981, 'Robust measures of location for directional data', *Technometrics* 23, 77–81.

Mahtab, M. A., D. D. Bolstad, J. R. Alldredge, and R. J. Shanley: 1972, 'Analysis of fracture orientations for input to structural models of discontinuous rocks', *U.S. Bureau of Mines* RI 7669.

Mardia, K. V.: 1972, *Statistics of Directional Data*, Academic Press, London.

Mardia, K. V.: 1975, 'Statistics of directional data (with discussion)', *Journal of the Royal Statistical Society* B 37, 349–393.

Mardia, K. V. and B. D. Spurr: 1973, 'Multi-sample tests for multi-modal and axial data', *Journal of the Royal Statistical Society* B 35, 422–436.

Schou, G.: 1978, 'Estimation of the concentration parameter in von Mises-Fisher distribution', *Biometrika* 65, 369–377.

Schuenemeyer, H. H., G. S. Koch Jr., and R. F. Link: 1972, 'Computer program to analyze directional data based on the methods of Fisher and Watson', *Mathematical Geology* 4, 177–202.

Spurr, B. D.: 1981, 'On estimating the parameters in mixtures of circular normal distributions', *Mathematical Geology* 13, 163–173.

Turner, E. J. and L. E. Weiss: 1963, *Structural Analysis of Metamorphic Tectonites*, McGraw-Hill, New York.

Vistelius, A. B.: 1966, *Structural Diagrams*, Pergamon, London.

Watson, G. S.: 1956a, 'Equatorial distributions on a sphere', *Biometrika* 52, 193–201.

Watson, G. S.: 1956b, 'Analysis of dispersion on a sphere', *Monthly Notices of the Royal Astronomical Society Geophysics Supplement* 7, 153–159.

Watson, G. S.: 1956c, 'A test for randomness of directions', *Monthly Notices of the Royal Astronomical Society Geophysics Supplement* 7, 160–164.

Watson, G. S.: 1966, 'The statistics of orientation data', *Journal of Geology* 74, 786–797.

Watson, G. S.: 1970, 'Orientation statistics in the earth sciences', *Bulletin of the Geological Institute University of Uppsala NS* 2, 73–89.

Watson, G. S. and E. J. Williams: 1956, 'On the construction of significance tests on a circle and the sphere', *Biometrika* 43, 344–352.

RICHARD S. JARVIS

TOPOLOGY OF TREE-LIKE NETWORKS

The study of tree-like networks has revealed some important insights into the spatial organization of geographic surfaces. Research has focused upon network topology, attempting to describe and explain the pattern or arrangement of branch elements that connect into a network. Network topology has also provided a convenient framework for storage of other measurements on surface geometric properties. This paper will examine the tree-like networks of river channels and ridges that may be used to characterize the topographic surface of fluvially-eroded terrain. Some of this work developed in economic geography, modeling spatial flows over potential surfaces (Warntz, 1966); and some aspects can be related to a theory of generalized geographic surface networks (Pfaltz, 1976). Topologic analyses of tree-like networks have found applications to spatial systems outside geography: including botanical networks of plant stems and roots (Thornley, 1977), physiological branching systems of bronchial airways and neural Purkinje cells (Hollingworth and Berry, 1975; Horsfield et al., 1971), and various engineering situations dealing with fluid flow through porous media (Liao and Scheidegger, 1969). Non-spatial applications include the study of evolutionary trees (Harding, 1971).

1. TREE-LIKE NETWORKS ON GEOGRAPHIC SURFACES

A geographic surface is defined by a continuous, single-valued function, $z = f(x, y)$, where the independent variables x and y jointly determine location within a geographic coordinate system. It is possible to develop surfaces of higher dimension, but this paper will only be concerned with topographic surfaces defined on two dimensions. The form of the surface may be represented, to a certain degree of precision, by a series of contour lines, each defined by the intersection of the surface with a plane of constant z value. The arrangement of these contour lines, projected onto a map, constitutes the topology of the surface, from which we can define a series of points, lines, and areas, whose spatial relations represent the structure of the surface. The contoured surface may contain such a wealth of information that problems of data retrieval and manipulation become overwhelming, and its spatial

271

Gary L. Gaile and Cort J. Willmott (eds.), Spatial Statistics and Models, 271–291.
© 1984 by D. Reidel Publishing Company.

structure remains incomprehensible. Extraction of certain tree-like networks embedded in the surface offers a means of simplification so that spatial structure can be recognized and interpreted.

The basic topology of a geographic surface has been determined by Warntz (1966, 1975) and Pfaltz (1976). Both authors acknowledge much earlier mathematical contributions by Euler, Cayley, Maxwell, and Morse. Surface form is represented by two orthogonal families of curves: contour lines already noted; and slope lines, indicating the path of steepest gradient at a point. There are three sets of points, known as points of equilibria, where surface gradient is zero: peaks, pits, and passes (Figure 1a). Peaks are local

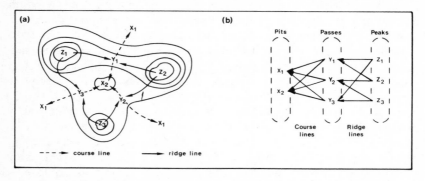

Fig. 1. Geographic surface topology: (a) contour map; (b) Pfaltz network.

maxima about which slope lines diverge. Pits are local minima with convergent slope lines. Together peaks and pits constitute Warntz's absolute extremum points. Passes are saddle points on the surface, where a single closed contour line crosses itself to form two loops. They are the low point of convergence between two adjacent peaks and the high point of divergence between two adjacent pits. Warntz termed passes "mixed extrema points". Spatial relationships between peaks, pits, and passes define two special types of slope line: ridge lines and course lines (Figure 1a.) Passes are connected to peaks by ridge lines, and to pits by course lines. Several useful graphs can be extracted from the network of these critical points and lines.

Surface topology can be described by a tripartite graph, which Mark (1979) has termed the Pfaltz graph of the surface (Figure 1b). This graph can be simplified by a process of abstraction, known in graph theory as a homomorphic contraction, replacing subgraphs by single points. Pfaltz shows how the structure of a surface may be clarified by abstracting and retaining critical points which correspond to the "macrostructure" of the surface, eliminating those points which represent a "local microstructure" (Pfaltz, 1976, p. 86).

While Pfaltz graphs offer great potential for modeling geographic surfaces they have yet to be widely applied in geomorphic studies of the topographic surface. Geomorphologists have focused upon the tree-like networks of river channels and topographic ridges. One factor contributing to this neglect is the spatial boundary of the surface. Pfaltz requires the function z to be constant everywhere on the boundary, defining a closed surface bounded by a single closed contour. This does not conform with the partitioning of space into drainage basins, traditionally regarded as the fundamental geomorphic unit in fluvial landscapes.

Warntz (1975) specifically relates surface topology to the spatial structure of fluvial landforms (Figure 2). Ridges connect peaks and bound drainage

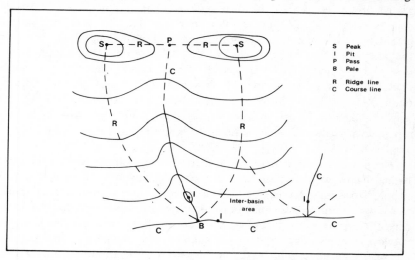

Fig. 2. Warntz network of a first-order drainage basin.

basins. River channels occupy portions of course lines, and course lines bound hills — defined as districts whose slope lines run to the same peaks. Ridges and courses form a skeleton of surface-specific points and lines (Peucker *et al.*, 1978), which is known as the Warntz network of the surface (Mark, 1975). In the simplest complete drainage basin, containing a single, unbranched (first order) stream, the Warntz network distinguishes two types of mixed extrema points: passes and pales (Figure 2). These points are topologically identical on a general geographic surface, so Pfaltz passes include both Warntz passes and pales. Warntz passes lie at the self-crossing point of a contour whose loops enclose two peaks. The course line from a pass must run downslope to a pit, but the basin mouth at a stream junction lies at the intersection of ridge lines and course lines, and so must be another kind of mixed extrema point known as a pale. The pale lies at the self-crossing point of an inloop type of contour, whose smaller loop lies entirely within the basin, and whose larger loop encloses the basin. Any continuous path through a Warntz network of connected ridge and/or course lines must encounter an alternating sequence of absolute extremum (peaks, pits) and mixed extrema (passes, pales) points.

Stream junctions have important implications in a Warntz network. The traditional geomorphic-hydrologic approach to landscape spatial structure treats the surface in terms of drainage basins, which collect and organize spatial flows. Basins are defined by outlets at stream junctions, where three courses meet at a pale, and so must three ridge lines. As soon as a basin is placed in its spatial context additional intersections of ridge lines appear on the boundary of inter-basin areas (Figure 2). These ridge intersections define new peaks, which must be connected to new passes, leading to new course lines, and so on. Warntz networks thus characterize the surface topology of drainage basins by an "infinite regress" where "new peaks require additional passes, and so on in new and continually regenerating cycles to the level of separated particles, at which level the concept of surface itself is no longer applicable" (Warntz, 1975, pp. 219–220).

The stream network mapped on a topographic surface defines threshold basins, below which course lines do not support spatial flows of the kind required to form a drainage basin. The mixed extrema points are the essential elements in defining a channel network. As Pfaltz (1976. p. 92) noted for his tripartite graphs: "it is the presence (or absence) of passes that constrains the network, not the peaks or pits. A topographic ridge emanating from a peak, or course from a pit, is represented in the surface network only if it terminates at a pass." Not all geomorphologists are comfortable with Warntz's notions of triple passes at junctions and infinite regress. Mark (1979) denies that these pits and passes exist on natural streams, at least as represented on small or medium scale terrain maps. He suggests a notion that streams represent not one course, but a bundle of parallel, infinitesimally close course lines.

In summary there have been two attempts to develop a theory for the topology of two-dimensional geographic surfaces, such as topography. Because stream channels and topographic ridges do not correspond exactly with course and ridge lines this work has yet to incorporate the study of tree-like networks in geomorphology and hydrology. The remainder of this paper will be concerned with these latter systems, identified as real features of the land surface, regardless of their correspondence to the general surface topology.

2. RIVER CHANNEL NETWORKS

Network topology has been the main framework for classification and morphometric analysis of drainage composition. Channel networks are defined as topologic trees, free from closed loops, disjunctions, and connections of more than three edges. Complications in nature, such as braiding, lakes, diversions, or deltas, must be resolved and the network graph made dendritic by omission or correction. The network is directed in that the direction of flow is fixed at all nodes, which are either junctions, sources, or the outlet. The edge connecting two nodes is a link, which forms the basic element of a channel network. A connected downstream sequence of links defines a flow path through the network. Junctions form the downstream confluence point of two tributary links and the upstream head of the resultant link. Sources lie at the head of unbranched links at the upstream limit of channel flow. At the downstream end of the entire network is the outlet, toward which all flows within the system are directed. Links which head at junctions are known as interior, while those which head at sources are exterior. The topologic characteristics of a channel network are obtained by counting nodes or links along flow paths through the network.

The position of a link in a channel network determines its two basic topologic attributes: magnitude and path length. All the topologic indices currently applied to channel networks stem from these two. The magnitude of a network is given by its number of sources, and the magnitude of a link by the number of sources ultimately tributary to it (Shreve, 1967). Path length, also known as link distance, denotes the number of links in the flow path from the head of the link in question to the network outlet (Jarvis, 1972; Werner and Smart, 1973). Any network property can be referenced to a link by assigning it the value for the subnetwork it drains. Thus a link of magnitude n drains a subnetwork of magnitude n. The path length of a link has nothing to do with the subnetwork headward, but any path length statistic which characterizes that subnetwork can be assigned to the link.

Network topologic indices do not have to be measured directly from the graph. This fortunate circumstance is made possible through use of a data

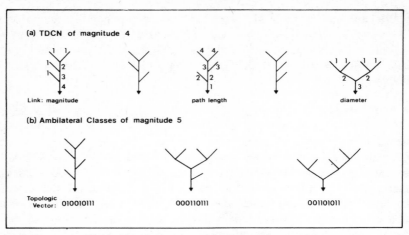

Fig. 3. Topologic properties of channel networks.

structure, known as the topologic vector, which stores the arrangement of links implicitly (Shreve, 1967; Smart, 1970, 1978; Ferguson, 1977). The network is stored in a sequence starting at the outlet and working headward, turning left at each junction and back at each source. An interior link is recorded by a zero, and an exterior link by a one, with each link only recorded on first traversal. The network can be reconstructed by reading the topologic vector from left to right and regenerating the sequence of left turns and returns (Figure 3). Algorithms for magnitude and path length utilize the fact that a link of magnitude n drains a subnetwork of $2n-1$ links, consisting of n exterior (ones) and $n-1$ interior (zeros). In the topologic vector an interior link at position j (from the left) branches into two tributaries at positions $j+1$ and $j+2m$, where m is the magnitude of the link in position $j+1$. The topologic vector can be transformed into a magnitude vector by working back through the binary string (from the right end), replacing each zero by the sum of the elements in the two tributary positions. The path length vector is derived from the magnitude vector by working through the string from the left end. The outlet link in position 1 is assigned path length 1, and an interior link at path length k branches headward into tributaries at path length $k+1$. Assigning link distances to the tributaries for each interior link will complete the path length vector.

Other topologic measures are derived from the magnitude and path length vectors. The diameter, d, and the mean source link distance, $\bar{h}_e$, are given by the maximum and mean values of the exterior path lengths in a network

(Jarvis, 1972; Werner and Smart, 1973). Each can be compiled as a network vector, where the value for a link refers to the subnetwork it drains. Path number vectors store the number of links at each path length from the outlet, with position from the left end of the vector indicating the path length (Werner and Smart, 1973). They can be compiled for all links in a network, and for interior and exterior separately. The maximum topologic width of a network is the largest value in the total path number vector (Kirkby, 1976). Strahler orders can also be obtained straightforwardly from the original topologic vector (Smart, 1970).

Although the topologic vector developed by Smart and described here is the most widely used, it is not the only binary string representation of network topology. Scheidegger (1967; see also Ranalli and Scheidegger, 1968) reversed the designation of zeros and ones, and employed right turns instead of left in recording. Kirkby (1976) records by generation, which is given by path length, and reads from left to right within a generation. Any topologic vector sequence provides a structure for data storage of associated link geometric attributes (Jarvis, 1977), with the retrieval algorithms depending on the sequence of link storage.

2.1. *The Random Model and Network Classification*

During the 1970s the study of channel network morphology has been dominated by the probabilistic-topologic approach of Shreve (1967, 1969, 1975) and Smart (1968). The random model is based on two postulates: (a) in the absence of strong geologic controls network topology is nearly random; and (b) interior and exterior link lengths are independent random variables and approximately independent of location in a network (Smart, 1978; Shreve, 1974). The first postulate asserts that topologically distinct channel networks of a given magnitude, known as TDCN, should occur with equal frequency. Its widespread empirical success underlies development of the random model and its extension to metric properties. The second postulate indicates that topologic path length should be an unbiased estimator of metric flow path length. However, formal testing of topological randomness is not without problems in real-world sampling situations.

A direct test of the random topology postulate requires enumeration of TDCN, and is specific to the magnitude sampled. The number of TDCN at magnitude n is given by

$$N(n) = \frac{1}{2n-1} \begin{bmatrix} 2n-1 \\ n \end{bmatrix} = \frac{1}{2n-1} \frac{(2n-1)!}{n![(2n-1)-n]!}$$

which becomes very large at fairly low magnitudes (Table I). If there are insufficient replicates for sampling at the given magnitude, a variety of classifications can be employed to group TDCN into a more manageable number of classes. Given numbers of TDCN in each class the random model can still be tested, by comparing observed frequencies of class membership with expected values under the assumption of equiprobable TDCN. Ambilateral classes group TDCN distinguished only by the right-left nature of one or more tributary junctions (Smart, 1969). Path lengths can be used to develop three more levels of classification: path number classes, which group TDCN with identical path number vectors; total path length classes, which group TDCN with the same total path length summed over all links; and diameter classes which group TDCN with the same diameter (Werner and Smart, 1973). Ambilateral classes coalesce into path number classes, and path number classes into total path length classes. In sampling a natural region of finite size, the number of network replicates decreases with increasing magnitude, and tests of the random model are forced to depend on classifications with fewer and fewer classes (Table I).

TABLE I
Number of Topologic Classes for Networks of Given Magnitude

Magnitude	TDCN	Ambilateral classes	Path number	Total path length	Diameters
3	2	1	1	1	1
4	5	2	2	2	2
5	14	3	3	3	2
6	42	6	5	5	3
7	132	11	9	8	4
8	429	23	16	12	5
9	1430	46	28	16	5
10	4862	98	50	21	6
15	2674440	4850	914	61	11
20	1.767×10^9	293547	16952	122	15
40	6.804×10^{20}	8.100×10^{12}	2.015×10^9	604	34

Classifications which group TDCN suffer an inevitable loss of information compared to complete enumeration of individual TDCN. The information content $H(x)$ of classification x can be measured by Shannon's formula

$$H(x) = - \sum_{i=1}^{n} p_i \log p_i,$$

where x contains n categories, each with associated probability p_i (Jarvis and Werritty, 1975). Class probabilities are given by the relative frequency of equiprobable TDCN. A ratio of $H(x)/H(\text{TDCN})$ shows the information retained by classification x compared to complete specification of individual TDCN classes (Figure 4). Information losses become very high even at fairly low magnitudes.

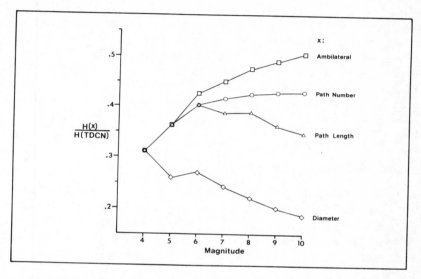

Fig. 4. Relative information content of network topologic classifications compared to specification of all TDCN for magnitudes 4 through 10.

Direct tests of the random topology model encounter two major difficulties: regional constraints on target population size; and interpretation of deviation from topologic randomness. Natural networks are sampled from a region whose extent is limited by the need to assume a homogeneous geologic and climatic setting, plus freedom from human interference with drainage patterns. The smaller the area over which these conditions are satisfied the smaller the target population of networks of any given magnitude. Regional size thus constrains the number of networks sampled and leads to information losses in network classification in order to test the model.

The random topology model offers a simple null hypothesis. Specification of an alternative hypothesis is left to the individual experimental design. There are two problems in interpreting deviations from the null hypothesis.

First, current geomorphologic theory is very vague about the ways in which non-random topologies might be generated. To ascribe a deviation from random topology to the presence of geologic controls merely establishes that the particular sampling context was inappropriate for a test of the random model. Further a regional sample of networks that conform to the hypothesis of topologic randomness may be disaggregated according to spatial criteria, such as orientation, into subsets that deviate from the model (Abrahams, 1975a). The second problem of interpretation concerns the classification used. Deviations from the model involve too many networks in some classes and too few in others. For classification by TDCN, ambilateral, and path number classes there is no single index on which to rank and compare classes. Total path length and diameter classifications can be interpreted on a scale of topologic structure (see Section 2.2), but these classifications suffer great information losses in testing the random model at any but the lowest magnitudes.

2.2. *Network Topologic Structure*

Network topologic structure can be characterized in terms of elongation, width, and asymmetry. Measures of elongation have been most widely tested empirically, particularly in connection with deviations from topologic randomness. Network width offers great promise for analysis of basin hydrologic responses. Asymmetry is a useful indicator of geologic influences on network morphology.

Elongation is defined from exterior link path lengths. For TDCN of magnitude n the most elongate structure would be associated with a path number vector of n elements

$$f(j) = 1, 2, 2, 2, \ldots, 2$$

giving the number of links at each path length $j=1$, n. The most compact structure would be associated with a path number vector of $m+2$ elements

$$f(j) = 1, 2, 4, 8, \ldots, 2^m, 2(n-2^m),$$

where m is the integral value of $\log_2 n$. Quantitative indices of topologic structure ranging between these extremes are given by the mean and maximum exterior path lengths, $\bar{h}_e$ and d respectively. For networks of given magnitude, the minimum values of $\bar{h}_e$ and d are associated with the most compact network structure, and maximum values with the most elongate structure. The two indices do not rank intermediate classes in exactly the same way (Smart, 1978). Solutions for the extreme values at any magnitude are given by Werner and Smart (1973).

The distributions of $\bar{h}_e$ and d in a topologically random population can be used to interpret observed deviations from the random model in terms of structural elongation or compaction. The random model also provides a yardstick for comparing observed structures even where there are insufficient replicates for a formal test. Simulation of equiprobable TDCN provides expected values and confidence intervals for $\bar{h}_e$ and d at any magnitude (Werner and Smart, 1973; Shreve, 1974). Observed networks can be compared with these random model expectations.

In order to compare network structures of different magnitudes, standardized structural measures are needed that allow for the increases in ranges and expected values of $\bar{h}_e$ and d with increasing magnitude. From simulated networks, Werner and Smart (1973) determined that these relationships could be described by power functions

$$\bar{h}_e = 1.63 \, n^{\,0.52}$$

and

$$d = 1.98 \, n^{\,0.59}.$$

Shreve also found from simulation that the exponent of the diameter-magnitude relation in a topologically random population decreases with increasing n, tending towards 0.5 (Shreve, 1974). To a reasonable approximation $\bar{h}_e/n^{0.5}$ and $d/n^{0.5}$ offer standardized structural measures, relatively independent of magnitude in a topologically random population. Both indices are scaled in the direction of compaction (low values) to elongation (high values).

Measures of topologic structural elongation lend themselves to spatial interpretation of network pattern through inferences to basin shape. In the absence of systematic spatial structure in link lengths or orientations, networks characterized as compact or elongate might be expected to occupy basins of corresponding planar shape. The standardized diameter $d/n^{0.5}$ is the topologic equivalent of planar shape indices of the form $L/A^{0.5}$ where L is some measure of basin length and A the basin area. Spatial variations in network structure within large basins indicate how tributary sub-basins are nested within the overall system (Jarvis and Sham, 1981). Downstream changes in network structure along the main stem of a network indicate a typical pattern where junctions of large tributaries are separated by sequences of small tributary inflows. Entrance of a large tributary fills the available space on that side of the main channel and precludes development of other large subnetworks in the immediate vicinity.

Another measure of network topologic structure that can be used in ways similar to those outlined for $\bar{h}_e$ and d is the maximum topologic width. Maximum width provides an index of structure scaled in terms of narrow to broad. Topologic width can be derived from a random walk representation of the channel network graph, with each TDCN represented by a distinct walk (Kirkby, 1976). The procedure is to start at the outlet and scan the network by generation (path length). Construct an x, y plot with x giving the total number of links scanned, and y increasing by one for each interior link and decreasing by one for each exterior link. Upward steps then indicate branching beyond the current generation, while downward steps show termination at this generation. The walk begins with an upward step, contains $2n-1$ steps for a network of magnitude n, and finishes with $y = -1$. The maximum height (y) of the walk is the topologic width of the network. Comparing observed networks with distributions simulated from a topologically random population allows identification of significantly broad or narrow structures.

Network asymmetry can be defined by a similar random walk representation, only scanning the network in the clockwise sequence of the Smart topologic vector. Ferguson (1980) defines the L index of topologic asymmetry as the maximum excess of interior links over exterior during the scan. Constructing the random walk as before, the maximum height for this scan defines the value of L. Ferguson derives expected values and confidence intervals for topologically random networks of any magnitude, so observed values can again be gauged against the yardstick of the random model. To some extent, the various structural measures are related since extreme asymmetry is only possible in narrow, elongated networks.

Drainage network structure has important implications for spatial organization of flows through the channel system. It influences the development of flood flow hydrographs and their moderation downstream. Kirkby (1976) showed that network topology could significantly affect both hydrograph peak flow and time of delay to peak, particularly in moderate and large sized basins. This kind of simulation modeling suggests that network topologic structure, involving maximum width and path length, offers great promise for future analysis of network influences on basin hydrologic responses.

2.3. Topologic Growth Models

Topologic growth models are concerned with the ways in which additional links can be attached to an existing network so that the network grows in size (magnitude). New links may be attached to existing interior or exterior links, with the assumption that these additions correspond to natural processes of headward bifurcation and lateral tributary development. Current knowledge of geomorphic process is such that relative probabilities of these different growth forms are unknown. In the absence of direct historical observation of network evolution, growth is modeled one link at a time, with various hypothetical probabilities assigned to different types of link attachment. Growth paths are established which identify each sequence of k link additions capable of transforming one topologic state (TDCN or ambilateral class of magnitude n) into another (of magnitude $n+k$) — though not all transformations are possible for given k and n. The build-up of different network states according to model specifications generates probabilities of topological classes at each magnitude that may be compared with natural samples. Rapid proliferation of possible states with increasing magnitude restricts empirical comparisons to small networks, up to about magnitude 6.

Several kinds of topologic growth models can be applied to channel networks. Dacey and Krumbein (1976) tested three models which specified the probabilities of an exterior link bifurcating (v_n), and an interior link developing a tributary to its right (u_n) or left (also u_n) for a network of magnitude n. For growth one link at a time

$$2(n-1)u_n + n v_n = 1.$$

In model A, only bifurcations of exterior links are allowed, and each possibility is equally likely ($u_n=0$, $v_n=1/n$). This generates TDCN that are equiprobable within a given ambilateral class, but not over the entire ensemble for the magnitude. These distributions were not satisfactorily fit by any natural networks examined. Model B allows only right and left tributary developments, with each of the $2n-1$ links in the network equally likely to spawn a tributary ($u_n=1/[2(2n-1)]$, $v_n=1/(2n-1)$). This leads to equiprobable TDCN consistent with Shreve's model of topologically random channel networks. Model C allows for equal probability of right and left tributary developments on interior links and bifurcations of exterior links ($u_n=v_n=1/(3n-2)$). Again, TDCN are equiprobable within a given ambilateral class but not over the ensemble for the magnitude. The sequence of models, A to B to C, shows a decrease in the contribution to growth of exterior link branching, and an increase in the proportion of structurally elongated networks. Dacey and Krumbein found most natural networks fitted either models B or C, or both. Their results are consistent with, but do not prove, that branching probabilities for links of the same type (interior or exterior) are equal and independent of position within the network.

Interpretations of tests of topologic growth models require great caution because identical probability distributions for TDCN or ambilateral classes can be generated by very different growth mechanisms. For example, the probabilities associated with model B (tributary development on all links) are also generated by Werner's S model (1972d), and a model of bifurcation with termination separately suggested by Smart (in Dacey and Krumbein, 1976) and Kirkby (1976). Werner's model is developed for mergers among channels growing downslope. The model by Smart and Kirkby has probabilities of bifurcation or termination at a source both equal to $1/2$, with growth continuing until all exterior links have been terminated. As with all attempts to infer evolutionary process from current form, Dacey and Krumbein note: "an empirical analysis comparing theoretical probabilities with observed frequencies of occurrence of topologic forms in natural drainage basins does not provide sufficient evidence to establish the types and frequencies of branching that produced the observed topologic forms" (1976, p. 159). There may also be other forms of network modification during growth, such as link abstraction (Abrahams, 1976), not incorporated in these models.

2.4. *Tributary Arrangements of Links and Chains*

There have been several refinements of the simple topologic distinction of interior and exterior link types. Sub-types have been identified, along with certain kinds of tributary arrangement along main channel flow paths. The purpose of these classifications is to elucidate spatial structure within a channel network. Some growth inferences have also been made, though less formal than the topologic growth models (see Section 2.3).

Three main concepts have been applied to the topology of tributary arrangements: the distinction between a mainstream and a tributary at a junction, made on the basis of subnetwork topologic size as given by magnitude or diameter; the notion of tributary "handedness" with regard to the mainstream; and the organization of a sequence of links along a flow path into a chain. James and Krumbein (1969) first defined mainstream paths, terminated where magnitude falls below ten, or the difference between main and tributary magnitudes below five. Along a mainstream, interior links were classified as cis, when bounded upstream and downstream by tributaries entering from the same side of the main channel, or trans, where bounding tributaries enter from the opposite side (Figure 5a). By extension, a sequence

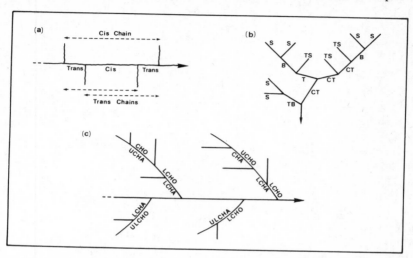

Fig. 5. Link types and chains: (a) cis and trans, after James and Krumbien (1969); (b) Mock link types (1971); (c) Flint tributary arrangements (1980).

of links along a mainstream bounded by same-side tributaries is a cis chain; one bounded by opposite-side tributaries is a trans chain. The relative frequencies of cis and trans links in nature provided the first significant deviation from Shreve's random model: trans links predominate (about 60%) in nature, while cis and trans are equiprobable in topologically random networks. An observed dearth of very short cis links in nature prompted the speculation that these elements may have been eliminated from an original equiprobable cis-trans distribution by lateral erosion and capture of sameside tributaries (James and Krumbein, 1969; Abrahams, 1975b). Alternatively short cis links may be excluded during headward growth because large tributaries preempt space for lateral development of same-side tributaries in their immediate vicinity (Smart and Wallis, 1971).

The idea of classifying links by the topologic setting of bounding tributary magnitudes was extended by Mock (1971) into a comprehensive system for all links in a network (Figure 5b). Exterior links are either source (S) or tributary source (TS), depending on their downstream confluence with a link of magnitude equal to (*S*) or greater than (*TS*) one. Four types of interior link are recognized. Bifurcating (*B*) and tributary bifurcating (*TB*) are bounded upstream by confluence of two links of equal magnitude, and merge downstream with a link of smaller (*B*) or equal/greater magnitude (*TB*). Tributary (*T*) and cis-trans (*CT*) links are bounded upstream by confluence of two links of unequal magnitude, and flow downstream into a link of equal/greater (*T*) or smaller (*CT*) magnitude. Mock derived probabilities of each type in a topologically random population. The classification has proved useful in studies of network geometry, with Abrahams (1977) finding a positive relation between abundance of *TS* links and relative relief. This suggests systematic deviation from random model expectations in surfaces of very high or very low relief.

A recent link classification, by Flint (1980), extends the concept of chains to entire flow paths from source to outlet. Geometric criteria, such as alignment, are needed to trace mainstreams through tributary junctions of equal magnitude. Flint also revises the notion of tributary handedness to distinguish branching away from the mainstream, termed obtuse, from that towards the mainstream, termed acute (Figure 5c). Chains extended to a source are unbounded at their upper end (UCHO for obtuse, UCHA for acute); and chains ending in larger streams are unbounded by a lower tributary (LCHO for obtuse, LCHA for acute). Where both these conditions hold there is no tributary bound at either end (ULCHO and ULCHA). Observed frequencies in this complex topologic-geometric classification lead Flint to some important discoveries about network spatial structures. Immediately above a sub-basin outlet, tributaries to the main channel of the sub-basin tend to develop on the outer side (obtuse). This bias persists through about three junctions, beyond which the James-Krumbein model of independent events on opposite sides of the channel prevails, with a preference for alternate-side tributaries (62.5% trans links). Towards the headwaters, the narrowness of the sub-basin helps create local asymmetries which favor same-side branches.

3. TOPOGRAPHIC RIDGE NETWORKS

Ridge networks have received much less attention than channel networks. This neglect probably stems from three main problems. First, there is nothing unique about ridge lines in terms of geomorphic process compared to immediately adjacent surface areas — in contrast to the distinction between overland flow and channel flow for streams. Ridges are residual features, created as a result of active surface modification by erosion elsewhere. Secondly, ridge lines are not explicitly portrayed on topographic maps, and have to be entirely inferred from contour crenulations identifying topographic divides. Thirdly, extraction of tree-like ridge networks from the general surface topology is difficult to match with topographic features.

The main attempt to apply a probabilistic-topologic approach to ridge networks has been by Werner. At first, he considered the network of link drainage area divides (1972a). This polygonal lattice was transformed into a tree-like network by separating ridge lines at the passes, leaving nodes at the peaks. Later, he identified ridges as topographic features from contour crenulations and related them to the channel network (1972b,c). Empirical data suggest a stochastic relationship interlocking exterior ridge and channel links, so that the frequency distribution of ridge networks is random once the basin magnitude and number of exterior ridge links are given. Finally, Werner (1973) defined the ridge network as the geometric dual of the channel network, with ridge lines between all pairs of adjacent exterior channel links (including the outlet link). Allowing for the difficulties in defining both sets of networks on a surface, Werner's work indicates that both ridge networks and channel networks are topologically random when examined in isolation, but given one pattern the other is non-random.

A different formulation of tree-like ridge networks was developed by Mark (1979), based on the Pfaltz network of a surface. Mark defines the ridge tree for a single hilltop, which is a closed surface with no pits. The network represents connections between peaks, with nodes for peaks and edges for the passes shared by bounding nodes (Figure 6). Hilltop magnitude is given by the number of peaks, and topologically distinct ridge trees correspond to topologically distinct Pfaltz graphs and Warntz networks for areas with no large pits. Mark finds these ridge trees are not equiprobable

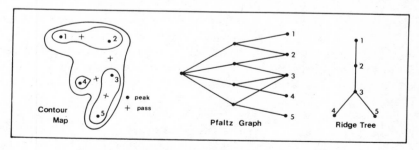

Fig. 6. Topographic ridge networks, after Mark (1981).

in nature, and develops a model for Pfaltz graph frequencies given by a random distribution of peaks within an elliptical field whose elongation can vary. Ridge networks are formed by connecting peaks in a minimum spanning tree. Simulation of peak distributions under varying elongation of the elliptical field gives the expected Pfaltz graph frequencies.

In a regional context, the optimum elongation value for goodness of fit of observed class frequencies to the model indicates the degree of ridge anisotropy within the topography. Mark found significant within-network ridge anisotropy in a region of mature landscape traditionally regarded as free from geologic controls. Preferred ridge orientation was attributed to imposition of elongated interfluves by well-developed master streams. The minimum spanning tree postulate may be explained by a tendency to minimize the surface-area: volume ratio of a hilltop (Mark, 1981).

There are problems in attempting to expand Mark's analysis, as he notes. As hilltop magnitude increases, the minimum spanning tree criterion becomes less meaningful. Many different topologies can be created with marginal differences in total edge length. The correspondence between elliptical field elongation and topographic ridge anisotropy deteriorates as boundary shape has less influence on topology near the center of the area. Also, the number of topologically distinct ridge trees increases rapidly with magnitude — for example 6, 11, 23, 47, and 106 classes for 6 through 10 peaks respectively. The same sample-size problems apply as for channel networks.

4. CONCLUSIONS

Tree-like networks of channels and ridges can be related to the general topology of a two-dimensional topographic surface. However, channels and ridges do not occupy all the course and ridge lines, and in practice their networks are defined on geomorphic criteria. General surface topology is still useful for topographic generalization and data storage. The probabilistic-topologic approach has explained many empirical features of channel network morphology. It can also be applied to ridge networks. Topology can be used to characterize the spatial structure of channel networks and to build simple models of network growth. Topologic structure affects drainage basin hydrologic responses, and geologic constraints are reflected in the spatial symmetry of channel and ridge tree-like networks. Topologic randomness need not imply spatial randomness. In an area of eastern Kentucky relatively free from geologic inhomogeneities, both the channel and ridge networks conform well to topologic randomness in their small headwater basins, but deviate from randomness in tributary channel arrangements and show non-random spatial distributions of channel network nodes along with ridge tree anisotropy (Mark, 1979; Smart, 1978; Krumbein and Dacey, 1973).

Dept. of Geography
State University of New York at Buffalo

BIBLIOGRAPHY

Abrahams, A. D.: 1975a, 'Topologically random channel networks in the presence of environmental controls', *Geological Society of America Bulletin* 86, 1459–1462.

Abrahams, A. D.: 1975b, 'Initial bifurcation process in natural channel networks', *Geology* 3, 307–308.

Abrahams, A.. D.: 1976, 'Evolutionary changes in link lengths: further evidence for stream abstraction', *Transactions of the Institute of British Geographers* 1, 225–230.

Abrahams, A.D.: 1977, 'The factor of relief in the evolution of channel networks in mature drainage basins', *American Journal of Science* 277, 626–646.

Dacey, M. F. and W. C. Krumbein: 1976, 'Three growth models for stream channel networks', *Journal of Geology* 84, 153–163.

Ferguson, R. I.: 1977, 'On determining distances through stream networks', *Water Resources Research* 13, 672–674.

Ferguson, R. I.: 1980, 'Topological asymmetry of drainage networks: the L index and its applications', *Journal of Geology* 88, 457–465.

Flint, J. J.: 1980, 'Tributary arrangements in fluvial systems', *American Journal of Science* 280, 26–45.

Harding, E. F.: 1971, 'The probabilities of rooted tree-shapes generated by random bifurcation', *Advances in Applied Probability* 3, 44–77.

Hollingworth, T. and M. Berry: 1975, 'Network analysis of dendritic fields of pyramidal cells in neocortex and Purkinje cells in the cerebellum of the rat', *Philosophical Transactions of the Royal Society* 270B, 227–264.

Horsfield, K., G. Dart, D. E. Olson, G. Filley, and G. Cumming: 1971, 'Models of the human bronchial tree', *Journal of Applied Physiology* 31, 207–217.

James, W. R. and W. C. Krumbein: 1969, 'Frequency distribution of stream link length', *Journal of Geology* 77, 544–565.

Jarvis, R. S.: 1972, 'New measure of the topologic structure of dendritic drainage networks', *Water Resources Research* 8, 1265-1271.

Jarvis, R. S.: 1977, 'Drainage network analysis', *Progress in Physical Geography* 1, 271–295.

Jarvis, R. S. and C. H. Sham: 1981, 'Drainage network structure and the diameter-magnitude relation', *Water Resources Research* 17, 1019–1027.

Jarvis, R. S. and A. Werritty: 1975, 'Some comments on testing random topology stream network models', *Water Resources Research* 11, 309–318.

Kirkby, M. J.: 1976, 'Tests of the random network model and its application to basin hydrology', *Earth Surface Processes* 1, 197–212.

Krumbein, W. C. and M. F. Dacey: 1973, 'Comments on randomness in spatial components of dendritic stream channel networks' in *Recent Researches in Geology*, Hindustan Publishing Corporation, Delhi, pp. 53–65.

Liao, K. H. and A. E. Scheidegger: 1969, 'Branching -type models of flow through porous media', *Bulletin of the International Association of Scientific Hydrology* 15(4), 137–145.

Mark, D. M.: 1979, 'Topology of ridge patterns: randomness and constraints', *Geological Society of America Bulletin* 90, 164–172.

Mark, D. M.: 1981, 'Topology of ridge patterns: possible physical interpretation of the minimum spanning tree postulate', *Geology* 9, 370–372.

Mock, S. J.: 1971, 'A classification of channel links in stream networks', *Water Resources Research* 7, 1558–1566.

Peucker, T. K., R. J. Fowler, J. J. Little, and D. M. Mark: 1978, 'The triangulated irregular network', *Proceedings of the Digital Terrain Models Symposium*, American Society of Photogrammetry, 516–540.

Pfaltz, J.: 1976, 'Surface networks', *Geographical Analysis* 8, 77–93.

Ranalli, G. and A. E. Scheidegger: 1968, 'A test of the topological structure of river nets', *International Association of Scientific Hydrology Bulletin* 13 (2), 142–153.

Scheidegger, A. E.: 1967, 'Random graph patterns of drainage basins', in *14th General Assembly, International Association of Scientific Hydrology*, Berne, Paper 157, pp. 415–425.

Shreve, R. L.: 1967, 'Infinite topologically random channel networks', *Journal of Geology* 75, 179–186.

Shreve, R. L.: 1969, 'Stream lengths and basin areas in topologically random channel networks', *Journal of Geology* 77, 397–414.

Shreve, R. L.: 1974, 'Variation of mainstream length with basin area in river networks', *Water Resources Research* 10, 1167–1177.

Shreve, R. L.: 1975, 'The probabilistic-topologic approach to drainage-basin geomorphology', *Geology* 3, 527–529.

Smart, J. S.: 1968, 'Statistical properties of stream lengths', *Water Resources Research* 4, 1001–1014.

Smart, J. S.: 1969, 'Topological properties of channel networks', *Geological Society of America Bulletin* 80, 1757–1774.

Smart, J. S.: 1970, 'Use of topologic information in processing data for channel networks', *Water Resources Research* 6, 932–936.

Smart, J. S.: 1978, 'The analysis of drainage network composition', *Earth Surface Processes* 3, 129–170.

Smart, J. S. and J. R. Wallis: 1971, 'Cis and trans links in natural channel networks', *Water Resources Research* 7, 1346–1348.

Thornley, J. H. M.: 1977, 'A model of apical bifurcation applicable to trees and other organisms', *Journal of Theoretical Biology* 64, 165–176.

Warntz, W.: 1966, 'The topology of a socio-economic terrain and spatial flows', *Regional Science Association Papers* 17, 47–61.

Warntz, W.: 1975, 'Stream ordering and contour mapping', *Journal of Hydrology* 25, 209–227.

Werner, C.: 1972a, 'Channel and ridge networks in drainage basins', *Proceedings of the Association of American Geographers* 4, 109–114.

Warner, C.: 1972b, 'Graph-theoretical analysis of ridge patterns', *Proceedings of the 22nd International Geographical Congress*, 943–945.

Werner, C.: 1972c, 'Patterns of drainage areas with random topology', *Geographical Analysis* **4**, 119–133.

Werner, C.: 1972d, 'Two models for Horton's law of stream numbers', *Canadian Geographer* **16** (1), 50–68.

Werner, C.: 1973, 'The boundaries of drainage basins for topologically random channel networks', *Proceedings of the Association of American Geographers* **5**, 287–290.

Werner, C. and J. S. Smart: 1973, 'Some new methods of topologic classification of channel networks', *Geographical Analysis* **5**, 271–295.

ROBERT F. AUSTIN

MEASURING AND COMPARING TWO-DIMENSIONAL SHAPES

1. INTRODUCTION

Much time and energy has been expended on the study of shape, a fundamental property of geographic phenomena. Interest has been especially strong in the fields of cartography, geomorphology, economic geography and political geography. While the reasons for the interest in the first two fields are self-evident, an explanation for the interest in the latter fields is appropriate.

Many of the models of twentieth century location theory and geography are derived in part from studies of central places and regional space packing. In combination, these have evolved into the notion of a hexagonal lattice of service areas for various human activities such as marketing and transportation, if the assumptions of the models are met. By definition, the actual shapes of the service areas are, in large part, a function of the nature of the surface on which the lattice of service areas develops. Therefore, most theoretical studies have concentrated on the mechanisms of service area generation on a real-world surface and then inferred the existence of a hexagonal lattice through such techniques as Thiessen polygons (Dirichlet regions) generated by a simulation of the same mechanisms on an isotropic surface.

It is clear that the shapes of service areas on a real-world surface cannot be expected to be regular hexagons. It is also clear, however, that if the principles underlying the notion of a hexagonal lattice are correct, certain aspects of that lattice *should* be present. The two most important aspects are compactness and contiguity. The first aspect — "compactness" is a "measure of nearness between surface elements of [a] figure" (Frolov, 1975, p. 677). This aspect derives from the concepts of threshold and range and the assumed efficient use of space. This last point is perhaps the single most important premise of economic location theory. In a sense these hexagons represent a compromise between circular service areas "overproviding" for the client population (intersecting ranges for a particular service) and similar service areas "underproviding" for the client population (tangent ranges), the key being the shape efficiency of the circle. In the game of chess, two equally matched opponents will most often play to a stalemate. In the game of location theory, suppliers and consumers (if equally matched) should also play to a stalemate,

293

Gary L. Gaile and Cort J. Willmott (eds.), Spatial Statistics and Models, 293–312.
© 1984 *by D. Reidel Publishing Company.*

a compromise of efficiency or compactness that is represented on an isotropic surface by a lattice of hexagons. Similarly, the second aspect — contiguity — derives from the first. In a hexagonal lattice of service areas, excluding boundary cases, each service area is contiguous with six other areas.

Shape is also the basic component of the morphological approach in political geography, an approach that may be defined as the study of the pattern, shape and structure of political areas. The morphological approach is an intuitively obvious way for geographers and planners to study the effects of physical, albeit often quite permeable, barriers on political areas. The approach is also one of the ways in which geographers and planners may examine the implications of physical shape for the internal organization of and the efficiency of service delivery within political areas (aspects of the classic form-process question).

The notion of efficiency in the use of space is a most important premise of political location theory as well. While the economic geographer might define this efficiency in terms of movement cost or time (for example, delivery costs for goods and services), the political geographer might be more interested, at the national level, in the speed with which troops may be dispatched to an international border or the difficulty of patrolling an irregular versus a regular (in the extreme case, circular) border. At the local level, the shape of an administrative area will to varying degrees influence, among other things, the efficiency of medical, educational, and social welfare service deliveries and the cost of building and maintaining a local transportation system.

It may also be argued that the shape of a political area influences to some extent the degree of political and social integration of the population. Although counter-examples may be cited, we see that in many cases compactness and, failing that, physical contiguity are directly related, along with size, to political and social cohesion. Other factors are certainly of great significance in this regard, yet a fragmented (or divided) state is quite obviously at a disadvantage.

Traditionally, political geographers attempted to address this topic using a small set of categories to classify the shapes of compact (Uruguay), elongated (Chile), prorupted (Afghanistan), fragmented (Malaysia), and enclave-perforated (West Berlin) areas, as well as areas shaped like boots, mittens, pork chops, snails, hooks, diamonds, and tear drops. Farther along the spectrum of description, Tyler and Wells (1971, p. 2) reported that one 1961 New York congressional district was called by critics "The Camel Biting the Tail of the Buffalo Which is Stepping on the Tail of the Dachshund." More recently these "descriptive methods have been replaced by a variety of more efficient mathematical techniques" (Muir, 1975, p. 53), as seen for example in the work of Massam (1975), Taylor (1973), and Morrill (1981).

Although in a general sense Muir's comment is true, there are certain restrictions that must be considered when using existing shape measures. Massam (1975, p. 16), writing in the same year as Muir, noted that "until recently there had been little theoretical work on the understanding of the properties of different sorts of shape measures." At an earlier date, Bunge (1966, p. 73) observed that only certain aspects of shape (and these not necessarily separate from other characteristics such as orientation) could be expressed by any of the shape measures that could be both easily calculated and easily interpreted. And the methods that do provide unique pairings of index numbers and shape are either difficult to interpret or difficult to calculate. Despite these limitations, it is possible to analyze selected *aspects* of shape, such as compactness, provided that we select appropriate measures. Moreover, recent work in Fourier analysis seems to be close to resolving at least some of the difficulties.

2. CLASSICAL MEASURES

Several reviews of shape measures have been published, of which those by Boots and Lamoureaux (1972), Whittington *et al.*, (1972), Frolov (1975), Moellering and Rayner (1979), and Austin (1983) are the most notable examples prepared by geographers. In the field of psychology, Zusne (1970) has reviewed such measures in the context of visual perception and Pavlidis and Feng (1977) have summarized the work on syntactic analysis. Rutovitz (1970) (cited by Moellering and Rayner (1979)) reviewed current research in the biological sciences. Moellering and Rayner (1979, p. 3) note reviews in the area of picture processing by Rosenfeld (1969), Duda and Hart (1973), and Gonzales and Wintz (1977).

A number of classification systems have been suggested for the various measures of shape, including the two-by-two matrix proposed by Boots (1971) which classes measures according to whether they refer to standard (*SS*) or nonstandard (*NS*) shapes and whether they are parametric (*P*) or nonparametric (*NP*). Frolov (1975) proposed a system of eight classes which groups measures according to the type of data used for calculation. The most important of these classes are reviewed here.

2.1. *Perimeter and Area-Based Measures*

The simplest measure in this class may be expressed:

$$S_p = P/A \tag{1}$$

where S_p is the perimeter-based measure, P is the length of the perimeter of a shape and A is the area of the shape (Figure 1). Minor variations of this general form also have been suggested, the variations most frequently involving assigning weights of one sort or another to the variables. Equation (1) may be restated for any reference circle, as

$$S_p = (2\pi r)/\pi r^2$$

and reduced to

$$S_p = 2/r.$$

From this, it is clear that the measure is scale dependent. More commonly, therefore, perimeter-based measures have been calculated (occasionally with scaling constants) as

$$S_p = P/P_c$$

where P_c is the circumference of the circle with an area equal to the area of the shape in question (Figure 1). Once again, minor variations have been suggested.

Examples of studies using or discussing measures in this class include those by Pounds (1963), East and Prescott (1975), Miller (1953), Morrill (1981), Richardson (1960), Schwartzberg (1966) and Duda and Hart (1973), as well as a number of 19th century German geographers (Frolov, 1975, pp. 678–680). Chorley *et al.*, (1957) proposed that a lemniscate could be used as the reference polygon (rather than a circle) in such a measure, and applied this modification to the study of drainage basins.

Measures of this type fall in the category of "maximum problems" in mathematics (Rademacher and Toeplitz, 1957, pp. 17–22, 139–46). A basic difficulty associated with their use is their extreme sensitivity to minute boundary irregularities or crenulations, which we might term the "fjord effect".

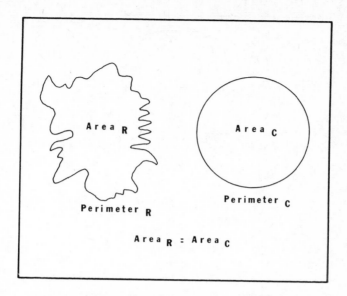

Fig. 1. Parameters of perimeter and area-based measures.

2.2. *Linear Dimension and Area-Based Measures*

Measures in this class are distinguished by the use of length and width measurements as well as area, usually with reference to some standard polygon. The measure used by Horton (1932) was

$$S_d = A/D^2 \qquad\qquad (2)$$

where S_d is the diameter-based measure and D is the long axis of the figure. This measure has often been restated and variously termed the Gibbs (1961), Cole (1964), or Haggett (1965) compactness ratio. In these modified expressions the measure is, in essence, an explicit comparison of the area of a region with the area of the circumcircle of the region. The area of a circle (πr^2) may be inserted in equation (2) and the value for a circle of S_d determined to be $\pi/4$. If this value is inverted and used as a scaling constant, equation (2) may be rewritten (with four decimal point accuracy) as

$$S_c = 1.2732\, A/D^2. \qquad\qquad (3)$$

Such an expression yields values ranging from 0 for a line to 1.0 for a circle

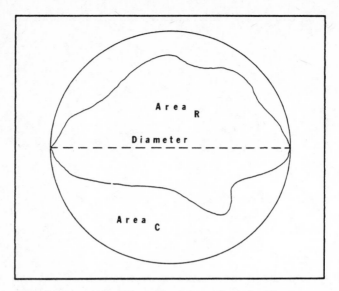

Fig. 2. Parameters of linear dimension and area-based measures

(or 0 to 100 if the most common scaling constant is used). A number of different shapes may have similar or identical index values, and, therefore, we cannot say that a particular region is shaped like another region or like some regular polygon simply because they have the same index values. However, we can say that a particular region is more or less compact than another.

The comparative lack of theoretical work on such classical shape measures is evidenced by the implicit assumption, by many authors, that the minor variations on this theme are significantly different measures, when in fact the only difference is a scaling constant. (For a brief discussion of the genesis of the index, see Boots, 1978 and Haggett, 1978; for a comment on that exchange, see Austin, 1982a). Blair and Biss (1967), for example, argue that there is a difference between the diameter of the circumcircle of a region used by Cole (1964) and the longest axis of a region defined by Haggett (1965) (cf. Horton, 1932). The difference is purely semantic, since every operationalization of the Gibbs/Cole/Haggett measure known to this author has implicitly assumed an equality. Indeed, Haggett's (1965, p. 227; Haggett *et al.,* 1977) own index value for an equilateral triangle can only be obtained by this assumption. Moreover, although perhaps widely realized, the fact that this measure is merely a special case (where the major and minor axes are equal) of the ellipse-based index discussed by Stoddard (1965) appears to have been unappreciated, and the larger family of curves into which this curve itself would fall has not been discussed in the geographic literature. An examination of this family (a subset of the conic sections) will prove quite profitable in future studies. Alternatively, this problem may be viewed as a specific example of what Rademacher and Toeplitz (1957, pp. 103–10) term "the spanning circle of a finite set of points." These authors discuss an algorithm (apparently first proposed by Chrystal, 1885) for solution of this "minimum problem" that is readily adapted to computer calculation.

The results from several studies using the modified measure shown in equation (3) have been summarized by Austin (1982a). In addition to its use in the studies already cited, this measure, either as shown or with minor variations, has been used by Schumm (1965), Krumbein (1941), Reock (1961), Austin (1981), Austin and Dowell (1982), Haggett (1965), Massam (1970), Pederson (1967), Hampson (1971), and Boots (1970). Bosch (1978) has used a version of this measure that also included the perimeter of the region.

2.3. *Radial Vector Measures*

Another type of shape index, the Boyce and Clark (1964) radial shape index, is in a sense related to the second class of compactness measures. The index is calculated by measuring the lengths of 16 (or more) equally spaced radials from the geometric center of an area to its boundary and determining the proportion that each radial contributes to the sum of the lengths (Figure 3). The absolute values of the difference between these percentages and the comparable percentages for a circle (for example, 6.25% if 16 radials are used) are then summed. In equation form

$$S_{rv} = \sum_{i=1}^{n} \left| (100 r_i / \sum_{i=1}^{n} r_i) - (100/n) \right|,$$

where r_i is the length of radial i and n is the number of radials. With 16 radials, values for S_{rv} range from 0 (for a circle) to 175 (for a line segment). With an infinite number of radials, the maximum value of S_{rv} is 200.

When it is calculated in this way, this index is more than the sophisticated compactness ratio implied by Blair and Biss (1967). As Cerny (1975, p. 21) noted, "with any finite number N of radials, measurements [sic] is actually

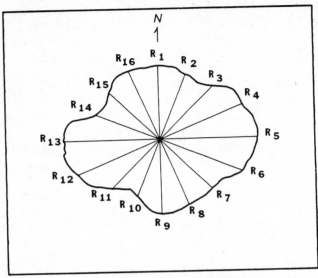

Fig. 3. Parameters of the Boyce and Clark radial vector measure.

of an N-sided polygon rather than the original shape with all its detail." In this regard, Dent (1972), using as vertices the ten points most frequently designated in a survey as necessary for the reconstruction of a shape (that is, ten "characteristic points"), has compared the Boyce-Clark index values for sixteen states with their corresponding 10-sided polygons. "A Pearson product-moment correlation yielded an r of + 0.97" (Dent, 1972, p. 398). Moreover, Cerny (1975, p. 26) states that "the chance of two shapes with the same index value, taken at random, being visually similar is considerably less than 0.01."

Boyce and Clark (1964) observed that from a methodological point of view, a more satisfactory measure in many cases would use radials from the *functional* center of a region (for example, the central business district of a metropolitan area). In this way, the index may be used to determine the accessibility of a central node (one definition of the spatial efficiency of a system). When the measure is calculated using a functional center, the range of values is 0 to 200 regardless of the number of radials, since the possibility of such a point being located at the end of a line segment must be admitted.

In addition to this sensitivity to the location of the center of the region, Cerny (1975) noted that index values will vary with the number of radials and their orientation. It is recommended that at least sixteen radials be used, since this is the number at which index values begin to stabilize, and also to permit comparison with the findings of other authors. For a similar reason, one radial should be oriented north (0°), with the others spaced at equal intervals (22.5° if exactly sixteen radials are used).

Compared to the measures discussed previously, this measure has seen restricted use. Studies that have examined the measure include Austin (1981), Stoddard (1965), Lo (1980), and Austin and Dowell (1982). Lo's (1980) application is particularly interesting since it demonstrates the utility of decomposing the measure to examine orientation. The radial shape index has also been used by Austin (1982b) in a study of temporal area specifically, and two-dimensional non-Euclidean metrics in general.

3. CONTEMPORARY DEVELOPMENTS

Concurrent with the development of the field of pattern recognition (Attneave and Arnoult (1956), Brown and Owen (1967), Granlund (1972), Hudson and Fowler (1966), Ledley (1964), Rosenfeld (1969), Stenson (1966), Zusne (1970); see Austin (1983) for more recent work), a much firmer theoretical foundation for the study of shape measures began to be constructed in the late 1960's. Built upon the theorems of several branches of mathematics, this foundation supported the development of a wide range of measures of shape. In general, few of these measures have seen widespread use.

There are several reasons for the comparative lack of subsequent empirical studies using these measures, including difficulties associated with calculation. Given the widespread availability of electronic digitizers and computers, this is in most cases an unsatisfactory explanation. Much more pressing issues are the difficulties associated with interpretation, including ambiguity of reference. In addition, many of these measures were created in order to examine particular aspects of shape (rather than the general form-process question), and subsequent use presumed similar interests. Moreover, some of the measures make quite stringent assumptions regarding the nature of the spatial data to be examined. Finally, and perhaps most important, these measures have been perceived by many geographers as advances toward the development of a much finer class of measures, rather than as end products in themselves. In this sense, a limited number of test applications is probably sufficient.

It is not possible to consider here all of the measures that have been suggested in recent years. Instead, examples of four approaches to measurement are considered.

3.1. *Inscribed Polygon Measures*

The best known example of this type of measure is the "shape sums" method proposed by Bunge (1966). This measure represents an extension of the concept of the reference shape discussed in Section 2 for the case of a circle. Bunge (1966) noted that a variety of polygons could be use as referents. He selected an octagon, on experimental grounds, as the most satisfactory shape for his purposes.

The method of measurement is relatively simple. Basically, an octagon with sides of equal length and angles of variable size is inscribed on the study shape. Each of the vertices of the inscribed octagon may be labelled consecutively for the sake of simplicity as V_1 through V_8. The first measurement is computed by measuring the distances between V_1 and V_3, V_2 and V_4, V_3 and V_5, and so on through V_8 and V_2 (that is, "lag one" vertex distances). These are then summed. The second measure is the sum of "lag two" distances (that is V_1-V_4, V_2-V_5, ..., V_8-V_3). The third measure is the sum of "lag three" distances. These three series (with the "lag zero" distances which are known at the outset) exhaust the set of such measurements for an octagon. The fourth, fifth, and sixth measurements are the sums of the squares of the lag one, lag two, and lag three distances respectively.

Once the eight points of tangency have been specified, computation is quite easy. However, the specification of these points is a rather cumbersome operation. (Bunge suggested a mechanical apparatus for this portion of the process.) More important, such a measure is actually only a description of the inscribed polygon. This means that although we may classify shapes, we may not (contrary to Bunge's assertion) reconstruct them. Finally, the set of six sums (or n-2 sums for an n-gon) is difficult to interpret. Beyond the original examples provided by Bunge (1966), it appears that the only published example of an application of this method was presented by Stoddard (1965).

3.2. *Moment Measures*

By "moment measures" is meant the group of measures derived from the distance (weighted or unweighted) of elements of a region from its center (generally defined as the barycenter, or "center of gravity"). Frolov (1975, p. 684) noted that a simple version of such measures was proposed as early as 1842 by J. H. von Thünen. Stewart and Warntz (1958a, 1958b) may be credited with the general (re-)introduction of such measures to the field of geography. Blair and Biss (1967) developed this concept and applied the related notion of the "dynamical radius" to the study of shape compactness. Their index of shape may be expressed in the form

$$S_{dr} = A / (2\pi \int_R r^2 \, dx dy)^{1/2},$$

where r in this case is the distance from a particular rectangular element of length dx and breadth dy to the center (however defined) of a region R. Although this measure has received some endorsement, the number of additional applications has been so restricted as to preclude complete evaluation.

The approach also has been rigorously elaborated for the study of shape by Massam (1970, 1975), Massam and Goodchild (1971), and Massam and Burghardt (1968) in a form which allows the weighting of elements and distances by population. In so doing, the measure provides a good description of shape efficiency in the context of central point accessibility (that is, degree of compactness and centrality of a point in terms of human population density). This measure may be expressed formally as

$$S_{mi} = A^2 / 2\pi I_a,$$

where I_a is the moment of inertia of the study region around its barycenter. Due primarily to its data requirements, and the specific nature of the questions for which it is best suited, this measure has served primarily as a conceptual tool and an impetus for further study.

3.3. Set-Theoretic Measures

The measures discussed in Section 2 were comparisons between a particular region and variously defined circles. Comparisons could just as well be made with any reference polygon (cf. Section 3.1). Lee and Sallee (1970) suggested that the specific reference polygon should be selected on the basis of the particular research problem at hand (for example, a lemniscate for the study of drumlins or an ellipse for the study of atolls). This notion could be realized by superimposing upon the study region some reference polygon with the same area as that region in such a manner that the intersection of the areas of the two shapes is maximized. For the set A_r (study region) and the set A_p (polygon)

$$S_{st} = 1 - \frac{A_r \cap A_p}{A_r \cup A_p},$$

where A_r is the area of the study region, A_p is the area of the reference polygon, $A_r = A_p$ and $A_r \cap A_p$ is maximized.

Interpreting values of this measure is comparatively simple. In the case of drumlins for example, a drumlin that is shaped exactly like a lemniscate will be completely covered by the reference lemniscate, and the measure of S_{st} will be 0. The greater the magnitude of S_{st}, (to a maximum of 1.0), the greater the deviation of the shape from the reference polygon. It must be remembered, however, that comparisons between areas and studies may be made *only* if the reference polygon has been completely specified and accurately duplicated.

3.4. *Harmonic Analysis*

The use of harmonic analysis in general and the Fourier series in particular within geography has been discussed by Moellering (1979, 1981, 1982) and by Moellering and Rayner (1979), who also provided a survey of similar efforts in other fields. Moellering and Rayner (1979, p. 25) noted that "as was shown by Fourier in 1807 (Fourier, 1822) so long as a series [of x and y coordinate pairs] is continuous and single-valued and has a finite set of maxima and minima it may be represented exactly by a set of sinusoids". This fact has been used to great advantage in the field of communication, for example, to analyze the open curves of electronic signals. More recently, it has been proposed that similar analysis could be performed on closed curves (that is, two-dimensional shapes).

Any curve may be approximately modeled by a sine wave with a given frequency ("width") and amplitude ("height"). The harmonic of a particular curve is an integral multiple of the fundamental frequency of that curve. By summing several harmonics, we may construct a complex curve. Put simply, harmonic analysis attempts to express through sines and cosines, and in this instance the Fourier series, the shape of a curve.

A number of approaches have been taken in harmonic analyses of shape. Certainly the most easily understood is that using polar coordinates. Basically, for any geometric shape there is a geometric center or barycenter ("center of gravity"). From this center, we may define a set of polar coordinates and then measure the radii to the boundary of the shape. In theory, an infinite number of radii may be measured, but more commonly an equally-spaced finite number of radii will actually be used. In this case, a *discrete* Fourier transform (as opposed to a continuous Fourier expression) is the appropriate technique. In the case of the studies by Blackwell *et al.*, (1982), the discrete

Fourier transform that is used is implemented in the FFTRC subroutine of the International Mathematical and Statistical Libraries as follows

$$x(K + 1) = \sum_{J=0}^{N-1} A(J + 1) \, e^{(2 \pi i J K)/N}$$

where $K = 0, 1, \ldots N/2$.

Here $A(1)$, $A(2)$, $\ldots A(N)$ are the input values to be transformed and $X(1)$, $X(2)$, $\ldots X(N)$ are the components of the discrete Fourier spectrum. The values of $X(N/2 + 2)$, $\ldots X(N)$ are obtained as the complex conjugates of the previously computed values by

$$X(N + 2 - I) = \text{CONJG}(X(I))$$

where $I = 2, \ldots N/2$.

The series of coefficients derived from these calculations constitute a description of shape that is reversible (that is, we may reconstruct the shape if given the series). The continuous series is theoretically infinite, while the discrete transform yields a finite series. In either case, the series may be truncated for all practical purposes at the fifth or sixth harmonic (Moellering and Rayner, 1970; Blackwell *et al.*, 1982).

At least two objections have been raised against this basic type of analysis. First, it has been argued that the results of the analysis are sensitive to the selection of the barycenter. Although this may have posed a problem in the past, new methods of defining the barycenter through triangulation have been proposed (Blackwell *et al.*, 1982) that appear to enhance stability (at least in the context of numerical analysis). The second objection is related to the complexity of shapes susceptible to this type of analysis.

In general, the majority of shapes analyzed by geographers are remarkably simple in most respects. The homogeneity of the degree of compactness of several hundred disparate study regions has been discussed by Austin (1982a). Mandelbrot (1975), whose work is introduced in Section 4.2, has suggested that the range of geomorphologic shapes is quite restricted. Nonetheless, it would be convenient to define our measures of shape in such a way as to accommodate various degrees of complexity. Several authors have noted that the method of Fourier analysis discussed above cannot deal with truly complex shapes, and have suggested alternatives that employ intrinsic functions in a complex plane. It appears that this rejection of the basic technique may have been premature. Blackwell *et al.*, (1982) have proposed that for complex shapes, values of rho may become negative for some values of theta. Conceptually this means that the curve has crossed itself, *but* a single value is retained. The overlap disappears when the series is subsequently plotted in x, y space.

Much additional research on the harmonic analysis of geographic regions will be necessary before the technique achieves widespread acceptance. It is, however, one of the most promising approaches considered to date.

4. FUTURE DIRECTIONS

The concept of shape is basic to virtually all geographic inquiry, and has been described as such by numerous geographers. However, the measurement of shape has proven to be an extremely difficult problem. Although the measures discussed in Section 3 appear promising, other approaches continue to be developed. Prediction is always a hazardous enterprise, but it is safe to say that two approaches developed originally by mathematicians will soon enter the geographic literature on shape. These approaches, concerned with graph theory and fractal dimensions, therefore deserve some comment.

4.1. *Graph Theory*

For several years, geographers have used graphs for the study of, for example, relative location (that is, connectivity). However, the power of graph theory (and its tools) has not yet been completely realized, let alone taken advantage of, by geographers. For this reason, graph theoretic methods should be considered as a possible future direction for studies of shape. (For a complete discussion of graph theory, see Harary (1969, 1978)).

One of the most obvious, if somewhat simple, applications of graph theory is to the problem of the fragmentation and puncturing of shapes. Much more interesting is the approach to shape recognition adopted by Pavlidis and Feng (1977). Known within the field of pattern recognition (as well as other fields including linguistics) as syntactic analysis, the method argues that shapes may be decomposed and the components analyzed using graph theoretic methods. (The components themselves may be subjected to further decomposition.) In this way, the structure of the shape may be studied and shapes may be classified by the results. To date, a very restricted set of applications has been published that are of immediate applicability in geography.

4.2. *Fractals*

A second relatively recent development in the study of shape has been discussed in detail by Mandelbrot (1975, 1976, 1977). The approach involves extraordinarily complex mathematical analysis. Basically, a Poisson-Brown stochastic model is fit to the object of study (say, a region) and the "fractal dimension" of the object is used as the measure of shape. The theory underlying the method is based on the concept of self-similarity and the joint concepts of "signal" and "noise" in communication (Clark and Gaile, 1973). Mandelbrot proposes to distinguish between signal and noise and in so doing to distinguish or characterize shape.

5. CONCLUSION

One very important question remains to be considered: For what specific purpose do we wish to measure shape? The answer to this question will suggest the best approach or approaches to the study of shape. A number of attributes have been described as desirable for an ideal measure of shape. In effect each of these attributes may constitute an answer to this question. It will suffice to consider three here.

5.1. Shape Reconstruction

It has been suggested that for a numerical measure of shape to be useful, it should be possible to reconstruct the shape from the measure alone in a manner analogous to reconstructing a line segment from a distance measure. (In both cases, orientation is assumed not to be an issue). A truly effective geographic information system should incorporate not only such information as is necessary for spatial correlations, but also that which is necessary for a visual display of results (for example, maps). It has been argued that a "reconstructable" shape measure would be useful for such purposes.

In fact, a much simpler method of reconstructing shapes is to simply store the coordinates of the region's boundaries. Such a data array may be thinned to any specified degree of generality — using such principles as parsimony, aesthetics, and the physical characteristics of the display device — and still be more accurate for this purpose than any conceivable summary measure. As demonstrated by the Laboratory for Applications of Remote Sensing at Purdue University, computer file space allocation is, for all practical purposes, irrelevant in this context (particularly when considered in relation to the amount of other data stored in such a system). The costs of reconstructing shape definitely favor simple coordinate storage.

5.2. *Single Index*

A second attribute that has been described as desirable is the ability to summarize shape in a single index. Lee and Sallee (1970) have proven that no unique single index measure is possible. There are two choices presently available for the description of shape: a "signature" consisting of a set of parameters or a series of unified parameters (such as the Fourier series).

5.3. *Limited Value Range*

Moellering and Rayner (1979, p. 9) stated that "an additional desirable property of such a shape measure is that the value of the parameter range between zero and one where zero is a straight line and one represents the index shape, usually a circle." This is an attribute that can clearly be gained by most of the measures considered through rather straight-forward transformations. For example, consider the radial shape index with a range of values from 0 for a circle to a maximum of 200 for a line (see 2.3 for a discussion of the range). The first step of the transformation — dividing by 200 — yields values from 0 to 1. The second step, which will invert the values in order to satisfy the criterion noted above, is specified by the function $f(x) = (1 - x)$.

5.4. *Summary*

The conclusion to be drawn from this discussion is that the attributes considered in Sections 5.1 and 5.3 are relatively unimportant, while the attribute considered in Section 5.2 is unattainable. The ability to compare shapes, or at least aspects of shapes, in an unambiguous and easily interpreted manner must be for the present the primary criterion by which a measure is evaluated. Only after comparison and classification has been completed (or is thoroughly underway) may analysis proceed. In this regard, Tobler's (1978) efforts, which employ the concept of isomorphism, may ultimately prove to be more useful than many of the techniques mentioned above.

Dept. of Geography
University of Missouri — Columbia

BIBLIOGRAPHY

Attneave, F. and M. Arnoult: 1956, 'The quantitative study of shape and pattern recognition', *Psychological Bulletin* 53(6), 452–71.

Austin, R. F.: 1981, 'The shape of West Malaysia's districts' *Area* 13(2), 145–50.

Austin, R. F.: 1982a, 'Reply to Boots and Blair', *Area* 14(2), 127–31.

Austin, R. F.: 1982b, 'A definition and estimate of temporal area', *Professional Geographer* 34(3), 297–304.

Austin, R. F.: 1983, 'Bibliography of measures of spatial shape', *Vance Bibliographies* (Public Administration Series).

Austin, R. F. and T. Dowell, 1982, 'The compactness and contiguity of Missouri's counties', presented to the Missouri Academy of Science.

Blackwell, P., J. Johannsen, S. Chang, and R. F. Austin: 1982, unpublished research on polar coordinate, discrete Fourier transforms.

Blair, D. J. and T. H. Bliss: 1967, 'The measurement of shape in geography: an appraisal of methods and techniques', *Bulletin of Quantitative Data for Geographers No. 11*, Department of Geography, Nottingham University.

Boots, B. N.: 1970, 'An approach to the study of patterns of cellular nets', *Discussion Paper No. 1*, Department of Geography, Rutgers University.

Boots, B. N.: 1971, 'The measurement of shape in geography', Department of Geography, Rutgers University, mimeograph.

Boots, B. N.: 1978, 'Haggett's shape index', *Area* 10(2), 86.

Boots, B. N. and L. F. Lamoureaux: 1972, *Working Notes and Bibliography on the Study of Shape in Human Geography and Planning*, Council of Planning Librarians, Exchange Bibliography No. 346.

Bosch, W.: 1978, 'A procedure for quantifying certain geomorphological features', *Geographical Analysis* 10(3), 241–47.

Boyce, R. R. and W. A. V. Clark: 1964, 'The concept of shape in geography', *Geographical Review* 54, 561–72.

Brown, D. R. and D. H. Owen: 1967, 'The metrics of visual form: Methodological dyspepsia', *Psychological Bulletin* 68(4), 243–59.

Bunge, W.: 1966, *Theoretical Geography* (second revised edition), Lund Studies in Geography, Series C, General and Mathematical Geography No. 1, Gleerup, Lund.

Cerny, J. W. : 1975, 'Sensitivity analysis of the Boyce-Clark shape index', *Canadian Cartographer* 12(1), 21–27.

Chorley, R. J., D. E. G. Malm, and H. A. Pogorzelski: 1957, 'A new standard for estimating drainage basin shape', *American Journal of Science* 255, 138–41.

Chrystal, G.: 1885, 'On the problem to construct the minimum circle enclosing n given points in a plane', *Proceedings of the Edinburgh Mathematical Society* 3, 30–33.

Clark, W. A. V. and G. L. Gaile: 1973, 'The analysis and recognition of shapes', *Geografiska Annaler* 55B(2), 153–63.

Cole, J. P.: 1964, *Study of Major and Minor Civil Divisions in Political Geography*, Department of Geography, University of Nottingham, mimeograph (presented to the 20th International Geographical Congress, Sheffield).

Dent, B. D.: 1972, 'A note on the importance of shape in cartogram communication', *Journal of Geography* 71(7), 393–401.

Duda, R. O. and D. E. Hart: 1973, *Pattern Classification and Scene Analysis*, John Wiley and Sons, New York.

East, W. G. and J. R. V. Prescott: 1975, *Our Fragmented World*, Macmillan, London.

Fourier, J. B. J.: 1822, *Theorie Analytique de la Chaleur* trans.: Freeman, A.: 1955, *The Analytical Theory of Heat*, Dover, New York.

Frolov, Y. S.: 1975, 'Measuring the shape of geographical phenomena: A history of the issue', *Soviet Geography Review and Translation* 16, 676−87.

Gibbs, J. P.: 1961, 'A method for comparing the spatial shapes of urban units', in J. P. Gibbs (ed.), *Urban Research Methods*, Van Nostrand, Princeton pp. 99−106.

Gonzales, R. and P. A. Wintz: 1977, *Digital Image Processing*, Addison Wesley, Reading.

Granlund, G. H.: 1972, 'Fourier preprocessing for hand print character recognition', *IEEE Transactions on Computers* C−21(2), 195−201.

Haggett, P.: 1965, *Locational Analysis in Human Geography*, Edward Arnold, London.

Haggett, P.: 1978, 'Reply to Boots', *Area* 10(2), 86−87.

Haggett, P., A. D. Cliff, and A. Frey: 1977, *Locational Analysis in Human Geography* (second edition), Edward Arnold, London.

Hampson, A.: 1971, *The Influence of Territorial Shape on Municipal Expenditures: England and Wales*, M. A. Thesis, Department of Geography, University of Denver.

Harary, F.: 1969, *Graph Theory*, Addison Wesley, Reading.

Harary, F.: 1978, 'On the history of the theory of graphs', pp. 1−17 in *New Directions in the Theory of Graphs*, University of Michigan Press, Ann Arbor.

Horton, R. E.: 1932, 'Drainage basin characteristics', *Transactions of the American Geophysical Union* 13, 350−61.

Hudson, J. C. and P. M. Fowler: 1966, 'The concept of pattern in geography', *Discussion Paper No. 1*, Department of Geography, University of Iowa.

Krumbein, W. C.: 1941, 'Measurement and geological significance of shape and round-ness of sedimentary particles', *Journal of Sedimentary Petrology* 11(2), 64−72.

Ledley, R.: 1964, 'High-speed automatic analysis of biomedical pictures', *Science* 146(3641), 216−23.

Lee, D. and T. Sallee: 1970, 'A method of measuring shape', *Geographical Review* 60(4), 555−63.

Lo, C. P.: 1980, 'Changes in the shapes of Chinese cities', *Professional Geographer* 32(2), 173−83.

Mandelbrot, B. B.: 1975, 'Stochastic models for the earth's relief, the shape and the fractal dimension of the coastlines, and the number-area rule for islands', *Proceedings of the National Academy of Science U.S.A.*, 72(10), 3825−28.

Mandelbrot, B.: 1976, 'Note on the definition and the stationarity of fractional gaussian noise', *Journal of Hydrology* 30(4), 407−09.

Mandelbrot, B.: 1977, *Fractals: Form, Chance and Dimension*, W. H. Freeman, San Francisco.

Massam, B. H.: 1970, 'A note on shapes', *Professional Geographer* 22(4), 197−99.

Massam, B. H.: 1972, *The Spatial Structure of Administrative Systems*, Association of American Geographers, Commission on College Geography Resource Paper No. 12.

Massam, B. H.: 1975, *Location and Space in Social Administration*, John Wiley, New York.

Massam, B. H. and A. F. Burghardt: 1968, 'The administrative subdivisions of Southern

Ontario: An attempt at evaluation', *Canadian Geographer* 12(3), 125–34.

Massam, B. H. and M. F. Goodchild: 1971, 'Temporal trends in the spatial organization of a service agency', *Canadian Geographer* 15(3), 193–206.

Miller, V. C.: 1953, *A Quantitative Geomorphic Study of Drainage Basin Characteristics in the Clinch Mountain Area, Virginia and Tennessee*, Columbia University, Department of Geology, Technical Report No. 3, Contract N6, O. N. R. Project NR 389–042.

Moellering, H.: 1979, 'A review of spatial shape measures', presented to the Association of American Geographers, Philadelphia.

Moellering, H.: 1981, 'An approach to the matching of cartographic shapes using dual axis fourier shape analysis', presented to the Association of American Geographers, Los Angeles.

Moellering, H.: 1982, 'A comparison of several harmonic measures of shape', presented to the Association of American Geographers, San Antonio.

Moellering H. and J. N. Rayner: 1979, *Measurement of Shape in Geography and Cartography*, Department of Geography, Ohio State University, Numerical Cartography Laboratory, NSF Grant No. SOC77–11318.

Morrill, R.: 1981, *Political Redistricting and Geographic Theory*, Association of American Geographers, Washington.

Muir, R.: 1975, *Modern Political Geography*, Macmillan, London, pp. 51–57.

Pavlidis, T. and H-Y. F. Feng: 1977, 'Shape discrimination', in K. S. Fu (ed.), *Syntactic Pattern Recognition, Applications*, Springer-Verlag, Berlin, pp. 125–45.

Pederson, P. O.: 1967, 'On the geometry of administrative areas', Universitetcenter, Copenhagen, mimeograph.

Pounds, N. J. F.: 1963, *Political Geography*, Mc-Graw Hill, New York, pp. 33–65.

Rademacher, H. and O. Toeplitz: 1957, *The Enjoyment of Mathematics*, H. Zuckerman (translator), Princeton University Press, Princeton.

Reock, E. E., Jr.: 1961, 'A note: Measuring compactness as a requirement of legislative apportionment', *Midwest Journal of Political Science* 5(1), 70–74.

Richardson, L. F.: 1960, 'A preliminary theory of geographical opportunities for fighting: Contiguity', in Q. Wright and C. C. Lienau (eds.), *Statistics of Deadly Quarrels*, Boxwood Press, Pittsburgh, pp. 288–291.

Rosenfeld, A.: 1969, *Picture Processing by Computer*, Academic Press, New York.

Rutovitz, D.: 1970, 'Centromere finding: Some shape descriptors for small chromosome outlines', in B. Meltzerand and D. Michie (eds.), *Machine Intelligence* 5, American Elsevier, New York.

Schumm, S. A.: 1956, 'Evolution of drainage systems and slopes in badlands at Perth Amboy, New Jersey', *Bulletin of the Geological Society of America* 67, 597–646.

Schwartzberg, J. J.: 1966, 'Reapportionment, gerrymanders, and the notion of compactness', *Minnesota Law Review* 50, 443–452.

Stenson, H. H.: 1966, 'The physical factor structure of random forms and their judged complexity', *Perception and Psychophysics* 1, 303–310.

Stewart, J. Q. and W. Warntz: 1958a, 'Physics of population distribution', *Journal of Regional Science* 1, 99–123.

Stewart, J. Q. and W. Warntz: 1958b, 'Macrogeography and social science', *Geographical Review* 48(2), 167–184.

Stoddard, D.: 1965, 'The shape of atolls', *Marine Geology* 3(5), 369–383.

Taylor, P. J.: 1973, 'A new shape measure for evaluating electoral district patterns', *American Political Science Review* 67(3), 947–950.

Tobler, W. R.: 1978, 'Comparison of plane forms', *Geographical Analysis* 10(2), 154–162.

Tyler, G. and D. I. Wells: 1971, 'The new gerrymander threat', *The American Federationist* 78, 1–7.

Whittington, G., K. S. O. Beavon, and A. S. Mabin: 1972, 'Compactness of shape: Review, theory and application', *Environmental Studies: Occasional Paper No. 7*, University of Witwatersrand, Johannesburg.

Zusne, L.:1970, *Visual Perception of Form,* Academic Press, New York, pp. 175–246.

PART II

SPATIAL MODELS

WILLIAM C. KRUMBEIN†

A SIMPLE STEP-BY-STEP APPROACH TO SPATIAL MODEL BUILDING [1]

Model building in the spatial sciences can be better understood and accomplished when the cognitive processes from which effective models evolve can be identified and segregated into a finite number of explicit, sequential steps. It sometimes is asserted that such a cascade of intellectual efforts could be deduced entirely from first principles but, as those who have built successful analogs to real-world processes would argue, such is not the case. Experience is essential to the understanding and, therefore, documentation of the model building process. Drawing from many years of experience and in full view of the scientific method, particularly its deductive theme, eight essential and sequential steps are presented in the hope that they may provide guidance to those who are new to mathematical model building. These steps are:

1. A particular problem is identified and selected for study. This step involves such background work as a preliminary literature scan, field observation(s), conversations with scientists who are familiar with the problem under consideration and so on.

2. A conceptual model (a mental picture) of the processes, responses and boundary conditions that characterize the problem is developed. Qualitative statements, diagrams, flow-charts, et cetera characteristically emerge from this stage.

3. The conceptual model is reduced into a set of discrete, verbal statements and each statement corresponds to at least one of the fundamental elements of the concept. Such statements include postulates, for example, that are relevant to the processes and their outcomes.

4. Each discrete verbal statement in Step (3) is formalized as an algebraic, probabilistic or other mathematical statement. The mathematical representations must be isomorphic with their corresponding verbal statements.

5. The verbal statements are "erased" and the purely mathematical relationships that exist among the symbolic expressions are condensed into one or more equations that can be solved by analytical or numerical methods. The end-product of this step represents the initial model.

6. Using such boundary conditions, theoretical or empirical values of

Gary L. Gaile and Cort J. Willmott (eds.), Spatial Statistics and Models, 315–319.
© 1984 *by D. Reidel Publishing Company.*

constants and parameters as may be available or can be estimated, the equations derived at Step (5) are solved.

7. The model is tested with observed data, especially those data that are specified by the model itself, including topological and metric outputs that must conform to real-world input.

8. Based upon the model's performance in Step (7), it is rejected, accepted or modified. For models that yield outputs that are acceptable first approximations, Step (8) begins a sequence of modification/refinement loops that retrace many of the above steps in the hope of producing a better version of the model.

Although the model-building process is described as a series of discrete steps in order to enhance conceptualization and discussion, it should be understood that the process, in fact, is a continuous one in which discontinuities between stages do not actually exist. In such a schema, the creative process generally flows from the top, down; however, refinement often involves multiple passes through subsets of the steps. In other instances, steps can be bypassed when sufficient knowledge already is available. The utility of these guidelines can be illustrated by the conceptual development of the well-known heat conduction model from a minimum number of premises.

A Simple Deterministic Model of Heat Flow Through a Solid Body

In this simple example, Step (1) is easily satisfied merely by stating that we wish to mathematically describe the flow of heat through a solid body. The model is then conceptualized for a system of interest (Step 2) — one that also can be realistically specified. For this, heat transfer through a thin, pure copper rod with a cross-sectional area (A) can easily be imagined. As part of the conceptualization, it will be assumed that the rod is fully insulated against heat loss to the surrounding environment and that a heat source (e.g., 100 °C) is applied at the initial end of the rod ($x = 0$, where x is the distance from the initial end (m) measured in the direction of the rod's major axis). At the far end of the rod ($x = 1$), a heat absorber is placed and it has a fixed temperature (e.g., 20 °C). These few initial conditions and assumptions are all that is necessary for a complete conceptualization of the heat conduction process.

Several postulates now can be made largely on the basis of common sense (Step 3). These are:

1. Heat flows from high to low temperatures.

2. The rate of heat flow normal to any cross-sectional area A depends on the temperature gradient in the x-direction.

3. The rate of heat absorption ($J s^{-1}$) by any unit volume of the rod (m^3) depends on (i) the difference in heat flow at both ends of the volume, i.e., normal to A at positions x and $x + \Delta x$ and (ii) the mass of the material in the unit volume (kg).

4. Heat flow is a function of both distance and time $- q(x, t)$.

In order to convert these verbal statements into mathematical expressions (Step 4), a set of symbols needs to be defined. Let temperature (°C) first be symbolized by T. A steady rate of heat flow in the x-direction (q_x) can then be described as

$$q_x \propto \frac{T_{x+\Delta x} - T_x}{(x + \Delta x) - x} . \qquad J s^{-1}$$

When position x is defined as the reference location 1 and position $x + \Delta x$ as datum 2, then

$$\frac{T_{x+\Delta x} - T_x}{(x + \Delta x) - x} = \frac{T_2 - T_1}{x_2 - x_1} = \frac{\Delta T}{\Delta x} . \qquad °C\ m^{-1}$$

Since, in the general case, T also varies with y, z, and t, and we may wish to evaluate the differential $(\Delta T/\Delta x)$ as Δx approaches zero, partial differential notation will be adopted; that is,

$$\frac{\partial T}{\partial x} = \lim_{\Delta x \to 0} \frac{\Delta T}{\Delta x} . \qquad °C\ m^{-1}$$

Partial notation allows for the explicit separation of heat flows that occur in the x, y and z directions as well as for variations in the flow as a function of time.

Drawing from postulates 1 and 2 above, the rate of heat flow into a segment of the rod beginning at x can be expressed as

$$q_x = -kA \frac{\partial T}{\partial x}\bigg|_x \qquad J s^{-1} \tag{1}$$

and out of the segment at $x + \Delta x$ as

$$q_{x+\Delta x} = -kA \frac{\partial T}{\partial x}\bigg|_{x+\Delta x} \qquad J s^{-1} \tag{2}$$

where k is the thermal conductivity of pure copper ($Wm^{-1} {}°C^{-1}$). Thermal conductivity (k) is a property of the material of interest and, for most applications, it is assumed to be independent of T. Its physical interpretation and units can easily be derived through the dimensional evaluation of equation (1) or (2). The rate of heat absorption by the segment then becomes

$$q_{x+\Delta x} - q_x = -kA \left[\frac{\partial T}{\partial x}\bigg|_{x+\Delta x} - \frac{\partial T}{\partial x}\bigg|_x \right]. \qquad J\,s^{-1} \qquad (3)$$

Recalling that mass equals density times volume and postulate 3(ii) above, the rate of heat absorption by the segment alternatively can be written as an explicit function of time:

$$q_{x+\Delta x} - q_x = -c\rho A \Delta x \frac{\partial T}{\partial t} \qquad J\,s^{-1} \qquad (4)$$

where $A\Delta x$ is the volume of the segment (m^3), ρ is the density of pure copper ($kg\,m^{-3}$) and c is a constant of proportionality — termed the specific heat ($J\,kg^{-1}\,{}°C^{-1}$). By equating equations (3) and (4), again converting Δx to ∂x and dividing through by $-kA\partial x$, the rates of heat gain or loss by the segment reduce to

$$\frac{\left[\frac{\partial T}{\partial x}\big|_{x+\Delta x} - \frac{\partial T}{\partial x}\big|_x \right]}{\partial x} = \frac{\partial^2 T}{\partial x^2} = c\rho k^{-1} \frac{\partial T}{\partial t}. \qquad {}°C\,m^{-2} \qquad (5)$$

From equation (5), the initial model of heat flow through the copper rod (Step 5) can be rewritten as

$$\frac{\partial T}{\partial t} = k\rho^{-1}c^{-1} \frac{\partial^2 T}{\partial x^2} = \alpha^2 \frac{\partial^2 T}{\partial x^2} \qquad {}°C\,s^{-1}$$

where α^2 is the thermal diffusivity of pure copper ($m^2\,s^{-1}$). This means that the time rate of change of the segment's temperature or internal energy is proportional by α^2 to the degree to which $\partial T/\partial x$ is nonlinear. It is worth noting that $\partial T/\partial t$ is clearly dependent on the ability of copper to transfer heat (α^2) — which, like k, is assumed to be independent of T.

Now that the initial model has been derived, initial and boundary conditions need to be specified (Step 6) in order that an experimental check on the model can be performed. Perhaps the most simplifying condition that can be prescribed is to evaluate model performance under "steady state" conditions. In other words, set $\partial T/\partial t = 0$ so that T will vary linearly with x. Needless to say, experimental data support the model's description of steady state heat flow (Step 7) and, therefore, this model is acceptable for steady state applications (Step 8). With accurate specifications of α^2 and the temperature profile, the model also well-describes conductive systems in which $\partial T/\partial t \neq 0$, called "transient", although further tests and modifications are in order (Step 8).

Even though the development of the one-dimensional (in x) heat conduction model is well-known, it is important in the spatial context since it is the general expression for virtually all one-dimensional diffusion. As long as α^2 can be specified for the medium of interest, heat flow can be adequately characterized. It also is worth mentioning that the model can easily be extended to two or three dimensions and, perhaps most importantly, to spatial diffusion processes that mimic heat flow. Many spatial diffusion systems are well-framed by this formulation.

NOTE

[1] This brief paper was compiled and written by Cort Willmott from handouts and notes taken during two of the late William C. Krumbein's lectures to the graduate seminar in "Spatial Model Building" that was given in the Department of Geography at UCLA during the winter of 1974. The course was jointly taught by James O. Huff and Krumbein and Gary Gaile and Cort Willmott numbered among the struggling students. We are grateful to Professor Krumbein for the inspiration that he unselfishly gave to those fledgling geographers – the editors.

ANDREW R. PICKLES AND RICHARD B. DAVIES

RECENT DEVELOPMENTS IN THE ANALYSIS OF MOVEMENT AND RECURRENT CHOICE

1. INTRODUCTION

Theories of choice, which geographers frequently entertain, suggest that an individual's choice is not only a function of the measurable characteristics of the individual and the choice set, but may also be a function of some unmeasurable component such as tastes, motivations and natural propensities (e.g., 'chronic movers', Morrison, 1970). In addition, choice is suggested to be a function of past behavior. Examples of such a relationship are the changing of choice probabilities as the result of learning from previous choices, growing loyalty or increasing inertia to change with repeated use of the same alternative and circumstances in which a change of choice is associated with a set of varying costs. In studies of migration, where choices are areas of residence, all of these forms of relationships may be expected to exist.

In spite of the clear demand for longitudinal data from a few geographers and other researchers, the vast majority of available data for the analysis of spatial choice processes remains cross-sectional. For example, census data provides data on current residential choice but almost nothing on previous residential choices or even exactly when the current residence was chosen. It is therefore of little surprise to find that much current research work continues to be performed using models and methods which are at best agnostic, at worst naive, as to the dynamic nature of the choice process. Within such data questions about the relationships between choices made at different times cannot be effectively examined. Even where individual longitudinal records are available, for example from activity and travel diaries, the inter-temporal relationships between choices have frequently been ignored, at least in part because of the inadequate development and poor awareness of appropriate models for such analysis. In such cases, the data have been aggregated over time to provide average choice probabilities for each individual, which are then analyzed using cross-sectional methods. There are, of course, notable exceptions in particular within the analysis of migration where a number of researchers have shown interest in determining the presence of 'duration of stay' effects and of 'cumulative inertia' (McGinnis, 1968). These studies have been reviewed elsewhere (Pickles, Davies and Crouchley, 1982). These

321

Gary L. Gaile and Cort J. Willmott (eds.), Spatial Statistics and Models, 321–343.
© 1984 by D. Reidel Publishing Company.

comments, nevertheless, should not detract from some recent developments that have been made in the analysis of cross-sectional data. However, it should be understood that where dynamic effects and unobserved variables are of importance, parameter estimates and predictions obtained from cross-sectional models may be quite misleading.

This paper is divided into several sections. Section 2 briefly outlines the task for cross-sectional analysis and describes some of the recent developments in aggregate data analysis, including the relationship between some of the aggregate models and models of individual choice. Section 3 introduces some models of individual choice and considers their application to individual data for a single observed choice or time period. Some of the problems of directly introducing past individual behavior as an explanatory variable are also described. Section 4 presents a general model, proposed by Heckman (1981) for the analysis of individual choice data when there are a series of choices observed for each individual. Estimation of the general model requires further specification, restriction and a rich data set before estimation becomes both computationally and statistically reasonable. This section proceeds to illustrate the variety of approaches by which this can be done. Section 5 summarizes remaining problems which require not only further technical solution, but also improvements in the theory of individual spatial choice to assist in the task of proper model specification.

The methods to be discussed are drawn from an area of research which is still undergoing vigorous growth. It should be understood that, as yet, there is often no accepted 'best approach' to a particular analysis. A variety of approaches are presented, which offer different theoretical and computational advantages. In future years, some of these methods will form the basis of both more refined and routine approaches whilst others may become little more than intellectual curiosities. However, they all offer valuable intellectual insights into the problem of analyzing such data.

2. SOME RECENT DEVELOPMENTS IN AGGREGATE METHODS FOR CROSS-SECTIONAL DATA

Perhaps, one of the more significant recent developments in aggregate level analysis has been the synthesis that has been achieved amongst a variety of previous models. Ledent (1981) and Wilson (1979) have shown how Alonso's theory of movement (Alonso, 1978) reduces to different members of Wilson's family of spatial interaction models (Wilson, 1971) under varying conditions. Such models estimate flows within a table of inter-state migration in a single step from the values of exogeneous variables and certain information about the marginal distributions or net migration constraints. Anas (1981) has shown that a doubly-constrained spatial interaction can be viewed as equivalent to a relatively simple form of multinomial logit model, an individual level method of analysis discussed in the next section. Anas points out that this not only provides a theoretical framework at the individual level for consideration of such spatial interaction models, but that both models may be estimated using either aggregate or individual level data.

An alternative approach to the analysis of such tables of flows first decomposes the table of flows into two elements, a symmetric component of flows and a skew-symmetric component. The prospect here is that relatively simple models may then be fitted to each of these components separately. Tobler (1979) and Constantine and Gower (1982) describe and apply a variety of models of this form.

The demometrics approach (e.g., Rogers, 1980) extends the demographic accounting methods into a multi-regional, multi-dimensional context. These methods, including the Rees-Wilson accounting framework, with its concern with minor flows (Rees and Wilson, 1977), are essentially transition matrix methods in which flows to destinations are determined as proportions of the populations at risk at the origins.

All these methods make very strong assumptions as to the nature of the individual process underlying the aggregate flow. The most unattractive of these assumptions are those of homogeneity — that all individuals share the same transition or choice probabilities, and Markovity — that the effect of each individual's past history on current transition or choice probabilities may be entirely summarized by the effect of their current state alone, if it has any effect at all. Not only is there much behavioral theory to suggest that such assumptions would be most unlikely to hold in practice, but the larger than expected variance in the observed flows which is frequently encountered, casts empirical doubt upon them (Flowerdew and Aitkin, 1982). However, examination of such individual level assumptions are most easily performed using individual level methods, which the next section introduces.

3. INDIVIDUAL LEVEL METHODS FOR SINGLE PERIOD CROSS-SECTIONAL DATA

The most commonly encountered models for examining individual level migration or choice data are variants of the general linear model with a discrete dependent variable. An appealing approach is to model the discrete variable in terms of continuous variable crossing thresholds. In a binary choice context, let $y(i)$ be an indicator variable for the choice of 1 or 0 by individual i, and

$$y(i) = \begin{cases} 1 \text{ if } y^*(i) \geqslant 0 \\ 0 \text{ otherwise} \end{cases}$$

where $y^*(i)$ is a continuous latent variable which, as shown below, may often be interpreted as a measure of relative utility.

The latent variable may be derived in a variety of ways. Consider an individual i who may obtain utility $u(i, 0)$ and $u(i, 1)$ from each of the two alternatives, where

$$u(i, 0) = \bar{u}(i, 0) + \epsilon(i, 0)$$

and

$$u(i, 1) = \bar{u}(i, 1) + \epsilon(i, 1)$$

and where $E[\epsilon(i, j)] = 0$ for all i and j.

The probability of choosing alternative 1 is given by

$$\Pr[y(i) = 1] = \Pr[\bar{u}(i, 1) + \epsilon(i, 1) \geqslant \bar{u}(i, 0) + \epsilon(i, 0)]$$

$$= \Pr[\bar{u}(i, 1) - \bar{u}(i, 0) \leqslant \eta(i)]$$

where $\eta(i) = \epsilon(i, 1) - \epsilon(i, 0)$.

If $\epsilon(i, 0)$ and $\epsilon(i, 1)$ are identically distributed with extreme value density functions (Johnson and Kotz, 1970, p. 272) then $\eta(i)$ has a logistic distribution function and

$$\Pr[y(i) = 1] = \Pr[y^*(i) \geqslant 0] = \frac{\exp[\bar{u}(i, 1)]}{\exp[\bar{u}(i, 0)] + \exp[\bar{u}(i, 1)]}$$

$$= \frac{\exp[\bar{u}(i, 1) - \bar{u}(i, 0)]}{1 + \exp[\bar{u}(i, 1) - \bar{u}(i, 0)]}$$

where $y^*(i) = \bar{u}(i, 1) - \bar{u}(i, 0) + \eta(i)$.

It is usually expected that differences in utilities between the alternatives are related to individual characteristics, differences in the characteristics of the alternatives available and other exogenous variables. Assuming a linear function, then

$$y^*(i) = \mathbf{Z}(i)\beta + \eta(i)$$

and

$$\Pr[y(i) = 1] = \frac{\exp[\mathbf{Z}(i)\beta]}{1 + \exp[\mathbf{Z}(i)\beta]} \quad \text{or} \quad \log \frac{\Pr[y(i) = 1]}{1 - \Pr[y(i) = 1]} = \mathbf{Z}(i)\beta,$$

where $\mathbf{Z}(i)$ is a vector of exogenous variables describing individual, environmental and alternative characteristics, and β is a vector of parameters. This is, of course, the familiar logit model.

If $\epsilon(i, j)$ are normally distributed, then $\eta(i)$ have a normal cumulative density function (CDF), giving rise to the probit model

$$\Pr[y(i) = 1] = \Pr[y^*(i) \geqslant 0] = \int_{-\infty}^{\mathbf{Z}(i)\beta} [1/(2\pi)^{1/2}] \exp\{-t^2/2\} \, dt.$$

When individuals can be grouped or where there are several observations on each individual, these models can be estimated using weighted least squares. Where only a single observation is available for some individuals or groups, then maximum likelihood estimation is necessary. The estimated parameters are those which optimize the following non-linear likelihood function for a sample of I individuals, written for the polytomous n choice context using an obvious extension of the previous notation

$$L = \prod_{i=1}^{I} \prod_{j=0}^{n-1} \Pr[y(i) = j]^{\delta(i, j)},$$

where $\delta(i, j) = \begin{cases} 1 \text{ if individual } i \text{ makes choice } j \\ 0 \text{ otherwise} \end{cases}$

The parameters estimated are asymptotically normally distributed with variance given by the diagonal elements of the negative of the inverse of the sample Hessian. The sample Hessian, or matrix of second derivatives of the likelihood function with respect to the parameters of the model, is calculated or estimated by virtually all non-linear optimization routines. In the binary context, parameter estimation and testing pose no great computational burden.

In the polytomous choice context, such as that required for a multi-regional migration model, the logit model offers considerable computational advantage. This is mainly due to the fact that, for the multinomial logit model, choice from several alternatives can be reduced to a problem involving the indepedent consideration of a series of binary comparisons

$$Pr\,[y(i) = 1] = \frac{\exp\,[\bar{u}(i,j)]}{\sum\limits_{j}\exp\,[\bar{u}(i,j)]} = \frac{\exp\,[\bar{u}(i,1) - \bar{u}(i,0)]}{\sum\limits_{j}\exp\,[\bar{u}(i,j) - \bar{u}(i,0)]}$$

$$= \frac{\exp\,\mathbf{Z}(i)\beta_1}{1 + \sum\limits_{j=1}\exp\,\mathbf{Z}(i)\beta_j}$$

However, this very powerful simplification implies a very restrictive assumption about individual behavior. The problem is that the model does not distinguish alternatives which are perceived to be similar from those which are perceived as very different. Thus, the addition of an alternative identical to a pre-existing alternative is assumed to attract individuals from all other alternatives rather than simply sharing in those individuals who had previously chosen the similar alternative (the 'red-bus blue-bus' problem, McFadden (1973)). This independence of irrelevant alternatives assumption (IIA), as it is known, may under particular circumstances be overcome by assuming the decision process to be nested. In such a model similar alternatives may be grouped together as a single alternative within an intergroup logit choice model with further models fitted for the intragroup choices (Hensher and Johnson, 1981). In the migration context, such a procedure might form two groups of states of those adjacent to the origin and those far from the origin for analysis at one level, followed by models examining the choice of state within each group. The probit model is able to incorporate correlations amongst the error terms and thus need not make the IIA assumption.

In addition, the multinomial logit model assumes that choice probabilities are the same for all observationally identical individuals. The covariance probit model, a random coefficient model proposed by Hausman and Wise (1978), attempts to model variations in tastes by allowing the coefficients of the model to be distributed according to a normal distribution over the population rather than fixed and identical for all individuals. For the model

$$y^*(i,j) = \mathbf{Z}(i,j)\bar{\beta} + \epsilon(i,j)$$

where $\epsilon(i,j) = \mathbf{Z}(i,j)v(i) + \eta(i,j)$, $\mathbf{Z}(i,j)$ is a $1 \times K$ vector of non-stochastic explanatory variables and $\bar{\beta}$ is a $K \times 1$ vector of the mean values for the coefficients of these explanatory variables.

The $K \times 1$ vector $\nu(i)$ of normally distributed random variables has elements $\nu(i, k)$ such that

$$E[\nu(i, k)] = 0$$

and

$$E[\nu(i, k)\nu(i', k')] = \begin{cases} \sigma_\nu(k) \text{ for } i = i' \text{ and } k = k' \\ 0 \quad \text{ for } i \neq i' \text{ or } k \neq k'. \end{cases}$$

Similarly $\eta(i, j)$ is a normally distributed random variable with

$$E[\eta(i, j)] = 0$$

and

$$E[\eta(i, j)\eta(i', j',)] = \begin{cases} \sigma_\eta(j) \text{ for } i = i' \text{ and } j = j' \\ 0 \quad \text{ for } i \neq i' \text{ or } j \neq j'. \end{cases}$$

The model allows individuals to have heterogenous responses with respect to how a change in an explanatory variable effects utility and choice. Estimation of the binary choice model can be performed without numerical integration, since the normal CDF and its inverse are available on many computers. However, each additional choice beyond two requires numerical integration in one further dimension, which becomes costly although approximation procedures are available.

The computational problems can be relieved if the problem can be framed in terms of an ordered response model (Amemiya, 1975). Such a model is more difficult to interpret in terms of utility, but in migration it may be readily understood through some notion of 'residential stress' (Huff and Clark, 1978) which can be relieved through the choice of one from a series of increasingly drastic alternatives.

In the application by Akin et al. (1979), the alternatives were no move, local move within a county and move outside of a county. The model is specified in a very similar way to the Hausman-Wise model, and indeed for binary choice is a special case of it. However, for n alternatives, the choice of each alternative is associated with some part of the same one-dimensional CDF, defined by $(n-1)$ thresholds $A(j)$, which are to be estimated from

$$y^*(i) = \mathbf{Z}(i)\bar{\beta} + \epsilon(i)$$

and

$$\epsilon(i) = \mathbf{Z}(i)\,\nu(i) + \eta(i),$$

where $\mathbf{Z}(i)$ is a $1 \times K$ vector of non-stochastic explanatory variables, $\bar{\beta}$ is as before, $\nu(i)$ is as before, and $\eta(i)$ is a normally distributed random variable with

$$E[\eta(i)] = 0$$

and

$$E[\eta(i)\,\eta(i')] = \begin{cases} \sigma_\eta & \text{for } i = i' \\ 0 & \text{for } i \neq i' \end{cases}$$

The choice probabilities for individual i for each of the alternatives 1 to n are given by

$$\Pr[i, 1] = \Pr[-\infty < y^*(i) < A(1)] = \int_{-\infty}^{(\mathbf{A}(1) - \mathbf{Z}(i)\bar{\beta})/C(i)} \phi(\lambda)\,d\lambda$$

$$\Pr[i, 2] = \Pr[A(1) < y^*(i) < A(2)] = \int_{(A(1) - \mathbf{Z}(i)\bar{\beta})/C(i)}^{(A(2) - \mathbf{Z}(i)\bar{\beta})/C(i)} \phi(\lambda)\,d\lambda$$

$$\Pr[i, n] = \Pr[A(n-1) < y^*(i) < \infty] = \int_{(A(n-1) - \mathbf{Z}(i)\bar{\beta})/C(i)}^{\infty} \phi(\lambda)\,d\lambda$$

where $\phi(\lambda)$ is the standard normal density and

$$C^2(i) = \sum_{k=1}^{k} \sum_{k'=1}^{k} Z(i, k)\,Z(i, k')\,\sigma_\nu(k, k') + \sigma_\eta^2.$$

In their application of the model, it is of interest to note that Akin *et al.* find significant heterogeneity, or non-zero variance in the coefficients $\sigma_\nu(k, k)$, which supported their contention that there are different decision making structures across households. In particular, though spouses income has an insignificant mean coefficient, the coefficient has significant variance. "In other words, even though on 'average' there is no effect, the probability of getting a

positive or negative effect for spouses incomes in some families is quite high."
(Akin *et al.*, 1979, p. 240).

As yet, none of the models have examined the role of previous choice
behavior on current decisions in any thorough fashion. The obvious approach,
and that proposed by Moss (1979) is to estimate a discrete choice model, for
example a multinomial logit model suitably nested, in which variables describing past behavior would simply be included amongst the exogenous variables.
In fact such variables, being determined by the previous outcomes of the
choice process itself, are endogenous. The incorporation of endogenous
variables pose severe estimation problems, variously referred to within the
stochastic process literature as 'spurious contagion' (Feller, 1967), 'spurious
high order effects' (Massy *et al.*, 1970) and the 'deficient diagonal' (Coleman,
1964). In general, this refers to the specification errors which arise where an
exogenous, possibly unobservable, variable has been omitted in the presence
of an endogenous variable. In the migration context, we may, for example,
have omitted a variable called 'conservatism' which is independent of all the
other exogenous variables but is negatively correlated with the probability of
moving. Cohorts with increasing duration of stay at current residence will
have an increasing proportion of individuals who are 'conservative' and, as a
result, the observed mobility rates for these cohorts will decline with increasing duration of stay. Therefore, current duration of stay will be positively
correlated with the omitted variable 'conservatism'. It is well-known that the
omission of a variable correlated with an included variable results in biased
estimation. Exactly similar arguments have been discussed in analysis of
unemployment duration (e.g. Lancaster and Nickell, 1980).

Some of the ideas required for the resolution of this problem have already
been introduced in the random coefficient models of this section, in which
additional variation across individuals, or heterogeneity, is allowed for over
and above that due to the included exogeneous variables.

4. METHODS FOR THE ANALYSIS OF PANEL DATA
WITH REPEATED OBSERVATIONS

Uncontrolled heterogeneity and duration dependence are just two of the
factors to be accounted for within a dynamic model. Heckman (1981)
considers a general dynamic model for a binary process of the following form

$$y^*(i, t) = Z(i, t)\beta + \sum_{j=1}^{\infty} \gamma(t-j, t)y(i, t-j) + \sum_{j=1}^{\infty} \lambda(j, t-j) \prod_{l=1}^{j} y(i, t-l)$$
$$+ G(L)y^*(i, t) + \epsilon(i, t) \tag{1}$$

where $i = 1, \ldots, I, t = 1, \ldots, T$ and $G(L)$ is a general lag operator.

$$y(i, t) = \begin{cases} 1 \text{ if } y^*(i, t) \geqslant 0 \\ 0 \text{ otherwise} \end{cases}$$

In this model, the latent variable is determined by five terms. The first term accounts for the effects of exogenous variables. The second term accounts for the effects of past history in the form of a finite order Markov model of a special form. The third term accounts for the cumulative effects of the most recent continuous experience in a state, introduced to capture the notion that occupation of a state may be associated with an accumulation process. This term might be rewritten as

$$\sum_{j=1}^{\infty} \lambda(j, t - j) \prod_{l=1}^{j} (1 - y(i, t - l))$$

to account for renewal effects such as cumulative inertia.

The fourth term accounts for habit persistence in which prior propensities to select a state (prior values of the latent variable) rather than prior occupancy of the state determine the current probability that a state is occupied (latent Markov model of Coleman, 1964).

Finally the error term $\epsilon(i, t)$ must account for all other individual variation. This model is very general and, hardly surprisingly, must be severely restricted before estimation becomes practicable given data and computational constraints.

We have seen that for estimation of duration dependence and, by implication, the other dynamic characteristics of the choice process, the effects of taste variation or omitted variables must be accounted for. The probit models of the previous section allowed for this variation through random slope coefficients. Such an approach could be used in analyzing how a preceding choice effects a subsequent choice (see for example Johnson and Hensher, 1981). An alternative approach is to consider these omitted factors as an additive component of variance, such that

$$\epsilon(i, t) = \tau(i) + \nu(i, t) \tag{2}$$

where $\nu(i, t)$ is independently and identically distributed with mean zero and variance σ_ν^2 and $\tau(i)$ is an individual specific effect whose values are distributed over the population according to some unknown density function independent of $\nu(i, t)$.

In the model, observationally identical individuals may make different choices for two reasons. Firstly, because of the error term $v(i, t)$, $y(i, t)$ is stochastic, reflecting the fact that the observable variables determine choice probabilities not choice deterministically. Secondly, different values for the individual specific component $\tau(i)$ mean that otherwise identical individuals will possess different choice probabilities. The effect of the variation in $\tau(i)$ is that the observationally identical population becomes distributed over possible values for the choice probability according to some unknown 'mixing distribution' rather than all sharing the same value (Figure 1). To model or account

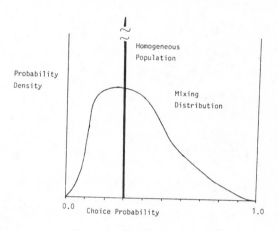

Fig. 1.

for the variation, there are two main approaches, which are sometimes equivalent, that can be taken according to whether the distribution over $\tau(i)$ is considered or the mixing distribution over the choice probabilities is examined directly.

Perhaps the most obvious approach is to allow each individual a fixed parameter $\tau(i)$ which is to be estimated. However, most panel data consists of a large number of individuals surveyed over a relatively small number of periods. Under such circumstances, a very large number of parameters must be estimated and maximum likelihood estimates of these parameters and other parameters of the model are inconsistent (Neyman and Scott, 1948; Heckman, 1981, p. 134). An elegant approach which gives consistent estimates of some parameters is the conditional likelihood approach of Anderson (1970, 1973).

Consider a binary choice logit model with fixed coefficients but with an individual specific 'fixed effect' $\tau(i)$. From equations (1) and (2)

$$\Pr[y(i, t) = 1 | Z(i, t), \tau(i)] = \frac{\exp(Z(i, t)\beta + \tau(i))}{1 + \exp(Z(i, t)\beta + \tau(i))}$$

$$= \frac{\exp(w(i, t))}{1 + \exp(w(i, t))}.$$

Suppose that $T = 2$, then the probability that $y(i, 2) = 1$, given that $y(i, 1) + y(i, 2) = 1$ is

$$\Pr[y(i, 2) = 1 | Z(i, t), \tau(i), y(i, 1) + y(i, 2) = 1]$$

$$= \frac{\Pr[y(i, 1) = 0, y(i, 2) = 1 | Z(i, t), \tau(i)]}{\Pr[y(i, 1) = 0, y(i, 2) = 1 | Z(i, t), \tau(i)] + \Pr[y(i, 1) = 1, y(i, 2) = 0 | Z(i, t), \tau(i)]}$$

$$= \frac{\exp(Z(i, 2)\beta + \tau(i))}{\exp(Z(i, 2)\beta + \tau(i)) + \exp(Z(i, 1)\beta + \tau(i))}$$

$$= \frac{\exp(w(i, 2) - w(i, 1))}{1 + \exp(w(i, 2) - w(i, 1))}.$$

This clearly does not depend on any part of $w(i, t)$ which remains constant from time period 1 to time period 2. It therefore provides a way of obtaining consistent estimates of the parameters for time varying exogenous variables, removing the effects of time constant exogenous variables and individual specific effects in particular. For this model, $\sum_{t=1}^{T} y(i, t)$, the count of choices of alternative 1 in the series, is a sufficient statistic for $\tau(i)$, allowing its effect to be removed by conditioning on that count.

Such an approach can be readily extended to a first order Markov model where exogenous variables are constant over time. This introduces a further problem concerned with the treatment of initial conditions of dynamic processes. Since, in a Markov chain, choice behavior depends on previous choice, the first observed choice can only be modeled using special, often undesirable, assumptions. A more acceptable approach is to model second and subsequent choices, conditional upon the first observed choice. If

$$\Pr[y(i, t) = 1 | Z(i), \tau(i), y(i, t-1)] = \frac{\exp(Z(i)\beta + \tau(i) + \gamma y(i, t-1))}{1 + \exp(Z(i)\beta + \tau(i) + \gamma y(i, t-1))}$$

then $y(i, 1)$, $\sum_{t=1}^{T} y(i, t)$ and $y(i, T)$ are sufficient statistics for $\tau(i)$.

Thus, for example with $T = 4$ and using an obvious notation for binary choice series

$$Pr[y(i, 2) = 1 | Z(i), \tau(i), y(i, 1) = 1, y(i, 4) = 0, \sum_{t=1}^{4} y(i, t) = 2]$$

$$= \frac{Pr[1100 | Z(i), \tau(i), y(i, 1) = 1]}{Pr[1100 | Z(i), \tau(i), y(i, 1) = 1] + Pr[1010 | Z(i), \tau(i), y(i, 1) = 1]}$$

$$= \frac{\exp \gamma}{1 + \exp \gamma}$$

providing a consistent estimator for the Markovian effect parameter γ. The approach can be extended to higher order Markov chains (Chamberlain, 1979).

The binary Markov model above is just one form (Brand Loyal) of such models examined by Massy $et\ al.$ (1970) using very similar testing procedures based on an empirical Bayes approach. These methods have been extended by Davies $et\ al.$ (1982a) to provide a family of independent tests for collections of binary series, which test for homogeneity, stationarity and the absence of renewal and Markov effects. These tests specify particular models of the process and assess their goodness of fit. This is done by comparing the choice frequencies predicted by the model for a particular 'experimental' period for individuals grouped according to their past behavior, with the observed frequencies. For example, for a nonstationary renewal process with no unobserved heterogeneity,

$$Pr[y(i, t) = 1] = \frac{\exp[Z(i, t)\beta + \lambda(d)]}{1 + \exp[Z(i, t)\beta + \lambda(d)]}$$

where d is the time since the last renewal.

In the case of no exogenous variables and with an obvious notation

$$Pr[y(i, 4) = 1 | 111] = Pr[y(i, 4) = 1 | 011] = Pr[y(i, 4) = 1 | 101]$$

$$= Pr[y(i, 4) = 1 | 001] = \frac{\exp[\alpha(4) + \lambda(0)]}{1 + \exp[\alpha(4) + \lambda(0)]} \tag{3}$$

and

$$Pr[y(i, 4) = 1 | 110] = Pr[y(i, 4) = 1 | 010] = \frac{\exp[\alpha(4) + \lambda(1)]}{1 + \exp[\alpha(4) + \lambda(1)]} \tag{4}$$

etc.

Thus under homogeneity, the conditional probabilities of equation (3) are all equal and so a test of the model is simply a contingency table of the frequency of choice 1 or 0 for each of the conditioning series types (similarly for equation (4)). For longer series, a limited number of exogenous variables might be used whilst leaving sufficient degrees of freedom to perform a test for residual heterogeneity.

To test for non-stationarity and non-zero order effects, the possibility of individual specific heterogeneity must be confronted. The approach adopted by Davies *et al.* (1982a) was to remove these effects by randomization. With no exogenous variables, these tests may also be reduced to contingency table tests.

These tests have been applied to migration data (Pickles *et al.*, 1982) and they showed (1) the inadequacy of simple disaggregation as a control for heterogeneity, (2) that non-stationarity is considerable and (3) that duration of stay effects, if they exist at all, may be rather smaller than expected.

The preceding analysis has made progress through the use of various conditional likelihood functions. An alternative approach is to use the marginal likelihood (see Chamberlain, 1979), found by integrating the likelihood conditional on values of the unknown variable(s) over their distribution in the population. This is the approach already inntroduced in the covariance probit model, in which the distribution of the unobservable component of the latent variable was assumed to be normal. Pickles *et al.* (1982) considered the distribution over the choice probabilities directly, rather than over some component of the latent variable. In their analysis of migration data, they assumed migration probabilities to be distributed according to a beta-distribution; a flexible distribution over the [0, 1] interval used by others (Massy *et al.*, 1970) and having some useful mathematical properties. For a stationary zero-order model, the probability of a particular sequence of moves and no moves from an individual drawn at random from a population, with migration probabilities distributed according to a beta density $b(p)$, is given by

$$
\Pr[y(1), y(2), \ldots, y(T)] = \int_0^1 \Pr(y(1), y(2), \ldots, y(T)|p)\, b(p)\, dp
$$

$$
= \int_0^1 \left\{ \prod_{t=1}^{T} p^{y(t)} (1-p)^{1-y(t)} \right\} p^{\alpha-1}(1-p)^{\beta-1} \frac{\Gamma(\alpha+\beta)}{\Gamma(\alpha)\,\Gamma(\beta)}\, dp
$$

$$
= \prod_{t=1}^{T} \left[\frac{\alpha + \sum\limits_{j=1}^{t-1} y(j)}{\alpha+\beta+(t-1)} \right]^{y(t)} \left[\frac{\beta + \sum\limits_{j=1}^{t-1} (1-y(j))}{\alpha+\beta+(t-1)} \right]^{1-y(t)}
$$

The parameters of the beta mixing distribution may be made functions of time invariant exogenous variables as in Heckman and Willis (1977) where

$$\alpha_i = \exp(\mathbf{Z}(i)\xi_\alpha)$$

and

$$\beta_i = \exp(\mathbf{Z}(i)\xi_\beta).$$

It should be noted that the model can be simply extended to the polytomous choice context (see Pickles 1982a for an application to housing choice). The mixing distribution methods can also be extended to a Markov model. Following the latent variable approach of equation (1) and for simplicity ignoring exogenous variables, a first order stationary Markov model may be represented by

$$\Pr[y(i, t) = 1 \mid \tau(i), y(i, t-1)]$$

$$= \frac{\exp[\tau(i) + \gamma y(i, t-1)]}{1 + \exp[\tau(i) + \gamma y(i, t-1)]}.$$

The probability of a particular binary choice series, noting the need to account for the initial condition, is given by

$$\Pr[y(i, 2), \ldots, y(i, T) \mid \tau(i), y(i, 1)]$$

$$= \prod_{t=2}^{T} \frac{\{\exp[\tau(i) + \gamma y(i, t-1)]\}^{y(i,t)}}{1 + \exp[\tau(i) + \gamma y(i, t-1)]}.$$

The probability of a particular choice series for a person selected from the population at random, given their first choice, is again found by integrating the likelihood conditional upon τ over $f(\tau \mid y(1))$, the conditional density of τ in the population

$$\Pr[y(2), \ldots, y(T) \mid y(1)] = \int_{-\alpha}^{\alpha} \prod_{t=2}^{T} \frac{\{\exp[\tau + \gamma y(t-1)]\}^{y(t)}}{1 + \exp[\tau + \gamma y(t-1)]} f(\tau \mid y(1)) \, d\tau. \quad (5)$$

From the point of view of a choice probability mixing distribution, individuals in a binary Markov process follow a transition matrix of the form

Choice at time t

		1	0
Choice at time $t-1$	1	$p(i)$	$1 - p(i)$
	0	$1 - q(i)$	$q(i)$

and therefore should be considered to be distributed according to a bivariate density function over possible values of both p and q. For such a model, the proportion of the population with each series type is

$$\Pr[y(2), \ldots, y(T) | y(1)] = \int_0^1 \int_0^1 \left\{ \prod_{t=2}^{T} p^{y(t)y(t-1)} (1-p)^{(1-y(t))y(t-1)} \right.$$

$$\left. q^{(1-y(t))(1-y(t-1))} 1 - q^{y(t)(1-y(t-1))} \right\} f(p, q | y(1)) \, dp \, dq \qquad (6)$$

requiring bivariate integration.

Equation (5) can be seen to be a special form of this Markov model in which

$$p(i) = \frac{\exp[\tau(i) + \gamma]}{1 + \exp[\tau(i) + \gamma]}$$

and

$$1 - q(i) = \frac{\exp[\tau(i)]}{1 + \exp[\tau(i)]} = \frac{\exp[\tau(i) + \gamma]}{\exp[\tau(i) + \gamma] + \exp[\gamma]}$$

$$= \frac{\exp[\tau(i) + \gamma] (1 + \exp[\tau(i) + \gamma])^{-1}}{\exp[\tau(i) + \gamma] (1 + \exp[\tau(i) + \gamma])^{-1} + \exp \gamma [1 + \exp(\tau(1) + \gamma)]^{-1}}$$

$$= p(i) [p(i) + (1 - p(i)) \exp \gamma]^{-1} = g(p(i)) \qquad (7)$$

Then

$$\Pr[y(2), \ldots, y(T) | y(1)] = \int_0^1 \left\{ \prod_{t=2}^{T} p^{y(t)y(t-1)} (1-p)^{(1-y(t))y(t-1)} \right.$$

$$\left. (1 - g(p))^{(1-y(t))(1-y(t-1))} g(p)^{y(t)(1-y(t-1))} \right\} f(p | y(1)) \, dp.$$

To obtain the more general Markov model of equation (6) within the latent variable framework of Heckman's model would require its extension to include two person specific components such that

$$\tau(i) = \begin{cases} \tau_0(i) \text{ iff } y(i, t-1) = 0 \\ \tau_1(i) \text{ iff } y(i, t-1) = 1 \end{cases}$$

and

$$E[\tau_j(i)\tau_{j'}(i')] = \begin{cases} \sigma_\tau(j, j') \text{ for } i = i' \\ 0 \qquad \text{ for } i \neq i'. \end{cases}$$

Some special Markov models have been applied to store choice by Crouchley *et al.* (1982a) and the general Markov model by Crouchley *et al.* (1982b). Actual estimation of the models requires an assumption concerning the parametric form of the distribution of the person specific effects in the population.

The results of the analysis of migration data using conditional likelihood methods suggested that non-stationarity cannot be ignored. Heckman (1981) considers a second error structure, for the general latent variable model with non-stationarity parameter $\alpha(t)$

$$\epsilon(i, t) = \alpha(t)\tau(i) + \eta(i, t)$$

which can also be examined as a time varying mixing distribution of the choice probability over the population. Davies *et al.* (1982c) consider a similar approach in a non-stationary zero-order choice model in which

$$\Pr[y(i, t) = 1] = \frac{\exp[\tau(i) + \alpha(t)]}{1 + \exp[\tau(i) + \alpha(t)]}.$$

With such a relationship, it has already been shown that choice probabilities can be functionally related (equations (7)) and series probabilities obtained using univariate integration where

$$\Pr[y(1), y(2), \ldots, y(T)] = \int_0^1 \prod_{t=1}^{T} g_t(p)^{y(t)} (1 - g_t(p))^{1-y(t)} f(p) \, dp$$

in which $g_1(p) = p$ and $g_t(p) = p[p + (1 - p)\exp \alpha(t)]^{-1}$.

An assumption of a parametric form for the distribution of unobservables or the choice probability mixing distribution is not, however, an unrestrictive assumption, particularly, as in most contexts, we have very little knowledge as to how these are likely to be distributed in the population. The addition of mass points or spikes to such distributions may add some flexibility (see Pickles *et al.*, 1982) but does not resolve this problem. A less restrictive approach is to model the distribution through its empirically estimated moments.

Consider a non-stationary zero-order choice model in which choice probabilities at time t are a simple linear function of those at time s; thus $p_t(i) = k_t p_s(i)$. Though $p_t(i)$ is not in general bounded to the $(0, 1)$ interval, this problem can be removed by appropriate selection of time s. Letting time s be time period 1, then for example

$$\Pr[y(1) = 1, y(2) = 1, y(3) = 0] = \int_0^1 p_1 p_2 (1 - p_3) f(p_1) \, dp_1$$

$$= \int_0^1 p_1 k_2 p_1 (1 - k_3 p_1) f(p_1) \, dp_1$$

$$= k_2 \int_0^1 p_1^2 f(p_1) \, dp_1 - k_2 k_3 \int_0^1 p_1^3 f(p_1) \, dp_1$$

$$= k_2 \mu_2' - k_2 k_3 \mu_3'$$

where $\mu_r' = \int_0^1 p_1^r f(p_1) \, dp_1 =$ the rth non-central moment about the origin of the mixing distribution $f(p_1)$. Estimation of the moments $\{\mu_r'\}$ must be made subject to constraints $0 \leqslant (\mu_b')^{a-c} \leqslant (\mu_c')^{a-b} (\mu_a')^{b-c} \leqslant 1$ for all $a \geqslant b \geqslant c \geqslant 0$ and $\mu_r' \geqslant \mu_{r+1}'$ in order to be feasible moments for a probability density function. Such moments are able to model any shape of density function without any of the restrictions of parametric assumptions. Indeed they can be used to identify appropriate parametric forms of, for example, the distribution of migration probabilities over the population (Crouchley et al., 1982).

Heckman (1981) considers a further form of individual specific component, referred to as 'generalized heterogeneity'.

$$\epsilon(i, t) = \rho \epsilon(i, t - 1) + \tau(i) + \eta(i, t).$$

With such a model, the individual specific effect evolves over time in a stochastic manner. Heckman argues that such an error structure cannot be examined in terms of a mixing distribution over choice probabilities. However, the usefulness of 'generalized heterogeneity' has yet to be demonstrated.

Some of the discrete time approaches and all of the essential ideas may be brought to bear on the analysis of continuous time duration data and the counts of events in continuous time counting processes. The model which has received widest attention is a continuous time renewal model in which the hazard rate is given by

$$h(i, t) = \nu(i) \, \psi_1(z(i)) \, \psi_2(t),$$

where $\psi_1(z(i))$ is some positive function of exogenous variables, $\psi_2(t)$ is a positive function of time since the last renewal, and $\nu(i)$ is a person specific term. The model has been discussed by a number of authors for single duration data such as length of unemployment (Lancaster, 1979; Heckman and Singer, 1981). Some particularly tractable forms may be found where $\nu(i)$ is assumed distributed according to a gamma density over the population and $\psi_2(t)$ is of a Gompertz or Weibull form. Such a model, extended to include non-stationarity and Markovian effects, has been applied to intra-urban residence history data, identifying significant duration of stay effects that varied with housing tenure type (Pickles, 1983). Alternatively, under certain circumstances, no distributional assumptions about the person specific term $\tau(i)$ need be made by using a conditional likelihood approach (Hausman, et al., 1981) to estimate the parameters associated with time varying exogenous variables.

No review of applied methods for dynamic analysis of panel data would be complete without some mention of the importance of the sampling scheme adopted within the data under analysis. It has already been noted that for dynamic processes, the initial conditions or the first observation must be treated with care. In fact, the problems thus posed vary from the trivial to the insoluble, depending on the particular sampling scheme adopted (Lerman and Mahmassani, 1981; Pickles, 1983). The collection of longitudinal data must be undertaken in a way which will maximize its potential usefulness, otherwise very considerable data wastage can occur (Ginsberg, 1979). Unfortunately, longitudinal sampling theory is as yet poorly developed and, whilst recommendations can be made to minimize the problems posed by initial conditions, the problem of attrition bias (see Heckman, 1976 and Davies et al., 1982b) and new entrants to the population remain severe.

5. SCOPE OF APPLICATION AND PROBLEMS

The preceding section has briefly introduced some of the methods available to begin the task of modeling dynamic individual behavior. Though many of the ideas and methods that have been presented may be unfamiliar, an intuitive understanding of the problems these methods attempt to overcome should be clear. Thus, the wide scope of geographical processes to which such models could be applied should be readily appreciated, for these methods are not limited to application to migration, housing and store choice studies reported but would be of importance in such tasks as geographical comparison of mortality rates (Vaupel et al., 1979; Manton et al., 1981) and changes in choice of journey to work transport mode (Johnson and Hensher, 1981).

However a number of problems remain, of which perhaps the most important is the severely restricted state space examined. Many choice processes of interest to geographers, e.g., many studies of inter-regional migration, involve choice amongst a large number of alternatives. Whilst some of these choice processes may be recast into more structured decision-making hierarchies, many aspects could not be examined using the binary choice methods which, for the most part, have been discussed in this review. Some of these methods are easily extended to polytomous choice, for example the beta-logistic model, but for many the computational problems become increasingly severe, frequently the result of the need to perform multi-dimensional, numerical integration. However, progress can be expected as the result of improved approximation techniques to the integration but also through further analytical development of the models.

Even within this limited state space, the models described are capable of incorporating a vast array of behavioral hypotheses. However, the data and computational demands required to distinguish amongst the many competing and partial theories of geographic choice are likely to be very large. Perhaps ironically, the further development of these methods will put an increasing pressure on the need for a more rigorous and comprehensive theory of search and choice. (Smith *et al.*, 1979). Such theoretical development might usefully draw upon search theory elsewhere, for example labor dynamics (see Flinn and Heckman, (1982), as Rogerson (1982) has done for application to migration.

Dept. of Geography (A.R.P.)   *Dept. of Town Planning* (R.B.D.)
Northwestern University   *Inst. of Science and Technology*
                                 University of Wales

BIBLIOGRAPHY

Akin, J. S., D. K. Guilkey, and R. Sickles: 1979, 'A random coefficient probit model with an application to a study of migration', *Journal of Econometrics* **11**, 233–246.

Alonso, W.: 1978, 'A theory of movements', in N. Hansen (ed.) *International Perspective on Structure, Change and Public Policy*, Ballinger, Cambridge, Mass.

Amemiya, T.: 1975, 'Qualitative response models', *Annals of Economic and Social Measurement* **4**, 363–372.

Anas, A.: 1981, 'Discrete choice theory, information theory and the mathematical logit and gravity models', Paper presented at the North American Meetings of the Regional Science Association, November 13th–15th, Montreal.

Anderson, E. B.: 1970, 'Asymptotic properties of conditional maximum likelihood estimators', *Journal of the Royal Statistical Scoiety* Series B **32**, 283–301.

Anderson, E. B.: 1973, *Conditional Inference and Models for Measuring*, Mentalhygiejnisk Forlag, Copenhagen.

Chamberlain, G.: 1979, 'Heterogeneity, omitted variable bias and duration dependence', Discussion Paper 691, Harvard Institute of Economic Research.

Coleman, J. S.: 1964, *Introduction to Mathematical Sociology*, Macmillan, New York.

Constantine, A. G. and J. G. Gower: 1982, 'Models for the analysis of inter-regional migration', *Environment and Planning* A 14, 477–497.

Crouchley, R., R. B. Davies, and A. R. Pickles: 1982a, 'A re-examination of Burnett's study of Markovian models of movement', *Geographical Analysis* 14, 260–263.

Crouchley, R., R. B. Davies, and A. R. Pickles: 1982b, 'Identification of some recurrent choice processes', *Journal of Mathematical Sociology* 9, 63–73.

Crouchley, R., A. R. Pickles, and R. B. Davies: 1982a, 'Dynamic models of shopping behaviour: testing the linear learning model and some alternatives', *Geografiska Annaler* B, 27–33.

Crouchley, R., A. R. Pickles, and R. B. Davies: 1982b, 'A family of Markovian models of recurrent choice', *Regional Science and Urban Economics* 12, 305–311.

Davies, R. B., R. Crouchley, and A. R. Pickles: 1982a, 'A family of hypotheses tests for a collection of short event series with an application to female employment participation', *Environment and Planning* A 14, 603–614.

Davies, R. B., R. Crouchley, and A. R. Pickles: 1982b, 'Some methods for the testing and estimation of dynamic models using panel data', *Environment and Planning* A (in press).

Davies, R. B., R. Crouchley, and A. R. Pickles: 1982c, 'Modelling the evolution of heterogeneity in residential mobility', *Demography* 19, 291–299.

Feller, W: 1967, *An Introduction to Probability Theory and its Application*, Wiley, New York.

Flowerdew R., and M. Aitkin: 1982, 'A method of fitting the gravity model based on the Poisson distribution', *Journal of Regional Science* 22, 191–202.

Flinn C. and J. Heckman: 1982, 'New methods for analysing structural models of labor force dynamics', *Journal of Econometrics* 18, 115–168.

Ginsberg, R. B.: 1979, 'Timing and duration effects in residence histories and other longitudinal data I: stochastic and statistical models', *Regional Science and Urban Economics* 9, 369–392.

Hausman, J., B. Hall, and Z. Grilliches: 1981, 'Econometric models for count data with an application to the patent-Rand D relationship, (mimeo), M.I.T., Cambridge, Mass.

Hausman, J. and D. A. Wise: 1978, 'A conditional probit model for qualitative choice: discrete decisions recognising interdependence and heterogeneous preferences', *Econometrica* 46, 403–426.

Heckman, J.: 1976, 'The common structure of statistical models of truncation, sample selection and limited dependent variables and a simple estimator for such models', *Annals of Economic and Social Measurement* 5, 475–492.

Heckman, J. J.: 1981, 'Statistical models for discrete panel data', in C. Manski and D. McFadden (ed.), *Structural Analysis of Discrete Data*, M.I.T. Press, Cambridge, Mass.

Heckman, J. J. and B. Singer: 1981, 'The identification problem in econometric models for duration data, (mimeo), University of Chicago.

Heckman J. J. and R. Willis: 1977, 'A beta-logistic model for the analysis of sequential labour force participation of married women', *Journal of Political Economy* 85, 27–58.

Hensher, D. A. and L. W. Johnson: 1981, *Applied Discrete Choice Modelling*, Halstead, New York.

Huff, J. O. and W. A. V. Clark: 1978, 'Cumulative stress and cumulative inertia: a behavioural model of the decision to move, *Environment and Planning* A 10, 1101–1119.

Johnson, L. W. and D. A. Hensher: 1981, 'Application of multinomial probit framework to a two period panel data set', (mimeo), Macquarie University, Australia.

Johnson, N. L. and S. Kotz: 1970, *Continuous Univariate Distributions – 1*, Houghton Mifflin, Boston.

Lancaster, T.: 1979, 'Econometric methods for the duration of unemployment', *Econometrica* 47, 939–956.

Lancaster, T. and S. Nickell: 1980, 'The analysis of re-employment probabilities for the unemployed', *Journal of the Royal Statistical Society* A 143, 141–165.

Ledent, J.: 1981, 'On the relationship between Alonso's theory of movement and Wilson's family of spatial interaction models', *Environment and Planning* A 13, 217–224.

Lerman, S. R. and H. Mahmassani: 1981, 'The econometrics of search' (mimeo), M.I.T. Cambridge.

Manton, K. G., M. A. Woodbury, and E. Stallard: 1981, 'A variance components approach to categorical data models with heterogeneous cell populations: Analysis of spatial gradients in lung cancer mortality rates in North Carolina Counties', *Biometrics* 37, 259–269.

Massy, D. F., D. B. Montgomery, and D. G. Morrison: 1970, *Stochastic Models of Buying Behavior*, M.I.T. Press, Cambridge.

McFadden D.: 1973, 'Conditional logit analysis of qualitative choice behaviour', in P. Zarembka (ed.), *Frontiers in Econometrics*, Academic Press, New York.

McFadden, D.: 1981, 'Econometric models of probabilistic choice', in C. Manski and D. McFadden (eds.), *The Structural Analysis of Discrete Data*, M.I.T. Press, Cambridge, Mass.

McGinnis, R.: 1968, 'A stochastic model of social mobility', *American Sociological Review* 23, 712–722.

Morrison, P. A.: 1971, 'Chronic movers and the future re-distribution of population: a longitudinal analysis', *Demography* 8, 171–184.

Moss, W. G.: 1979, 'A note on individual choice models of migration', *Regional Science and Urban Economics* 9, 333–343.

Neyman, J. and E. Scott: 1948, 'Consistent estimates based on partially consistent observations', *Econometrica* 16, 1–32.

Pickles, A. R.: 1982, Applications of Stochastic Process Models to Intra-Urban Migration in Cardiff. Unpublished PhD, University of Wales, Cardiff.

Pickles, A. R.: 1983, 'The analysis of residence histories and other longitudinal panel data: a continuous time Markov renewal model incorporating exogenous variables', *Regional Science and Urban Economics* 13, 171–285.

Pickles, A. R., R. Crouchley, and R. B. Davies: 1982, 'Non-participants in choice processes: an application to intra-urban migration', *Area* 14, 43–50.

Pickles, A. R., R. B. Davies, and R. Crouchley: 1982, 'Heterogeneity, non-stationarity and duration-of-stay effects in migration', *Environment and Planning* A 14, 615–622.

Rees, P. and A. G. Wilson: 1977, *Spatial Population Analysis*, Arnold, London.

Rogers, A.: 1980, 'Introduction to multi-state mathematical demography', *Environment and Planning* A 12, 487–498.

Rogerson, P.: 1982, 'Spatial models of search', *Geographical Analysis* 14, 217–228.

Smith, T. R., W. A. V. Clark, J. Huff, and P. Shapiro: 1979, 'A decision making search model of intra-urban migration', *Geographical Analysis* 11, 1–2.

Tobler, W. R.: 1979, 'Estimation of attractivities from interactions', *Environment and Planning* A 11, 121–127.

Vaupel, J. W., K. G. Manton, and E. Stallard: 1979, 'The impact of heterogeneity in individual frailty on the dynamics of mortality', *Demography* 16, 439–454.

Wilson, A. G.: 1971, 'A family of spatial interaction models and associated developments', *Environment and Planning* A 3, 1–32.

Wilson, A. G.: 1980, 'Comments on Alonso's theory of movement', *Environment and Planning* A 12, 727–732.

JAMES O. HUFF

DISTANCE-DECAY MODELS OF RESIDENTIAL SEARCH

1. INTRODUCTION

For the past several years I have been attempting to describe and explain residential mobility and residential search behavior. My objective in this paper is to investigate a series of simple distance-decay models which are designed to predict where a household will look for a new residence within an urban area. The proposed models, although couched in residential search terms, are potentially applicable to other human activities involving the selection of an alternative from a set of spatially distributed possibilities.

The residential search models are predicated upon the assumption that the household uses sources such as newspapers, friends, and real estate agents to acquire indirect information on selected attributes of vacancies. Certain vacancies are rejected solely on the basis of the indirect information provided while others are considered to be viable possibilties. The household proceeds to visit vacancies in this possibility set until a new residence is found or the household stops searching. Members of the possibility set which are located near critical nodes in the household's search space — nodes such as the prior residence and work place — are assumed to have a greater chance of being visited than possibilities which are further away. The search patterns generated by the proposed models are therefore a function of the underlying distribution of vacancies in the possibility set and the spatial biases in the household's actual search behavior.

The first portion of the paper is devoted to the discussion of several distance-decay functions which have been applied in the description of residential search behavior and other types of human behavior as well. The paper then focuses attention on the combination rules or the trade-offs made by a household when search is with reference to more than one key node or location in the household's search space. The final section of the paper is devoted to an empirical example which shows that the abstract search models can be calibrated and evaluated given information on the observed search pattern and the distribution of vacancies in the possibility set.

Gary L. Gaile and Cort J. Willmott (eds), Spatial Statistics and Models, 345–366.
© 1984 *by D. Reidel Publishing Company.*

2. SINGLE REFERENCE POINT MODELS

The closest thing to a law that we as geographers have studied and elaborated upon is the so-called distance-decay effect by which we mean that the intensity of interaction between two places decreases at a decreasing rate with increasing distance between the places. In the case of residential search behavior, we expect that the intensity of search will tend to decline with increasing distance from key reference points in the household's search space — reference points such as the prior residential location, location of the work place, and the locations of friends and acquaintances. The purpose of this section is first to establish a general model of the search process and then to derive specific distance-decay functions from additional assumptions about the search process.

2.1. *The General Model*

The first assumption in the general search model is that all vacancies in the region can be assigned to one of two disjoint sets: the set of vacancies, N, which cannot be rejected without direct investigation by the household; and the set, R, which can be rejected solely on the basis of indirect information from sources such as newspapers and real estate agents. The conceptual and methodological problems associated with the definition of the possibility set, N, for any given household are not addressed in this paper. Suffice it to say that the search model cannot be operationalized until an unambiguous assignment rule is given. See Burnett (1980) and Pipkin (1978) for a general review of the choice set problem; and see Huff (1982) for a discussion of the problem in the residential search context.

Given that a vacancy, x, is a member of the possibility set, N, the probability that x is the jth vacancy visited by a household during the course of its search is assumed to be proportional to $\theta(x) = f(s(x))$ where $s(x)$ is the distance between the vacancy, x, and the fixed reference point, a, and f is a function which decreases at a decreasing rate as s increases. The above assumptions imply that

$$P_r\,[w_j = x] = \begin{cases} \theta(x)/\,T(a, N), x \in N \\ 0,\, x \notin N \end{cases}$$

where w_j is the jth vacancy visited in the search sequence and

$$T(a, N) = \sum_{k \in N} \theta(k).$$

From this general search model, we may derive a number of testable inferences concerning the characteristics of the search pattern generated by the model. The inferences are in terms of measurements taken on the search patterns generated by the models. Two general classes of measurements are used to summarize the patterns:

a) occupancy or membership measurements — observed vacancies are assigned to one of n mutually exclusive areas or neighborhoods in the city; and

b) distance and/or directional measurements
   i) taken over the set of observed vacancies, and
   ii) taken with respect to an external reference point (present location, workplace, realtor location).

Both classes of measurements may be further differentiated depending upon the decision to include the ordering of observed vacancies as an aspect of the measurement problem.

The expected pattern of search generated by the simple distance-decay model may be summarized as follows:

1. If the domain of search is partitioned into a set of mutually exclusive areas or neighborhoods, then the probability that the jth vacancy seen in the search occurs in area i is

$$p(i, j) = p(i) = \sum_{k \in N_i} \theta(k)/T(a, N)$$

where N_i is the subset of vacancies located in area i which are members of the possibility set, N.

2. Since $p(i, j) = p(i)$, the number of vacancies seen in area i during a search sequence of length w is binomially distributed with parameters $(p(i), w)$.

3. The probability that the jth vacancy seen in the search sequence is a distance $s \leqslant s^*$ is

$$p(s^*, j) = p(s^*) = \sum_{\substack{k \in N \\ s(k) \leqslant s^*}} \theta(k)/T(a, N)$$

4. The ith moment of the distribution of distances between the reference point, a, and the vacancies seen during a given search sequence is

$$m_i(a) = \sum_{k \in N} s^i(k) \theta(k)/T(a, N)$$

5. If $s(j, k)$ is the distance between two vacancies, j and k, then the ith moment of the interpoint distances between the vacancies seen in a search sequence is

$$m_i^* = \sum_{\substack{j \in N \\ k \neq j}} \sum_{k \in N} s^i(j, k) \theta(k) \theta(j) / T(a, N, N)$$

where

$$T(a, N, N) = \sum_{\substack{j \in N \\ k \neq j}} \sum_{k \in N} \theta(k) \theta(j).$$

2.2. *Special Cases*

The general model cannot be evaluated until we have specified the form of the distance decay function, $\theta(x)$. Several candidates come readily to mind and are briefly discussed in this section.

If we invoke awareness space concepts and follow Wolpert's (1965) argument that the household will tend to concentrate search in already familiar areas, then the negative exponential function would be a good candidate for $\theta(x)$. Begin by assuming that the probability of visiting a vacancy $x \in N$ is proportional to the household's familiarity with the area immediately surrounding x. A household's familiarity with an area is assumed to decline with increasing distance between the area and the household's prior residence; and the rate of change in familiarity at a distance s from the prior residence is assumed to be proportional to the familiarity at that distance such that

$$\frac{\partial \Phi(s)}{\partial s} = -\lambda \Phi(s)$$

where $\Phi(s)$ is the households's familiarity with locations at a distance s from the prior residence, a.

The implication from the above assumption is that

$$\Phi(s) = \Phi(0) e^{-\lambda s}.$$

The probability of visiting a vacancy x at a distance $s(x)$ from the prior residence is therefore

$$\Pr[\omega_j = x] = \begin{cases} e^{-\lambda s(x)}/T(a, N), x \in N \\ 0, x \in N \end{cases} \tag{1}$$

where

$$T(a, N) = \sum_{k \in N} e^{-\lambda s(k)} \text{ and } \lambda \leqslant 0.$$

When a single workplace is involved and the principal focus of search is the workplace location, the negative exponential form will still be appropriate if we assume that the probability of visiting a vacancy, $x \in N$, is inversely proportional to the perceived travel cost associated with a commute between x and the workplace and if we further assume that commuting costs increase exponentially with distance.

If a zone of indifference exists around the workplace as Getis (1969) has suggested and the decision to investigate a vacancy reflects the fact that vacancies within this zone decline in attractiveness with increasing distance, then the probability of seeing a vacancy $x \in N$, which is a distance $s(x)$ from the workplace, a, is

$$P_r[w_j = x] = \begin{cases} \mu / T(a, N), & s(x) < s^* \\ \mu e^{-\lambda(s(x) - s^*)} / T(a, N), & s(x) \geqslant s^* \end{cases}$$

where s^* is the maximum extent of the zone of indifference around the work place and

$$T(a, N) = \int_0^{s^*} \mu g(s)\, ds + \int_{s^*}^{\infty} \mu e^{-\lambda(s - s^*)} g(s)\, ds,$$

$g(s)$ being the number of vacancies in N that are a distance s from the workplace, a, and $\lambda \geqslant 0$.

If the household uses a space-covering type search strategy as might be the case if the primary information source were "For Sale" or "For Rent" signs, then a more appropriate form of the distance-decay function should be an intervening opportunities model similar to the original Stouffer model (1940). We begin by ordering all vacancies in N in terms of their respective distances to the reference point, a, such that the vacancy $x \in N$ has order $x(k)$ which means that k vacancies are closer to a. It is assumed that the household visits the closest vacancy in N which has been identified during the course of its indirect search — and that every vacancy in N has a probability, a, of having been identified. The above assumption implies that

$$P_r[w_j = x] = \begin{cases} a(1-a)^k / T(a, N), x \in N \text{ with order } x(k) \\ \\ 0, x \notin N \end{cases}$$

where

$$T(a, N) = \sum_{k=0}^{n-1} a(1-a)^k = 1-(1-a)^n, a \geq 0,$$

with n being the number of vacancies in the possibility set, N.

In view of the space covering nature of the search process described by the intervening opportunities model, it may be important to consider the effects of sampling without replacement. Assuming that the household deletes a vacancy from the potential choice set once it has seen the vacancy and decided that it is inappropriate, the probability that a vacancy x is the jth element of the search sequence will necessarily increase as vacancies nearer the anchor point are seen and rejected. In formal terms,

$$P_r[w_j = x \mid w_i \neq x, i < j \wedge y(j, k) = \ell] = a(1-a)^{k-\ell} / 1-(1-a)^{n-j+1}$$

where $y(j, k)$ is the number of k nearest vacancies to the anchor point which are members of N and have already been seen and rejected during the search sequence $w_1, \ldots, w_{j-1}$.

This version of the model implies that the household will tend to first search intensively near the residence (or some other anchor point); but, as the nearby possibilities are rejected, search will tend to occur in areas at an increasing distance from the anchor point. The expected location of the vacancy ultimately chosen by the household will depend upon the probability of terminating the search process. As the probability of success increases, the expected number of vacancies seen in the search sequence necessarily decreases which implies that the expected distance between the anchor point and the new residence will decline.

As is always the case in these models, a critical question is the determination of the parameters which govern the shape of the distance decay function (λ or a in the cases discussed). Speare, Goldstein, and Frey (1975) have argued that the territorial scope of search is not only a function of the household's "awareness space" as proposed by Brown and Moore (1970) but is also a function of the kinds of residential stresses on the household which originally precipitated the decision to begin searching for a new residence. For example, if a household is dissatisfied with the size of its current residence, but is very satisfied with its current location within the city, then the search space is likely to be heavily focused on the possibilities in the immediate neighborhood. The point of this discussion is that the parameter (λ or a) is likely to be a function of household attributes taken in conjunction with characteristics of the current residence.

3. MULTIPLE REFERENCE POINT MODELS

When a household has two or more reference points in its search space, the problem becomes one of determining the relative importance of each anchor point in focusing search. The household may also trade-off the distances from the respective reference points differently depending upon the nature of the anchor points. If, for example, the two reference points represent the location of the current residence and the realtor who is responsible for showing some but not all of the houses seen by the household, then the resulting search pattern may be bimodal with relatively high densities near the two reference points. On the other hand, if the two reference points represent the work places of two employed household members, then the intensity of search may be highest along the axis through the two workplaces.

In view of the possible differences in search behavior arising from different combinations of anchor points, several specific forms of the multiple reference point model are presented. The cases are designed to illustrate the possible effects that critical nodes in a household's awareness or activity space have upon the pattern of search as well as upon the conditional nature of search in which the past pattern of search affects subsequent search bahavior.

3.1. *Multi-centric Search Model*

A two-stage decision process is hypothesized in which the household first selects a point of reference or an anchor point and then proceeds to search in the immediate vicinity of that point until the household decides to focus its search around a different reference point.

In order to fully specify the model, the number and locations of the potential reference points must be known. The obvious candidates for inclusion in the reference point set would be the current residence, the work place(s) or school location, and the residences of relatives. The probability $p(i, j)$, of choosing to use a reference point, i, when searching for w_j must also be established as well as the rules governing the decision to visit a particular vacancy given that search is focused around the reference point.

To simplify matters, it is assumed that the decision to focus search around a reference point i is an independent trials process with μ_i being the probability that reference point i is selected. Once a reference point is selected, the search for a vacancy is described by the single reference point model outlined in Section 2. The resulting form of the model is

$$P_r[w_j = x] = \sum_i \mu_i \, \theta_i(x) / T(a_i, N) \tag{2}$$

where $\Sigma_i \, \mu_i = 1$ and $\theta_i(x)$ is described by one of the special cases outlined in Section 2. For example, if a negative exponential distance-decay function were hypothesized, then

$$\theta_i(x) = e^{-\lambda_i s_i(x)}$$

where $s_i(x)$ is the distance between the vacancy, x, and the reference point, i and $\lambda_i \geqslant 0$.

The search pattern generated by the multicentric model will necessarily be a function of the number and location of the reference points with vacancies in the search sequence clustered around each reference point and with the number of vacancies in each cluster roughly proportional to μ_i. This general observation is necessarily conditional upon the underlying distribution of vacancies in the possibility set, N. The formal properties of the expected search pattern generated by the multicentric model are similar to the five properties derived for the single reference point model outlined in Section 2.1. In each instance, the multicentric distance-decay function can be directly substituted for the single-center, distance-decay function;

$$\sum_{\varrho} \mu_\varrho \, \theta_\varrho(k) / T(a_\varrho, N)$$

is substituted for

$$\theta(k) / T(a, N)$$

in each of the five properties of the expected search pattern.

Barrett's (1973) work on residential search indicates that the distance decay parameters may vary as a function of the household's current location within the city (λ or a decreasing with increasing distance from the CBD) if the reference point is the current residence. The distance-decay parameters also tend to vary as a function of socioeconomic status and ethnicity, with low status and minority populations having relatively high parameter values (see Brown and Holmes 1971). The relative importance of the current residence as measured by the parameter μ as well as the associated distance-decay parameter may also be a function of the length of stay in the current residence and the household's level of satisfaction with the surrounding neighborhood.

3.2. Shifting Reference Point Model

If one of the reference points in the search space is the last vacancy seen and is therefore a shifting reference point, the resulting model is a set of rules or assumptions concerning the trade-off between the household's tendency to visit vacancies near the last vacancy seen. The key premise in this particular model is that the residential search process consists of a series of outings or epochs. Each epoch begins at or with reference to a fixed reference point, a_i, which means that the first vacancy seen during each epoch is selected on the basis of its distance from the fixed reference point. All subsequent vacancies seen during a given epoch are selected on the basis of their locations relative to the last vacancy seen by the household. The decision to terminate an epoch is assumed to be an independent trials process where termination at any point occurs with probability, β.

The formal statement of the model is

$$P_r[w_{j+1} = x] = \begin{cases} \sum_i \mu_i \, \theta_i(x)/T(a_i, N), j=0 \\ \\ \beta \sum_i \mu_i \, \theta_i(x)/T(a_i,N) + (1-\beta) \, \theta_j(x)/T(w_j,N), j \geqslant 1 \end{cases}$$

where $\theta_j(x)$ is the distance-decay function for the shifting reference point, w_j.

The search process will tend to generate a series of clusters with the number of clusters depending upon the length of the search sequence, and the probability of terminating an outing or epoch. The clusters will become increasingly distinct (the distance between clusters increases relative to the distance between members of a cluster) as the distance-decay parameters get larger and β gets smaller. The number of clusters and the compactness of each cluster will also depend upon the underlying distribution of vacancies in N

and the nature of this distribution will play an increasingly important role in the structure of the search pattern as β approaches zero.

The resulting search behavior is akin to Gould's (1966) conceptualization of the search process in which a distinction is made between space covering (with reference to the fixed reference point) and space organizing search (with reference to the last vacancy seen). Gould's conceptualization would also appear to argue for the adoption of an intervening opportunities model for search near the shifting reference point and the negative exponential model as a descriptor of the space covering phase.

The distance decay parameter for the shifting reference point and the parameter β are likely to be dependent upon the type of information source employed by the household and the associated amount of location specific information provided by that source. If a household relies heavily upon For Sale or For Rent signs as a source of information for example, then the distance-decay parameter would be much larger than would be the case if the primary source is the newspaper. The probability of ending a search outing or epoch is also a function of the household's dissatisfaction with the current residence which is reflected in the household's search rate (number of vacancies seen per time period). As the search rate increases, the length of any given outing will tend to increase (β declines).

3.3. Elliptical or Teardrop Search Patterns

An argument already employed to motivate one of the single reference point models is that households tend to concentrate search in already familiar areas. This general observation is bourne out in Barrett's Toronto study (1973) and serves as the basis for the multiple reference point model presented in this section.

The probability of visiting a given vacancy in the possibility set is assumed to be proportional to the household's familiarity with the area immediately surrounding the vacancy. The household's familiarity with an area, $\Phi(s_1, s_2, \ldots)$, is assumed to be a function of that area's distance, s_i, from each of the key reference points, a_i, in the household's activity space. The rate of change in familiarity at a distance s_i from a reference point, a_i, is assumed to be proportional to the household's familiarity with the area such that

$$\frac{\partial \Phi(s_1, \ldots, s_i, \ldots)}{\partial s_i} = -\lambda_i \Phi(s_1, \ldots, s_i, \ldots)$$

for all reference points a_i. The implication of the above assumption is that

$$\Phi(s_1, \ldots, s_i, \ldots) = \exp \left[-\sum_i \lambda_i s_i + c_0 \right].$$

Since the probability of visiting a vacancy $x \in N$ is proportional to $\Phi(x)$, the household's familiarity with the area immediately surrounding x, it follows that

$$P_r[w_j = x] = \exp \left[-\sum_i \lambda_i s_i(x) \right] / T(a_1, \ldots a_i, \ldots, N) \qquad (3)$$

where

$$T(a_1, \ldots a_i, \ldots, N) = \sum_{k \in N} \exp \left[-\sum_i \lambda_i s_i(k) \right]$$

When only two reference points are involved, a_1 and a_2, the familiarity surface and the intensity of search will have elliptical contour lines with a_1 and a_2 as foci if $\lambda_1 = \lambda_2$. If the household's activity space is oriented primarily around a_1, then $\lambda_1 > \lambda_2$ which implies that the contours would be distended in the direction of a_1 resulting in a "teardrop" shaped search pattern. The highest concentration of vacancies seen by the household would tend to occur along the axis connecting the two reference points with an orientation toward the dominant point (a_1 in this case). The predicted elliptical or teardrop shape of the search space is consistent with Brown and Holmes' findings in their study of household search behavior in Columbus, Ohio (1971).

Although the form of the distance-decay function has been derived from assumptions concerning the household's familiarity with a location, the model would also describe the expected search behavior of households with two working members outside the home. If the anchor points are the two workplaces and the decision to investigate a given dwelling is a function of the weighted sum of distances to the respective workplaces, then the model predicts that the household is likely to concentrate its search along a line drawn between the two workplaces. The parameters, λ_1 and λ_2, in this instance reflect the difficulty or the cost attached to the respective journeys to and from work. As the parameter values increase, search would be more concentrated along the axis between the two workplaces with an orientation toward the workplace of the household member with the highest per unit travel cost.

A slightly different form of the joint distance-decay function emerges if we assume that the probability of visiting a vacancy $x \in N$ is inversely proportional

to the sum of the actual or perceived travel costs between the vacancy x and
the designated reference points (two workplaces for example). If $\Gamma_i(x)$ is the
travel cost function associated with each reference point i, then the above
assumption implies that

$$P_r[w_j = x] = [\sum_i \Gamma_i(x)]^{-1} / \sum_{k \in N} [\sum_i \Gamma_i(k)]^{-1}.$$

In this version of the model, the household has a tendency to concentrate
search around an intermediate point between the reference points. The result
is to be expected since the model is a probabilistic version of Weber's plant
location model which generates a minimum transportation cost solution.

Thus far, it has been tacitly assumed that all the reference points in the
household's search space exert a positive influence on search behavior. In
some instances, however, the household may actively avoid certain locations
or areas of the city. The so-called "white flight" phenomenon serves as one
rather important example of avoidance behavior. The avoidance of locations
in or near congested areas would also be an example of search behavior which
is negatively influenced by a reference point.

For those reference points, $\hat{a}_\varrho$, avoided by the household during search,
we define a function

$$\Psi(x) = c_0 + \sum_\varrho \delta_\varrho \exp(-s_\varrho(x)/\delta_\varrho)$$

which is a measure of the intensity of the household's dissatisfaction with the
area surrounding a vacancy x located a distance $s_\varrho(x)$ from an undesirable
reference point $\hat{a}_\varrho$. For reference points, a_j, which attract the household,
$\Phi(x)$, as defined at the beginning of this section, is taken to be a measure of
the attractiveness of the area surrounding x.

If we assume that the probability of visiting a vacancy $x \in N$ is directly
proportional to $\Phi(x)$ and inversely proportional to $\Psi(x)$, then the resulting
model is

$$P_r[w_j = x] = \Phi(x)\,\Psi(x)^{-1}/T(a_1 \ldots, a_j, \hat{a}_1, \ldots \hat{a}_j, N).$$

The resulting search pattern will again tend to have an elliptical or teardrop
shape for one positive and one negative reference point but the intensity of
search in this instance will be oriented away from the negative reference point.

4. EMPIRICAL EXAMPLE

Although the primary purpose of this paper is to model the spatial aspects of residential search, I will briefly digress into the realm of reality to indicate how the models may be evaluated when we have data on actual search behavior. A single case study will suffice for illustrative purposes and in this instance the household under study was searching for a new residence in the San Fernando Valley of Los Angeles during the spring of 1979. In a retrospective interview, the household was asked to indicate the locations (to the nearest cross-street) of the vacancies visited during the search process. Figure 1 shows

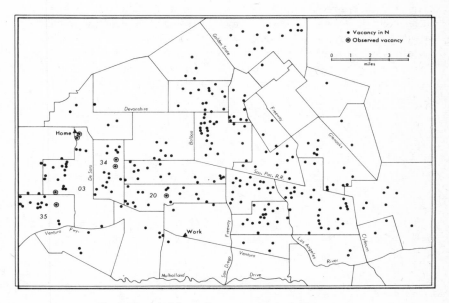

Fig. 1. Household search pattern and possibility set (N).

the pattern of vacancies seen by the household and the locations of the prior residence as well as the workplace location. During the course of the interview, the household also indicated that it was searching for a house in the $85—90,000 price range. The possibility set, N, is assumed to contain only those vacancies in the San Fernando Valley which are in the household's price range. The distribution of all such vacancies occurring at one point in time during the spring of 1979 is shown in Figure 1. The data serving as the basis for this empirical example were collected as part of a much more extensive study of residential search in the San Fernando Valley. A summary of the main theoretical and empirical findings from the study can be found in a series of articles by W. A. V. Clark, T. R. Smith, P. Shapiro, and myself (Huff, 1983; Clark, 1981; Smith *et al.*, 1979; Clark and Smith, 1982).

The observed search pattern, in conjunction with information on the distribution of vacancies in the household's possibility set, serve as the basis for estimating the parameters in the search models. The parameters are estimated using standard maximum likelihood methods. Given maximum likelihood estimates for the parameters, the expected search pattern generated from the model is compared to the observed search pattern. Since there is little reason to expect that the household would look at the same vacancies if it were to repeat the residential search process, the models are evaluated in terms of their respective abilities to generate an expected search pattern which is similar but not necessarily identical to the observed pattern. The comparison between expected and observed patterns is in terms of the area and distance related measures of the sort outlined in Section 2.1 for the single reference point case.

4.1. *Single Reference Point Model*

The specific form of the single reference point model to be calibrated is the familiar negative exponential case given in equation (1) where the reference point, *a*, is the location of the prior residence. The model has a single parameter, λ, to be estimated using maximum likelihood methods.

The search model in question characterizes search as a simple independent trials process which implies that the probability of visiting a sequence of vacancies, $w = \{w_2, \ldots w_m\}$, is simply

$$L = \prod_{j=1}^{m} P_r[w_j]$$

where $P_r[w_j]$ is the probability of observing vacancy w_j. If we now think of the search sequence w as the sequence actually observed by our sample household, then function, L, is an intuitively appealing likelihood function where $P_r[w_j]$ is as given in equation (2). The value of λ which maximizes L, thus maximizing the probability that the observed search sequence would be generated by the model, is $\lambda = .43$.

The model is first evaluated against the observed pattern in terms of its ability to predict the number of vacancies seen in area *i* during a search sequence of length seven (the household investigated seven vacancies) where the areas are the thirty-six community areas shown in Figure 1. The predicted probability of visiting a vacancy in area i is

$$p(i) = \sum_{k \in N_i} e^{-.43s(k)} / T(a, N)$$

where N_i is the number of vacancies in N which are located in area i. The predicted probabilities for the areas containing vacancies actually observed by the household are given in column 2 of Table I.

TABLE I

Predicted probability of searching in a given area

	Search model			
	Null hypothesis	Single reference	Multicentric	Elliptical
Community area	$\lambda = 0.0$	$\lambda_H = .43$	$\mu = .91$ $\lambda_H = .51$ $\lambda_W = .98$	$\lambda_H = .58$ $\lambda_W = .25$
03	.08	.44	.45	.40
34	.06	.21	.19	.28
20	.07	.05	.07	.08
35	.04	.05	.05	.02
All other areas	.75	.25	.24	.22

Since we are assuming that search is an independent trials process, the expected number of vacancies seen in each area i is $\mu_i = wp_i$ and the associated variance is $\sigma_i^2 = wp_i(1-p_i)$. As can be seen from Table II, the model performs reasonably well since on the average it assigns five of the seven vacancies to the correct area (% correct in Table II); whereas under the null hypothesis that the distance decay effect is negligible ($\lambda = 0.0$), less than two out of seven vacancies are correctly assigned. However, the model does tend to underpredict the expected number of vacancies in areas which are in the general vicinity of the reference point (areas 34, 20, and 35) while over-predicting the intensity of search both in the immediate area surrounding the reference point (area 03) and in the remainder of the search domain beyond the general vicinity of the prior residence.

The second set of measures used to evaluate the simple distance decay

TABLE II

Observed and predicted number of vacancies visited in each community area

Community area	Observed number of vacancies	Predicted by search model			
		Null hypothesis $\lambda = .00$	Single reference $\lambda_H = .43$	Multicentric $\mu = .91$ $\lambda_H = .51$ $\lambda_w = .98$	Elliptical $\lambda_H = .58$ $\lambda_w = .25$
03	3	.55 (.71)[a]	3.12 (1.32)	3.16 (1.31)	2.79 (1.40)
34	2	.43 (.64)	1.46 (1.07)	1.32 (1.03)	1.92 (1.18)
20	1	.48 (.67)	.32 (.55)	.48 (.67)	.57 (.72)
35	1	.31 (.55)	.37 (.59)	.35 (.58)	.15 (.38)
all other areas	0	5.22 (1.14)	1.73 (1.14)	1.69 (1.13)	1.57 (1.10)
% correctly predicted		25%	74%	74%	78%

[a] Numbers in parentheses ( ) are the standard deviations around the predicted value.

model are summarized in Table III. Measures are taken on the distance between an observed or predicted vacancy, w_j, and
a) the prior residence, a_1,
b) the work place, a_2,
c) the mean center, $(\bar{x}, \bar{y})$, of the pattern, a_3, and
d) the other vacancies in the search pattern.
Given the relevant distance measures, the observed and predicted patterns may be summarized in terms of the fixed point moments, $m_i(a_1)$, $m_i(a_2)$, and $m_i(a_3)$ as given by $m_i(a_j) = \Sigma_{k \in N} s^i(j, k) e^{-\lambda s_1(k)} / T(a_1, N)$, where $s^i(j, k)$ is the ith power of the distance between reference point a_j and vacancy k; $s_1(k)$ is the distance between the prior residence, a_1, and vacancy k; and $T(a_1, N) = \Sigma_{k \in N} e^{-\lambda s_1(j)}$.
The last three rows in Table III are the first three moments of the intervacancy distances for the vacancies in the expected and observed search

TABLE III
Distance measures on observed and predicted search patterns

I. First three moments of the distances between vacancies in the search pattern
and the prior residence (H)[a]

	Observed pattern	Null hypothesis $\lambda = .0$	Single reference $\lambda_H = .43$	Multicentric $\mu = .91$ $\lambda_H = .51 \; \lambda_w = .98$	Elliptical $\lambda_H = .58 \; \lambda_w = .25$
$m_1 \, (H)$	2.40	7.95	2.40	2.55	2.40
$m_2 \, (H)$	11.78	107.70	12.38	14.85	12.00
$m_3 \, (H)$	67.28	1650.75	86.85	117.75	75.22

II. First three moments of the distances between vacancies in the search pattern
and the work location (w).

$m_1 \, (w)$	6.22	6.15	6.75	6.45	6.15
$m_2 \, (w)$	56.10	58.28	64.42	61.35	54.98
$m_3 \, (w)$	527.70	612.75	637.50	606.00	515.48

III. First three moments of the distances between vacancies in the search pattern
and the mean center of the pattern $(\bar{x}, \bar{y})$.

$m_1 \, (\bar{x}, \bar{y})$	2.18	5.18	2.25	2.40	2.10
$m_2 \, (\bar{x}, \bar{y})$	7.35	43.20	9.82	11.25	7.72
$m_3 \, (\bar{x}, \bar{y})$	28.95	408.00	61.35	72.00	37.50

IV. First three moments of the inter-point distances between the vacancies in
the search pattern.

$m_1{}^*$	3.22	7.05	3.22	3.45	3.00
$m_2{}^*$	17.18	86.25	19.88	22.88	15.75
$m_3{}^*$	102.30	1231.50	161.40	195.00	104.32

[a] Moments are measured in miles.

pattern. The interpoint moments for the single reference point model are
determined as follows:

$$m_i{}^* = \sum_{j \in N} \sum_{\substack{k \in N \\ k \neq j}} s^i(j, k) \, e^{-\lambda s_1 (j)} \, e^{-\lambda s_1 (k)} / T(a_1, N, N)$$

where

$$T(a_1, N, N) = \sum_{j \in N} \sum_{\substack{k \in N \\ k \neq j}} e^{-\lambda s_1 (j)} \, e^{-\lambda s_1 (k)}.$$

A comparison of the first moments for the observed pattern and the first moments predicted from the baseline case and the simple negative exponential case (Columns 1, 2, and 3 in Table III) generally supports the earlier conclusion that the simple distance-decay model provides a reasonably accurate description of the observed search pattern in both relative and absolute terms.

Although the model performs very well when evaluated in terms of the first moments of the distance measures, an analysis of the higher order moments suggests that the model may be mis-specified. In every instance, the second and third moments predicted from the model exceed the observed values. The implication is that the model is overpredicting the intensity of search very near the reference point and is also overpredicting the possibility of search at relatively large distances from the key reference point since the observed and predicted first moments are almost identical for three of the four distance measures. This conclusion is corroborated by the area-based results which pointed toward the same pattern of over- and underprediction.

Systematic errors such as those already outlined may arise from several rather different sources. The first possibility is that the possibility set has not been correctly specified. For example, if the household only considers vacancies in the West Valley and we have defined the search domain as the entire San Fernando Valley, then the model would necessarily overpredict the probability of searching in the East Valley. The second possibility is that the negative exponential distance-decay function is inappropriate. Given our results, a linear distance-decay function would appear to be an attractive alternative. The third possibility is that more than one reference point has an effect upon the observed search behavior. In particular, the workplace may exert an added influence upon the search pattern which is not incorporated in the simple distance-decay model. It is this third possibility which is investigated in the next section.

4.2. *Multiple Reference Point Models*

The multiple reference point models are clearly a more complex characterization of the search process than were the single reference point models. What we do not know, until the models are evaluated against observed search behavior, is whether the multiple reference point models provide substantially better descriptions of the search pattern. One example can hardly serve as a basis for a definitive statement in this regard but it can provide insights into how the multiple reference point model is likely to perform. The search pattern under study is the same pattern described in the earlier case study and is shown in Figure 1. In this instance, however, the observed pattern is compared against the expected patterns generated by the multicentric model and an elliptical model. The specific versions of these two models assume the existence of two key reference points, a_1 — the prior residence and a_2 — the workplace; and both reference points are assumed to have a positive influence on search behavior. The distance-decay function used in both models is again the negative exponential.

The multicentric model (equation 2) is a three parameter model when search is conducted with reference to prior residence, a_1, and workplace, a_2. The three parameters, μ, λ_1 and λ_2, are all assumed to be positive and are estimated using maximum likelihood methods; the likelihood function being

$$L = \prod_j P_r[w_j]$$

and

$$P_r[w_j] = \mu\,[e^{-\lambda_1 s_1 (j)}/T(a_1, N)] + (1-\mu)\,[e^{-\lambda_2 s_2 (j)}/T(a_2, N)]$$

where $s_1(j)$ or $s_2(j)$ are the distances between vacancy w_j and the prior residence or the workplace and

$$T(a_i, N) = \sum_{k \in N} e^{-\lambda_i s_i(k)}.$$

An exhaustive grid search of the three dimensional parameter space was used to determine the values of μ, λ_1 and λ_2 which maximize L. The likelihood function is maximized when

$\mu = .91,$
$\lambda_1 = .51,$ and
$\lambda_2 = .98.$

The multicentric model is evaluated in the same general fashion as the single reference point model; and the results are summarized in column four of Tables II and III. Although the multicentric model generates an expected search pattern which closely resembles the observed pattern, the summary area and distance measures indicate that the single reference point model (summarized in column 3 of the tables) does as well or better as a descriptor of the observed search pattern. It would appear that the increase in complexity and in the number of parameters to be estimated cannot be justified in this instance.

The other multiple reference point model under discussion is the elliptical model (equation 3) which states that the probability of visiting a vacancy w_j is

$$P_r[w_j] = e^{-\lambda_1 s_1 (j) -\lambda_2 s_2 (j)} / T(a_1, a_2, N)$$

where λ_1 and λ_2 are assumed to be positive and

$$T(a_1, a_2, N) = \sum_{k \in N} e^{-\lambda_1 s_1 (k) -\lambda_2 s_2 (k)}.$$

The parameter values which maximize the likelihood function are

$\lambda_1 = .58$, and
$\lambda_2 = .25$.

The elliptical model generates an expected search pattern, as summarized in the last column of Tables I, II, and III, which is almost indistinguishable from the observed search pattern. In contrast to the multicentric model, the elliptical model is a marked improvement over the single reference point model in two major respects. The second and third moments for the distance measures given in Table III are in much closer accord with the observed moments which suggests that the mis-specification problems encountered in the single reference point model can be resolved through the inclusion of the workplace as a secondary reference point in the elliptical model. Secondarily, the inclusion of the workplace as a reference point also materially improves the correspondence between the observed and predicted moments for the distance to the workplace.

When all is said and done, what can be concluded from the empirical example, particularly in view of our rather small sample size? I have worked through this example primarily for pedagogical purposes. The first objective was to show how simple and more complex search models of the type outlined in the main body of the paper can be calibrated given information on observed search behavior and the distribution of vacancies in the possibility set. The second objective was to show how inferences pertaining to area based occupancy measures and distance measures taken on the search pattern may be used first to summarize important features of the pattern and second to evaluate the models in terms of their capacities to reproduce the main features of the observed pattern. The third objective was to highlight the importance of the combination rules which govern the roles played by the various reference points in the multiple reference point models. To date, we have been preoccupied with the form of the distance-decay function in our single reference point models and I wished to show that the mis-specification problem could stem from a failure to recognize that more than one reference point may be influencing the observed behavior.

5. CONCLUDING REMARKS

The residential search models proposed in this paper represent an effort to take what we know or suspect about the spatial aspects of residential search and to express these ideas in formal terms. Inferences pertaining to the search patterns generated by these models are derived, thus providing a means of directly comparing the outcomes of differing conceptualizations of the search process. These inferences also provide a mechanism for discriminating between the various models since they can be judged against observed search behavior.

The reference point models have two premises in common: the first is that the intensity of search tends to decline with increasing distance from key nodes in the household's search space and the second is that the spatial distribution of possibly acceptable vacancies has an important influence upon the distribution of vacancies visited by the household. The formal models suggest several different search processes which satisfy these two general conditions while resulting in very different search patterns. Aside from an explicit description of the expected search pattern arising from the interaction between distance decay effects and the underlying distribution of possibilities, the reference point models are of interest because they provide a formal link between the role of distance in the residential search process and previously observed or conjectured search patterns.

Dept. of Geography
University of Illinois

ACKNOWLEDGEMENTS

Support from N.S.F. Grant Soc 77–27362 is gratefully acknowledged.

BIBLIOGRAPHY

Barrett, F.: 1973, *Residential Search Behavior*, Geographical monograph 1, York University Press, Toronto.

Brown, L. and J. Holmes: 1971, 'Search behavior in an intraurban context: a spatial perspective', *Environment and Planning* 3, 307–326.

Brown, L. and E. G. Moore: 1970, 'The intra-urban migration process: a perspective', *Geografiska Annaler* 52B, 1–13.

Burnett, K. P.: 1980, 'Spatial constraints-oriented approaches to movement', *Urban Geography* 1, 53–67.

Clark, W. A. V.: 1981, 'On modelling search behavior', in D. Griffith and R. MacKinnon (eds.), *Dynamic Spatial Models*, Sijthoff and Noordhoff, Rockville.

Clark, W. A. V. and T. Smith: 1982, 'Housing market search behavior and expected utility theory II: the process of search', *Environment and Planning A* 14, 717–737.

Getis, A.: 1969, 'Residential location and the journey from work', *Proceedings of the Association of American Geographers* 1, 55–59.

Gould, P.: 1966, 'Space searching procedures in geography and the social sciences', Social Science Research Institute Working Paper #1, University of Hawaii.

Huff, J.: 1982, 'Spatial aspects of residential search', in W. A. V. Clark (ed.), *Modelling Housing Market Search*, Croom Helm, London.

Pipkin, J.: 1978, 'Fuzzy sets and spatial choice', *Annals of the Association of American Geographers* 68, 196–204.

Smith, T., W. A. V. Clark, J. O. Huff, and P. Shapiro: 1979, 'A decision making and search model for intraurban migration', *Geographical Analysis* 11, 1–22.

Smith, T. and W. A. V. Clark: 1980, 'Housing market search: information constraints and efficiency', in W. A. V. Clark and E. G. Moore (eds.), *Residential Mobility and Public Policy*, Sage, Beverly Hills.

Speare, A., S. Goldstein, and W. Frey: 1975, *Residential Mobility and Metropolitan Change*, Ballinger, Cambridge.

Stouffer, S.: 1940, 'Intervening opportunities: a theory relating mobility and distance', *American Sociological Review* 5, 845–867.

Weber, A.: 1909, *Theory of the Location of Industries*, University of Chicago Press, Chicago.

Wolpert, J.: 1965, 'Behavioral aspects of the decision to migrate', *Papers of the Regional Science Association* 15, 159–169.

ERIC S. SHEPPARD

THE DISTANCE-DECAY GRAVITY MODEL DEBATE

1. INTRODUCTION

The gravity model has been by far the most popular mathematical description of human spatial interaction. The purpose of this paper is not to review its usage in general (Carrothers, 1956; Tocalis, 1978), but only to discuss one statistical question; the difficulties associated with accurately estimating the tendency of trips to decrease as distance increases by use of ordinary least squares (OLS) regression models applied to observed data. This introductory section will outline the nature of the problem and of the debate that has developed in the last ten years.

The gravity model may be stated as

$$I_{ij} = G \cdot p_i^\alpha \, p_j^\gamma \, d_{ij}^{-\beta}, \tag{1}$$

where I_{ij} is the number of trips from origin i to destination j; P_i is some measure of the propensity of trips to be generated at i; P_j is a measure of the propensity of destination j to attract trips; d_{ij} is some measure of the physical separation of j from i; and G, α, γ and β are parameters to be estimated from empirical data.

Before discussing statistical questions, there are some important conceptual issues relating to the use of this model to be raised. First, it is a model of aggregate human spatial action. It is a formulation that has a history of describing well the regularities of aggregate interaction patterns and there is a correspondingly long history of attempts to underpin it with an explanation based in individual behavior. The principal difficulty of such attempts to construct a theory for the gravity model is based in a problem that has puzzled sociologists for years, and has become known as the "ecological fallacy." This "fallacy" stresses the danger of attempting to apply generalizations about human action gained from aggregate data, which summarize the overall acts of a large number of heterogeneous people, to make inferences about how individuals act.

Indeed, three very different conceptions of individual action can all be made consistent with the aggregate results of the gravity model. The first,

Gary L. Gaile and Cort J. Willmott (eds.), Spatial Statistics and Models, 367–388.
© 1984 *by D. Reidel Publishing Company.*

and most common, approach is to conceive of spatial interaction as the result of conscious choice between destinations in a situation where the constraints on choice are not severe. That this approach has dominated the literature is unfortunate, partly because the more sophisticated the conceptions of spatial choice the less plausible they become as explanations of the gravity model, and partly because this emphasis on free choice limits the types of questions asked in a way that is ideologically biased in favor of *status quo* maintaining social values (Sheppard, 1978, 1979b, 1980). The second approach would explain a decay of trips with increasing distance as a result of spatial action being highly constrained, with those making longer trips being that part of the population subject to fewer constraints (Stetzer and Phipps, 1977). The third approach would explain this distance effect on interaction as being due to increasing divergence in cultural values with increased distance, in turn allowing research to focus on how such values are societally determined. More cannot be said about these issues here except to stress once more the danger of following the tradition of equating human interaction with acts based solely on conscious individual rational choice. To avoid such connotations, we shall talk of human action rather than human behavior.

The other major point to notice is that there are many ways of defining the concepts of the propensity to generate trips, the attractiveness of a destination, and physical separation, introduced in equation (1). For brevity, we shall call the first two of these concepts "populations" or "masses," and the third concept "distance," although in practice each term may be an aggregate of several attributes that may not, say, include population at all. Thus, for example the "spatial structure of populations" refers to the spatial distribution of those attributes affecting trip generation propensity or destination attractiveness. What these attributes will be will depend, of course, on the type of spatial interaction under study.

The principal contribution of the gravity model is to separate the factors accounting for spatial interactions into three groups; those factors that are *in situ* attributes of the origin (P_i), those that are *in situ* attributes of the destination, and those that are attributes of the relative location of i with respect to j. If the gravity model can be accurately estimated, then, the term $d_{ij}^{-\beta}$ in equation (1) would express the effect of relative location on interaction, separating this from the less purely geographical concepts P_i^α and P_j^γ. In fact, the concept of "distance decay," the propensity for trips to decrease as distance increases, refers to $d_{ij}^{-\beta}$, and β itself is often thought of as a measure of the friction of distance. The larger β is, the more rapidly trips decrease as distance increases (Figure 1).

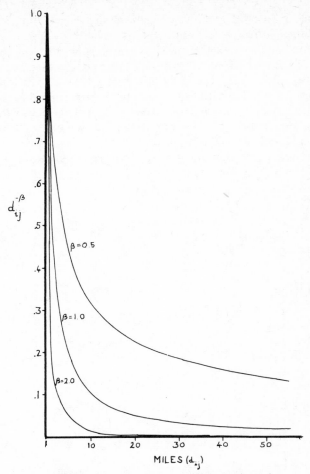

Fig. 1. Distance-decay functions: different values of β.

The importance of separating the term $d_{ij}^{-\beta}$ from the population terms can be easily seen. If empirical data on the number of trips travelling various distances are simply plotted against distance we would not obtain an accurate measure of how distance affects interaction. This is because if, for example, attractive places happen to be located a long way from large origins, a lot of long distance trips would result giving particular shape to the frequency distribution of trips against distance. But, if attractive destinations are close to big origins, a very different shape would result (Figure 2). Clearly, what is happening here is that the spatial structure, or relative location, of populations profoundly affects the number of trips made of any given length. If we wish to isolate the "pure" effect of relative location on interaction, i.e. the distance decay effect, from the distortions introduced by the spatial structure of populations, then we would like the empirical parameter β to measure this effect alone. Thus, the size of β should be independent of the spatial structure of populations if we are to interpret it as a measure of the "true" distance decay of trips with increasing distance.

Methods of fitting least squares regression equations to interaction data

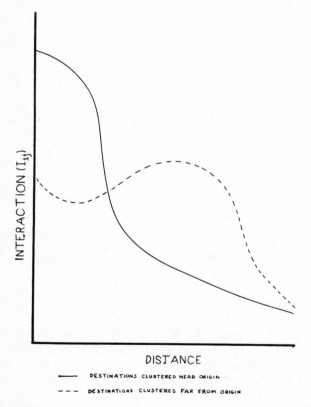

Fig. 2. Variability, by origin, in the relation between destinations and distance in a spatial system.

have been employed in an attempt to isolate these various factors. Regression methods may be applied by taking logarithms of both sides of equation (1). If this is done

$$\log (I_{ij}) = G + \alpha \log (P_i) + \gamma \log (P_j) - \beta \log (d_{ij}). \tag{2}$$

If data for three explanatory variables and the dependent variable are collected, then least squares regression methods can be used to attempt to estimate the various parameters by fitting the following equation as closely as possible to the observed data in logarithmic form. If the true relationship in a population of data takes the form of equation (2), and if a sample is collected from that population, then estimates of the population parameters may be obtained by

$$\log (I_{ij}) = \hat{G} + \hat{\alpha} \log (P_i) + \hat{\gamma} \log (P_j) - \hat{\beta} \log (d_{ij}) + \epsilon_{ij}. \tag{3}$$

Here $\hat{G}$, $\hat{\alpha}$, $\hat{\gamma}$ and $\hat{\beta}$ are least squares sample estimates of the respective population parameters in equation (2), based on the data sample collected. ϵ_{ij} is the estimate of the residual error unaccounted for by this model.

The question of debate is whether the OLS estimate $\hat{\beta}$ is indeed independent of the spatial structure of populations. Despite some early doubts expressed by Porter (1956), it was believed for many years that $\hat{\beta}$ did indeed solely represent the true distance decay effect. Thus, equation (3) was estimated in very many studies. In practice, it was frequently remarked that the estimate $\hat{\beta}$ varied considerably and unpredictably from one study to the next, but this was generally regarded as being due to differences in true distance friction levels that could not be captured by such a simple aggregate model. Such differences might reflect differences in behavior or in the nature of the constraints faced by individuals. However, Curry (1972) took a different view. He argued that the very way in which the model is formulated, with its inclusion of a product of the population terms (equation (1)) suggested that "the non-zero exponent on distance has nothing to do with friction, and everything to do with the map pattern, ... any 'calibration' is specific to a particular pattern of origins and destinations and may be substantively meaningless," (1972, p. 132). If he is right, the immediate implication is that much of the 'unpredictable' variation in $\hat{\beta}$ may simply be due to the fact that the spatial pattern of origins and destinations is different in each study area.

Given the traditional importance of the gravity model in geography, this proposal generated considerable interest and controversy that will be detailed in the following sections. Basically, the only way in which the $\hat{\beta}$ estimator may be affected by the spatial structure of population is if some of the statistical assumptions made in the use of the regression methods are violated. If these assumptions are true, then $\hat{\beta}$, like all least squares regression estimates, is a best linear unbiased estimator (BLUE). Thus, a review of the debate will be preceded by a discussion of these assumptions. The various ways in which the spatial structure of populations can lead to such violations will then be the focus of discussion, followed by what conclusions can be drawn to date in a controversy that is still continuing.

One final point is worthy of note before proceeding: the frequent use of origin-specific estimates of $\hat{\beta}$. A number of researchers have tried to simplify the problem by fitting equation (3) separately to the sub-sample of interactions from a particular origin i. Thus, for each i the regression equation applied to such a sample of data becomes

$$\log{(I_{ij})} = \hat{G}_i + \hat{\gamma}_i \log{(P_j)} - \hat{\beta}_i \log{(d_{ij})} + \epsilon_{ij}. \tag{4}$$

Here the term $\alpha \log{(P_i)}$ may be left out as it is the same for all data in the sub-sample. Just as other researchers found $\hat{\beta}$ to vary from one study area to the next, so also $\hat{\beta}_i$ seemingly varies significantly from one origin to the next within a study area. Clearly, this is a symptom of the same problem; if spatial structure helps account for variations in $\hat{\beta}$, then presumably it should also account for observed differences in $\hat{\beta}_i$.

2. ORDINARY LEAST SQUARES REGRESSION AND THE GRAVITY MODEL

The purpose of using multiple regression, then, is to obtain an accurate estimate of the parameter β from equation (2) (as well as an accurate estimate of α and γ). There are two aspects of "accuracy" in this context. First, we wish β to capture only the distance decay effect, separating this from origin and destination specific factors in the sense described in the previous section. Second, we wish our estimate of β to be both *unbiased* and *consistent*. It will be an unbiased estimate if, when $\hat{\beta}$ in equation (3) is estimated several times, each using a different moderately sized sample, these estimates average out to be equal to the true value of β. It will be consistent if, as the size of the sample becomes infinitely large, the multiple regression OLS estimate of β converges on the true value. For these conditions to be met, there are a series of assumptions about multiple regression that must be satisfied in any application of equation (3). If these are not all met, then some, or all, of the desirable properties will be lost. Thus, it it worth examining the assumptions in detail.

a) The observed values of the explanatory variables should be free of measurement error, and non-stochastic. If not, then parameter estimates will be biased in moderate sized samples, although they are at least consistent.

b) *No multicollinearity.* The various explanatory variables should not be highly correlated with one another. If such correlations are high, parameter estimates are still unbiased, but a further problem occurs. Our estimates of the variance of the parameter values from one sample to another become excessively large. This means that any test of significance for the parameters is more likely than it should be to decide that the parameter is not significant (i.e., it does not differ significantly from zero). This conservative bias in significance tests can imply that we will be forced to reject distance as being a significant explanatory factor in situations where it is in fact important.

c) The expected value of the residual associated with any observation is zero. If this were not the case, and the residuals seemed to be consistently positive, or negative, for particular observations, then this would indicate that some explanatory factor is missing. Our model would then be incorrect, or *mis-specified,* since either it is incomplete, or the mathematical nature of the relationships between the variables are wrongly formulated. Mis-specification always implies our parameter estimates will be both biased and inconsistent, because they are attempting to adjust for the incorrect specification. In this case, inaccuracy in the first sense as described above leads to inaccuracy in the second sense.

d) *Homoscedasticity.* The variance of the residuals is approximately the same for all observations. If this is not true, then once again the parameter estimates are unbiased, but the estimates of the variances of these parameters are again biased.

e) *Autocorrelated residuals.* The residuals from the regression should be purely stochastic and should bear no relation to one another. In the context of spatial data, it may be that residuals located near to one another take on similar (or opposite) values; i.e. they are positively (or negatively) autocorrelated. The implications of this violation of the multiple regression assumptions on the validity of OLS parameter estimates will depend on how this problem came about. If autocorrelation occurs because a variable is missing from the regression that has a distinctive geographical pattern, then the problem is one of mis-specification giving rise to biased and inconsistent parameter estimates; estimates that are once again inaccurate in the first sense. However, if autocorrelation in residuals is not due to a missing variable but is simply a property of the residuals, a property that should have been taken into account in how the residuals were specified in equation (2), then parameter estimates are unbiased. But in this latter case, there is still a problem; estimates of the variances of the parameters tend to be too small, making significance tests excessively liberal. The implication would then be that distance might be retained as a significant explanatory factor of human spatial action even though in reality it is not important. This is a case where inaccuracy can occur even if $\hat{\beta}$ is independent of the spatial structure of origins and destinations.

f) *Residuals uncorrelated with explanatory variables.* Just as they should not be systematically related to each other, the residuals should also not be related to any of the explanatory variables. If such relations do exist, the parameter estimates are biased and inconsistent. The existence of a problem here is often a case of mis-specification where the explanatory variables are themselves influenced by values of the dependent variable; a case of causality running in both directions.

g) *The normality assumption.* The residuals should be normally distributed around the expected mean of zero for any given combination of values of explanatory variables (see Johnston, 1978, p. 41). If this assumption is violated, it has no effect whatsoever on the parameter estimates or their variances. It does, however, indicate that tests of significance should be treated with extreme caution, as normality is necessary if we are to place full confidence in the results of t-tests and F-tests.

Summarizing the above list, the two sources of inaccuracy are: mis-specification [assumptions c), part of e) and f)], which I shall call a conceptual bias, and assumption violations producing problems despite the fact that the original model is properly specified [assumptions a), b), d), the remainder of e), and g)] which could be called a *technical inaccuracy,* In this second case, the actual estimates are not biased in a statistical sense. However, it is true that in assumptions b), d) and e) the OLS estimates are no longer the best estimates possible, giving rise to a *de facto* inaccuracy; an inaccuracy reinforced by the danger of making erroneous statements about the significance of mass or distance effects.

Suppose that all the variables influencing interaction are included in P_i, P_j and d_{ij}, and an OLS regression is then fit to the data. Clearly, we have then avoided any mis-specification that may occur as a result of missing variables. However, despite that, it is still possible for conceptual bias to creep into our estimates of $\hat{\beta}$ simply because we may have formulated the mathematical relations between the various variables incorrectly — which is another kind of mis-specification problem. In either event, if things are mis-specified then the possibility exists that as OLS procedures attempt to fit the wrong model to the data $\hat{\beta}$ may become confounded with included or excluded mass effects. The result would be that $\hat{\beta}$ measures more than the 'true' distance decay effect. In short, inaccuracy of the first kind, or *conceptual bias* would then exist. We wish to avoid this at all costs, which implies that mis-specification should not occur if we are to interpret $\hat{\beta}$ as a distance decay parameter. The core of the debate thus has to do with what kinds of mis-specification problems can occur, and how these can be avoided in our search for $\hat{\beta}$ values that have substantive meaning. If mis-specification cannot be avoided, then $\hat{\beta}$ is of little theoretical value since it can change every time the geography of the study area changes. Technical inaccuracy can also lead to interpretations of $\hat{\beta}$ that are erroneous, but not because of confusion introduced as a result of using an incorrect model. In principle, this inaccuracy can be fixed by appropriate modifications of the methodology of regression in order to adjust to the violated assumptions, and may have little to do with non-independence of masses and distance. Once such adjustments are made, and if no conceptual bias exists, then $\hat{\beta}$ may indeed be interpreted as the 'true' distance decay effect. Since technical inaccuracy is less problematic, it will be dealt with first, before moving on to discuss conceptual bias introduced as a result of mis-specification.

3. SOURCES OF TECHNICAL INACCURACY

Of the five sources of technical inaccuracy, non-fixed explanatory variables, multicollinearity, heteroscedasticity, autocorrelated residuals (not due to mis-specification), and non-normality, only the second one has received detailed attention in the distance-decay gravity model debate. This, in fact, was the source of original debate. When Curry (1972) originally suggested the problem, his statements were taken to be a discussion of the problem of multicollinearity by Cliff *et al.* (1974). Their concern was with the possibility of inaccuracy in OLS estimates of β in a situation where a linear correlation exists between P_j and d_{ij}. For example, consider an urban area where population densities decline systematically with distance from the CBD. If a gravity model is fitted to telephone calls emanating from downtown, then there will be a correlation between destination population and distance, two of the explanatory variables in equation (2). Cliff *et al.* correctly argued that this problem would not bias OLS estimates of β unless the correlation were so high that the computational procedures of OLS regression break down.

There was considerable discussion of this question (Cliff *et al.*, 1974, 1975, 1976; Curry *et al.*, 1975; Sheppard *et al.*, 1976) particularly revolving around attempts to use a simulation model to prove the point. Although this is of interest for reasons of its own right, indicating problems that must be faced with simulation modeling in general, it is of little direct relevance, since it emerged that the two groups of authors were discussing different issues. Curry had been concerned all along with the possibility of bias due to mis-specification of the mathematical relationship between masses and distance. In the end an aggrement on the basic issues was reached:

> Much of the disagreement . . . seems to hinge upon our interpretation of Curry's original (1972) paper. We felt Curry implied . . . that the OLS estimators were biased *even when the model was correctly specified* . . . We have sought to demonstrate that this is not so. If Curry (1972) was concerned *solely* with the effect of mis-specification on the estimation problem — a restriction which we feel was not made clear in the original paper — then we are in agreement . . . .
>
> (Cliff *et al.* (1976), p. 341; emphasis in original)

Although questions of conceptual bias are thus not related to the existence of multicollinearity, the inaccuracies that come from this problem are of some interest. The spatial structure of the populations will determine whether or not their correlation with distance is high. Where correlations are high, and multicollinearity is a problem, the distance or mass variables may erroneously be rejected as being apparently insignificant. Thus in one study area, where correlations are high, the distance decay effect may be rejected, while in another area where little multicollinearity exists, it may be regarded as significant. These different conclusions can occur even if the estimated values for $\hat{\beta}$ are very similar in the two areas and the "true" distance effect is identical, because estimates of the standard error of $\hat{\beta}$ differ. Similarly, within a study area such as the city described above, if the model is fit separately for each origin, the significance of $\hat{\beta}$ may be rejected for flows from the CBD and accepted as important at suburban origins, just because of the different levels of multicollinearity in each case. Clearly, such differing conclusions are purely a statistical illusion brought on by the differing spatial structures.

This type of influence of spatial structure on the statistical *significance* of the distance decay effect is in principle avoidable by identifying the existence of multicollinearity and correcting for it. However, as Fotheringham (1980) points out, there is no clear notion of how much multicollinearity must exist before the problem must be corrected for. This is a problem associated with using multiple regression in any context that has not been well solved by statisticians. Although there is little discussion of measurement error in the explanatory variables, heteroscedasticity, autocorrelation and non-normality with respect to distance decay parameters, the principle would be the same here. First, violations of the assumptions must be tested for and identified, and the investigator should be confident that no mis-specification exists. Second, the regression methodology should be adjusted accordingly, attempting Generalized Least Squares methods for heteroscedasticity and autocorrelation (Johnson, 1972; Hepple, 1976); and non-parametric tests in the event of non-normality (another issue that is rarely discussed in the standard textbooks). Apparently, the only solution for measurement error is to avoid it and maximize sample size (Koutsoyiannis, 1978).

A most important point, however, is that these solutions will only give good estimates of the distance decay effect if the original model is not mis-specified. If mis-specification exists, in the sense that the simple model of equation (3) is unable to properly separate distance and origin or destination effects from one another, then all that these solutions will do is give a more accurate estimate of a parameter that is conceptually biased in the first place. This is why mis-specification is so important; if the parameter is conceptually biased, an accurate estimate of its value will be of limited use because it cannot be interpreted as a pure distance decay effect despite its technical accuracy.

4. MIS-SPECIFICATION

4.1. *Symptoms of Mis-Specification*

If it is indeed the case that the OLS estimate $\hat{\beta}$ in equation (3) is affected by both the "true" distance decay effect and by the spatial configuaration of origins and destinations, then this type of mis-specification should show up in empirical regressions in two ways. First, there should be significant and unpredictable variation in the estimated values of $\hat{\beta}$ from one study to the next. This has certainly been the case (Carroll and Bevis, 1957; Olsson, 1970), and has been a major drawback for those wishing to give the gravity model theoretical status. However, this cannot be convincing evidence of mis-specification, since such variations may also be due to different travel behavior, different constraints, different trip purposes, etc. The question of how much of this unpredictability is due to mis-specification can only be fully answered if the conceptual bias can be identified and eliminated. Second, if equation (3) is fit separately to flows from each origin in the spatial system, to give origin-specific estimates of the distance decay effect as shown in equation (4), then these should also vary from origin to origin. This is because the relationship between opportunities and distance is different for each origin (Figure 3). This variability would be somewhat more convincing as evidence of mis-specification since the other factors are likely to be less variable within a study area than between study areas. Once again, there is substantial evidence of this variability (Gould, 1975; Leinbach, 1973; O'Sullivan, 1977); evidence that in fact stimulated the research of Johnston on this subject.

4.2. *Mis-Specification: Applying the Wrong Theory*

One way in which mis-specification can lead to biased parameter estimates is if human spatial action generated by one theory is mistakenly thought to be due to another theory. The research of Johnston (1973) on bias in estimating distance-decay parameters illustrates this. He developed simulation experiments where trips were generated by an intervening opportunities model, and then looked at what happened if a researcher erroneously attempted to fit a gravity model to these data. Mathematically, the model that is fit, separately for each origin i, is the following regression:

$$\log (\overset{\circ}{I}_{ij}) = \hat{A}_i + \hat{\gamma}_i \log (P_j) - \hat{\beta}_i \log (d_{ij}) + \epsilon_{ij} \tag{5}$$

whereas in actual fact

$$\log (\overset{\circ}{I}_{ij}) = B + \theta_i \log (P_j) - \delta_i \log (O_j) + \epsilon_{ij}.$$

Here O_j is the number of destinations closer to i than j in any direction.

Obviously, as distance increases so does the number of intervening opportunities. Thus, the gravity model will provide a good fit to the intervening opportunities data. However, just as the relation between masses and distance varies from one origin to the next (Figure 3), so will the relationship between intervening opportunities and distance. Thus, in the event that an observer mistakenly applies the gravity model to intervening opportunities data, the $\hat{\beta}_i$ coefficient will differ from one origin to the next as the model attempts to approximate the variation in opportunities by a variation in distance. Because the covariance of distance and opportunities differs for each origin, it is inevitable that $\hat{\beta}$ will also differ. The resulting effects have been amply illustrated by Johnston (1975a, b; 1976).

It can in fact be shown mathematically that when this mistake is made,

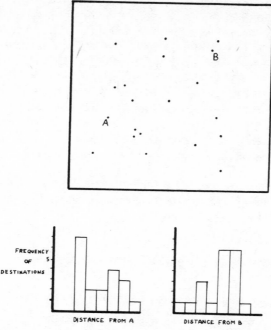

Fig. 3. Variability, by origin, in the relation between destinations and distance in a spatial system.

the estimate of $|\hat{\beta}_i|$ from equation (5) is in fact inversely related to the variance of log (d_{ij}) about origin i (Sheppard, 1979a, p. 133 theorem 2). In other words, the more that destinations cluster close to an origin i, the larger $|\hat{\beta}_i|$ will be (i.e., the greater the apparent distance decay effect). This result can then be used in practice to see whether there is in fact a negative correlation between $|\hat{\beta}_i|$ and the variance of log (d_{ij}). If so, that would suggest that this type of mis-specification may in fact be occurring. Sheppard (1979a) finds that such a negative correlation does exist in the data of O'Sullivan (1977), but not in that of Leinbach (1973) or Gould (1975).

It is tremendously difficult in practice to determine whether or not a gravity model is being mistakenly fit to intervening opportunities data, or *vice versa*. Typically, due to the relation between opportunities and distance, both models fit the same set of data almost as well as one another. In addition, we rarely know enough about the human spatial action under study to choose one theory over the other *a priori*. If, however, after calculating OLS regression equations for the gravity model on origin specific data, a negative correlation is found between $|\hat{\beta}_i|$ and var (log (d_{ij})), then that indicates that the wrong model may be in use because the data may in fact be the result of interaction based on intervening opportunities. Such an interpretation could be placed on O'Sullivan's results (Sheppard, 1979a). But, it should be emphasized that this is only one possibility. We simply do not know enough about the problem to say what other types of mis-specification could produce the same effect. In addition, the mathematical proof referred to above has only been proven for a situation where P_j is constant for all j, with only the relative location of the various destinations being variable from one origin to the next.

In this context, the work by Fotheringham (1980) should be noted. He discusses the mis-specification error associated with fitting equation (5) to data generated by the relationship:

$$I_{ij} = A - c_i\, d_{ij} + \epsilon_{ij}.$$

Again, the spatial structure significantly biases OLS estimates of $\hat{\beta}$.

4.4. *Mis-Specification: The Convolution of Populations and Distances*

When Curry (1972) revived the debate about whether or not parameter $\hat{\beta}$ in equation (3), as estimated by OLS regression, captures the 'true' distance decay effect and only this effect, his misgivings stemmed from the similarity between the product of origin and destination terms in the numerator of the gravity model, and the expression for the spatial autocorrelation in a map of destinations and origins. With the help of some elementary mathematics, these misgivings can be made more precise.

Suppose that a study area has been divided into a set of regular squares or hexagons between which spatial interactions are to be modeled, and let the term r_s refer to the level of spatial autocorrelation between the populations of those cells that are distance s apart. Now, the formula for spatial autocorrelation of one variable at different locations parallels the equation for correlation between two variables:

$$r_s = \frac{\sum\limits_{i=1}^{n_s} (P_i - \bar{P}_s)\,(P_{i+s} - \bar{P}_s)/n_s}{\sum\limits_{j=1}^{n} (P_j - \bar{P})^2/n}.$$

Here P_{i+s} is the population of a cell s units of distance from i, n_s is the total number of pairs of locations distance s apart, $\bar{P}_s$ is the mean population of all cells that are in this set of paired comparisons, n is the total number of cells in the study area ($n \geq n_s$), and $\bar{P}$ is the mean population averaged over all cells in the study area.

By expanding the brackets for the numerator, and taking advantage of the fact that the denominator is simply the variance of the set of populations, which will be denoted here by the symbol σ_p^2:

$$r_s = \{ \sum_{i=1}^{n_s} P_i P_{i+s} - 2 \sum_{i=1} P_i \bar{P}_s^2 + n_s \bar{P}_s^2 \} / n_x \, \sigma_p^2.$$

But,

$$2 \sum_{i=1}^{n_s} P_i \bar{P}_s = 2 \bar{P}_s \sum_i P_i,$$
$$= 2 \bar{P}_s \bar{P}_s n_s,$$

since

$$\bar{P}_s = \frac{1}{n_s} \sum_{i=1}^{n_s} P_i.$$

Therefore,

$$r_s = \{ \sum_i P_i P_{i+s} + n_s \bar{P}_s^2 \} / n_s \sigma_p^2. \tag{6}$$

In general, the autocorrelation in populations tends to be high at short distances and lower at greater distances away, since locations closer together tend to be more similar. Thus, in practice, r_s is typically inversely related to distance, s. Now σ_p^2 is constant for all s, in general $\bar{P}_s$ will not vary systematically with s, and n_s will tend to decline as s increases. When asking, then, what it is in equation (6) that brings about a decline in r_s with distance most attention must be concentrated on the first term, $\sum P_i P_{i+s}/n_s$. Since n_s is declining, and r_s typically declines as distance s increases, then the product $P_i P_{i+s}$ must also be declining significantly. Thus, we may conclude from all of this that the product of populations is strongly related to distance simply due to the spatial autocorrelation of population, in line with Curry's intuition (1972; Curry et al., 1975; Sheppard, 1979a). Further, since typically the spatial structure of populations differs from one study area to the next, it may well be that spatial autocorrelation will also differ. Thus, the relation between the product of populations and distance can vary from one study area to the next if (as is generally the case) the spatial structure is not identical.

Now consider the problem of fitting a gravity model to interaction in such a hypothetical study area. Also assume, for simplicity, that the interaction parameters for the mass terms, α and γ, are identically equal to one. Then

$$I_{ij} = P_i P_j d_{ij}^{-\beta} . \qquad (7)$$

Further, let us aggregate all pairs of cells distance s apart in this study area to create one composite observation on interaction at distance s (Curry et al., 1975; Sheppard, 1979a):

$$\sum_{i=1}^{n_s} I_{i,\ i+s} = \sum_{i=1}^{n_s} P_i P_{i+s}\, s^{-\beta},$$

where $s = d_{i,\ i+s}$ is the distance apart. One such observation could be created for each possible distance interval and the set of such observations could then be entered into an OLS regression model to estimate β:

$$\log\left(\sum_i I_{i,\ i+s}\right) = A + \log\left(\sum_i P_i P_{i+s}\right) - \hat{\beta} \log s + \epsilon_{i,\ i+s}, \qquad (8)$$

for all $s = 1, \ldots, S$.

Our conclusions from equation (6) would show that the second term on the right hand side here is related to distance. Intuition is readily confirmed if equation (6) is rearranged so that

$$\sum_i P_i P_{i+s} = r_s\, n_s\, \sigma_p^2 + n_s\, \bar{P}_s^2,$$

which is then substituted into (8) to yield:

$$\log\left(\sum_i I_{i,\ i+s}\right) = A + \log\left(r_s\, n_s\, \sigma_p^2 + n_s\, \bar{P}_s^2\right) - \hat{\beta} \log\,(s) + \epsilon_{i,\ i+s}. \qquad (9)$$

This shows that both the second and the third terms are related to distance, each in a different way.

In equation (8) no coefficient was assigned to the product of populations expression since α and γ were assumed to be equal to one in equation (7). However, in practice OLS regression would only reproduce this value of one if the additive functional relation in equation (8) is well behaved. But unfortunately, that need not be the case because our two explanatory variables are both functions of distance.

As one extreme example, suppose $r_s = s^{-\lambda}$. Then equation (8) becomes

$$\log \left(\sum_i I_{i,\ i+s} \right) = A + \log[s^{-\lambda}\, n_s\, \sigma_p^2 + n_s\, \overline{P}_s^2] - \hat{\beta} \log (s) + \epsilon_{i,\ i+s}$$

$$= A - \lambda \log (s) + \log [n_s\, \sigma_p^2 + s^{\lambda}\, n_s\, \overline{P}_s^2] - \hat{\beta} \log (s) + \epsilon_{i,\ i+s}.$$

The result is an equation with two different terms related to distance in reality, whereas the equation used to estimate this, equation (8), only has one term. As a result, $\hat{\beta}$ in equation (8) will attempt to capture some of these other effects. In the words of Cliff *et al.* (1975, p. 287):

"when [this] mixed additive-multiplicative model ... is wrongly specified as [3] ... the estimates [of $\hat{\beta}$ will be] all over the place as the linear form struggles to calibrate the non-linear form."

In general, the function relating r_s to distance is often quite complex, even in apparently simple examples (Sheppard, 1979a, p. 129). If r_s is related to distance in some way, then it must also be related to the explanatory variable, log s, in equation (9). However, this is likely to be a non-linear relationship. When two variables are strongly non-linearly related, their simple correlation can still be very small, so an inspection of the correlation between $\log(s)$ and $\log (\Sigma P_i\, P_{i+s})$ would not reveal the existence of a problem. However, the problem is still there; a problem caused by trying to fit a linear model to a relationship that is in fact non-linear.

What implications are to be drawn from this? The spatial autocorrelation function, r_s, will differ from one study area to the next as it depends on the spatial structure of opportunities. Thus, for two study areas with different spatial structures the effects of this bias on the OLS estimate of $\hat{\beta}$ in equation (8) will in all likelihood be different. As a result, one would expect that $\hat{\beta}$ would alter from one study to the next even if the 'true' distance decay effect has not changed. What is not known, however, is how severe this effect will be. Recall that the argument was developed under the assumption $\alpha = \gamma = 1$. Thus, the severity of the effect will depend on α and γ and also on the relationship between r_s and distance. There is much work to be done before we know much about conditions under which this bias is significant. However, the potential effects of spatial structure in biasing OLS estimates of $\hat{\beta}$ when the model is mis-specified cannot be ignored. The work of Johnston showed how much effect mis-specification may have in producing different biases in $\hat{\beta}$ for different spatial structures.

The important point is that this mis-specification will always be present if equation (3) is used to estimate gravity-like interactions, except when all populations are equal at all origins and destinations, or alternatively when the masses are randomly distributed in space. Even in these last cases, if origin-specific gravity models are fitted (equation (5)), the bias will still exist, affecting each $\hat{\beta}_i$ estimate differently because each origin has a different location relative to the set of destinations. Thus, we would expect that conceptual bias due to this type of mis-specification would always be present in origin-specific OLS regression estimates of the gravity model. Ultimately, as Cliff *et al.* (1975, p. 287) suggest, the only solution is first to estimate the nature of the relationship between spatial autocorrelation and distance, r_s, for each study area or each origin-specific regression. Then this information should be entered into equation (9) by replacing r_s with this function. Finally, non-linear regression estimates of all relevant parameters would have to be obtained. This has not yet been attempted, so there is no practical evidence about the importance of this bias. Alternatively, if the relationship between distance and mass terms is more explicit, it is possible to derive some clear idea at least about the nature and possibly the direction of bias (Baxter, 1983).

4.3. *Mis-Specification: Interaction Feedback Effects*

As a third example of how mis-specification can occur, consider assumption f) of OLS regression models discussed above; that the residuals should not be correlated with values of any explanatory variables. This assumption can be violated if it is assumed that causality only runs in one direction, from explanatory variables, X, to dependent variable, Y, in a situation when in fact Y also has a causal effect on X. For example, if

$$Y = A + BX + \epsilon, \tag{10}$$

and

$$X = C + DY + U \tag{11}$$

where ϵ and U are the residual errors, then substituting (10) into (11) gives

$$X = C + DA + DBX + D \cdot \epsilon + U.$$

In other words, X is related to ϵ, the residual in the initial regression equation (10), which is a violation of the assumption. This is known as simultaneous equation bias; bias that occurs when one way causality is assumed in a situation where both variables affect each other. Better estimates of the regression coefficients can then be obtained if methods such as two stage least squares

(2SLS) or indirect least squares (ILS), are used instead of the standard OLS approach.

It is highly plausible that this type of mis-specification may occur in spatial interaction studies. This will be the case if it is not only true that interactions depend on the spatial structure of the populations, but it is also the case that the size of those populations are themselves dependent on the level of spatial interaction. This effect of interactions feeding back to affect the spatial structure is obviously central in models of migration, and can frequently be the case for other types of interaction. Fotheringham and Webber (1980) provide an example of this type of bias, in the following way:

$$\log (I_{ij}) = \alpha + \gamma_1 \log (P_i) + \gamma_2 \log (P_j) - \beta \log (d_{ij}) + \epsilon_{ij} \qquad (12)$$

and

$$\log (P_i) = \mu + \phi \sum_j \log (I_{ij}) + u_i \qquad (13)$$

They prove mathematically that unless $\phi = 0$ in equation (13), or ϵ_{ij} are all exactly equal to zero, an OLS estimate of β in equation (12) will be biased as it ignores the determinants of P_j in equation (13) (see Fotheringham and Webber, 1980, p. 36). They then investigate the error associated with estimating β in (12) using simple OLS, compared to the results of using 2SLS to simultaneously estimate both equations together. Their empirical example was the level of inter-state migration flows, 1949–50, from "large" to small states. They find that the OLS estimate of β gave a value of 0.592, whereas the value of the distance coefficient from 2SLS estimation was 0.968; very different answers that turned out also to be significantly different statistically. Thus, in this case an empirical example does exist, and it suggests that the effects of simultaneous equation bias are quite large.

There are standard econometric methods for obtaining better estimates than those from OLS when simultaneous equation bias is present, as noted above (see also Meyer, 1974; O'Sullivan, 1971). These methods are well-known, and easily used although there is much controversy as to whether they provide improvements that are worth the extra effort with large equation systems and small samples. Solution of this problem, however, does not eliminate other possible sources of bias, such as the one described in the previous section. As was suggested there, that bias may be endemic in any study area where the destination populations are spatially autocorrelated.

5. CONCLUSIONS

In the debate about how to obtain meaningful estimates of distance decay effects, it seems that conceptual bias poses significantly more problems than technical inaccuracy. Three possible sources of conceptual bias due to mis-specification have been noted, one being due to the application of incorrect theories, the second being due to the geography of populations, and the third resulting from an incomplete theory. Clearly, any or all of these may be present in any study, presenting a considerable problem for any researcher since none of them are easy to identify. The first and third are relatively easy to deal with once they are identified; they are standard problems facing any researcher attempting to use regression to empirically test a theory. We as yet have no solution for the second problem, and very little idea of how much bias is introduced because of this. The reason no solution exists is because this is not a standard statistical problem, but rather arises from the geographical nature of the problem. This is, however, an unfortunate situation as the problem stems from the spatial autocorrelation of population, and is thus endemic to almost any study area. Thus, there is some important research still to be done on the topic.

There is also the possibility of other mis-specification problems that have not yet been identified. Mis-specification is a major difficulty in using the gravity model because of its poor theoretical basis. If we had good theory to tell us how interactions occur and what affects both their occurrence and any possible estimation methods, then it would be a simple matter to apply this knowledge. But, when a theory is being sought while at the same time it is being calibrated against data, then it is all but impossible to narrow down *a priori* the number of ways mis-specification may occur. This leaves any researcher with a formidable task, as it represents the situation where empiricist reasoning is at its weakest: "One thing . . . which has been repeatedly stressed by all the contributors to the debate, is the very great weakness of geographical theory in this area to guide us, and the large volume of work that remains to be undertaken," (Cliff *et al.*, 1976, p. 342).

Dept. of Geography
University of Minnesota

BIBLIOGRAPHY

Baxter, M.: 1983, 'Model mis-specification and spatial structure in spatial interaction models', *Environment and Planning A* 15, 319–28.
Carroll, J. D. and H. W. Bevis: 1957, 'Predicting local travel in urban regions', *Papers of the Regional Science Association* 3, 183–197.

Carrothers, G. A. P.: 1956, 'An historical review of the gravity and potential concepts of human interaction', *Journal of the American Institute of Planners* 22, 94–102.

Cliff, A. D., R. Martin, and J. K. Ord: 1974, 'Evaluating the friction of distance parameter in gravity models', *Regional Studies* 8, 281–286.

Cliff, A. D., R. Martin, and J. K. Ord: 1975, 'Map pattern and friction of distance parameters: reply to comments by R. J. Johnston, and by L. Curry, D. A. Griffith and E. S. Sheppard', *Regional Studies* 9, 285–288.

Cliff, A. D., R. Martin, and J. K. Ord: 1976, 'A reply to the final comment', *Regional Studies* 10, 341–342.

Curry, L.: 1972, 'A spatial analysis of gravity flows', *Regional Studies* 6, 131–147.

Curry, L., D. A. Griffith, and E. S. Sheppard: 1975, 'Those gravity parameters again', *Regional Studies* 9, 289–296.

Fotheringham, A. S.: 1980, *Spatial Structure, Spatial Interaction and Distance-Decay Parameters*, Unpublished Ph. D. Dissertation, McMaster University, Hamilton.

Fotheringham, A. S. and M. J. Webber: 1980, 'Spatial structure and the parameters of spatial interaction models', *Geographical Analysis* 12, 33–46.

Glickman, N. J.: 1976, 'A note on simultaneous equation estimation techniques: Application with a regional econometric model', *Regional Science and Urban Economics* 6, 275–288.

Gould, P.: 1975, 'Acquiring spatial information', *Economic Geography* 51, 87–99.

Hepple, L. W.: 1976, 'A maximum likelihood model for econometric estimation with spatial series', in I. Masser (ed.), *Theory and Practice in Regional Science*, London Papers in Regional Science, vol. 6, Pion, London.

Johnston, J.: 1972, *Econometric Methods* 2nd ed., McGraw-Hill, New York.

Johnston, R. J.: 1973, 'On frictions of distance and regression coefficients', *Area* 5, 187–191.

Johnston, R. J.: 1975a, 'Map pattern and friction of distance parameters: A comment', *Regional Studies* 9, 281–283.

Johnston, R. J.: 1975b, *The World Trade System: Some Enquiries into its Spatial Structure*, G. Bell & Sons, London.

Johnston, R. J.: 1976, 'On regression coefficients in comparative studies of the friction of distance', *Tijdschrift voor economische en sociale geografie* 67, 15–28.

Johnston, R. J.: 1978, *Multivariate Statistical Analysis in Geography*, Longman, New York.

Koutsoyiannis, A.: 1978, *Theory of Econometrics: An Introductory Exposition of Econometric Methods*, Barnes and Noble, New York.

Leinbach, T. R.: 1973, 'Distance, information flows and modernisation: some observations from West Malaysia', *The Professional Geographer* 25, 7–11.

Meyer, D. R.: 1974, 'Use of two stage least squares to solve simultaneous equation systems in geography', in M. Yeates (eds.), *Proceedings of the 1972 Meeting of the I.G.U. Commission on Quantitative Geography*, McGill-Queen's University Press, Montreal, pp. 101–112.

Olsson, G.: 1970, 'Explanation, prediction and meaning variance: an assessment of distance interaction models', *Economic Geography* 46, 223–233.

O'Sullivan, P. M.: 1971, 'Forecasting interregional freight flows in Great Britain', in M. D. I. Chisholm, A. E. Frey, and P. Haggett (eds.), *Regional Forecasting*, Butterworth, London, pp. 443–450.

O'Sullivan, P. M.: 1977, 'On gravity and eruptions', *The Professional Geographer* 29, 182–185.

Porter, R.: 1956, 'Approach to migration through its mechanism', *Geografiska Annaler* 38, 13–45.

Sheppard, E. S.: 1978, 'Theoretical underpinnings of the gravity hypothesis', *Geographical Analysis* 10, 386–402.

Sheppard, E. S.: 1979a, 'Gravity parameter estimation', *Geographical Analysis* 11, 121–132.

Sheppard, E. S.: 1979b, 'Notes on spatial interaction', *The Professional Geographer* 31, 8–15.

Sheppard, E. S.: 1980, 'The ideology of spatial choice', *Papers of the Regional Science Association* 45, 197–213.

Sheppard, E. S., D. A. Griffith, and L. Curry: 1976, 'A final comment on mis-specification and autocorrelation in those gravity parameters', *Regional Studies* 10, 337–339.

Stetzer, F. and A. G. Phipps: 1977, 'Spatial choice theory and spatial indifference: a comment', *Geographical Analysis* 9, 400–403.

Tocalis, T. R.: 1978, 'Changing theoretical foundations of the gravity concept of human interaction', in B. J. L. Berry (ed.), *Perspectives in Geography 3: The Nature of Change in Geographical Ideas*, Northern Illinois University Press, DeKalb.

ROGER W. WHITE

PRINCIPLES OF SIMULATION IN HUMAN GEOGRAPHY

1. INTRODUCTION

Human geographers, like everyone else, are trying to understand a world which is complex and constantly changing. For the most part, however, the methods which are available to them are only appropriate to a simple, static world. Simulation analysis is the exception. It is the natural language for handling complex, dynamic systems realistically.

Hagerstrand (1957) is the pioneer in the use of simulation techniques in human geography, with his paper on migration in rural Sweden. Morrill (1962) was also an early user, simulating the development of central place systems. In addition, by the 1960's simulation modeling of urban traffic flows had become widespread, and was used by planners and traffic engineers to design optimal traffic control systems. These applications, while certainly geographical in nature, were largely ignored by geographers, who seemed, in fact, to forget simulation analysis as statistical methods came to dominate the field.

Recently, however, there has been a revival of interest in the technique, especially among those working in the area of urban systems. In this field, there has been much progress in the past few years in developing models relating urban structure to urban processes, and there has been a corresponding development of analytical techniques, primarily in the area of differential topology, for dealing with these models.[1] However, it is often the case that even the new mathematical techniques are inadequate for the task of elucidating the behavior of the models. And, if we cannot determine what a model implies about the system being modeled, then it is of little value, regardless of how plausible it may appear. Simulation analysis provides a way out of this difficulty, since it can reveal the behavior of any model in as much detail as desired (or until the computer account is exhausted). For example, both Coelho and Wilson (1976) and White (1977, 1978a, b) have used simulation techniques to examine the behavior of models of the retail system. Aspects of these models will be discussed in detail in Sections 2–4. Allen and Sanglier (1979, 1981, 1983) have also developed ambitious, but promising simulation models of urban systems. These stochastic models

389

Gary L. Gaile and Cort J. Willmott (eds.), Spatial Statistics and Models, 389–416.
© 1984 *by D. Reidel Publishing Company.*

describe the dynamic interrelationships of a number of phenomena, such as employment in each of several sectors in each urban center, economies of scale, competition of cities for migrants, and urban growth. While the models themselves are interesting, the simulation analysis has not been carried far enough to map out the characteristic behavior of the models.

Industrial location is another area in which applications of simulation analysis are beginning to appear. Two economists, Nelson and Winter, have been engaged in a reformulation of the theory of the firm using a dynamic modeling approach. While their initial work used analytical techniques for exploring the behavior of the models (see e.g., Winter 1971 and Nelson and Winter 1975), they subsequently turned to simulation modeling (Nelson, et al. (1976). Following their methods, Weinberg and Schmenner (1977) have developed a simulation model of business location decisions in an urban area. In their model, relocation decisions are driven by land shortages due either to expanded demand or to the need to adopt new technology. White (1982) has also developed a simulation model of industrial location. In this model, locational decisions depend on both access to information about sites and characteristics of the sites themselves. The aim is to simulate the development of new manufacturing regions.

In spite of the recent increase in interest in simulation modeling among human geographers, the existing applications are still too few to make a review article worthwhile. Therefore, the approach taken here is to illustrate simulation modeling by developing three examples of the use of the technique in the study of urban retail systems.[2] The first example is a practical planning application in a specific city; the second is an exploration of the role of the central business district, and the third is an application to the development of a general theory of retail systems. In order to reveal more clearly the similarities and differences between practical and theoretical applications, and incidentally to save the reader the trouble of mastering the details of three models, we use the same basic model throughout.

This approach also permits us to concentrate not on the model itself, but on the principles and tricks of the trade of good simulation modeling. In fact, throughout this chapter the major emphasis is placed on pointing out the characteristics of a good simulation analysis. This point is most important, for in using simulation, as opposed to cookbook techniques like statistical tests, the modeler has essentially a free hand. Almost anything can be programmed into a computer and run as a simulation model, and it is easy, even tempting, to construct a grandiose model which takes everything into consideration, and which, thanks to arbitrary adjustments, even mimics a real-world situation. Yet such an ad hoc model will produce spurious or misleading results and explain nothing. On the other hand, used carefully, with honesty and good judgement, simulation analysis is a powerful, useful tool as well as an art.

2. A PLANNING APPLICATION

The first example is an application of simulation modeling to a planning problem in St. John's, Newfoundland. St. John's, like many North American cities, experienced a decline of its Central Business District following the construction of several large suburban shopping malls. This has led to a concern that the size, location, and timing of new malls should be controlled in order to prevent serious declines in existing centers. Such a policy has been followed successfully in other areas, notably Ontario. However, success depends on the ability to predict with reasonable accuracy what the effect of a proposed center will be. In order to make such predictions, we need both a model which can simulate the actual urban retailing system, and data descriptive of the St. John's system to use in that model. We outline first the necessary available data and then describe the model.

2.1. *Data*

Figure 1 shows the St. John's area divided into census tracts, as well as the location of the major shopping centers. Center 1 is the Central Business District (CBD), and Centers 2–6 are more recent outlying shopping malls. Center 7 is a proposed mall. The sizes of these centers are shown in Table I. These data will be part of the input to the model.

From the census and other sources, we have data on total disposable income in each census tract, and these can be converted to estimates of total expenditures on retail goods and services by residents of each tract. We also have, from traffic studies, data on average travel time from a representative point in each tract to each of the seven centers.

2.2. *The Model*

The standard Lakshmanan-Hansen model of spatial interaction[3] is the basis of the simulation model of the retailing system. This model states that the crude attraction of a retail center for some population is proportional to the size of the center and inversely proportion to some power of distance

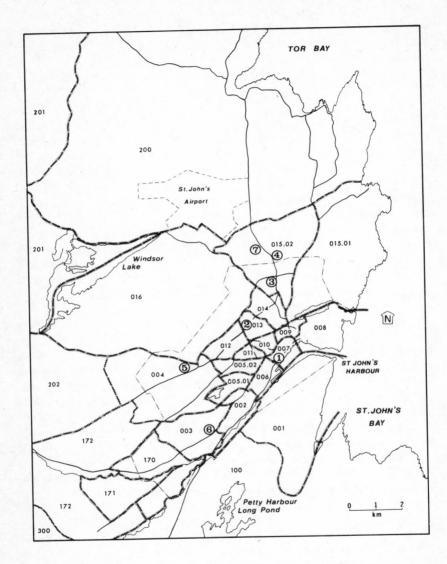

Fig. 1.   Metropolitan St. John's, Newfoundland: major retail centers and census tracts.

TABLE I
Major Shopping Centers, St. John's, Newfoundland

Center	Size (m^2 GLA)
1 (CBD)	86,990
2	5,440
3	8,790
4	9,290
5	35,160
6	42,750
7 (proposed)	40,000

to that center; and the *relative* attraction of the center is given by the ratio of its crude attraction to the total attraction of all competing centers in the system. Thus

$$I_{ij} = (S_j/D_{ij}^n) \left/ \sum_j (S_j/D_{ij}^n) \right. \tag{1}$$

where I_{ij} is the proportion of total retail purchases by residents of census tract i which are made in center j. S_i is the size of center j measured in square meters of gross leasable floorspace. D_{ij} is the distance from census tract i to center j measured in travel time. n is a parameter (constant) to be calibrated to the situation in which the model is applied.

The relative flow of expenditures given by equation (1) can be converted to an absolute figure by multiplying by the total volume of expenditures (E_i) on retail goods and services by residents of census tract i. From the retailer's point of view, this is the revenue received from residents of that tract. Total revenue (R_j) received by retailers in center j is then given by

$$R_j = \sum_i E_i I_{ij}. \tag{2}$$

The success of a center is determined not only by its revenue but also by the costs incurred in generating those revenues. We will assume that costs (C_j) are a simple function of the size of the center

$$C_j = a + b_j S_j^m.$$

The constant a represents a threshold level of costs, and the parameter m determines whether we are dealing with a case of diseconomies of scale

$(m > 1)$, constant returns to scale $(m=1)$ or economies of scale $(m < 1)$. Profit (P_j) is simply the difference of revenue and cost:

$$P_j = R_j - C_j.$$

The model as it has been outlined so far is sometimes used in a planning context to estimate the effect of a proposed shopping center on existing facilities. The model is first calibrated to the existing situation, and then equations representing the new center are added and the new profit levels for each center calculated. If the result shows the proposed center likely to be unprofitable, or, on the other hand, profitable, but likely to threaten the survival of one of the existing centers, planning permission may be denied.

In this form the model is static, but it can be transformed into a dynamic simulation model by adding assumptions about the behavior of retailers in response to varying profit levels. Let us assume that if a center is profitable it will grow, either because existing businesses will expand or because other firms will be attracted to it. Similarly, if it is incurring a loss it will shrink, because some establishments will close or more to another location. If we take this adjustment of center size to be strictly proportional to profit, then we can write

$$t+1 S_j = {}^t S_j + g (R_j - C_j)$$

and

$$t+1 S_j = {}^t S_j + g \left(\sum_i E_i \left(({}^t S_j / D_{ij}^n) / (\sum_j {}^t S_j / D_{ij}^n) \right) - (a + b_j \, {}^t S_j^m) \right) \quad (3)$$

where g is the growth factor, expressing the number of square meters a center expands (or contracts) per dollar of profit (or loss) per time period. Notice that since the distances (D_{ij}) between the various residential zones and the retail centers are fixed, the only variables in this equation are the center sizes $({}^t S_j)$, and these must be written with the time index, t, since they may change from one time period to the next.

Substituting into equation (3) data on retail expenditures (E_i), travel time (D_{ij}) and center sizes (S_j) for St. John's for the year the new mall was to be opened, 1981, we can now calculate estimates of center sizes in the next time period (1982). We then substitute the 1982 sizes back into equation (3) to predict values for 1983, and so on. The model thus generates a series of sizes for each of the seven centers.

After a number of years, or iterations of the model, the system will normally approach a new equilibrium position, that is, the centers will achieve stable sizes. The predicted sizes for two of the centers, the CBD and the proposed mall, are shown in Figure 2. In this case, the CBD is shown

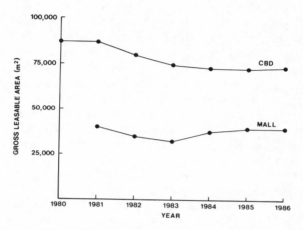

Fig. 2. Predicted sizes of central business district and proposed mall, 1981–86.

to suffer a significant decline in the three years following the opening of the mall, and then to stabilize, while the new center undergoes a slight contraction during the first year but then regains its initial size during the third year. The other five centers (not shown) are not seriously affected.

2.3. *Evaluation of the Model*

Having outlined a simple form of the simulation model and shown the types of results that are generated, we now examine certain aspects of the model more closely and discuss several desirable modifications. The first matter which deserves attention is the value of the constants or parameters in equation (3). Where do these come from? Ideally their values are available from previous empirical studies of shopping trip behavior, in the case of the distance exponent "n", and studies of retail center cost function in the case of the cost parameters a, b and m. In practice, because both origin-destination studies of traffic flow and surveys of shoppers are fairly common, and because both can be used to calibrate an interaction model like that in equation (1), usable values for n are often available. Detailed cost data, on the other hand, are rarely available, and so it is not usually possible to determine the value of all three cost parameters empirically.[4] This problem, however, provides an opportunity to deal with another difficulty involving calibration of the model.

The values of each of the parameters used, taken individually, should be empirically reasonable. But in addition, the behavior of the model as a whole should be representative of the situation we are modeling. Because no model can be a perfect representation of reality, it is possible, or rather likely, that using the best individual calibration of the various parameters would result in a model which, in its behavior, is not optimally calibrated to the situation being modeled. Specifically, in the case we are examining, we would like to start off with a model calibrated so that it is approximately in equilibrium before the seventh center is added. We assure this by manipulating the cost parameters. First, we simplify the problem by setting the fixed cost parameter, a, equal to zero. Then, we use what data are available to determine (or make a best guess of) the value of m. Since this parameter is important in the qualitative behavior of the system (in that it determines whether the model represents increasing, constant, or decreasing returns to scale), it is important that it have a value at least within the range necessary to represent the appropriate effect (e.g., diseconomies of scale). In other words, we are not completely free to manipulate its value. However, the remaining parameters, b_i, are essentially scaling factors and have no effect on the qualitative behavior of the model. Thus, they can be assigned a suitable set of values (each center having a different value) to assure that the model is approximately in equilibrium before the introduction of the new center. Of course, there may be situations where it is appropriate to start the simulation with the model in disequilibrium. But in that case, in order to establish the effect of the new center on the system, it will be necessary to run the model over the entire period of interest, without the proposed center, and then re-run it with the new center included.

Turning now to desirable modifications of the model, we will examine first the growth mechanism. The approach used in equation (3), in which growth (or decline) is assumed to occur simply in proportion to profit (or loss), is useful because it is simple; but this simplicity is perhaps of greater value in the theoretical applications discussed in Sections 3 and 4 than in the present planning application context because the mechanism is not very realistic. Retailers do not react to every minor fluctuation in profits by expanding or contracting. In fact, there is considerable inertia. Businesses may endure subnormal profits or even losses for some time, hoping for an improvement in conditions, or they may sit on excess profits waiting to see if the good times are more than a temporary aberration. Thus, realistically, the simple constant of proportionality (g) should be replaced by a threshold criterion (e.g., retail centers expand or contract in proportion to profits or losses greater than some threshold amount), with perhaps a delay criterion also (e.g., profits or losses must be greater than the threshold value for at least two time periods before a center reacts).

Another modification which would be appropriate in the case of a city undergoing significant growth during the period being simulated, would be to treat the total expenditures on retail goods by census tract as variables rather than constants. In other words, E_i, which appears in equations (2) and (3) as a constant with its value read in as part of the input data, would be replaced by an expression such as

$$E_i (1 + r_i)^t$$

to represent a situation in which real retail expenditures from census tract i are growing at a rate of r_i per time period t. Normally, of course, each census tract would have a different growth rate.

Finally, it is desirable to alter the model so that its structure reflects our knowledge that every model is in error to some degree. In this case, although there are many possible sources of error, for example in the calibration of the parameters, it is likely that the major source of error is in the estimation of the relative volumes of interaction, I_{ij}. Since the standard techniques for calibrating the interaction equation, equation (1), yield estimates of the size of error (e.g., regression analysis gives us the standard error of the estimate), the most convenient method for dealing with the problem is to introduce into the interaction equation a random error term, normally distributed, with a mean value of zero and a variance as estimated in the calibration procedure. The growth equation, (3), would now read

$$^{t+1}S_j = {}^tS_j + g \left(\sum_i E_i \left((({}^tS_j/D_{ij}^n) / \sum_j ({}^tS_j/D_{ij}^n)) + e_i \right) - (a + b_j \, {}^tS_j^m) \right),$$

where e_i is the stochastic error term. Now, of course, every time the simulation model is run, it will produce a different set of center sizes, even though the initial conditions are the same for all runs. Consequently, the model must be run a sufficient number of times to permit us to establish a statistical description of its behavior. Specifically, we should be able to determine for each center at each time period the mean and standard deviation of estimated center size. In other words, we are able to put confidence limits around our estimates of center sizes. This is important, since it would be unwise to base a planning decision, such as a decision to deny permission for the proposed mall, on the results of a simulation model without having any idea as to the accuracy or reliability of those results.

This procedure of running a model many times in order to build up a picture of its behavior is known as sensitivity analysis. In the example just discussed, we have in effect performed a sensitivity analysis on the random variate, e_i. But we could go further. For example, we could examine the effect of changing the variance of e_i. To do so, it would be necessary to run the model a number of times for each of a range of values for the variance. The number of runs required can become large. In addition, we should also examine the effect of the other parameters in the model, especially those like n and m which determine the qualitative structure of the model. The reason for a sensitivity analysis of the parameters is that we can never know that we have exactly the right values for them; indeed, in many cases, we may have had to guess at values. And yet, the results of the model may be extremely sensitive to the values of some parameters; that is, small changes in some parameters may produce large changes in the results. If that is the case, and we are unable to specify the values of those parameters accurately, then the model is essentially useless, since the results will largely be artifacts of the incorrectly specified parameters. A good model is one which is not sensitive to variations in parameter values which lie within the range of calibration errors. Such a model is called robust. In Section 4, we will see the idea of robustness extended to the *form* of the model.

The need for sensitivity analysis creates a requirement for simplicity in the model. In the case of stochastic models, many runs are necessary for each value of each parameter to be tested, and there may be many parameters. For example, in the basic model represented by equation (3) there are 11 parameters ($g, n, m, a, b_1, \ldots, b_7$). Furthermore, it may be necessary to test for interaction effects between pairs or groups of parameters. In particular, this is necessary where two or more parameters are involved in non-linearities in the model, as are n and m in equation (3). In this case, results from a branch of algebraic topology known as catastrophe theory show that certain changes in the values of these parameters, together, but not separately, can cause sudden and often peculiar changes in the behavior of the model. Since to test for interaction effects it is necessary to test a number of different values of one parameter for each value assigned to the other, the number of runs required may quickly become very large.

Both common sense and mathematical results may be used judiciously to reduce the number of runs required in a sensitivity analysis. Nevertheless, it is easy to build models with so many parameters that adequate sensitivity analysis becomes virtually impossible. There is always a temptation to make models more complex. This is especially true in the case of applied models, since greater realism lies in greater complexity. For example, we just proposed using a large number of parameters in the interest of greater realism. Most of these, specifically the growth rates for retail expenditures in the census tracts (r_i), would have a straightforward effect and would not require much sensitivity testing. However, the threshold parameter suggested for the growth criterion would require considerable analysis. The point is that it is easy to build a model so "realistic" that its behavior is, practically speaking, unknowable. Unnecessary complexity should always be resisted.

3. AN EXPLORATORY APPLICATION

In the second example, we use the same retail center model (with a few minor modifications) but apply it not to a particular city, but to a class of cities, with the aim of exploring some of the general characteristics of intra-metropolitan retail systems. Thus, concern is not with prediction, but with understanding, and this new point of view raises several issues which will be considered in more depth in Section 4.

The problem we are concerned with is, what does the general model of retail centers imply about the role of the central business district? This is now a generic question, not a question about a specific city. We therefore apply the model to data representing a variety of "generalized" cities. Again, we use the model represented by equation (3).

This time, however, since we are not interested in matching the behavior of the model to a particular city, but only in determining certain aspects of the general behavior of the model, it is no longer necessary to calibrate every parameter and initial condition to particular, empirically determined magnitudes; for many of them either the values can be set arbitrarily, or they can be assigned in any way that preserves certain proportions.

We specify the model as follows:

(1) The cost parameters a and b_i are set to zero and one respectively, while m is assigned various values greater than one. In other words, we eliminate threshold costs and assume that all centers have identical cost functions characterized by diseconomies of scale. We will examine the grounds for this latter assumption below.

(2) The distance decay parameter n is assigned a value of one. This is

toward the low end of the range of empirically established values and such a value characterizes major, high order retail centers.[5] Since our primary objective is to examine the role of the central business district, it is appropriate to use a value for this parameter that is characteristic of the CBD and its major competitors.

(3) Rather than deal with census tracts, we assume the urban area is divided into a large number of equal-area zones. Total buying power (E_i) in each zone is determined by distance of the zone from the city center (CBD) with the relationship taking the familiar negative exponential form established by Muth and others:

$$E_i = \alpha e^{-\beta D}{}_{i0},\qquad\qquad(4)$$

where for this example we assume $\alpha = 1$, $\beta = .18$, and D_{i0} is the distance from zone i to the CBD. $\beta = .18$ is within the range of values which to characterize population density in American cities of $0.5-1.0$ million population.[6] By using the same value, we are in effect ignoring systematic variations in per capita income.

(4) The CBD is assumed to be located at either the center of the simulated area (the standard configuration) or at the midpoint of one edge (the coastal city configuration). Centers other than the CBD are located around it in an orderly way, as shown in Figure 3 for the standard configuration.

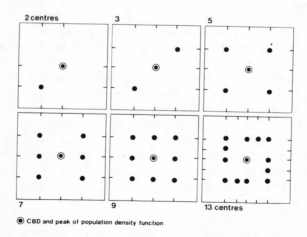

⊙ CBD and peak of population density function

Fig. 3. Configurations of centers used in central business district simulations.

In the application of the model to St. John's, each iteration represented a year, and the results were displayed as a series of timepaths by which the system regained equilibrium after being disturbed by the addition of a new center. In the present example, we are interested only in the equilibrium position, and we characterize the behavior of the model by the types of equilibrium position attained. We take this approach primarily because it simplifies the calibration problem considerably. Since we are dealing with a system which (as it has been parameterized here) is known to display equifinality,[7] we can use any set of initial sizes for the centers. More importantly, it is not necessary to determine what value of the growth parameter would represent a year; we can choose any convenient value. Of course, if we were to make a change in the type of growth mechanism, as outlined previously, then we could no longer assume that the results would be the same.

Since several parameters, as well as the initial conditions in the form of the number and configuration of centers, were manipulated, it is not possible to present a fully comprehensive set of outcomes. However, the results described here are representative of the behavior of the system.

As stated previously, we assume that the system is characterized by diseconomies of scale ($m > 1$). There are two reasons for this. First, sensitivity analysis shows that for values of $m < 1$ all centers except one disappear, and for $m = 1$ all centers except the CBD become insignificant in size. Since such results are clearly not in accord with what we observe in actual cities, we must conclude either that one or more of the other parameters (in particular a and b_i) have been given unrealistic values, or that $m > 1$, or, of course, that there is something more fundamentally wrong with the model. We ignore this last possibility, and there are good reasons, as will become clear in the next section, for believing that the value of n is appropriate. The question of whether it is reasonable to set all b_i's equal is more troublesome, and will be taken up again below.

The second reason for assuming that $m > 1$ is empirical. With respect, at least, to planned centers, for which some cost data are available, the evidence is that developments larger than neighborhood centers are in fact characterized by diseconomies of scale. For example, according to data published by the Urban Land Institute (1969) for 101 community shopping centers, with a median size of 14,300 square meters of gross leasable area, the median capital cost was $137.80 per square meter. This may be compared to $203.40 per square meter for the median regional shopping center, with an area of 49,200 square meters. Operating costs were also lower for the smaller centers: $6.35 per square meter for the community centers compared to $7.50 per square meter for the regionals. For newer centers, those less than four years old, the differences were even greater: capital costs of $131.30 per square meter for the community centers versus $252.75 for the regionals, and operating costs of $4.95 per square meter for community centers compared to $7.50 for the regional centers. These cost differentials were evident in every region of the United States and in Canada also. And, they are only marginally reduced by adjustments to the figures to account for under-reporting of capital costs by the smaller centers. Finally, we may mention one other figure which may reflect costs while also taking into account the fact that larger centers tend to generate more sales per square meter. For most tenant categories, both rent and rent plus other tenant charges as a percentage of sales were higher in regional than in community centers.

Proceeding on the assumption that retail centers are in fact characterized by diseconomies of scale, we examine the effect of the size of the diseconomies. Three values of m are used, 1.05, 1.1 and 1.2. The effect of the diseconomies is then measured by the size of the CBD relative to the total size of all centers. The results depend on (1) the total number of centers present, (2) the configuration of the centers, and (3) the value of the distance decay parameter, β, in the income distribution function (equation 4). A representative set of outcomes is shown in Figure 4 where relative size of the CBD is shown as a function of the number of centers present, for each of the three levels of scale diseconomies, for the configurations shown in Figure 3 and for $\beta = .18$. When only one center is present, that center naturally accounts for 100% of the retail activity regardless of cost conditions. As the number of centers increases, the absolute spread between the relative sizes of the CBD under conditions of high and low diseconomies, respectively, increases, until, when five centers are present, the CBD accounts for only 34% of retail activity under conditions of high diseconomies ($m=1.2$), but accounts for 66% under low diseconomies ($m=1.05$). However, as the number of centers is increased beyond five, the spread in CBD size decreases. With 13 centers, CBD size ranges from 12% for $m=1.2$ to 30% for $m=1.05$. Relative CBD size decreases very slowly as the number of centers increases beyond 12. Interestingly, for seven relatively self-contained metropolitan areas in the U.S. Midwest, with 1970 urbanized area populations ranging from 500,000 to 1.1 million, the mean number of Major Retail Centers as defined in the 1967 Census of Business was 14.1, and the mean proportion of total retail sales accounted for by the CBD ranged from 8.1% to 16.3%, with a median of 12.2%. This last figure corresponds almost exactly with the simulation result for $m=1.2$.

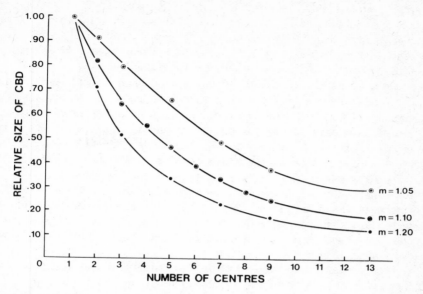

Fig. 4. Relative size of central business district as a function of number of centers, for three levels of diseconomies of scale.

As the locations of the peripheral centers are changed, relative CBD size changes as well. Some indication of the relationship is given in Table II which shows the effect of moving the peripheral center in a two center

TABLE II
Distance – size relationship for a two center system:
$m = 1.1, \beta = .18$

Distance of Peripheral center from a corner of map	Relative size of CBD
.125	.975
.250	.940
.375	.885
.500	.815
.625	.729
.750	.635
.875	.544

system progressively closer to the center of the map. In this example, distance is measured as a fraction of the total distance from the corner to the center of the map, CBD size is shown as a fraction of the total size of both centers, $m = 1.1$, and $\beta = .18$. As expected, for higher values of β, the relative CBD sizes are greater, and conversely for lower values.

On the basis of these results, it would seem that the model rules out cases in which extremely peripheral centers are of large size, a situation which is common in American urban areas. However, a series of experiments was run in which differential cost structures were introduced. Specifically, for the CBD the cost parameter b_i was raised to $b_i = 1.1$, while for the other (peripheral) centers, the value $b_i = 1$ was retained. In every case, under this cost regime, the CBD was insignificant in size compared to the peripheral centers. It is somewhat disturbing that such a modest change in the value of this cost parameter should have such a large effect on the equilibrium structure, for such a result implies that it may be impossible to distinguish the role of m and b_i, and thus that the explanation of urban retail structure provided by the model is weaker than we might hope.

Let us turn now to the case of the "coastal city", in which the peak of the population distribution lies at the midpoint of one edge of the map. Table III shows results for a two center system as the position of the peripheral

TABLE III
Distance — size relationship for a two-center "coastal" system:
$m = 1.1, \beta = .18$

Distance of peripheral center from CBD	Relative size of CBD
.04	.42
.10	.26
.16	.18
.26	.18
.36	.25
.50	.37
.62	.50
.72	.63

center is moved from a point near the CBD progressively farther away. Distance is measured as a fraction of the total distance from the CBD to the opposite edge, and again, CBD size is relative to total size of both centers,

$m = 1.1$ and $\beta = .18$. In this particular case, if the secondary center is located anywhere between the CBD and a point 62% of the way to the opposite edge of the map, at equilibrium it will be larger than the CBD. For larger values of β, relative CBD sizes are grater, and vice versa.

In the present example, the optimum location for a center, in the sense that it is the location which maximizes equilibrium center size, is at a point about one quarter of the way from the CBD to the opposite edge. In a coastal city with a diameter of 12 miles, this would represent a point about 3 miles inland.

One of the assumptions hidden in the interaction equation is that transportation is equally available between all pairs of points in the area. In most cities, especially in past times, this was clearly not the case. Nevertheless, in a few cases the transportation constraints were less severe, and in those instances we see events similar to those appearing in the simulation results. For example, in Manhattan, transit has long been uniformly good in a north-south direction, and this has probably permitted the shift of the main retail center by stages from its original downtown location to its current position some three miles further north.

In general, this use of the simulation model to examine the role of the CBD must be considered exploratory, and we learn at least as much about the strength and weaknesses and behavior of the model as we do about urban retailing systems. In both cases, the most important result is a series of questions, with perhaps some suggestions of answers. In the case of the model, the most important question concerns the sensitivity of the results to the values of the cost parameters, b_i. This problem may be a manifestation of a deeper problem analogous to the problem of identifiability in econometric procedures: while in algebraic terms the model may be unambiguous, in applications it may be difficult or impossible to distinguish the roles of two sets of parameters like b_i and m.

In the case of the retailing system, we have found that the model suggests both that it is possible to predict the relative size of the CBD and that an eccentric CBD will migrate toward the geographical center of the urban area if transporation and topographic conditions permit. If such suggestions are substantiated by future tests, then the model in effect provides an explanation of these phenomena, for it displays the mechanism by which the relative size of the CBD and its location are related to such underlying factors as the cost structure of centers and spatial interaction propensities of consumers. Once the model has been reasonably well developed and substantiated for some domain of application, then it, together with its predictions, constitutes a theory of these phenomena. The predictions are read as hypotheses, or, if well substantiated, laws, and the model is the explanatory mechanism. We will examine such a case in the next section.

4. AN APPLICATION TO THEORY BUILDING

The final application consists of an extensive sensitivity analysis of the parameters of the retail center model. The purpose is to discover relationships between the parameters and the form of the retailing that are both significant and sufficiently robust to be reliable. In particular, the goal is to show that the model represented in equation (3), and a certain set of results of that model, together constitute a theory of retail systems, or in other words, a central place theory; and that the theory is able to answer some of the basic questions concerning retailing systems, such as the size and spacing of centers, and the nature of the hierarchy of centers. Because the analysis is very extensive, only the highlights will be discussed here. A fuller account appears in White (1977, 1978a).

We begin by applying equation (3) in the context of a system of twenty retail centers located as shown in Figure 5. For simplicity, we assume that

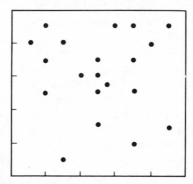

Fig. 5.   Configuration of centers used in central place theory simulations.
Figures 5, 6, 7 and Table IV are reprinted by permission from Roger W. White, 'Dynamic Central Place Theory: Results of a Simulation Approach', *Geographical Analysis* 9 (1977), 226–43.

buying power is uniformly distributed in the area (i.e., that all E_i are equal) and that all centers initially have the same size. In addition, we assume initially that the fixed cost parameter $a = 0$, that all $b_i = 1$, and that the marginal cost parameter $m = 1$. Letting the distance decay parameter, n, range over values from 0.5 to 3, approximately the range of empirically observed values, and continuing the simulation through sufficient iterations to reach equilibrium, we observe the results shown graphically in Figure 6 and in Table IV.

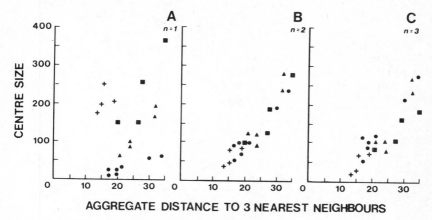

Fig. 6. Relationship between center size and aggregate distance to three nearest neighbors for three systems: (a) $n=1$; (b) $n=2$; (c) $n=3$. Distance to edge is indicated as follows: 5, circle; 10, triangle; 15, square; 20–22.5, cross.

We characterize the location of such centers by two measures. The first, the aggregate distance to the three nearest centers, is a measure of the local situation of a center. The second, the distance to the nearest edge of the simulated region, is a measure of the degree of centrality of the particular center within the region. Examining Figure 6B and 6C, we see that for higher values of the parameter n, specifically $n=2$ and $n=3$, only the local situation of a center, its location with respect to its immediate neighbors, is important as a determinant of center size; the closer a center is to its immediate neighbors, the smaller it is. How central or peripheral a center is within the whole region has no bearing on its size. For low values of n, such an $n=1$, (Figure 6A), both locational characteristics are important in determining the success of a center. Using multiple regression analysis to describe the relationship between center size and these two measures of location for a series of values of n (Table IV), we see that it is in the neighborhood of $n = 1.8$ that regional centrality ceases to be a significant determinant of center size.

This bifurcation in the behavior of the simulation model in the neighborhood of $n = 1.8$ is an extremely robust result. Sensitivity analysis shows

TABLE IV

Coefficients of the regression equation for center size against aggregate distance and distance to edge

Distance Decay Parameter	Intercept	Aggregate Distance	Distance to edge	Mult. R
	PART A – Gravity equation			
1. $n = 1$	−222.16	7.86	14.01	0.93
2. $n = 1.1$	−225.11	8.92	12.16	0.93
3. $n = 1.2$	−220.80	9.72	10.18	0.94
4. $n = 1.3$	−209.17	10.23	8.19	0.94
5. $n = 1.4$	−194.76	10.49	6.40	0.95
6. $n = 1.5$	−177.46	10.52	4.86	0.95
7. $n = 1.6$	−162.29	10.53	3.52	0.95
8. $n = 1.7$	−147.69	10.44	2.46[a]	0.95
9. $n = 1.8$	−143.35	10.47	1.90[a]	0.94
10. $n = 1.9$	−123.72	10.18	(0.92)	0.95
11. $n = 2$	−135.78	10.85	(0.82)	0.95
12. $n = 3$	− 70.40[a]	9.29	(−1.89)	0.91
	PART B – Negative exponential equation			
13. $n = 0.1$	−266.46	10.15	13.24)	0.93
14. $n = 0.2$	−127.55[a]	11.51	(−1.41)	0.85

Note: Dependent variable is sector size. Fixed cost = 0. All values are significant at the 0.0005 level unless otherwise indicated; figures in parentheses are not significant at the .05 level.

[a] Significant at the .05 level.

that changes in initial center sizes and locations, changes in cost parameters, and changes in the growth factor all leave this bifurcation phenomenon intact. Furthermore, it is even possible to substitute alternative forms of the interaction equation and the same bifurcation appears, mutatis mutandis. For example, if we substitute the widely used negative exponental interaction equation,

$$^tI_{ij} = \frac{^tS_j e^{-nD_{ij}}}{\sum_i {}^t S_j e^{-nD_{ij}}}$$

for equation (1) when deriving equation (3), then the simulation results are as described by lines 13 and 14 of Table IV. For the low value of n (n=0.1), both locational measures are determinants of center size; for the higher value (n=0.2), only aggregate distance to the nearest centers is significant.[8]

If the bifurcation phenomenon did not have such a robust character, it would be of little interest, since we would have to dismiss it as a spurious artifact of one parameterization or formulation of the model, and therefore of no empirical significance. Specifically, the gravity equation and the negative exponential equation are used almost interchangeably to describe spatial interaction. Furthermore, we can claim that the simulation model provides an explanation of certain center size phenomena by relating these to underlying characteristics of the spatial behavior of consumers. But, if we could make this claim only for one form of the model, and not for another one of apparently equal validity, then the claim would not be convincing for the explanation would appear ad hoc.

So, far we have identified an extremely robust bifurcation in the behavior of the simulation model and spoken of explanation. But what exactly are the empirical phenomena which might be explained by this behavior? To answer this question, we examine the role of the fixed cost parameter, a, which controls the expression of the bifurcation effect.

When $a = 0$, all centers present at the beginning of the run survive at equilibrium. When $a > 0$, however, some centers are eliminated, and other things being equal, the larger a, the more centers disappear. For $a > 0$, then, the pattern of location of centers at equilibrium differs form the initial pattern. Figure 7 shows typical equilibrium patterns of centers corresponding

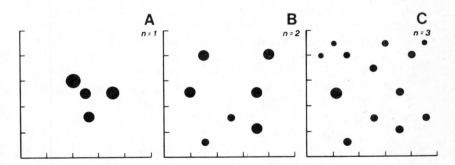

Fig. 7.   Equilibrium pattern of centers for three systems: (a) n=1; (b) n=2; (c) n=3. Area of circle is proportional to size of center.

to three values of n. In each case, the initial pattern was that shown in Figure 5. The original pattern is still evident in the case of $n = 3$ (Figure 7C), where the relatively great friction of distance gives the center a degree of protection against competition. For higher values of a, more centers are eliminated, and the equilibrium patterns for $n = 3$ are similar to those for $n = 2$. In the case of $n = 2$ (Figure 7B), the centers which disappear, are for the most part those which are nearer to other centers (e.g., most of those in the crowded top half of the map in Figure 5), so that the resulting distribution is relatively regular. On the other hand, for $n = 1$ (Figure 7A), the centers which survive tend to be fewer, larger, and more centrally located. In general, for high values of the interaction parameter ($n > 1.8$) centers tend to be regularly spaced and of roughly similar sizes; while for low values ($n < 1.7$) centers tend to be few, large and centrally located.

Empirically, values of n tend to vary with the type of good or service for which customers are travelling. Generally, establishments offering high order goods (e.g., women's clothing stores) have customer interaction fields characterized by low values of n, while those offering low order goods (e.g. drugstores of food stores) are associated with high values of n. Thus, the type of retail activity being simulated is represented in the model by the value of n, as well as, perhaps, the values of certain other parameters, especially a. It is now simple to include several types of retail activity in a single model: add a set of equations (with the appropriate values of n and a) for each activity. When this is done, at equilibrium there will be various combinations of activities in centers of various sizes, depending on initial conditions and parameter values. However, because of the bifurcation phenomenon, there will be only two fundamental *types* of centers:

(1) a smaller number of centers containing most of the higher order (low n) activity. These centers would have a large degree of redundancy in their offering of the high order goods; for example, they would have many clothing stores.

(2) a larger number of centers, relatively evenly spaced with respect to the population distribution, offering primarily low order goods (high n) and having little redundancy in their offerings.

This result seems to be substantiated by the available data. Figure 8 shows the results of a cluster analysis of two retail systems, one in Cape Town, South Africa, and the other in Snohomish county, Washington; the Snohomish county data are Brian Berry's from his classic paper on the central place system of that county. The analysis was carried out by Beavon (1977) for these and other systems. In every case, the results are similar. In both 8A and

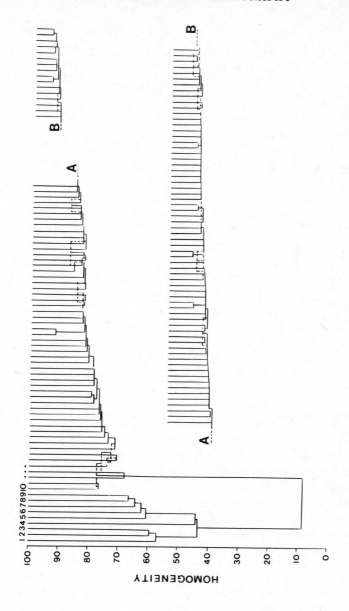

Fig. 8A. Cluster analysis of 143 retail centers: Cape Town, South Africa.

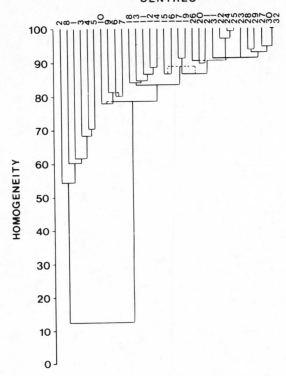

Fig. 8B. Cluster analysis of 32 retail centers: Snohomish county, Washington.

8B, the retail system falls neatly into two types of centers, a small group of large centers (Centers 1–9 in Figure 8A and Centers 2, 8, 1, 3, 4, 5, in 8B), and a much larger group of smaller centers.[9]

We have, then, in this section, developed an example of the way in which the simulation model can be used as the foundation of a theory of retailing systems. Briefly, the procedure is as follows:

    (1) perform exhaustive sensitivity analyses in order to discover the robust features of the model's behavior;

    (2) look for an emirically feasible interpretation of the robust features; that is, develop them as hypotheses;

    (3) test the hypotheses

None of these steps is trivial. A comprehensive, brute force sensitivity analysis may require impossible amounts of computer time; to get reliable results in a reasonable amount of time requires good judgement and some prior insight into the behavior of the model, perhaps from analytical techniques. Similarly, to interpret the results of the model in such a way that they become testable hypotheses may in some cases take considerable effort. For example, it might appear simple to test the bifurcation effect depending on n in the form in which it was presented in Figure 6 and Table IV, but this is not the case. Problems of finding good functional definitions, for example of centrality within the region ("Distance from edge of map") make it difficult to establish an unambiguous test. Translated into a type-of-center effect, as was done, the phenomenon is easier to test, but in fact the test that was presented still suffers from a lack of rigor in several respects.

5. A GENERAL ASSESSMENT OF SIMULATION MODELING

In the preceding three sections, we have examined a particular model of retail systems. It is apparent that the model is useful in a wide variety of applications, ranging from practical to theoretical, and that it is a rich source of insight into the nature of retail systems. But the model itself is simply a set of equations, either difference equations, as in equation (3), or an analogous set of differential equations. Why, then, is it necessary to use simulation analysis rather than analytical techniques in order to manipulate the model? For example, if we are interested in knowing the equilibrium position of the system, why not use algebraic techniques to solve equations (3) for $S_j(t)$, the set of trajectories shown in Figure 2, or why not rewrite equation (3) as equivalent differential equations and integrate? The simple answer is that, in this case, as in the case of many other complex, nonlinear models, no analytical solution is possible. If this seems surprising, recall that even for the simple Weber transport cost minimization problem, no analytical solution is available if there are more than three raw material/market sites. On the other hand, with the model cast in the form of a simulation routine, it is relatively simple to calculate system trajectories. Similarly, using simulation techniques it is a relatively straightforward matter to elucidate the structural properties of the model by means of a sensitivity analysis of the parameters; whereas analytical techniques for structural analysis, such as catastrophe theory, can give only general insights, and then only for certain types of systems. In a word, for dealing with complex models, simulation analysis is more practical.

Another virtue of the simulation model discussed in this paper and others like it is obvious; the model is based on relationships which can be, and in many cases have been, empirically determined. We refer especially to the interaction equation (equation 1), but also to the cost and income distribution equation (4). In this sense, then, the model is simply a logical device for deducing the implications of empirically established relationships. And if the facts as described by these relationships change, then the model changes as well to reflect the new (or newly discovered) state of affairs. One consequence is that we lose some of the elegance, but also some of the sterility, of the other two classes of models dealing with the same phenomena, traditional central place theory and the New Urban Economics. In the case of central place theory, the assumptions regarding the spatial behavior of consumers and the cost structures of retailers cannot be made to reflect empirical findings. If they were, the mechanism for generating the regular geometry which constitutes the output of the theory would be destroyed. Similarly, in the New Urban Economics, such typical assumptions as monocentricity and smooth rent and density gradients — assumptions which inevitably lead to unrealistic if not trivial results — are also seen as necessary. Unlike central place theory, however, where the assumptions are required to preserve the results, in this case the assumptions are needed to preserve the possibility of using an analytic approach. If the specifications of the models were designed to reflect relevant empirical findings, the models would typically be too complex to handle analytically.

The commitment to analytic models is often defended on the grounds that a theory, to be useful, must be simple: that if it were complex enough to be realistic, it would be as difficult to understand as reality itself, and therefore offer no insights. Unfortunately, it often seems that the simple theory is just simplistic. Perhaps a better criterion is that the conceptual structure of the theory should be simple, at least simple enough to be clear, without requiring that the detailed structure be simple. In addition, it has been proposed by Levins and others that a useful theory must be robust; that is, its predictions or output must not in general be highly sensitive to small changes in its specifications. This amounts to a second criterion: that in the output there be a simplicity or clarity of structure in spite of a complexity of detail.

The simulation model which has been examined in this paper essentially seems to satisfy both criteria. The conceptual structure, as it is based on revenue and cost functions for centers competing in space, is quite simple. Similarly, in spite of the countless variations in initial conditions, parameter values, and even in the form of certain functions, several regularities are almost invariably evident amid the plethora of details in the output. For example, we have seen that a dichotomy between concentrated and dispersed patterns dependent on the value of a single interaction parameter survives a change in the form of the interaction equation itself (from power function to negative exponential), a change in income distribution (from negative exponential to uniform) and, in most cases, a change in the cost function. It is the presence of these basic robust features in the output — this simplicity — together with the subtlety and flexibility provided by the complexity of detail, that provides the strength and utility of a good simulation model.

Dept. of Geography
Memorial University of Newfoundland

NOTES

[1] For a good review of both models and the new techniques see A. Wilson (1981).

[2] In taking this approach, we are following one of the basic tenets of simulation analysis, which is that the general principles are revealed through the collection of specific cases.

[3] This model, widely used by transportation engineers and planners, is simply another version of the gravity model. We use here the form which is likely to appear most familiar to geographers, but other formulations, such as the negative exponential, may equally well be used.

[4] Indeed, it was only an assumption that costs can be reasonably represented by a polynomial with three parameters, although this assumption permits a great deal of flexibility.

[5] We will return to this point in Section 4.

[6] In fact, $\beta = .18$ is toward the low end of the range which Muth found to characterize cities in this size class in 1950, but values have been declining steadily since that data.

[7] That is, it moves to the same equilibrium state regardless of the initial values of the variables.

[8] In terms of empirical calibrations of interaction equations, values of 0.1 and 0.2 for n in a negative exponential equation roughly correspond to values of 1 and 2 respectively in a gravity equation.

[9] In Figure 8, each center or group of centers is represented by a vertical line. The horizontal lines connecting centers or groups show how similar the centers or groups are, as measured on the index of homogeneity (vertical axis). Thus in Figure 8A, centers 1–9 can all be joined into a single group at the .43 level of homogeneity, and all other centers form another group at the .67 level, but these two groups can only be joined at the .08 level.

BIBLIOGRAPHY

Allen, P. M. and M. Sanglier: 1979, 'A dynamic model of growth in a central place system', *Geographical Analysis* 11, 256–272.

Allen, P. M. and M. Sanglier: 1981, 'A dynamic model of growth in a central place system – II', *Geographical Analysis* **13**, 149–164.

Allen, P. M. and M. Sanglier: 1984, 'A dynamic model of growth in a central place system – III', *Geographical Analysis* **15** (forthcoming).

Beavon, K. S. O.: 1977, *Central Place Theory: A Reinterpretation*, Longmans, London.

Coelho, J. D. and A. G. Wilson: 1976, 'The optimum size and location of shopping centres', *Regional Studies* **10**, 413–421.

Hagerstrand, T.: 1957, 'Migration and area', in D. Hannerberg, T. Hagerstrand, and B. Odeving (eds.), *Migration in Sweden: A symposium*, Lund Studies in Geography Ser. B. 13, Gleerup, Lund, pp. 27–158.

Lakshmanan, T. R. and W. G. Hansen: 1965, 'A retail market potential model', *Journal of the American Institute of Planners* **31**, 134–143.

Morrill, R. L.: 1962, 'Simulation of central place patterns over time', in K. Norborg (ed.), *Proceedings of the I.G.U. Symposium in Urban Geography, Lund, 1960*, Gleerup, Lund, pp. 104–120.

Muth, R. F.: 1961, 'The spatial structure of the housing market', *Papers and Proceedings of the Regional Science Association* **7**, 207–220.

Nelson, R. R. and S. G. Winter: 1975, 'Factor price changes and factor substitution in an evolutionary model', *Bell Journal of Economics and Management Science* **6**, 466–486.

Nelson, R. R. S. G. Winter, and H. L. Schuette: 1976, 'Technical change in an evolutionary model', *Quarterly Journal of Economics* **90**, 92–118.

Weinberg, D. H. and R. W. Schmenner: 1977, 'An evolutionary model of business location decisions: An early report', Paper presented to the American Economic Association – Econometric Society, New York.

White, R. W.: 1977, 'Dynamic central place theory: Results of a simulation approach', *Geographical Analysis* **9**, 226–243.

White, R. W.: 1978a, 'The simulation of central place dynamics: Two sector systems and the rank-size distribution', *Geographical Analysis* **10**, 201–208.

White, R. W.: 1978b, 'Morphogenesis in geographical systems: Results in the modelling of retail structures', Paper presented to the I.G.U. Working Group in Systems Analysis and Mathematical Models, Lagos.

White, R. W.: 1982, 'Regional Industrialization: An evolutionary approach', in L. Collins (ed.), *Industrial Decline and Regeneration*, Univ. of Edinburgh, pp. 203–213.

Wilson, A. G.: 1981, *Catastrophe Theory and Bifurcation: Applications to Urban and Regional Systems*, Croom Helm, London.

Winter, S. G.: 1971, 'Satisficing, selection, and the innovating remnant', *Quarterly Journal of Economics* **85**, 237–261.

JOHN N. RAYNER

SIMULATION MODELS IN CLIMATOLOGY

1. CLIMATE AND SIMULATION

During the last two decades there has been an explosion of research and publications dealing with simulation of atmospheric processes. Just a listing of those works would fill the space allotted to this paper. Consequently, the following is a highly selective review of the topic and the reader should refer to the references cited for more details and a more extensive literature list. On the other hand, the coverage is broad and, following the philosophy of the author, encompasses much which would be classified by some as meteorology. That is, he makes no clear distinction between meteorology and climatology and considers these subjects to be part of an integrated continuum. Durst (1951) recognized this in his definition, "The physical problem of synoptic forecasting and climatology is the same, for climate is but the synthesis of weather." Synthesis of weather in Landsberg's (1960) definition is "... the collective state of the earth's atmosphere for a given place within a specified interval of time." For Lorenz (1975), "Climate may be identified with a set of statistics of an ensemble of many states of the atmosphere." If we accept these descriptions, a true understanding of climate must of necessity involve the instantaneous states, so frequently we find climatologists involved in studies which are normally classified as meteorology. Geographers, whose interests lie in climatology, are part of the same current research milieu and many are engaged in simulating aspects of the atmosphere. The number has grown substantially since the author's short survey in 1974 (Rayner, 1974) and currently a non-exhaustive list would include: Arnfield, Bach, Barry, Brazel, Davies, Dozier, Hay, Henderson-Sellers, Hobgood, Lockwood, Outcalt, Parkinson, P. J. Sellers, Suckling, Terjung, Tyson and Williams.

In this paper, the word simulation is used in the broadest sense to indicate the artifical reproduction of some aspects of reality. It should be noted that this is not in line with atmospheric science where a distinction is made between *simulation*, which starts from fictitious initial fields, and *weather prediction*, which starts with the observed state of the atmosphere (Mesinger and Arakawa, 1976). The reasons for simulation as used here are three-fold:

417

Gary L. Gaile and Cort J. Willmott (eds.), Spatial Statistics and Models, 417–442.
© 1984 *by D. Reidel Publishing Company.*

prediction, understanding and control. Prediction involves diagnostic studies as well as future states of the atmosphere. For example, the accuracy of mapping past precipitation patterns in mountainous zones of sparse observations may be significantly enhanced by simulation (Colton, 1976). Prediction of the future encompasses a wide spectrum of intervals from minutes for tornado paths to thousands of years for ice advance. An understanding of these events is the ultimate aim of atmospheric science. Not only is it philosophically satisfying but it is necessary before any planned control of the atmosphere can proceed. For example, an accurate simulation model of the tropical atmosphere is required for the evaluation of hurricane modification hypotheses and is one of the goals of the First GARP Global experiment (FGGE) (GARP,1978).

2. TYPES OF SIMULATION MODELS

Various types of simulation models may be recognized. The *hardware* model has been used extensively and with great success in fluid mechanics (National Committee, 1972) and the same principles were applied early to atmospheric circulation (Fultz, 1951). However, the extent to which fluid flowing on a sphere may be reproduced in the laboratory is limited. Similarly, there are problems in studying photochemical and cloud processes in controlled experiments where walls must be artificially introduced. As a result, hardware models have been excluded from this review. The class *mathematical* models may be subdivided into a continuum of *purely statistical* to *purely theoretical*. The purely statistical model, for example the simple regression model which estimates surface solar radiation from cloud amount (Black, 1954), is very valuable for prediction but adds little to our understanding of the process. Consequently, the very large number of simulation models of this type has been omitted. At the other extreme the purely theoretical model, although it may be considered to be the ideal, is difficult to find. Usually, at some point in a model, some process must be parameterized by a statistical and/or empirical quantity. Thus, while the models discussed below are theoretically-based, they have been modified to some degree by empirical input. The extent of this "contamination" can be judged only by an examination of the basic physics included in the model. As outlined above, climate is identified with a set of statistics of a time ensemble so output of instantaneous theoretical models must ultimately be summarized. In one class of model, the *statistical-dynamical* one, the dynamical equations are themselves subject to statistical modification (Saltzman, 1978).

Theoretically-based mathematical models are composed of one or more equations which have to be solved for the simulation to proceed. The solution in simple cases may be obtained analytically but generally in the complex atmospheric models, which are often nonlinear, a numerical procedure must be adopted. Hence, the types of models discussed in the following have been restricted to theoretically-based numerical models.

3. CLASSIFICATION

Models may be classified according to a number of different and overlapping criteria. The ultimate product is an estimate of an *atmospheric element*, such as radiation, temperature, evaporation, mass (water vapor, CO_2, aerosols, etc.), pressure, and wind. For an understanding of the resulting statistics of that element, *process* dictates that the physics be expressed within the equations. These equations may apply to a number of *dimensions*, from one to three in space and one in time. Further subdivision is possible if the estimate is made for a single point in space and/or a single solution in time. For example, some temperature simulations solve for an equilibrium which may be a constant. In that case, time may be thought of as having no dimensions. The range of *scales* studied varies from the single point in space to the whole atmosphere and from a single point in time to geological eras. Parallel to scale, sometimes it is convenient to group according to the *phenomenon* or system. Thus, to identify a few, we study boundary layer turbulent transfer, tornadoes, sea breezes, urban heat islands, pollutant diffusion, tropical cyclones, Rossby waves, and the general circulation. Finally, models may be classified according to the *fidelity* with which they represent reality and according to their *complexity*. Simple models tend to deal with a single element at a single point, whereas complex models, such as general circulation models, incorporate many elements and processes over the whole atmosphere. As a variation, Terjung (1976) used *level of methodology* in his review of models in climatology. In the following pages, simulation models will be discussed according to element in Section 5 and according to scale and phenomenon in Section 6.

4. GENERAL POINTS ON NUMERICAL SIMULATION

Atmospheric events are time and space dependent. Consequently, the mathematics required to describe the processes involved are partial differential equations (Thompson, 1961; Haltiner and Williams, 1980). Although some may be solved analytically, by analogue computers, by finite element methods and by spectral methods, the current standard procedure is to convert the partial derivatives to finite difference forms which are amenable to computation on the digital computer. A large literature exists on these steps (Richtmyer and Morton, 1967; Kreiss and Oliger, 1973; GARP, 1976) but a few elementary yet basic principles will be outlined here.

One of the simplest equations frequently used to illustrate these points is that for the conduction of heat. First discussed by Fourier it has been intensively studied analytically by Carslaw and Jaeger (1959). A short and easily understandable derivation of the equation is given by Sellers (1965):

$$\frac{\partial T}{\partial t} = \frac{1}{c} \frac{\partial}{\partial z} \left(k \frac{\partial T}{\partial z} \right) = \kappa \frac{\partial^2 T}{\partial z^2}, \tag{1}$$

where T is temperature (K), z is length (m), k is the thermal conductivity ($J\ s^{-1}\ m^{-1}\ K^{-1}$) and c is the soil heat capacity ($J\ m^{-3}\ K^{-1}$). If k can be assumed to be constant with depth $k/c = \kappa(m^2\ s^{-1})$, the thermal diffusivity. Equation (1) states that the rate of change of temperature with time is proportional to the rate at which the temperature gradient changes with respect to distance.

4.1. Finite Differencing

As we know, $\partial T/\partial t = \Delta T/\Delta t$ as Δt approaches zero, ($\Delta T = T_2 - T_1$; $\Delta t = t_2 - t_1$), but it is clearly an approximation as Δt becomes large. The error may be investigated by expanding T, which is assumed to be a function of t written $T[t]$, as a Taylor series:

$$T[t+\Delta t] = T[t] + \Delta t \frac{\partial T[t]}{\partial t} + \frac{(\Delta t)^2}{2!} \frac{\partial^2 T[t]}{\partial t^2} + \frac{(\Delta t)^3}{3!} \frac{\partial^3 T[t]}{\partial t^3} + \dots . \tag{2}$$

or

$$T[t-\Delta t] = T[t] - \Delta t \frac{\partial T[t]}{\partial t} + \frac{(\Delta t)^2}{2!} \frac{\partial^2 T[t]}{\partial t^2} - \frac{(\Delta t)^3}{3!} \frac{\partial^3 T[t]}{\partial t^3} + \dots . \tag{3}$$

Each equation gives one simple finite difference form for $\partial T[t]/\partial t$. For example from equation (2)

$$\frac{\partial T[t]}{\partial t} = \frac{T[t+\Delta t] - T[t]}{\Delta t} - \frac{\Delta t}{2!} \frac{\partial^2 T[t]}{\partial t^2} - \frac{(\Delta t)^2}{3!} \frac{\partial^3 T[t]}{\partial t^3} - \dots$$

$$= \frac{T[t+\Delta t] - T[t]}{\Delta t} + O[(\Delta t)] .$$

In words, the direct substitution of a finite difference for a partial derivative involves a *first order error*, the error being called a *truncation error*. A more accurate form may be obtained by subtracting equation (3) from equation (2)

$$\frac{\partial T[t]}{\partial t} = \frac{T[t + \Delta t] - T[t - \Delta t]}{2\Delta t} - \frac{(\Delta t)^2}{3!} \frac{\partial^3 T[t]}{\partial t^3} - \cdots$$

$$= \frac{T[t + \Delta t] - T[t - \Delta t]}{2\Delta t} + O[(\Delta t)^2]$$

which involves a *second order error*. Further refinements, which include more terms of T in the finite difference representation and hence higher computational cost, are possible. Recently, Campana (1979) has shown that higher order differencing applied to the National Meteorological Center's prediction models does improve forecasts. Many general circulation models (GCM's), such as the third generation NCAR model, now use fourth order differencing (Williamson and Browning, 1973).

For the second derivative on the right hand side of equation (1), the equivalent of equation (2) and equation (3) may be added to give

$$\frac{\partial^2 T[z]}{\partial z^2} = \frac{T[z + \Delta z] - 2T[z] + T[z - \Delta z]}{(\Delta z)^2}$$

and so on.

4.2. *Stability and Convergence of the Finite Difference Scheme*

Through the use of direct differencing, equation (1) may be written

$$\frac{T[z, t + \Delta t] - T[z, t]}{\Delta t} = \frac{\kappa(T[z + \Delta z, t] - 2T[z, t] + T[z - \Delta z, t])}{(\Delta z)^2}.$$

Let $\kappa \Delta t/(\Delta z)^2 = \lambda$, then

$$T[z, t + \Delta t] = \lambda T[z + \Delta z, t] + (1 - 2\lambda)T[z, t] + \lambda T[z - \Delta z, t]. \quad (4)$$

It can easily be shown that the *stability* of the result is dependent upon λ which is a function the relative magnitudes of Δt and Δx for a given diffusivity. If λ is greater than 0.5, the result is unstable. Figure 1 shows two simulations using equation (4) for the third level of five layers (six levels)

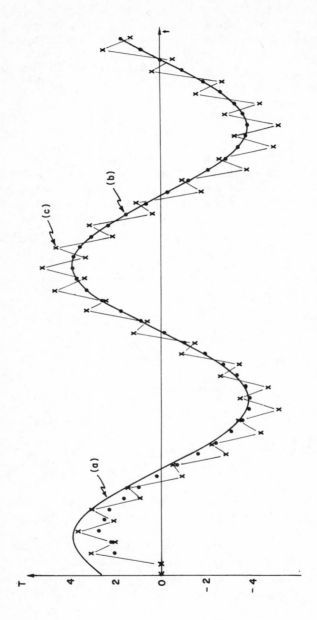

Fig. 1. Time plots of soil temperature simulations at level 3 in a 5 level system. (a) Analytical solution. (b) Numerical calculation, λ = 0.45. (c) Numerical calculation, λ = 0.56.

of soil. For *initial conditions*, the temperature at all levels except the top is assumed to be zero. As *boundary conditions*, the bottom level is held constant while the top is subject to a sinusoidal oscillation with an amplitude of 1 starting at a maximum. The system is allowed (forced) to pass through two complete cycles. When $\lambda = 0.45$, the digital results match the analytical solution which is available for this problem. When $\lambda = 0.56$, the solution continues to oscillate. Arnfield (1978) used the stable version in his surface climate simulation.

Alternatives are available to circumvent such instabilities. One approach is to use an implicit scheme where $T[t]$ is given in terms of $T[t + \Delta t]$ at each level. Then solution involves a set of simultaneous equations. This approach has been used by Outcalt *et al*. (1975) and Terjung and O'Rourke (1980a, b) in their simulations of thermal regimes of rather different surfaces.

Another important consideration is that the finite difference approximation eventually converges on the correct solution. In the example in Figure 1, the iteration does lead to *convergence* within two cycles. We should expect the same result had different initial conditions been used. The time the system takes to converge is known as the *relaxation time*.

4.3. *Grids*

Generally, it is convenient to use a uniform rectangular grid but there are situations where it is necessary or more logical to use other formats. For global circulation modeling, a 5 × 5 latitude by longitude grid is often selected. It must be modified as the poles are approached, however, and frequently gridpoints are skipped and smoothing applied (Williamson and Browning, 1973). In rotating systems such as tornadoes and tropical cyclones, a cylindrical coordinate system has some advantages (Wipperman *et al*. 1969; Anthes *et al*., 1971). For limited area models, the outer boundary creates a problem and often a wider spacing is used for the outer rows and columns of points (Lavoie, 1972; Pielke, 1974).

Various vertical coordinates have been adopted as independent variables (Sundqvist, 1979, Vol. II). The obvious choice, geometric height z, presents problems in areas of irregular topography where the horizontal finite difference terms cannot be calculated because the constant z surface vanishes into the ground. Also, if hydrostatic equilibrium cannot be assumed, vertical motion must be obtained by an indirect method. Pressure as a coordinate has the advantage that it simplifies the equations and vertical motion is given directly by the continuity equation. On the other hand, the same problem exists at the earth's surface which is now a variable in the p system. The sigma system (σ), originally suggested by Phillips (1957), which normalizes pressure by dividing it by the surface pressure, has distinct advantages in that the air-surface interface is 1 everywhere and the problem of topography is removed. Kasahara (1974) has generalized sigma for other variables and the third generation NCAR GCM, as opposed to the earlier ones, uses normalized height. The GFDL, NMC, Rand, GISS and Meteorological Office global circulation models all use sigma (GARP, 1974).

4.4. *Parameterization*

Where the basic physics are too complex, their inclusion too costly, or the systems are smaller than the grid cell size can resolve, the processes are summarized or *parameterized* in mathematical form. Obviously to be useful the components of the final expression must be derivable from available data (GARP, 1972). Sometimes the parameters are generated within the model itself and sometimes they are entered from independent studies.

To illustrate the procedure, we may consider the vertical transfer of sensible heat at the earth's surface. If molecular diffusion can be ignored, the transfer is the result of small eddies carrying varying quantities of sensible heat vertically. Averaged over an area, the vertical flux may be written as

$$H = c_p \overline{\rho w \theta} \tag{5}$$

where H is heat flow (W m^{-2}), c_p is specific heat at constant pressure (J kg^{-1} K^{-1}), ρ is density (kg m^{-3}), w is vertical wind (m s^{-1}), θ is potential temperature (K), and the bar represents averaging. Unfortunately, ρ, w and θ cannot be simulated or measured in practical situations so some other approach must be adopted (see Oke, 1978, Appendix A2 for a discussion of some alternatives). In general circulation models, the standard approach has been to follow the aerodynamic method and replace equation (5) by

$$H = -c_p \rho C_D |V| \Delta\theta \tag{6}$$

where C_D is the drag coefficient (dimensionless), $|V|$ is the magnitude of the horizontal wind at the lowest atmospheric level in the model (m s^{-1}), and $\Delta\theta$ is the difference between the potential temperatures at the lowest level and the surface (K) (Houghton, 1976). C_D is frequently entered as a constant for all surfaces and conditions but recent schemes estimate it within the model (Deardorff, 1972). Clearly equation (6) is a gross simplification of equation (5) and it is recognized as such. Therefore, while parameterization will remain a necessary element in most models, efforts are directed at improving them (see references in Section 6.2).

4.5. *Predictability and Sensitivity*

Lorenz (1975) has introduced the idea of two kinds of prediction. In running a climate model we assume that, regardless of the initial conditions, it will asymptotically approach the same state (i.e., converge) by which we may characterize the climate. If we use the boundary conditions of the existing real atmosphere, then we should expect the statistics of the model to approach those of the real atmosphere and, as with the weather forecast models we ought to be able to predict future climate. This is what Lorenz identifies as climatic prediction of the *first kind*. It raises the problem of the validation of climate models. How realistic are the results of the simulations? In complex models, the statistics will vary through time and on the interval of time used. Also, in systems which have a large inertia, such as the oceans, it is unclear how long the relaxation time is. If a constant season can be used, the troposphere alone comes to equilibrium after about two months and the stratosphere after about six months. When the annual cycle is included this time is increased for the atmosphere to several years (Smagorinsky, 1979). In addition, there are regional variations. Chervin (1980a; b) using an NCAR model showed that the characteristic time between effectively independent sample values is small in the tropics and increases with latitude. Exceptions were found at 20–30° S west of Africa, S. America and Australia where autocorrelation is high and in the N. Pacific and N. Atlantic where it is low. Recently, research has been directed at assessing the extent to which the larger models do simulate climate. For example, Blackman and Lau (1980), analyzing statistics generated by the GFDL-GCM, found that regional contrasts, the location of centers of action and storm tracks, and the transport by transient systems over the oceans were simulated with some skill. However, significant differences from the observed state showed up in the amplitude of the transient fluctuations in the upper troposphere, the location of the planetary scale waves, the eddy activity in middle and high latitudes and the depth of the Aleutian and Icelandic lows.

Lorenz (1968) has also questioned whether the atmosphere has a unique set of statistics. If it does and one set of boundary conditions regardless of the initial conditions produces one set of statistics, then it is called a *transitive system*. On the other hand, if different initial conditions and the same boundary conditions produce a different set of statistics, then it is an *intransitive* system. Experiments involving dishpans to simulate the atmosphere display both transitive and intransitive characteristics (Fultz *et al*., 1959). As a third alternative, if the system responds like a transitive system for long periods before it changes, Lorenz has named it an *almost intransitive* system. Such a system could account for what is called climatic change.

Usually climate change is thought of as being forced by some external change in the boundary conditions. Simulation involving such forcing is named by Lorenz (1975) climatic prediction of the *second kind*. It has been a very popular form of research and the literature on the *sensitivity* of climate to different boundary conditions is very large (GARP, 1979; Barry *et al*., 1979). Researchers have attempted to estimate the effect of changing solar radiation (Sellers, 1969; Budyko, 1969; Wetherald and Manabe, 1975; Pollard *et al*., 1980), CO_2, (Schneider, 1975; Marland and Rolty, 1979) O_3, NO_2, stratospheric H_2O and aerosols (Ramanathan and Coakley, 1978) chlorofluromethanes (Dickinson and Chervin, 1979; Crutzen, 1979), thermal pollution (Washington and Chervin, 1979), volcanic dust (Hunt, 1977), pollution (Koenig, 1975), dust (Russell and Grams, 1975), albedo (Charney *et al*., 1977; Williams, 1975) and topography during the Ice Age (Williams *et al*., 1974). Unfortunately, without a measure of the validity of the model the results of the simulations, although extremely valuable and interesting, must remain tentative. The atmosphere and earth is such a complex system that the relationship between the cause and the effect is difficult to unravel. The processes are nonlinear and numerous feedback processes may come into play. Several coupling mechanisms have been discussed by Schneider and Dickinson (1974) and recent research has investigated biosphere-albedo feedback (Cess 1978; Cess and Wronka, 1979), sea surface temperature (SST) feedback (Chervin *et al*. 1980), and cloud feedback (Wetherland and Manabe, 1980; Schneider *et al*., 1978).

Sensitivity studies are also important in assessing the factors which control climate and lead to a better understanding of climate. A prime example is the continuing discussion over the role of orography and land and sea differences (GARP, 1980; Grose and Hoskins, 1979). Despite many modeling attempts since the first by Charney and Eliassen (1949) to separate the topographic and thermal effects, the issue is still not resolved. It demonstrates that current simulation models are not yet sophisticated enough to provide definitive answers to many of the basic questions climatologists ask.

5. SURVEY OF MODELS BY ELEMENT

5.1. *Radiation*

Radiative transfer depends upon emission, absorption, scattering, and transmission by the atmospheric constituents. In turn, these processes are functions of the type and amount of the constituent, the wavelength of radiation, the pressure and the temperature. Because the band structure of radiation is highly complex, even when modeled (see Tiwari, 1978, for the infrared), direct numerical integration over wavelength and height is not usually attempted. Instead, spectrally average models have been developed.

Rogers (GARP, 1972) points out that approximations to radiative transfer used in general circulation numerical models are mostly of the longwave radiation chart type. The Manabe and Strickler (1964) approach used in the GFDL model (Holloway and Manabe, 1971) is very similar to the one developed by Yamamoto (1952). That is, spectrally integrated estimates of transmissivity of water vapor and carbon dioxide are plotted as functions of temperature and optical depth of each constituent. The atmospheric flux is then proportional to an area on the chart delimited by the plot of optical depth and temperature which are derived from an atmospheric sounding or from simulation. For a general circulation model, this integration is, of course, performed numerically. For longwave radiation, the early NCAR models used Sasamori's (1968) procedure which also was adopted from Yamamoto, but the third generation models (GARP, 1979) have incorporated new processes developed by Ramanathan and Dickinson including water vapor continuum bands with e-type absorption, ozone and carbon dioxide bands, and cirrus cloud and ground emissivities which are spectrally dependent.

Solar radiation is dealt with in a similar manner with absorption being calculated as a function of the optical thickness of water vapor, ozone, carbon dioxide and oxygen. Scattering is often assigned to a single layer and in earlier models was reduced to a constant. The complexity of cloud effects depends upon the parameterization of clouds and the number of layers in the model (Ramanathan and Coakley, 1978).

The results of such numerical simulations not only supply estimates of the instantaneous radiative diabatic heating, they can provide various statistics for the description of components of the general circulation. Manabe and Strickler (1964) have simulated and presented (their Figure 14) the vertical and latitudinal distribution of solar heating by season, and Newell *et al*. (1970), based partly on calculations by Rogers, have similarly illustrated the net radiation.

Different parameterizations are used when a single absorbing surface is of interest. Energy models of the earth-atmosphere reduce the expression of net radiation to

$$I(1 - \alpha) - \Delta L,$$

where I is extraterrestrial solar radiation, α is the earth-atmosphere albedo and ΔL is the terrestrial emission of longwave radiation. The latter two are empirically derived (Sellers, 1969).

For the earth's surface, I has to be modified to take into account atmospheric transmission as well as surface albedo. The surface receipt of solar radiation is then given by a spectrally integrated form of Bouguer's, Beer's or Lambert's law:

$$S = I \cos z \prod_{i=1}^{n} (\psi_i) \tag{7}$$

where S is the direct beam solar radiation (W m^{-2}), I is the extraterrestrial flux (W m^{-2}), z is the zenith angle, Π is the symbol for "product of" and ψ_i is the transmission of each constituent (dimensionless).

In surface climate simulations Outcalt (1971) and Terjung and O'Rourke (1980a) used three empirically derived ψ's (Brooks, 1959) representing absorption and scattering by water vapor and dry air and scattering by dust. Houghton (1954), in using equation (7), included absorption and scattering by water vapor and aerosols and Rayleigh scattering. Also, he took account of downward scattering and clouds. This method was followed by Davies *et al.* (1975) who gave

$$K\downarrow = I \cos z \; \psi_{wa} \psi_{da} (\psi_{ws} \psi_{rs} \psi_{ds} + 1) \frac{1}{2} \prod_{i=1}^{n} \psi_{ci} \tag{8}$$

for global solar irradiance, where w, d, r, a, and s stand for water, aerosol, Rayleigh absorption and scattering respectively and ψ_{ci} is the cloud transmission for layer i. The transmissions are obtained empirically with the only measurements needed being hourly cloud layer heights, types and amounts, and estimates of precipitable water. Suckling and Hay (1976) modified equation (8) to take account of multiple reflections.

In irregular terrain and in cities, the receipt of solar radiation is influenced by the zenith and azimuth angles of the slope and by reflections from adjacent surfaces. Dozier (1980), using a variety of sources for the transmissions as functions of wavelength, has developed a model which may be integrated over wavelength and time to produce direct and diffuse clear-sky solar radiation at a point. Slope, view-factor and reflection are taken into account. Nunez (1980) also includes clouds with his terrain calculations. Terjung and Louie (1973) reported on a similar solar radiation model for an urban area and demonstrated significant differences between urban and non-urban surfaces. Arnfield (1976, 1982) introduced a more general model for urban structures with varying albedos and multiple reflections. More recently, Terjung and O'Rourke (1980a) have refined their model and now include dual reflections.

Radiation chart (Elsasser, 1942; Yamamoto, 1952) type calculations may be employed for longwave radiation at the surface but these do need observed or simulated atmospheric profiles of temperature and humidity. Many recent models instead use a semi-empirical formula (e.g., see Brutsaert, 1975) which requires only temperature and vapor pressure at screen level. The surface simulation models of Outcalt and Terjung now use Brutsaert's formula. For terrain, Dozier and Outcalt (1979) take into account reflections and emissions from other slopes under clear skies while Nunez (1980) includes clouds but must input temperature and humidity. For the urban area, Terjung and O'Rourke (1980a) apply a similar technique with internally generated radiation, temperature and humidity, whereas Arnfield (1982) presents a more detailed radiative model with external forcing of radiation and temperature.

5.2. *Temperature*

Temperature is simulated using the principle of the conservation of energy. In the free atmosphere where temperature is also related to thickness, the rate of temperature change may be written

$$\frac{\partial T}{\partial t} = A - (\gamma_s - \gamma)w - u\frac{\partial T}{\partial x} + v\frac{\partial T}{\partial y} \quad , \tag{9}$$

where T is temperature (K), t is time (s), A is diabatic heat divergence ($T\,s^{-1}$), ($\gamma_s - \gamma$) is the difference between the wet adiabatic and environmental lapse rates (k m^{-1}) and u, v and w are the velocities (m s^{-1}) in the x, y and z (m. east, north, up) directions. The first term on the right involves the radiative and turbulent sensible and latent heat flux divergences. The second term is the convection and the third term the horizontal advection.

Complex models which evaluate these terms usually contain only limited surface parameterization of A so the accuracy of their prediction of surface temperature is limited. Consequently, everyday temperature forecasts depend on regression equations whose independent variables, such as 850–1000 mb thickness, are produced by the deterministic model.

Global energy balance studies of the Sellers (1969) type and surface simulations of the Myrup (1969) type, model the A term in equation (9) in more detail. Sellers' model is one-dimensional in the sense that it considers the average temperature of the earth as a function of latitude only. Another category in the one-dimensional class calculates the average temperature profile. Here, radiative divergence is modified by convective adjustment. A thorough review of this approach has been published by Ramanathan and Coakley (1978). At the surface, the conservation equation is

$$R_N + LE + H + G = 0, \tag{10}$$

where R_N is the net radiation, LE and H are the latent and sensible turbulent heat fluxes and G is subsurface conduction. Outcalt and Terjung and their associates write the terms in equation (10) as functions of temperature and then solve by iterative procedures.

5.3. Cloud and Precipitation

Large scale models use grid intervals that dictate that clouds must be parameterized and many early models used zonal climatological means. Often clouds are incorporated as simple functions of humidity. One NCAR parameterization sets low level cloudiness at

$$C_l = 2.4 \, RH - 1.6 \qquad 0.2 \leqslant C_l \leqslant 0.8$$

with additional restrictions that vertical velocity w be > -2 cm s^{-1} and RH be > 0.75 (Washington and Williamson, 1977). For precipitation in the same model, a distinction is made between convective and stable conditions. In the latter, a percentage (to take account of the grid region) of the saturation specific humidity is subtracted from the actual amount. Any excess is assumed to fall as precipitation. Convective precipitation is handled in a manner developed by Kuo (1965) for a tropical cyclone model. Similar methods are used by the National Weather Service but the calculated precipitation is only one of the inputs used in its quantitative precipitation forecasts.

Smaller scale models have had much greater success. Lavoie's (1972) mesoscale system using the primitive equations, averaged for one layer on a 6 × 12 km grid for Lake Erie, produced precipitation patterns which correlated well with observations. Pielke (1974) developed a three-dimensional model having 8 levels on an 11 × 11 km grid for the study of sea breezes over S. Florida. A modified version (Pielke and Mahrer, 1978) displays high correlation between predicted and observed zones of shower activity but not the specific location of showers. In another study using a two-dimensional (x, z) model, Colton (1976) simulated realistic orographically-induced precipitation in northern California.

Since the early work of Malkus and Witt (1959) a large body of research on the simulation of individual clouds has been published. See Cotton (1979) for a recent review of cloud physics and Court (1979) for precipitation.

5.4. Evaporation

As indicated in Section 4.4, it is currently impractical to simulate the variables in equation (5). The equivalent equation for water vapor is

$$E = \overline{\rho w q},$$

where E is evaporation (kg m^{-2} s^{-1}), ρ density (kg m^{-3}), w vertical wind (m s^{-1}) and q specific humidity (kg kg^{-1}). In general circulation models the aerodynamic equation is written in the form of equation (6)

$$E = -\rho C_D |V| \Delta q. \tag{11}$$

Theory suggests that different drag coefficients should be used for the different fluxes of momentum, sensible heat, and moisture and for different conditions. Arya (1977) has reviewed various parameterizations and concludes that Deardorff's (1972) scheme is the best currently available. Lavoie (1972), in his microscale model, defines the drag coefficient for moisture as

$$C_D'' = (K_E/K_M)C_D,$$

where the K's are the eddy diffusivities for moisture and momentum and C_D refers to momentum.

An alternative to equation (11) is the analog of molecular diffusion

$$E = -\rho K_E \frac{\partial \overline{q}}{\partial z}. \tag{12}$$

Myrup (1969) used this parameterization and then set K_E equal to K_M which in turn is derived from the neutral wind profile. Outcalt (1971) initially followed this formulation but later (Outcalt, 1972) modified it according to Fleagle and Businger (1963) to take account of different profiles. Simulations for high tundra conditions revealed that the model gave results which correlated well with observations (Brazel and Outcalt, 1973).

Arnfield (1978) employed the canopy resistance concept, and Terjung and O'Rourke (1980b) use a similar approach, as did Sellers and Lockwood (1981) in their analyses of the effects of interception on the water balance. Current research appears to be continuing along that line (Ziemar, 1979).

5.5. *Pressure and Wind*

Pressure and wind are related by the equation of motion but, excepting in its very simplest form of the geostrophic balance, this equation does not give the distribution of one of these variables solely in terms of the other. Consequently, only relatively complex models which solve a whole set of atmospheric equations, can simulate deterministically wind and pressure.

6. SURVEY OF MODELS BY SCALE AND PHENOMENON

The largest scale models deal with the atmosphere as a whole or with a single hemisphere. Schneider and Dickinson (1974) put them in a hierarchy on the basis of the number of dimensions and reviewed each in turn. Consequently, only a limited discussion on those models will proceed here.

6.1. *The General Circulation Model (GCM)*

Richardson (1922) foresaw the development of the GCM with "computers ... needed to race the weather for the whole globe" but it was not until the mid-1940's that this part of his "fantasy" came true. The equations Richardson developed are essentially the ones used today. Thompson (1961) has briefly reviewed the history of the subject and Kasahara (1977) has presented a summary of the basic equations, numerical methods and parameterizations in current use. Many aspects are also presented in Haltiner and Williams (1980) and the GARP publications. In the present paper, many of the comments at the end of Section 4.5 refer to GCM's.

It should be recognized that every major country of the world has at least one GCM in operation for everyday weather forecasting. The military and research establishments have others. Current research involves the validation of the models (Chervin, 1981) as well as sensitivity studies (see Section 4.5). Work is also progressing on improving parameterization and on including more processes. For example, Parkinson (Parkinson and Washington, 1979) has successfully modeled the growth, movement, and decay of sea-ice in a form suitable for easy incorporation into the NCAR GCM and Parkinson and Herman (1980) have reported on sea-ice simulations based on fields generated by the GLAS GCM. Oceans clearly have significant interaction with the atmosphere and coupled models appear to be one route in future research. Indeed, Manabe *et al.* (1975) and Washington *et al.* (1980) have already reported on ocean-atmosphere with sea-ice models.

GCM's usually have been developed by teams of researchers and programmers for extremely large and fast computers so climatologists tend to think that they are out of their reach. Some of the simpler ones, however, such as the Mintz-Arakawa two level model can be programmed and run by an individual on limited computing resources. The 1971 version including the programs are readily available from Gates *et al.* (1971).

A different class of climate model is one which is based on time-averaged equations. A definitive review of these, known as statistical-dynamical models, including a detailed classification is given by Saltzman (1978).

6.2. *Planetary Boundary Layer, PBL*

Considerable attention has been paid to the planetary boundary layer because a realistic parameterization is needed for the atmospheric models and because it controls the eddy fluxes from the surface. As Busch *et al.* (1976) point out there are two approaches. One parameterizes the PBL for model input (equation 11). The other models the PBL with several levels and computes the fluxes within the model. The problem is that such formulae are not easily related to the broader model. The usual solution is to use the mean gradients and eddy coefficients (equation 12). Because the equation is needed to close the complete set of equations this is known as a closure scheme. Equation (12) is a first order closure. Recent research has been directed at second order schemes (Wyngaard *et al.*, 1974; WMO, 1979; Paegle, 1979; Haltiner and Williams, 1980).

6.3. *Tropical Cyclones*

Initial attempts at simulating cyclones were made by Berkofsky (1960), Kasahara (1961) and Estoque (1962). In general, existing research utilizes the primitive equations in two or three dimensions. The axisymmetric group includes systems developed by Rosenthal (1978) whereas the three-dimensional approach is typified by the work of Anthes (1972) and Kurihara and Tuleya (1974). Excepting for the adjustment for boundaries, the latter use a set of equations very similar to GCM's. Realistic parameterization of cloud development is crucial and the three-dimensional models do simulate spiral rainbands. Various sensitivity studies have been conducted including one by Hobgood (1976) with the Anthes (1972) model in which evaporation over land was directly related to soil saturation. The results suggest that most of the dissipation of tropical cyclones after landfall is attributable to the reduction of evaporation.

6.4. *Mesoscale Models*

Flow in the lower atmosphere with simple relief has been studied successfully from an analytical standpoint in two dimensions by Scorer (1949) and in three dimensions by Crapper (1959). However, with irregular topography and/or heating numerical simulation is necessary. One of the earliest models was by Estoque (1961) for the sea breeze. Driven by a sinusoidal heating function over land with zero wind at the boundary the initially calm two-dimensional atmosphere developed a strong sea breeze circulation in the afternoon. Similar two-dimensional models have been created for cities (Olfe and Lee, 1971; McElroy, 1973; Bornstein, 1975). More realistic three-dimensional analogs have also been evolved. The St. Louis region heat island has been simulated by Vukovich *et al.* (1976, 1980), Lake Erie storms by Lavoie (1972) and Florida sea breezes by Pielke (1974).

6.5. *Local Surface Climate Simulation*

The original idea of a surface climate simulator was introduced by Halstead *et al.* (1957) who built an analog computer to solve equation (10). Myrup (1960) adapted the theory to a digital mode and it was taken up by Outcalt in 1971. Since that time, Outcalt and his associates have employed the technique in studying a variety of problems from needle ice development to urban thermal regimes. Terjung too, with his associates, used the same model in his urban simulations as have Arnfield (1978) and Tappen *et al.* (1981).

6.6. *Thunderstorms and Tornadoes*

Like tropical cyclones cumulus cells and tornadoes have been analysed using axisymmetric models (Ogura, 1962; Murray, 1970; Ogura and Takahashi, 1971; Smith and Leslie, 1980; Kuo and Raymond, 1980). Recently, interest in cumulus clouds has increased because of their "frictional" effect on the tropical meridional circulation and hence on the general circulation (Thompson and Hartman, 1979; Helford, 1979). Schlesinger (1975, 1980), who developed a three-dimensional model of a thunderstorm, has concentrated upon the dynamics of the storm, specifically the effect of wind shear on the cell.

7. POSTSCRIPT

Numerical simulation modeling can be a valuable and productive method of enquiry in all facets of climatology. Indeed, because the atmosphere is a complex system with many variables interacting nonlinearly with one another, this may be the only mode of process analysis. For a given element or phenomenon, there are multiple approaches based on different assumptions and utilizing different parameterizations. The above survey therefore has of necessity been superficial in its discussion of the models selected for inclusion (many have been omitted) and no attempt has been made to review critically the merits of them. Actually an objective comparison of similar models is difficult because, as pointed out by Kreitzberg (1979), many of the details of the computer models themselves are practically never documented in a formal way. There are exceptions, of course, where the programs are published (Gates *et al.*, 1971; Outcalt, 1971). For anyone interested in pursuing this line of research adapting someone else's program is one of the easiest ways to start. For my part, I wish to thank Professor Richard A. Anthes for providing me in the early 1970's with copies of his tropical cyclone models.

Dept. of Geography
The Ohio State University

REFERENCES

Anthes, R. A.: 1972, 'Development of asymmetries in a three dimensional numerical model of the tropical cyclone', *Mon. Wea. Rev.* **100**, 461–476.
Anthes, R. A., J. W. Trout, and S. L. Rosenthal: 1971, 'Comparisons of tropical cyclone simulations with and without the assumption of circular symmetry', *Mon. Wea. Rev.* **99**, 759–766.

Arnfield, A. J.: 1976, 'Numerical modelling of urban surface radiative parameters', in J. A. Davies (ed.), *Papers in Climatology: the Cam Allen Memorial Volume*, Discussion paper #7. Geography, McMaster Univ.

Arnfield, A. J.: 1978, 'An improved surface climate simulation model', *Assoc. Amer. Geog. Program Abstracts* 43.

Arnfield, A. J.: 1982, 'An approach towards estimation of the surface radiative properties and radiation budgets of cities', *Physical Geography* 3, 97–122.

Arya, S. P. S.: 1977, 'Suggested revisions to certain boundary layer parameterization schemes used in atmospheric circulation models', *Mon. Wea. Rev.* 105, 215–227.

Barry, R. G., A. D. Hecht, J. E. Kutzbach, W. D. Sellers, T. Webb, and P. B. Wright: 1979, Climatic change. *Reviews of Geophysics and Space Physics* 17, 1803–1813.

Berkofsky, L.: 1960, 'A numerical model for the prediction of hurricane formation,' *Geophys. Res. Papers* #67, Geophysical Research Directorate, U. S. Air Force.

Black, J. N.: 1954, 'The distribution of solar radiation over the earth's surface', *Archiv fur Meteorologue, Geophysike und Bioklimatologie* 7.

Blackman, M. L. and N. C. Lau: 1980, 'Regional characteristics of the northern hemisphere wintertime circulation: a comparison of the simulation of a GFDL general circulation model with observations', *J. Atmos. Sci.* 37, 497–514.

Bornstein, R. D.: 1975, 'The two-dimensional URBMET urban boundary layer model', *J. Meteor.* 14, 1459–1477.

Brazel, A. J. and S. I. Outcalt: 1973, 'The observation and simulation of diurnal evaporation contrast in an Alaskan alpine pass', *J. Appl. Meteor.* 12, 1134–1143.

Brooks, F. A.: 1959, *An Introduction to Physical Microclimatology*, Univ. of California Press, Davis.

Brutsaert, W.: 1975, 'On a derivable formula for longwave radiation from clear skies', *Water Resources Research* 11, 742–745.

Budyko, M. I.: 1969, 'The effect of solar radiation variations on the climate of the earth', *Tellus* 21, 611–619.

Busch, N. E., S. W. Change, and R. A. Anthes: 1976, 'A multilevel model of the planetary boundary layer suitable for use with mesoscale dynamic models', *J. Appl. Meteor.* 15, 909–919.

Campana, K. A.: 1979, 'Higher order finite-differencing experiments with a semi-implicit model at the National Meteorological Center', *Mon. Wea. Rev.* 107, 363–376.

Carslaw, H. S. and J. C. Jaeger: 1959, *Conduction of Heat in Solids*. Clarendon Press, Oxford.

Cess, R. D.: 1978, 'Biosphere-albedo feedback and climate modeling', *J. Atmos. Sci.* 35, 1765–1768.

Cess, R. D. and J. C. Wronka: 1979, 'Ice ages and the Milankovitch theory: A Study of interactive climate feedback mechanisms', *Tellus* 31, 185–192.

Charney, J. G. and A. Eliassen: 1949, 'On a physical basis to numerical prediction of large-scale motions in the atmosphere', *J. Meteor.* 6, 371–385.

Charney, J., W. J. Quirk, S-H. Chow, and J. Kornfield: 1977, 'A comparative study of the effects of albedo change on drought in semi-arid regions', *J. Atmos. Sci.* 34, 1366–1385.

Chervin, R. M.: 1980a, 'Estimates of first-and second-moment climate statistics in GCM simulated climate ensembles', *J. Atmos. Sci.* 37, 1889–1902.

Chervin, R. M.: 1980b, 'On the simulation of climate and climate change with general circulation models', *J. Atmos. Sci.* 37, 1903–1913.

Chervin, R. M.: 1981, 'On the comparison of observed and GCM simulated climate ensembles', *J. Atmos. Sci.* **38**, 885–901.

Chervin, R. M., J. E. Kutzbach, D. D. Houghton, and R. G. Gallimore: 1980, 'Response of the NCAR General circulation model to presented changes in ocean surface temperature. Part II: Midlatitude and subtropical changes', *J. Atmos. Sci.* **37**, 308–332.

Colton, D. E.: 1976, 'Numerical simulation of the orographically induced precipitation distribution for use in hydrologic analysis', *J. Appl. Meteor.* **12**, 1241–1251.

Cotton, W. R.: 1979, 'Cloud physics: a review for 1975–1978 IUGG Quadrennial Report', *Reviews of Geophysics and Space Physics* **17**, 1840–1851.

Court. A.: 1979, 'Precipitation research, 1975–1978', *Reviews of Geophysics and Space Physics* **17**, 1165–1175.

Crapper, G. D.: 1959, 'A three-dimensional solution for waves in the lee of mountains', *J. Fluids Mech.* **6**, 57–76.

Crutzen, P. J.: 1979, 'Chlorofluromethanes: threats to the ozone layer', *Reviews of Geophysics and Space Physics* **17**, 1824–1832.

Davies, J. A., W. Schertzer, and M. Nunez: 1975, 'Estimating global radiation', *Bound.-Layer Meteor.* **9**, 33–52.

Deardorff, J. W.: 1972, 'Numerical simulation of weather and climate', *Mon. Wea. Rev.* **100**, 93–106.

Dickinson, R. E. and R. M. Chervin: 1979, 'Sensitivity of a general circulation model to changes in infrared cooling due to chlorofluromethanes with and without prescribed zonal ocean surface temperature change', *J. Atmos. Sci.* **36**, 2304–2319.

Dozier, J.: 1980, 'A clear-sky spectral solar radiation model for snow-covered mountainous terrain', *Water Resources Research* **16**, 709–718.

Dozier, J. and S. I. Outcalt: 1979, 'An approach toward energy balance simulation over rugged terrain', *Geographical Analysis* **11**, 65–85.

Durst, C. S.: 1951, 'Climate – the synthesis of weather', *Compendium of Meteorology*. American Meteorological Society. Boston, pp. 967–975.

Elsasser, W. M.: 1942, 'Heat transfer by infrared radiation in the atmosphere', *Harvard Meteorological Studies* #6.

Estoque, M. A.: 1961, 'A theoretical investigation of the sea breeze', *Quart. J. Roy. Meteor. Soc.* **87**, 136–146.

Estoque, M. A.: 1962, 'Vertical and radial motions in a tropical cyclone', *Tellus* **4**, 394–402.

Fleagle, R. G. and J. A. Businger: 1963, *An Introduction to Atmospheric Physics*. Academic Press, New York.

Fultz, D.: 1951, 'Experimental analogies to atmospheric motions. *Compendium of Meteorology*. American Meteorological Society, Boston, pp. 1233–1248.

Fultz, D., R. R. Long, G. V. Owens, W. Bohan, R. Kaylor, and J. Weil: 1959, 'Studies of thermal convection in a rotating cylinder with implications for atmospheric motions', *Meteorological Monographs* **4**, #21.

GARP: 1972, 'Parameterization of sub-grid scale processes', ICSU/WMO *GARP Publication Series* #8.

GARP: 1974, 'Modelling for the First GARP Global Experiment', ICSU/WMO *GARP Publication Series* #14.

GARP: 1976, 'Numerical methods used in atmospheric models volumes I and II', ICSU/WMO *GARP Publication Series*. #17.

GARP: 1978, 'Numerical modelling of the tropical atmosphere', ICSU/WMO *GRAP Publication Series* #20.

GARP: 1979, 'Report of the JOC study conference on climate models: performance, intercomparison and sensitivity studies', ICSU/WMO *GARP Publication Series* #22 (2 volumes).

GARP: 1980, 'Orographic effects in planetary flows', ICSU/WMO. *GARP Publication Series* #23.

Gates, W. L., E. S. Batten, A. B. Kahle, and A. B. Nelson: 1971, *A Documentation of the Mintz-Arakawa Two-Level Atmospheric Circulation Model*, R-877-ARPA, Rand, Santa Monica.

Grose, W. L. and B. J. Hoskins: 1979, 'On the influence of orography on large-scale atmospheric flow', *J. Atmos. Sci.* **36**, 223–236.

Haltiner, G. J. and R. T. Williams: 1980, *Numerical Prediction and Dynamic Meteorology*. Wiley, New York.

Halstead, M. H., R. L. Richman, W. Corey, and J. D. Merryman: 1957, 'A preliminary report on the design of a computer for micrometeorology', *J. Meteor.* **14**, 308–325.

Helfard, H. M.: 1979, 'The effects of cumulus friction on the January Hadley circulation by the GLAS model of the general circulation', *J. Atmos. Sci.* **36**, 1827–1843.

Henderson-Sellers, A.: 1980, 'A simple numerical simulation of urban mixing depths', *J. Appl. Met.* **19**, 215–218.

Hobgood, J. S.: 1976, 'An examination of the sensitivity of a three-dimensional tropical cyclone model to changes in surface parameterization', Unpublished MA paper. Geography, The Ohio State University, Columbus.

Holloway, J. L. and S. Manabe: 1971, 'Simulation of climate by a global general circulation model', *Mon. Wea. Rev.* **99**, 335–370.

Houghton, H. G.: 1954, 'On the heat balance of the northern hemisphere', *J. Meteor.* **11**, 1–9.

Houghton, J. T.: 1976, *The Physics of Atmospheres*, Cambridge Univ. Press, Cambridge.

Hunt, B. G.: 1977, 'A simulation of the possible consequences of a volcanic eruption on the general circulation of the atmosphere', *Mon. Wea. Rev.* **105**, 247–260.

Kasahara, A.: 1961, 'A numerical experiment on the development of a tropical cyclone', *J. Meteor.* **18**, 259–282.

Kasahara, A.: 1974, 'Various vertical coordinate systems used for numerical weather prediction', *Mon. Wea. Rev.* **102**, 509–522 and *Mon. Wea. Rev.* **103**, 664.

Kasahara, A.: 1977, 'Computational aspects of numerical models for weather prediction and climate simulation', *Methods in Computational Physics* **17**, 2–66.

Koenig, L. R.: 1975, 'A numerical experiment on the effects of regional atmospheric pollution on global climate', *J. Appl. Meteor.* **14**, 1023–1036.

Kreiss. H., and J. Oliger: 1973, 'Methods for the approximate solution of time dependent problems', ICSU/WMO *GARP Publication Series*, #10.

Kreitzberg, C. W.: 1979, 'Observing, analyzing, and modeling mesoscale weather phenomena', *Reviews of Geophysics and Space Physics* **17**, 1852–1871.

Kuo, H-L.: 1965, 'On formation and intensification of tropical cyclones through latent heat release by cumulus convection', *J. Atmos. Sci.* **22**, 40–63.

Kuo, H.-L. and W. H. Raymond: 1980, 'A quasi-one-dimensional cumulus cloud model and parameterization of cumulus heating and mixing effects', *J. Atmos. Sci.* **108**, 991–1009.

Kurihara, Y. and R. E. Tuleya: 1974, 'Structure of a tropical cyclone developed in a three-dimensional numerical simulation model', *J. Atmos. Sci.* **31**, 893–919.

Landsberg, H.: 1960, *Physical Climatology*, Gray Printing Co., DuBois.

Lavoie, R. L.: 1972, 'A mesoscale model of the lake-effect storm', *J. Atmos. Sci.* **29**, 1025–1049.

Lorenz, E. N.: 1968, 'Climatic determinism', *Meteorological Monographs* **8**, #30, 1–3.

Lorenz, E. N.: 1975, 'Climate predictability', *GARP Publication Series* #16, 132–136.

Malkus, J. S. and G. Witt: 1959, 'The evolution of a convective element: a numerical calculation', *The Atmosphere and the Sea Ice Motion*, Rockefeller Inst. Press, N.Y., pp. 425–439.

Manabe, S. and R. F. Strickler: 1964, 'Thermal equilibrium of the atmosphere with a convective adjustment', *J. Atmos. Sci.* **21**, 361–385.

Manabe, S., K. Bryan, and M. J. Spelman: 1975, 'A global-atmosphere climate model. Part I: The atmospheric circulation', *J. Phys. Oceanography* **5**, 3–29.

Marland, G. and R. M. Rolty: 1979, 'Carbon dioxide and climate', *Reviews of Geophysics and Space Physics* **17**, 1813–1824.

McElroy, J. L.: 1973, 'A numerical study of the nocturnal heat island over a medium mid-latitude city (Columbus, Ohio)', *Bound.-Layer Meteor.* **3**, 442–453.

Mesinger, F. and A. Arakawa: 1976, 'Numerican methods used in Atmospheric models', ICSU/WMO *GARP Publication Series* #17, Vol. 1.

Murray, F. W.: 1970, 'Numerical models of a tropical cumulus cloud with bilateral and axial symmetry', *Mon. Wea. Rev.* **98**, 14–28.

Myrup, L.: 1969, 'A numerical model of the urban heat island', *J. Appl. Meteor.* **8**, 908–918.

National Committee for Fluid Mechanics Films: 1972, *Illustrated Experiments in Fluid Mechanics*, The MIT Press, Cambridge.

Newell, R. E., D. G. Vincent, T. G. Doplick, D. Ferruzza, and J. W. Kidson: 1970, 'The energy balance of the global atmosphere', in G. A. Corby (ed.), *The global circulation of the atmosphere*, Royal Meteorological Society, London, pp. 42–90.

Nunez, M.: 1980, 'The calculation of solar and net radiation in mountainous terrain', *J. Biogeography* **7**, 173–186.

Ogura, Y.: 1963, 'The evolution of a moist convective element in a shallow, conditionally unstable atmosphere: a numerical calculation', *J. Atmos. Sci.* **20**, 407–424.

Ogura, Y. and T. Takahashi: 1971, 'Numerical simulation of the life cycle of a thunderstorm cell', *Mon. Wea. Rev.* **99**, 895–911.

Oke, T. R.: 1978, *Boundary Layer Climates*, Halstead, New York.

Olfe, D. B. and R. L. Lee: 1971, 'Linearized calculations of urban heat island convection effects', *J. Atmos. Sci.* **28**, 1374–1388.

Outcalt, S. I.: 1971, 'A numerical surface climate simulator', *Geographical Analysis* **3**, 379–393.

Outcalt, S. I.: 1972, 'The development and application of a simple digital surface-climate simulator', *J. Appl. Meteor.* **11**, 629–636.

Outcalt, S. I., C. Goodwin, G. Weller, and J. Brown: 1975, 'Computer simulation of snowmelt and soil thermal regime at Barrow, Alaska', *Water Resources Research* **11**, 709–715.

Paegle, J.: 1979, 'Boundary layer physics and turbulence – theoretical aspects', *Reviews of Geophysics and Space Physics* **17**, 1782–1792.

Parkinson, C. L. and G. P. Herman: 1980, 'Sea-ice simulations based on fields generated by the GLAS GCM', *Mon. Wea. Rev.* **108**, 2080–2091.

Parkinson, C. L. and W. M. Washington: 1979, 'A large scale numerical model of sea ice', *J. Geophys. Res.* **84**, 311–337.

Phillips, N. A.: 1957, 'A coordinate system having some special advantages for numerical forecasting', *J. Meteor.* **14**, 184–185.

Peilke, R. A.: 1974, 'A three-dimensional numerical model of the sea and land breezes over S. Florida', *Mon. Wea. Rev.* **102**, 115–139.

Pielke, R. A. and Y. Mahrer: 1978, 'Verification analysis of the U. of Virginia three-dimensional mesoscale model prediction over S. Florida for 1 July 1973', *Mon. Wea. Rev.* **106**, 1568–1589.

Pollard, D., A. P. Ingersoll, and J. G. Lockwood: 1980, 'Response of zonal climate-ice sheet model to the orbital perturbations during the Quarternary ice ages', *Tellus* **32**, 302–319.

Ramanathan, V. and J. A. Coakley: 1978, 'Climate modelling through radiative models', *Reviews of Geophysics and Space Physics* **16**, 465–489.

Rayner, J. N.: 1974, 'Climatology and simulation', *Proceedings of the Association of American Geographers* **6**, 109–112.

Richardson, L. F.: 1922, *Weather Prediction by Numerical Process*, Cambridge Univ. Press, Cambridge, Dover edition. 1965.

Richtmyer, R. D. and K. W. Morton: 1967, *Difference Methods for Initial-value problems*, Interscience, Wiley, New York.

Rosenthal, S. L.: 1978, 'Numerical simulation of tropical cyclone development with latent heat release by resolvable scales I: Model description and preliminary results', *J. Meteor.* **35**, 258–271.

Russell, P. B. and G. W. Grams: 1975, 'Application of soil optical properties in analytical models of climate change', *J. Appl. Meteor.* **14**, 1037–1043.

Saltzman, B.: 1978, 'A survey of statistical-dynamical models of the terrestrial climate', *Advances in Geophysics* **20**, 183–304.

Sasamori, T.: 1968, 'The radiative cooling calculation for application to general circulation experiments', *J. Appl. Meteor.* **7**, 721–729.

Schlesinger, R. E.: 1975, 'A three-dimensional numerical model of an isolated deep convective cloud: Preliminary results', *J. Almos. Sci.* **32**, 934–957.

Schlesinger, R. E.: 1980, 'A three-dimensional numerical model of an isolated thunderstorm. Part II: Dynamics of updraft splitting and mesovortex couplet evolution', *J. Atmos. Sci.* **37**, 395–420.

Schneider, S. H.: 1975, 'On the carbon dioxide-climate confusion', *J. Atmos. Sci.* **32**, 2060–2066.

Schneider, S. H. and R. E. Dickinson: 1974, 'Climate modeling', *Reviews of Geophysics and Space Physics* **12**, 447–493.

Schneider, S. H., W. M. Washington, and R. M. Chervin: 1978, 'Cloudiness as a climatic feedback mechanism: effects on cloud amounts of prescribed global and regional surface temperature changes in the NCAR GCM', *J. Atmos. Sci.* **35**, 2207–2221.

Scorer, R. S.: 1949, 'The theroy of waves in the lee of mountains', *Quart. J. Roy. Meteor. Soc.* **75**, 41–56.

Sellers, P. J. and J. G. Lockwood: 1981, 'A computer simulation of the effects of differing crop types on the water balance of small catchments over long periods', *Quart. J. Roy. Meteor. Soc.* **107**, 395–414.

Sellers, W. D.: 1965, *Physical Climatology,* Univ. of Chicago Press, Chicago.

Sellers, W. D.: 1969, 'A global climatic model based on the energy balance of the earth-atmosphere system', *J. Appl. Meteor.* **8**, 392–400.

Smagorinsky, J.: 1979, 'Overview of the climate modelling problem', ICSU/WMO *GARP Publication Series #22*, 1–12.

Smith, R. K. and L. M. Leslie: 1979, 'A numerical study of tornadogenesis in a rotating thunderstorm', *Quart. J. Roy. Meteor. Soc.* **105**, 107–127.

Suckling, P. W. and J. E. Hay: 1976, 'Modelling direct, diffuse, and total solar radiation for cloudless days', *Atmosphere* **14**, 298–308.

Sundqvist, H.: 1979, 'Vertical coordinates and related discretization', ICSU/WMO *GARP Publication Series #17*, Vol. II, 1–50.

Tappen, N. J., P. D. Tyson, I. F. Owens and W. J. Hastie: 1981, 'Modelling the winter urban island over Christchurch, New Zealand', *J. Appl. Meteor.* **20**, 365–376.

Terjung, W. H.: 1976, 'Climatology for geographers', *Annals Assoc. Amer. Geogr.* **66**, 199–222.

Terjung, W. H. and S. S-F. Louie: 1973, 'Solar radiation and urban heat islands', *Annals Assoc. Amer. Geogr.* **63**, 181–207.

Terjung, W. H. and P. A. O'Rourke: 1980a, 'Simulating the causal elements of urban heat islands', *Bound.-Layer Meteor.* **19**, 93–118.

Terjung, W. H. and P. A. O'Rourke: 1980b, 'An economical canopy model for use in urban climatology', *Int. J. Biometeor.* **24**, 281–291.

Thompson, P. D.: 1961, *Numerical Weather Analysis and Prediction.* Macmillan, New York.

Thompson, S. L. and D. L. Hartman: 1979, "Cumulus friction': estimated influence on the tropical mean meridional circulation", *J. Atmos. Sci.* **36**, 2022–2026.

Tiwari, S. N.: 1978, 'Models for infrared atmospheric radiation', *Advances in Geophys.* **20**, 1–85.

Vokovich, F. M., J. W. Dunn, III, and B. W. Crissman: 1976, 'A theoretical study of the St. Louis Heat Island: The wind and temperature distribution', *J. Appl. Meteor.* **15**, 417–400.

Vukovich, F. M. and W. J. King: 1980, 'A theoretical study of the St. Louis Heat Island: Comparisons between observed data and simulation results on the urban heat island circulation', *J. Appl. Meteor.* **19**, 761–770.

Washington, W. M. and R. M. Chervin: 1979, 'Regional climatic effects of large-scale thermal pollution: Simulation studies with the NCAR general circulation model', *J. Appl. Meteor.* **19**, 3–16.

Washington, W. M., A. J. Semtner, G. A. Meehl, D. J. Knight, and T. A. Mayer: 1980, 'A general circulation experiment with coupled atmosphere, ocean and sea-ice model', *J. Phys. Oceanography* **10**, 1887–1980.

Washington, W. M. and D. L. Williamson: 1977, 'A description of the NCAR global circulation models', *Methods in Comp. Physics* **17**, 111–172. (General Circulation Models of the Atmosphere, J. Chang, ed.)

Wetherald, R. T. and S. Manabe: 1975, 'The effects of changing the solar constant on the climate of a general circulation model', *J. Atmos. Sci.* **32**, 2044–2059.

Wetherald, R. T. and S. Manabe: 1980, 'Cloud cover and climate sensitivity', *J. Atmos. Sci.* **37**, 1485–1510.

Williams, J.: 1975, 'The influence of a snow cover cover on the atmospheric circulation and its role in climatic change: Analysis based on results from the NCAR global circulation model', *J. Appl Meteor.* **14**, 137–152.

Williams, J., R. G. Barry, and W. M. Washington: 1974, 'Simulation of the atmospheric circulation using the NCAR global circulation model with Ice Age boundary conditions', *J. Appl. Meteor.* **13**, 305–317.

Williamson, D. L. and G. L. Browning: 1973, 'Comparison of grids and difference approximations for numerical weather prediction over a sphere', *J. Appl. Meteor.* **30**, 264–274.

Wippermann, F., L. Berkofsky, and A. Szillinsky: 1969, 'Numerical experiments on the formation of tornado funnel under an intensifying vortex', *Quart. J. Roy. Meteor. Soc.* **95**. 689–702.

WMO: 1979, 'The planetary boundary layer', WMO #530 *Techn. Note* #165. (ed., G. A. McBean.)

Wyngaard, J. C., O. R. Cote, and K.-S. Rao: 1974, 'Color modelling of the atmospheric boundary layer', *Advances in Geophysics* **18A**, 193–211.

Yamamoto, G.: 1952, 'On a radiation chart', *Science Reports* of the Tohoku U. 5, 4, 9–23.

Ziemer, R. R.: 1979, 'Evaporation and transpiration', *Reviews of Geophysics and Space Physics* **17**, 1175–1186.

CORT J. WILLMOTT

ON THE EVALUATION OF MODEL PERFORMANCE IN PHYSICAL GEOGRAPHY

1. INTRODUCTION

Following the lead of Haggett and Chorley (1967), Rayner (1974), Terjung (1976), Strahler (1980) and many others, physical geography has adopted a "model-based paradigm" and, as a result, the development and application of a wide variety of models is now commonplace within virtually every sub-field from geomorphology to bioclimatology. Within climatology, many models have a predominately deductive genesis while other models are collages of statistical and empirical reasoning and, in a few cases, "best-fit" functions are extracted from data with seemingly little regard for the safe-guards of a deductive stance. Still other models combine the mathematics of probability theory with empirically derived probabilities to create stochas-tic simulation models, e.g., Markov or Monte Carlo models. These categories of models are, by no means, mutually exclusive (or exhaustive for that matter) and a number of recent models may be considered combinatorial in that they incorporate two or more of the above-mentioned strategies into a single model.

Regardless of how one classifies models, or the type of system being modeled, perhaps the major purpose of any quantitative analog is to estimate events in space and time from some initial conditions and input variables. It follows that the degree to which model-predicted events approach the mag-nitudes of measured or otherwise reliably and independently derived observa-tions, relative to the "cost" required to produce a model's estimates, is one of the most important indicators of a model's value. This is not the only criterion which can be used to evaluate model performance since some models, such as explanatory models (Mather *et al.,* 1980), often do not have prediction as their major goal. In such situations, a "scientific" — rather than a statistical — evaluation may be more appropriate (Fox, 1981) although most successful model evaluation efforts are blends of both approaches. When statistical or quantitative evaluations of model performance are required, however, model-estimated events must be compared to independently measured or other reliable data in a meaningful way. As there is no consensus in the physical geographic literature on how to evaluate model performance

443

Gary L. Gaile and Cort J. Willmott (eds.), Spatial Statistics and Models, 443–460.
© 1984 *by D. Reidel Publishing Company.*

or compare the predictive abilities of two or more models, this paper attempts to survey and analyze commonly applied procedures, and set out some guidelines which can be used for comparing model-predicted values and reliable data. Consistent with most of the physical geographic literature, it is assumed that events can be represented as scalar quantities even though the description of many physical geographic processes is more realistically made with vector or tensor assignments.

My discussion will begin with the more subjective or visually oriented techniques of data-plots and sensitivity analysis. This will be followed by a brief description of important, univariate summary statistics and an examination of commonly applied correlation measures. The next portion of the text will compare and contrast a variety of commonly applied difference or error measures. Many of my points are illustrated in the final section of the main text with an exemplary evaluation of the performances of four climatic models that estimate monthly evapotranspiration.

2. GRAPHICS AND SENSITIVITY ANALYSIS

It may sound elementary to state that the first rule of data analysis (and similarly the analysis of those data that pertain to model performance) is to look at the data, but such is apparently not the case as so many quantitative, geographic papers under-utilize this almost axiomatic, statistical practice. The problem is particularly acute among geography's model builders who rarely provide meaningful visual representations of a model's ability to accurately characterize reality. In the past, such a deficiency was understandable as our data sets were large and our techniques for graphing or mapping data were cumbersome. Today, however, with the widespread availability of digital computers and easy-to-use graphics software and hardware, large data sets no longer pose a significant barrier to the visual display and analysis of geographic data.

When model-predicted events are being compared to reliable data (usually measured), geographers can employ a variety of graphical techniques to help illuminate the model's ability to correctly predict. Scatterplots between the model-predicted (P), and observed or reliable (O) variables are particularly helpful in uncovering a variety of systematic differences between O and P as well as those troublesome extreme cases. Plots of O and P over time (time-series plots) or space provide slightly more information than the scatterplots although they can be difficult to interpret when O and P are highly variable series. Graphs of ($P - O$) and other types of residual plots can likewise illuminate important patterns that would otherwise be overlooked when distilled in a table of summary statistics. The selective use of such data-display graphics, of course, is required for publication but there is very little to impede a researcher from using a wide variety of graphics during the various stages of model development and refinement. Data-display graphics are perhaps of greatest value during this time as they allow for a much more complete, albeit less exacting, presentation of model performance than the commonly used summary measures. The use of graphics supplements information contained within the various summary and evaluatory quantitative indices, and it can help characterize deviations from scientific expectations (Fox, 1981). When used in conjunction with a graphic display, sensitivity analyses can also help clarify a model's scientific credibility.

Sensitivity studies most often involve varying one of the functionally independent variables through its domain, while holding the other independent variables constant at representative levels, in order to observe the effects upon a dependent variable. Once again, the results are often best understood when visually presented — usually in the form of a graph where the abscissa is the independent variable of interest and the ordinate is a dependent variable. In the geographic case, a response-surface may be developed because the variables are inextricably tied to the dimensions of longitude and latitude. Sensitivity analyses are limited, however, since the results are frequently highly dependent upon the prescribed (often arbitrarily) background conditions , i.e., initial conditions and independent variables that are held constant. The results, therefore, should be interpreted with caution.

Data-display graphics and the visual display of sensitivity analyses can significantly enhance a researcher's understanding of a model when they are used in conjunction with the appropriate quantitative indices. Such visual aids represent the first level of exploration into model performance while summary univariate statistics comprise the second level.

3. SUMMARY UNIVARIATE MEASURES

Of all the summary indices available to describe variables, the two that continually emerge as the most informative, with respect to interval and ratio scale data, are the mean and standard deviation which describe position and scale, respectively. These measures have the concomitant advantages of being well-understood by most geographers and used in the computation of a variety of more special purpose, model evaluation indices — such as the parameters associated with a simple linear regression between O and P. For these reasons, the observed $(\overline{O})$ and predicted $(\overline{P})$ means and respective standard deviations $(s_o$ and $s_p)$ should always be computed and reported as part of a cadre of model evaluation graphics and quantitative indices.

4. CORRELATION MEASURES

Calculating and reporting quantitative measures of correlation between O and P has become, within the geographic literature, the most popular means of demonstrating the ability of models to accurately predict. Pearson's product-moment correlation coefficient (r) or its square, the coefficient of determination (r^2), is usually selected for the task even though it may not describe the "true" or underlying correlation between O and P as well as other correlation measures (Rutherford, 1973). Nonetheless, since r and r^2 have the historical interia of being commonly reported and they are generally representative of those types of relationships which can be characterized by most standardized measures of correlation, r and r^2 will be discussed and evaluated as if they are exemplary of the class of standardized measures of correlation.

Described by Willmott (1981), the essence of the problem associated with the use of r or r^2 for model evaluation is that they are completely insensitive to a wide variety of additive and proportional differences that can exist between O and P. This can easily be illustrated by considering two extreme cases. On the one hand, it is possible to obtain extremely high values of r or r^2 when O and P are quite dissimilar. Take, for instance, a special case where two hypothetical model-predicted time-series $(P^A$ and $P^B)$ are compared with an observed time-series (Figure 1a and 1b). Even though it is visually evident that P^A and P^B deviate substantially from O, the correlations between P^A and O, and P^B and O equal 1.0 — suggesting that r and r^2 are insufficient for making evaluations of accuracy, i.e., where accuracy is defined as the degree to which P assumes the magnitude of O. At the other extreme, it is possible for low or even negative values of r to occur simultaneously with relatively small differences between O and P — if the mean of at least one of the variables is stationary and the deviations about that mean are unsystematic. In other words, the "noise" level within O or P is high relative to any systematic-linear relationship that exists between O and P. This can be illustrated by computing and plotting three hypothetical time-series (one observed and two predicted) where the prescribed means are similar in magnitude and the deviations are produced by a pseudo-random number generator (Figure 1c and 1d). While the r's associated with P^A and P^B are perfect, those that attempt to describe the predictive abilities of P^C and P^D

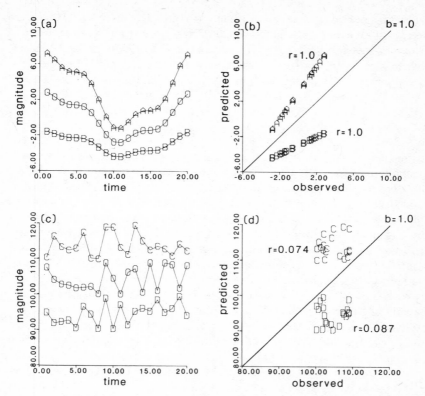

Fig. 1. Six hypothetical time-series — four predicted and two observed — are scatter-and time-series plotted ($N = 20$). Within graphs (a) and (b), the elements of model-predicted variables P^A and P^B are represented by A's and B's, respectively, while an O is used to depict the observed variable. Graphs (c) and (d) alternatively display relationships between model-predicted variables P^C and P^D and the corresponding observed time-series where C's, D's and O's indicate the respective data points. Perfect correlations exist between P^A, P^B and their corresponding O while P^C, P^D, and their associated O are almost entirely uncorrelated.

are very low even though it could be argued convincingly that the relative accuracies of P^A and P^B are not higher than those of P^C and P^D.

Recent model comparisons within solar climatology document the supposition that r and r^2 are insufficient to make meaningful distinctions between model-predicted variates (Powell, 1980) while other studies (Willmott and Wicks, 1980) empirically demonstrate how the magnitudes of r or r^2 may indeed be misleading. Most cases, which fall somewhere in between the above-described extremes, have indeterminate mixes and proportions of the various kinds of interrelationships that occur between O and P. As a result, the relationships between the magnitudes of r or r^2 and model performance are ill-defined which indicates that r and r^2 are inappropriate statistics — at best — for making quantitative comparisons between O and P.

5. DIFFERENCE MEASURES

Difference or "error" measures for evaluating model performance are generally derived from the variable $(\mathbf{P} - \mathbf{O})$ or $\mathbf{D}$, which is a vector of differences between the corresponding values of P_i and O_i, and each measure is scaled in a distinct way in order to describe particular characteristics of $\mathbf{D}$. Measures of average difference have been used most often although recent proposals by Fox (1981) and Willmott (1981), for instance, recommend the computation and interpretation of measures that describe features of $\mathbf{D}$ other than central tendency. Still other authors (Atwater and Ball, 1978; Johnson and Bras, 1980) have proposed and used a variety of *ad hoc* "absolute" (usually in the units of O and P) or "relative" (usually dimensionless) difference measures. Within this section of the paper, the more descriptive, exemplary or commonly used difference measures will be introduced and evaluated. The discussion will begin with the absolute measures followed by a review of selected relative indices.

Two average difference measures, that generally are accepted to be representative of $\mathbf{D}$, are the root mean square error (RMSE) and the mean absolute error (MAE). These measures take the form

$$\text{RMSE} = [N^{-1} \sum_{i=1}^{N} (P_i - O_i)^2]^{0.5} \tag{1}$$

and

$$\text{MAE} = N^{-1} \sum_{i=1}^{N} |P_i - O_i|, \tag{2}$$

where N is the number of cases. The former measure (equation (1)) has appeared intermittently within the environmental and physical science literature, albeit with increasing frequency over the past decade (e.g., Jensen, 1973). Geographers, on the other hand, have been slow to adopt RMSE, although there are an increasing number of exceptions (e.g., Willmott and Wicks, 1980; Suckling and Hay, 1976; Burt *et al.*, 1980). A quite different history is associated with the mean absolute error, which is rarely computed or reported in either the science or geographic literature, even though it is less sensitive to extreme values than RMSE because it avoids any physically artificial exponentiation. From a statistical-mathematical perspective, however, RMSE has the advantage of being more amenable to mathematical decomposition and analysis as well as to statistical interpretation. While the latter advantage may, in fact, not be an advantage at all (this assertion is addressed in the next section), RMSE's mathematical assets have proved helpful in the derivation of other useful measures (Willmott, 1981). In order to augment the information provided by RMSE or MAE, a few recent efforts have been directed toward the quantification of the major types or sources of error (e.g., Fox, 1981; Willmott, 1981).

Fox (1981), for instance, proposed that the important sources of error were characterized by the first (MBE) and second (s_D^2) moments of the distribution of the differences while Willmott (1981) recommended that the average "systematic" ($RMSE_s$) and "unsystematic" ($RMSE_u$) portions of RMSE encapsulate pertinent information on the nature of the error contained in P. Fox's (1981) indices are

$$MBE = N^{-1} \sum_{i=1}^{N} (P_i - O_i) \tag{3}$$

and

$$s_D^2 = (N-1)^{-1} \sum_{i=1}^{N} (P_i - O_i - MBE)^2 . \tag{4a}$$

When N is large, s_D^2 can be estimated from

$$s_D^2 \simeq RMSE^2 - (\bar{P} - \bar{O})^2 . \tag{4b}$$

Willmott's (1981) suggested measures take the general form

$$RMSE_s = [N^{-1} \sum_{i=1}^{N} (\hat{P}_i - O_i)^2]^{0.5} \tag{5}$$

and

$$RMSE_u = [N^{-1} \sum_{i=1}^{N} (P_i - \hat{P}_i)^2]^{0.5} , \tag{6}$$

where $\hat{P}_i = a + b\, O_i$ and a and b are the parameters associated with an ordinary least-squares (OLS) simple linear regression between O and P.

While MBE and s_D^2 describe the frequency distribution of $\mathbf{D}$, they do not identify the sources of error relative to the perfect prediction line, i.e., when $\mathbf{D}$ is the null vector. At the same time, MBE and s_D^2 provide virtually no additional information about $\mathbf{D}$ when RMSE, $\bar{P}$ and $\bar{O}$ are reported since MBE $= \bar{P} - \bar{O}$ and s_D^2 is a simple function of RMSE, $\bar{P}$ and $\bar{O}$ (4b). It can be concluded that MBE and s_D^2 are often redundant descriptions of $\mathbf{D}$ and, therefore, of marginal utility.

Under the propositions that P is dependent upon O and O is error free, the average error described by RMSE can be unambiguously partitioned into RMSE_s and RMSE_u. With a prior calculation of RMSE, it is only necessary to compute one of these two sources of error since they are related by

$$\mathrm{RMSE}^2 = \mathrm{RMSE}_s^2 + \mathrm{RMSE}_u^2. \tag{7}$$

An economical approach is to first estimate the unsystematic error from one of the computational forms of equation (6), e.g., $\mathrm{RMSE}_u = [s_p^2 - (bs_o)^2]^{0.5}$ or $\mathrm{RMSE}_u = [(1 - r^2)\, s_p^2]^{0.5}$, and then obtain RMSE_s from equation (7). Alternatively, when the additive, proportional and interdependent components of RMSE_s are of interest and/or already calculated, RMSE_s may be computed directly according to formulae given by Willmott (1981) and then equation (7) may be solved for RMSE_u. Knowledge of the magnitudes of RMSE_s and RMSE_u can be extremely helpful to the model-builder or -user when he or she is deciding whether or not a model is acceptable. That is, not only should RMSE be low but, since a "good" model ought to explain most of the systematic variation in O, RMSE_s should be relatively small while RMSE_u should approach RMSE. These indices also can be informative when used in a relative form — as will be discussed in the next few paragraphs.

Measures of relative error are usually dimensionless and most often they take the form of ratios between an absolute difference measure such as RMSE and a summary statistic that describes O. A variety of more exotic measures of relative difference could easily be conceived, but the computational and apparent interpretational simplicity of the simple ratio measures have an allure which has given them an advantage and insured them a place in the scientific literature. There are a number of important problems associated with the simple measures, however, and they will be considered along with recommendations for alternative formulations.

Most relative difference measures are derived from the supposition that the magnitude of error (usually average error) can be more fully appreciated when it is compared to the central tendency or dispersion present in O. As a result, the vast majority of indices reported are related to $\mathrm{RMSE}/\bar{O}$ or $(\mathrm{RMSE}/s_o)^2$ (e.g., Johnson and Bras, 1980; Davies, 1981) — particularly the former. In fact, $\mathrm{RMSE}/\bar{O}$ perhaps is the most popular measure of relative difference. While such measures have an obvious intuitive appeal, their general utility is questionable since they are unbounded, making interpretations of magnitude rather speculative and they can be unstable when $\bar{O}$, s_o or N is near zero. Within climatology, for example, time-series of ground heat flux and atmospheric counterradiation often exhibit means and standard deviations, respectively, near zero and, therefore, the values of $\mathrm{RMSE}/\bar{O}$ or $(\mathrm{RMSE}/s_o)^2$ or similar indices may be misleading. Another point to consider is that the error in prediction usually is inextricably related to *both a* and *b* and, subsequently, to *both* $\bar{O}$ and s_o. The tacit ascription of all the error represented by RMSE to either $\bar{O}$ or s_o, as evidenced by the computation and interpretation of $\mathrm{RMSE}/\bar{O}$ or $(\mathrm{RMSE}/s_o),^2$ is not then a sound practice. In order to circumvent these and other problems associated with the commonly used simple, relative error indices as well as with r and r^2, Willmott (1981) proposed some alternative formulations.

Given that error cannot be uniquely attributed to any of the well-known distributional parameters such as $\bar{O}$ and s_o, a more comprehensive basis of comparison is/was needed. Willmott (1981) assumed that the magnitude of the error (i.e., RMSE) was linked to both O and P and that a comprehensive and representative basis of comparison, consequently, would have to be derived from both O and P. Consistent with the development of RMSE_s and RMSE_u, Willmott (1981) postulated that O, and therefore $\bar{O}$, was error-free. For any set of paired observations, the maximum possible or potential distance that they could be apart then can be described by $(|P_i - \bar{O}| + |O_i - \bar{O}|)$. When this term is squared and summed over all observations it becomes a sort of potential error variance (PE) and $(0 \leqslant \mathrm{RMSE}^2 \leqslant N^{-1}\,\mathrm{PE})$. It follows that a descriptive relative error measure that reflects the overall-relative degree to which O is approached by P can be defined as

$$d = 1 - \frac{N \cdot \mathrm{RMSE}^2}{\mathrm{PE}} \ . \tag{8}$$

The index of agreement (d) varies between 0.0 and 1.0 where a value of 1.0 expresses perfect agreement between O and P and 0.0 describes complete disagreement. Since d is a dimensionless and bounded measure, it is easier to interpret than the relative measures discussed above although no single measure is sufficient to evaluate model performance.

Relationships described by equations (5), (6) and (7) make possible the description and interpretation of at least two more useful, relative measures. That is, the proportion of MSE ($RMSE^2$) that arises from systematic differences between O and P can be described by $(RMSE_s/RMSE)^2$ while the unsystematic proportion is $(RMSE_u/RMSE)^2$ or $[1 - (RMSE_s/RMSE)^2]$. Information about the degree to which model-induced errors are systematic or not offers an important supplement to $RMSE_s$ and $RMSE_u$ as well as facilitates cross-comparisons between different models and reliable data sets regardless of their associated units.

A summary recommendation is that researchers compute and report a minimum number of the most descriptive measures from each of the main categories, i.e., from the summary univariate measures, and the absolute and relative difference measures. It is further suggested that $\bar{O}$, $\bar{P}$, s_o, s_p, N, a, b, RMSE, $RMSE_s$, $RMSE_u$ and d represent an array of indices that (1) is comprehensive in its description of the interrelationships between O and P, and (2) provides enough information that a variety of other indices, e.g., $(RMSE_s/RMSE)^2$ or even r^2, can easily be computed for special purposes. When the above measures are used in conjunction with data-display graphics and sensitivity analysis, they are thought to be sufficient for the evaluation of a wide variety of physical geographic models.

6. STATISTICAL SIGNIFICANCE

It can be correctly surmised from my omission of references to the statistical significance of any of the measures previously discussed that (1) a descriptive, scientific evaluation of model performance is sufficient and (2) the computation, reporting and interpretation of statistical significance is generally unnecessary and can be misleading. With regard to the evaluation of model performance, it may be helpful to compute and report the magnitude of a test statistic (e.g., t, F or χ^2) associated with a difference measure as well as the observed significance level (α_0), but to interpret values of α_0 which are larger or smaller than an arbitrary cutoff (commonly $\alpha = 0.05$ or $\alpha = 0.01$) as "significant" or "insignificant" is entirely inappropriate. There is simply *no* significant difference between those observed significance levels that are in proximity to one another but fall on opposing sides of an arbitrary cutoff. If all the important assumptions for such a hypothesis test were known to be satisfied, then a determination of the significance of α_0 and the associated difference measure could be made with greater confidence. Since the degree to which assumptions have been violated and the power of a test is often as much a function of the test which has been selected, the frequency distributions of the sample(s) and N as it is of the true relationships between O and P, an interpretation of the significance or insignificance of α_0, and subsequently of real-world relationships between O and P, is often unwise. It is alternatively proposed that interpretations of the relationships between O and P should be based upon the axioms of algebra, knowledge about the sensitivity of the magnitudes of the difference measures to patterns that can exist within $\mathbf{D}$, understanding of the model which produced P and the reliability of the model-input data and O as well as of the computational scheme employed. A detailed understanding of the real-world processes that the model is attempting to describe is essential.

7. A COMPARISON OF FOUR EVAPOTRANSPIRATION MODELS

In order to illustrate the relative utility of the above-described evaluation methods, four climatic models that estimate monthly evapotranspiration from weather data and site information were compared. Using model-predicted and observed data which were interpolated from graphs given by Jensen (1973), representative procedures developed by Papadakis, Christiansen, Jensen-Haise and Thornthwaite are evaluated. Virtually no attempt is made to describe the physical-mathematical bases of these models as the focus of this paper is on the methods of evaluation. If the reader would like to examine a complete description and alternative comparison of these models, it is suggested that Jensen (1973) be consulted. My discussion will begin with an evaluation of model performance through selected graphics, followed by a quantitative assessment of these models' ability to accurately estimate lysimeter-derived (measured), monthly evapotranspiration.

Scatterplots of lysimeter-derived monthly evapotranspiration (O) versus model-predicted monthly evapotranspiration (P) were plotted since they represent one of the most comprehensive and informative graphic means of displaying both systematic and anomalous relationships between O and P (Klucher 1978, for example, relied almost exclusively on scatterplots to compare models that predicted solar irradiance on tilted surfaces). Four scatterplots are presented (Figure 2) — one for each model — where O_i and P_i represent average monthly values which were drawn from ten stations described by Jensen (1973).[1] Since evapotranspiration measurements are often taken only during the growing season, 16 observations were not available and these missing values necessarily reduced the total number of observed cases (N) to 104. Another data deficiency reduced N to 101 for comparisons

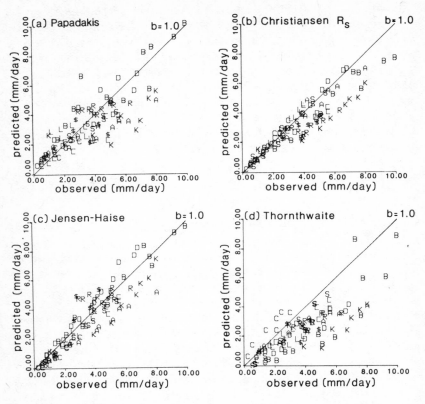

Fig. 2. Scatterplots of monthly lysimeter-derived (observed) evapotranspiration at ten stations versus four model-predicted variables for those same months and station locations. The model-predicted variables were generated by the models of Papadakis, Christiansen, Jensen-Haise and Thornthwaite – graphs (a), (b), (c) and (d), respectively – and a unique symbol is used to identify observations associated with a particular station. The stations and their corresponding plot symbols (given in parens) are: Aspendale, Australia (A); Brawley, California (B); Copenhagen, Denmark (C); Coshocton, Ohio (⊏); Davis, California (D); Kimberly, Idaho (K); Lompoc, California (L); Ruzizi Valley, Zaire (R); Seabrook, New Jersey (S); and South Park, Colorado ($).

of the Thornthwaite model (Table I). The four predicted variables (P) then contain model-derived estimates of O that were made by Jensen (1973) from published descriptions of the methods of Papadakis, Christiansen, Jensen-Haise and Thornthwaite. The Christiansen method is actually one that Jensen

TABLE I

Quantitative measures of evapotranspiration model performance[a]

	Summary univariate measures				Simple linear OLS regression coefficients		Difference measures				
	$\bar{O}$	$\bar{P}$	s_O	s_p	N	a	b	MAE	RMSE	$RMSE_s$	$RMSE_u$	d
Padadakis	3.65	3.30	2.17	1.84	104	0.76	0.70	0.96	1.28	0.74	1.05	0.89
Christiansen R_s	3.65	3.18	2.17	1.77	104	0.40	0.76	0.65	0.94	0.69	0.64	0.94
Jensen-Haise	3.65	3.38	2.17	2.20	104	−0.04	0.94	0.69	0.89	0.30	0.84	0.96
Thornthwaite	3.74	2.44	2.13	1.56	101	0.22	0.59	1.44	1.81	1.56	0.92	0.79

[a] The terms N, b and d are dimensionless while the remaining measures have the units mm day^{-1}.

(1973) refers to as the "Christiansen R_s" model since it requires solar irradiance (R_s) as an input.

Each scatterplot presents the pair-wise plotting of a single model-derived P with O for the above-mentioned ten stations (Figure 2). Within each scatterplot, data points corresponding to a particular station are identified by a unique character in order that within-environment and between-environment relationships can be comprehended. Perhaps one of the major shortcomings of such scatterplots, when the variables are time-series, is that the temporal relationships between events may not be apparent unless a time-identifying mark or symbol can be plotted at each data point. Whether or not a goal is to uniquely distinguish between each time-period or station for that matter, scatterplots become progressively less able to uniquely identify each data point and, therefore, to describe "all" relationships as the number of cases increases. Of course, when important relationships cannot be adequately represented by a single graphic medium, additional graphics such as time-series plots should be produced and interpreted. For purposes of this discussion, however, it is believed that the scatterplots adequately serve to illustrate the potential utility of data-display graphics.

With respect to the perfect prediction line (i.e., when $a = 0.0$ and $b = 1.0$), general error patterns associated with each of the four models are apparent (Figure 2). The methods of Jensen-Haise and Christiansen, for example, exhibit substantially less scatter about the perfect prediction line than either Papadakis or Thornthwaite, although the Christiansen model appears to systematically underpredict peak evapotranspiration — particularly at Brawley and Kimberly. Christiansen's model does quite well, however, during periods of low evapotranspiration (less than 3.0 mm/day). Papadakis' predictions exhibit a scatter of points similar to Thornthwaite's method but Thornthwaite's values are usually low. None of the scatterplots convincingly suggest that any of the four relationships between O and P are fundamentally nonlinear which indicates that it is reasonable to conduct the evaluation of model performance within the linear frame. More detailed interpretations of these (or other) graphs could readily be made by making use of information about the nature of the models, data reliability and site information but, once again, such is beyond the scope of this paper. What should be evident is that a wide variety of functional relationships between O and P as well as anomalies (which often are not apparent within the summary quantitative measures) can be identified and interpreted from data-display graphics — although roughly. Such visual aids concomitantly provide a crude means that can be used to rank models. Comparisons of models, with respect to the degree or magnitude of error or accuracy, however, can only be made through the careful evaluation of selected interval or ratio scale indices although graphics will help in the interpretation of such quantitative measures.

Interpretation of the summary position and scale parameters, i.e., $\bar{O}, \bar{P}, s_o$ and s_p, as well as of N, allows for a somewhat crude comparison of models (Table I). A quick glance at the four predicted means and $\bar{O}$, for example, indicates that all the models underpredicted — on the average — with the Jensen-Haise method posting the smallest average error (-0.27) while the Thornthwaite procedure yielded the largest difference (-1.3) (Table I). The degree to which s_p approaches s_o provides an indication of how well the models reproduce the observed variance. Once again, the Jensen-Haise approach seems superior while Thornthwaite's model does not well-describe the observed variability. Such simple measures should not be over interpreted but the variety of sites from which observations were drawn and the moderately large number of cases tend to support the conclusion that the values of $\bar{O}, \bar{P}, s_o$ and s_p are characteristic of these models' performances over a wide range of environments and times of the year.

Two measures which are neither univariate summary indices or difference measures, the slope (b) and intercept (a) of the simple linear, OLS regression between O and P, can be interpreted although their primary value lies in the fact that a variety of more representative measures can be efficiently computed when a and b are known. One major problem associated with the interpretation of a and b is that they are not mathematically independent of one another even though it is occasionally inferred that a only describes additive error and b proportionality error. A secondary but related problem can be exemplified in the following way: clearly, the four models could be ranked in terms of a and b but the researcher would then have to resolve the problem that those two ordinal variables whose elements are the ranks are not perfectly rank-correlated with one another or with ordinal variables derived from other measures (Table I). Since a and b are functionally linked $(a = \bar{P} - b\bar{O})$, it is suggested that they be only loosely interpreted although one would like a to approach 0.0 and b to approach 1.0.

Difference measures, on the other hand, supply both rigorous and versatile information about overall model performance. By and large, the average difference indices, i.e., RMSE, MAE, and d, agree with regard to the four models' ability to estimate O, although there are exceptions. Both RMSE and d suggest that the formulations of Jensen-Haise and Christiansen are highly accurate, with the former being the most accurate, while the models of Papadakis and Thornthwaite are substantially less reliable with Thornthwaite's method exhibiting the highest overall error. The magnitudes of MAE generally concur with RMSE and d, however, they (MAE) are lower than RMSE and they point to Christiansen's approach as being the most accurate. These minor discrepancies are both related to the fact that the quantity $(P_i - O_i)$ is squared during the computation of RMSE and d, which has the effect of weighting the influence of extreme values and inflating MSE. In most situations, when the frequency distribution of $\mathbf{D}$ is not unusual, RMSE and MAE are colinear and, therefore, it is sufficient to report either measure although I prefer RMSE as it is (1) a more conservative measure of accuracy, (2) more commonly reported in the literature and (3) often useful in the computation of other indices such as $RMSE_s$, $RMSE_u$ and d. From the interpretation of RMSE, MAE, and d as well as of the summary univariate measures and scatterplots, it can be safely concluded that the Jensen-Haise and Christiansen models provide accurate estimates of monthly lysimeter-derived evapotranspiration for a variety of environs and times of the year while Papadakis' and, to a greater degree, Thornthwaite's procedure are relatively inaccurate. These interpretations can be refined by considering the information contained within $RMSE_s$ and $RMSE_u$.

By partitioning RMSE into $RMSE_s$ and $RMSE_u$, it is possible to develop some prognoses that may be useful if a goal of the performance evaluation is to select a base-line model which is potentially better than the others, or to decide whether or not a particular version of a model is likely to be improved by tuning. Since refinements to a model ordinarily produce systematic responses in P, most such modifications should have relatively little impact on the magnitude of $RMSE_u$. As a result, the magnitude of $RMSE_u$ can be interpreted as a measure of a model's potential accuracy with respect to estimating O. Christiansen's framework then emerges as potentially the most accurate while Jensen-Haise's and Papadakis' approach lose some of their appeal. The Thornthwaite model promises to become much more competitive — following refinement. These interpretations are supported by the ratio measures $(RMSE_s/RMSE)^2$ and $(RMSE_u/RMSE)^2$ which suggest, for example, that only 11% of the error associated with the Jensen-Haise method could be excised if the model was tuned whereas 74% of the error contained within Thornthwaite's estimates might be removed. When the above-described difference measures are interpreted together with the summary univariate indices and data-display graphics, they are sufficient to evaluate a wide spectrum of models.

8. CONCLUDING REMARKS

With an increasing number of quantitative models being developed and used by physical geographers, the need to adequately evaluate model performance has expanded and become an important but little researched problem. It is particularly important for the discussion of model evaluation to be enlarged in order that a consistent and rational set of procedures may soon be established. In recognition of the paucity of literature on the topic, this paper has attempted to describe and evaluate a number of the commonly used methods and formulate and illustrate an array of procedures which can be used for comparing model-predictions to observed or otherwise reliable data.

It has been argued that correlations between observed (O) and model-predicted variables (P), as exemplified by Pearson's r and r^2, are insufficient to distinguish between competing models and not consistently related to the accuracy of model performance. Correlation coefficients may in fact be misleading measures of model performance. It has been alternatively suggested that certain difference or error indices, such as the mean absolute error (MAE), the root mean square error (RMSE), the systematic root mean square error ($RMSE_s$), the unsystematic root mean square error ($RMSE_u$) and the index of agreement (d), represent an adequate and preferable set of measures that may be used for quantitative evaluations of model performance. These difference measures should be accompanied by the observed and predicted means and standard deviations, respectively, as well as by appropriate data-display graphics and perhaps sensitivity analyses. When model performance is evaluated through the combinatorial interpretation of the appropriate difference measures, summary univariate statistics and data-display graphics, the absolute and relative abilities of a model to estimate O become virtually unmistakable. At the same time, there is no good reason to test the various difference measures for statistical significance because the degree of reliability of such tests is most often unknown. Model performance should simply be interpreted through the scientific and mathematical evaluation of the physical and computational processes that gave rise to O and P. In order to illustrate the above-described principles and procedures, four exemplary evapotranspiration models were briefly evaluated. Beyond this preliminary statement, a number of studies need to be conducted.

One major precept that needs to be studied is the assumption that O is error free, since the degree to which this assumption is true or reasonable can significantly effect the quantitative measures and their interpretation. Thornthwaite's evapotranspiration model, for instance, would appear much more accurate if actual evapotranspiration was overestimated owing to incorrect assumptions about the degree to which lysimeter-derived estimates are representative of areally integrated evapotranspiration or measurement error. At the same time, since many of the most interesting physical geographical problems are manifested as two-dimensional scalar, vector or tensor fields, a number of more creative graphic and quantitative methods will have to be developed to evaluate the output from more sophisticated models. Furthermore, quantitative procedures which incorporate the cost (in the broadest sense) associated with using a model into the evaluation process should be developed. One model, for example, may be slightly more accurate than another model but because the former requires more computing time and input variables that are difficult to obtain, the latter may be a "better" model. The evaluation of the model performance represents a relatively new and exciting area of research within the quantitative environmental sciences.

Dept. of Geography
University of Delaware

ACKNOWLEDGMENTS

Cartographic and computational assistance from Susan E. Marshall and Julia Bartoshesky is most gratefully acknowledged.

NOTE

[1] The stations are: Aspendale, Australia; Brawley, California; Copenhagen, Denmark; Coshocton, Ohio; Davis, California; Kimberly, Idaho; Lompoc, California; Ruzizi Valley, Zaire; Seabrook, New Jersey and South Park, Colorado.

BIBLIOGRAPHY

Atwater M. A. and J. T. Ball: 1978, 'A numerical solar radiation model based on standard meteorological observations', *Solar Energy* 21, 163–170.

Burt, J. E., J. T. Hayes, P. A. O'Rourke, W. H. Terjung and P. F. Todhunter: 1980, 'Water: A model of water requirements for irrigated and rainfed agriculture', *Publications in Climatology* 33, 1–119.

Davies, J. A.: 1981, *Models for Estimating Incoming Solar Irradiance*, Canadian Climate Centre, Downsview, pp. 1-101 (unpublished manuscript).

Fox, D. G.: 1981, 'Judging air quality model performance', *Bulletin of the American Meteorological Society* 62, 599–609.

Haggett, P. and R. J. Chorley: 1967, 'Models, paradigms and the new geography', in R. J. Chorley and P. Haggett (eds.), *Models in Geography*, Methuen, London, pp. 19–41.

Jensen, M. E. (ed.): 1973, *Consumptive Use of Water and Irrigation Water Requirements*, American Society of Civil Engineers, New York.

Johnson, E. R. and R. L. Bras: 1980, 'Multivariate short-term rainfall prediction', *Water Resources Research* 16, 173–185.

Klucher, T. M.: 1978, *Evaluation of Models to Predict Insolation on Tilted Surfaces*, N.A.S.A. Lewis Research Center, Cleveland, pp. 1–8, (NASA TM-78842).

Mather, J. R., R. T. Field, L. S. Kalkstein, and C. J. Willmott: 1980, 'Climatology: The challenge for the eighties', *Professional Geographer* 32, 285–292.

Powell, G. L.: 1980, *A Comparative Evaluation of Hourly Solar Global Irradiation Models*, Unpublished Ph. D. dissertation, Arizona State University, Tempe.

Rayner, J. N.: 1974, 'Climatology and simulation', *Proceedings of the Association of American Geographers* 6, 109–112.

Rutherford, B. M.: 1973, 'The accuracy, robustness and relationships among correlational models: A Monte Carlo simulation', York University Department of Geography, *Discussion Paper No. 8*, pp. 1–39.

Strahler, A. N.: 1980, 'Systems theory in physical geography', *Physical Geography* 1, 1–27.

Suckling, P. W. and J. E. Hay: 1976, 'Modelling direct, diffuse, and total solar radiation for cloudless days', *Atmosphere* 14, 298–308.

Terjung, W. H.: 1976, 'Climatology for geographers', *Annals of the Association of American Geographers* 66, 199–222.

Willmott, C. J.: 1981, 'On the validation of models', *Physical Geography* 2, 184–194.

Willmott, C. J. and D. E. Wicks: 1980, 'An empirical method for the spatial interpolation of monthly precipitation within California', *Physical Geography* 1, 59–73.

INDEX OF NAMES

461

INDEX OF NAMES

INDEX OF SUBJECTS

THEORY AND DECISION LIBRARY

An International Series in the Philosophy and Methodology
of the Social and Behavioral Sciences

Editors:

Gerald Eberlein, *University of Technology, Munich*
Werner Leinfellner, *University of Nebraska*

18. A. Rapoport, W. E. Stein, and G. J. Burkheimer, *Response Models for Detection of Change.* 1978, vii + 200 pp.
19. H. J. Johnson, J. J. Leach, and R. G. Mühlmann (eds.), *Revolutions, Systems, and Theories: Essays in Political Philosophy.* 1978, x + 198 pp.
20. Stephen Gale and Gunnar Olsson (eds.), *Philosophy in Geography.* 1979, xxii + 470 pp.
21. Maurice Allais and Ole Hagen (eds.), *Expected Utility Hypotheses and the Allais Paradox: Contemporary Discussions of Decisions Under Uncertainty With Allais' Rejoinder.* 1979, vii + 714 pp.
22. Teddy Seidenfeld, *Philosophical Problems of Statistical Inference: Learning from R. A. Fisher.* 1979, xiv + 246 pp.
23. L. Lewin and E. Vedung (eds.), *Politics as Rational Action.* 1980, xii + 274 pp.
24. J. Kozielecki, *Psychological Decision Theory.* 1982, xvi + 403 pp.
25. I. I. Mitroff and R. O. Mason. *Creating a Dialectical Social Science: Concepts, Methods, and Models.* 1981, ix + 189 pp.
26. V. A. Lefebvre, *Algebra of Conscience: A Comparative Analysis of Western and Soviet Ethical Systems.* 1982, xxvii + 194 pp.
27. L. Nowak, *Property and Power: Towards a Non-Marxian Historical Materialism.* 1983, xxvii + 384 pp.
28. J. C. Harsanyi, *Papers in Game Theory.* 1982, xii + 258 pp.
29. B. Walentynowicz (ed.), *Polish Contributions to the Science of Science.* 1982, xii + 291 pp.
30. A. Camacho, *Societies and Social Decision Functions. A Model with Focus on the Information Problem.* 1982, xv + 144 pp.
31. P. C. Fishburn, *The Foundations of Expected Utility.* 1982, xii + 176 pp.
32. G. Feichtinger and P. Kall (eds.), *Operations Research in Progress.* 1982, ix + 520 pp.
33. H. W. Gottinger, *Coping with Complexity.* 1983, xv + 224 pp.
34. W. Gasparski and T. Pszczołowski (eds.), *Praxiological Studies.* 1983, xiv + 418 pp.
35. A. M. Yaglom and I. M. Yaglom, *Probability and Information.* 1983, xx + 421 pp.
36. F. M. Wuketits, *Concepts and Approaches in Evolutionary Epistemology.* 1984, xiii + 307 pp.
37. B. F. Stigum and F. Wenstøp (eds.), *Foundations of Utility and Risk Theory with Applications.* 1983, x + 492 pp.
38. V. V. Kolbin, *Macromodels of the National Economy of the USSR.* 1984, forthcoming.
39. H. J. Skala, S. Termini, and E. Trillas (eds.), *Aspects of Vagueness.* 1984, viii+ 304 pp.
40. G. L. Gaile and C. J. Willmott (eds.), *Spatial Statistics and Models.* 1984, x + 482 pp.
41. J. van Daal and A. H. Q. M. Merkies, *Aggregation in Economic Research.* 1984, xiv + 321 pp.